1,000,000 Books

are available to read at

www.ForgottenBooks.com

Read online
Download PDF
Purchase in print

ISBN 978-1-330-10534-4
PIBN 10027016

This book is a reproduction of an important historical work. Forgotten Books uses state-of-the-art technology to digitally reconstruct the work, preserving the original format whilst repairing imperfections present in the aged copy. In rare cases, an imperfection in the original, such as a blemish or missing page, may be replicated in our edition. We do, however, repair the vast majority of imperfections successfully; any imperfections that remain are intentionally left to preserve the state of such historical works.

Forgotten Books is a registered trademark of FB &c Ltd.
Copyright © 2018 FB &c Ltd.
FB &c Ltd, Dalton House, 60 Windsor Avenue, London, SW19 2RR.
Company number 08720141. Registered in England and Wales.

For support please visit www.forgottenbooks.com

1 MONTH OF
FREE
READING

at
www.ForgottenBooks.com

By purchasing this book you are eligible for one month membership to ForgottenBooks.com, giving you unlimited access to our entire collection of over 1,000,000 titles via our web site and mobile apps.

To claim your free month visit:

www.forgottenbooks.com/free27016

* Offer is valid for 45 days from date of purchase. Terms and conditions apply.

English
Français
Deutsche
Italiano
Español
Português

www.forgottenbooks.com

Mythology Photography **Fiction**
Fishing Christianity **Art** Cooking
Essays Buddhism Freemasonry
Medicine **Biology** Music **Ancient**
Egypt Evolution Carpentry Physics
Dance Geology **Mathematics** Fitness
Shakespeare **Folklore** Yoga Marketing
Confidence Immortality Biographies
Poetry **Psychology** Witchcraft
Electronics Chemistry History **Law**
Accounting **Philosophy** Anthropology
Alchemy Drama Quantum Mechanics
Atheism Sexual Health **Ancient History**
Entrepreneurship Languages Sport
Paleontology Needlework Islam
Metaphysics Investment Archaeology
Parenting Statistics Criminology
Motivational

ACADEMICAL LECTURES

ON THE

JEWISH SCRIPTURES AND ANTIQUITIES.

VOL. IV.

ACADEMICAL LECTURES

ON THE

JEWISH SCRIPTURES

AND

ANTIQUITIES.

By JOHN GORHAM PALFREY, D. D., LL. D.

VOL. IV.

HAGIOGRAPHA AND APOCRYPHA.

"Si quis, in lege Domini die ac nocte meditatus, majus habuit studium, majus ingenium, otium, gratiamque, et potest de præsenti probabilius aliquid dicere, non invideo, non aspernor. Quin potius cupio ab eo discere quod ignoro, et libenter me discipulum profitebor, dummodo doceat, et non detrahat. Nihil enim tam facile quam otiosum et dormientem de aliorum labore ac vigiliis disputare." — *Hieron. in Mich.* ii.

BOSTON:
CROSBY, NICHOLS, AND COMPANY,
111 WASHINGTON STREET.

NEW YORK:
CHARLES S. FRANCIS AND COMPANY.
1852.

2 N . 1893

From the Library of
Prof. A. P. PEABODY 82

Entered according to Act of Congress, in the year 1852, by
JOHN GORHAM PALFREY,
in the Clerk's Office of the District Court of the District of Massachusetts.

CAMBRIDGE:
METCALF AND COMPANY,

CONTENTS

VOLUME FOURTH.

LECTURE LIV.

GENEALOGIES, AND REIGN OF DAVID.—THE FIRST BOOK OF CHRONICLES.

LECTURE LV.

HISTORY FROM DAVID'S TIME TO THE CAPTIVITY.—THE SECOND BOOK OF CHRONICLES.

LECTURE LVI.

EZRA AND NEHEMIAH.

LECTURE LVII.

FIRST AND SECOND BOOKS OF ESDRAS.

LECTURE LVIII.

THE TIME OF THE ASMONÆAN BROTHERS. — THE FIRST BOOK OF THE MACCABEES.

LECTURE LIX.

SECOND AND THIRD BOOKS OF THE MACCABEES.

LECTURE LX.

THE BOOK OF JOB.

LECTURE LXI.

THE PSALTER.

LECTURE LXII.

THEOLOGY, DEVOTION, AND MORALITY OF THE PSALMS.

LECTURE LXIII.

MESSIANIC PSALMS, AND PSALMS QUOTED IN THE NEW TESTAMENT.

LECTURE LXIV.

THE CANTICLES, AND THE GNOMOLOGICAL BOOKS.

LECTURE LXV.

TOBIT, PRAYER OF MANASSEH, AND JUDITH.

LECTURE LXVI.

BARUCH AND DANIEL.

LECTURE LXIX.

THE BOOK OF ESTHER.

LECTURE LXX.

HISTORY OF THE LATER JEWISH KINGDOM, AND CONCLUSION.

ERRATA.

Page	41, *line* 34, *for* וַיֵּשְׁבוּ ,	*read* וַיִּשְׁבּוּ .
"	41, " 34, " וַיֵּשְׁבוּ ,	" וַיִּשְׁבּוּ .
"	61, " 10, " transcript from,	" duplicate of.
"	68, " 35, " § 196,	" "Einleit.," § 196.
"	79, " 28, " poured,	" and poured.
"	86, " 8, " height,	" intended height.
"	91, " 5, " plural,	" singular.
"	142, " 30, " because it,	" because he.
"	263, " 36, " Supplem. ad Lex. Hebraic.,	" apud Rosenmüller, "Scholia in Psalm.," Prolegom. p. lxiv.
"	291, " 33, " former,	" latter.
"	330, " 20, " same class, while,	" same class. While
"	330, " 22, " loss. No,	" loss, no.
"	351, " 12, " the Philo,	" "the elder Philo."
"	351, " 13, " Caligula,	" the Greek-Egyptian kings.
"	352, " 5, " have,	" had.
"	366, " 13, " fourth,	" third or fourth.
"	446, " 38, " Vol. II. p. 197,	" Vol. I. p. 197.

LECTURES

JEWISH SCRIPTURES AND ANTIQUITIES.

LECTURE LIV.

GENEALOGIES, AND REIGN OF DAVID.

THE FIRST BOOK OF CHRONICLES.

JEWISH CLASSIFICATION OF THE SACRED BOOKS. — TITLES OF THE BOOKS OF CHRONICLES. — GENERAL STATEMENT OF THEIR CONTENTS. — SOURCES OF THE COMPILER'S INFORMATION. — DATE AND DESIGN. — DEFECTS AND REDUNDANCIES. — TENDENCY TO THE MARVELLOUS. — CONTRADICTIONS OF EARLIER RECORDS. — GENEALOGIES FROM ADAM TO THE GRANDCHILDREN OF ABRAHAM AND THE DUKES OF EDOM. — GENEALOGIES IN THE LINE OF JUDAH, WITH PARTICULARS NOT ELSEWHERE FOUND. — GENEALOGIES FROM DAVID TO THE DESCENDANTS OF ZERUBBABEL. — FRAGMENTARY GENEALOGIES, THROUGH FIVE CHAPTERS, OF JUDAH, SIMEON, REUBEN, GAD, MANASSEH, LEVI, ISSACHAR, BENJAMIN, NAPHTALI, EPHRAIM, AND ASHER. — LIST OF RESIDENTS IN JERUSALEM AND OTHER CITIES. — DEFEAT, DEATH, AND BURIAL OF SAUL. — ACCESSION OF DAVID TO THE MONARCHY OF THE TWELVE TRIBES. — HIS CAPTURE OF JERUSALEM. — LISTS OF HIS "MIGHTY MEN." — HIS REMOVAL OF THE ARK. — ERECTION OF HIS PALACE. — INCREASE OF HIS FAMILY. — HIS VICTORIES OVER THE PHILISTINES. — HIS PROPOSAL TO BUILD A TEMPLE. — HIS SUCCESSFUL WARS. — LIST OF HIS PRINCIPAL COURTIERS. — HIS CENSUS OF THE PEOPLE. — HIS PUNISHMENT FOR THAT PROCEEDING. — HIS PURCHASE OF A SITE FOR THE FUTURE TEMPLE. — ASSOCIATION OF SOLOMON WITH HIM IN THE ROYALTY. — HIS PROVISIONS FOR THE ERECTION OF THE TEMPLE. — HIS ARRANGEMENTS FOR THE POLITICAL AND ECCLESIASTICAL ADMINISTRATION. — HIS DEATH.

WE have examined the Law and the Prophets. The books remaining for our consideration are those belonging to the two collections of *Hagiographa* and

Apocrypha. The division of the Jewish sacred books under the heads of Law, Prophets, and Hagiographa is as old, at least, as the time of Jerome; * how much more ancient, we know not, though it appears to be recognized in the language of the New Testament.†

Among the Hagiographa are reckoned by the Jews the two books called by us "Chronicles." A literal version of their Hebrew title is "Records [or Events] of the Days." Gesenius translates it "Daily Affairs," or "A Journal of Affairs." ‡ The word "Annals," though of a different derivation, would well represent the sense. The Alexandrine version, with no propriety, designates the work by a name intimating that it is a collection of facts *omitted* in the other records of the same period.§

The First Book of Chronicles contains genealogical tables, with anecdotes interspersed, extending over the time from Adam to Ezra, and bringing down the lineage of a few families to a later period. Then follows an account of the death of Saul, and a full history of the reign of David. The Second Book relates to the period from the death of David to the destruction of the city by Nebuchadnezzar. Its main subject, after the time of the revolt, is the history of the southern kingdom, that of the northern being treated scarcely any further than as it connects itself with the former.

The compiler of these books names some, at least, of the sources of his information. He refers to books called the "Chronicles of King David," the "Book

---

* Comp. Vol. I. pp. 39, 40.

† Luke xxiv. 44. The prologue to Ecclesiasticus in like manner refers to " the Law, and the Prophets, and *the rest of the books.*"

‡ " Lexicon," *ad verb.* דָּבָר .

§ Τὰ Παραλειπόμενα.

of Samuel the Seer," the "Book of Nathan the Prophet," the "Book of Gad the Seer," the "Prophecy of
Abijah the Shilonite," the "Book of Iddo the Seer,"
the "Book of Shemaiah the Prophet," the "Story of
the Prophet Iddo," the "Book of Jehu the Son of
Hanani," the "Book of the Kings of Israel," the
"Vision of Isaiah the Prophet, the son of Amoz," the
"Story of the Book of the Kings," and the "Book of
the Kings of Judah and Israel." * This Book of the
Kings, which he repeatedly mentions, could not have
been that which is now in our hands under that name,
since sometimes, when the reader is referred to it for
more full information, the record is found to be more
concise than that in the Chronicles.† It appears probable that he was not even acquainted with that book.‡

   We have no information as to the authorship of the
compilation. The opinion which anciently prevailed
to some extent, ascribing it to Ezra, is without any
good authority.§ The time of its production is fixed
with considerable probability at a period not much
later than the year 536 B. C. If the last verses are
genuine, it must be dated as late as that time, since
they mention the proclamation of Cyrus permitting
the Jewish exiles to return and rebuild their city.
Chaldee forms of orthography frequently occur, and

---

   * 1 Chron. xxvii. 24; xxix. 29; 2 Chron. ix. 29; xii. 15; xiii. 22;
xx. 34; xxiv. 27; xxxii. 32.

   † E. g. 2 Chron. xxv. 1–26, comp. 2 Kings xiv. 1–20; 2 Chron. xxvii.
1–9, comp. 2 Kings xv. 32–38. See also 1 Chron. ix. 1 for a statement
which does not accord with the contents of our Books of Kings.

   ‡ Yet I have sometimes thought that references of this description in the
Books of Kings were to the books called by us the Books of Chronicles, and
vice versâ; — references, however, if it were so, made hastily and negli-
gently, not by the original compilers respectively, but by a later hand or
hands. This idea, I think, deserves more consideration than, since the time
when it occurred to me, I have been able to give it.

   § Also the genealogy of Ezra, as recorded in his own book (vii. 1, et seq.),
has fewer generations, by seven, than that in 1 Chron. vi. 3, et seq.

there are words of Chaldee and Persian derivation; *
circumstances which point to the same date. One
genealogy is continued as far as the time of Alexander the Great, but this is thought to be a later interpolation.† The purpose of a considerable portion of
the book appears to have been, to acquaint the Hebrews, on their return, with their ancestry, the authorized modes of worship, and the proper places of settlement for the respective tribes.

Some judgment in respect to the degree of completeness and finish of this history may be formed from
the following facts. Among the genealogies there is
none of the tribes of Zebulun and Dan; while, on the
other hand, there are two of Benjamin.‡ A list of
only twenty-three high-priests is given, for a period of
nine hundred years.§ The genealogy of the Levitical
tribe is most minutely detailed, and is brought down
to the destruction of Jerusalem. That of the tribe of
Judah is tolerably full, and the lineage of David is
continued to the end of the fourth century before
Christ. No mention is made of David's separate reign
of seven years over the tribe of Judah, except in a
brief note in one of the lists of his descendants.||

As we proceed, we shall observe a striking characteristic of this book as compared with the Books of
Samuel and Kings to be, that it delights more than
they in the marvellous; — a fact which well accords
with that of its more recent composition, since it is in
the common course of things for legends preserved by
tradition to acquire more and more of a marvellous
character, the longer they continue in currency.

An examination of the Books of Chronicles will

---

* E. g. בּוּץ, *cotton* (1 Chron. xv. 27) ; אֲדַרְכֹּנִים, *darics* (1 Chron. xxix. 7).
† 1 Chron. iii. 19 – 24.
‡ vii. 6 – 12 ; viii. 1 – 40 ; comp. also ix. 35 – 44.
§ vi. 3 – 15. || iii. 4.

lead to some important conclusions bearing on the principles of interpretation of the Old Testament. It will show that the Old Testament cannot be taken throughout as an infallible guide in the matters of history of which it treats, since in different parts it contradicts itself; and it will show that earlier books, which must have been in the hands of the author of Chronicles when he wrote, could not have been regarded by him as possessing the same absolute authority which in later times has been attached to them, inasmuch as, in that case, instead of contradicting, he would have copied them, or made his statements conform to theirs. And if further, in the sequel of my remarks, I frequently point out discrepancies which are merely verbal and of no material moment, it is with a view to the observation of facts tending to determine the relation of the books to each other in respect to a separate origin and different authority.

The first four verses of the book contain, without any introduction or explanation, a list of thirteen names. They are the same as those recorded in the fifth chapter of Genesis as designating the line of patriarchs from Adam to Noah and his sons.* The next nineteen verses are a literal copy, with the exception of a few omissions and one variation, of the tenth chapter of Genesis.† Four verses next exhibit the names in the line from Shem to Abraham, agreeably to the fuller account in Genesis.‡ Here, again, the

---

* In our English version, there appears a little difference, as Sheth, Jered, Enosh, Kenan, Henoch (Chron.), for Seth, Jared, Enos, Cainan, Enoch (Gen.); but the names in the original Hebrew are the same.

† The omissions are of biographical and geographical notices recorded in Gen. x. 1, 5, 9 – 12, 18 – 21, 30 – 32. Uz, and Hul, and Gether, and Mash [Meshech] are in Genesis (x. 23) represented as grandsons of Shem; in Chron. (i. 17) as his sons.

‡ Gen. xi. 10 – 27.

fact that each succeeding name in the catalogue represents a son of the preceding, is left to be supplied by
the reader's own knowledge of the history. The lists
of Ishmael's children, of Abraham's children by Ke-
turah, and of the children of two of these latter, are
extracted without alteration from the corresponding
record in Genesis.* The chapter concludes with a
catalogue of descendants from Abraham in the line of
Esau, of "the sons of Seir," whom they dispossessed
of their territory, and of Dukes of Edom, also taken
from that book, but with considerable variations.†
    The second chapter, after naming the sons of Ja-
cob and Judah, records the descendants from Zerah,
one of the latter, and more fully the descendants from
Hezron, Zerah's nephew, in the lines of Hezron's five
sons, Jerahmeel, Ram (whose line is traced to King
David, with the mention of David's brothers, sisters,
and nephews), Chelubai (or Caleb), Segub, and Ashur.
A large part of the matter contained in this chapter
is not found in any earlier book. The compiler must
have relied on sources of information which have not
been transmitted to our times. ‡

---

* 1 Chron. i. 28–33 ; comp. Gen. xxv. 2–4, 13–15.— I make no account of the change of the letter ר for ד in the name *Hadar* (30), a various reading of frequent occurrence in this book.

    † i. 34–54; comp. Gen. xxxvi. 10–43. Timna, represented in Chron-
icles (36) as the son of Eliphaz, was according to Genesis (12) his concubine. There is a number of variations, consisting in the change of one or
two letters in a name, but it would be a waste of pains to specify them.

    ‡ The facts briefly stated in ii. 1–5 are recorded in Gen. xxxv. 23–26,
xxxviii. 3–30, xlvi. 12. The passage ii. 9–12 is a copy of Ruth iv. 19–
22. Authority for ii. 13 is found in 1 Samuel xvi. 6–9 ; and for ii. 16, 17,
in 2 Sam. ii. 18, xvii. 25, except that in the verse last named the father of
Amasa is said to have been " Ithra, an Israelite," while in the parallel passage he is called " Jether, the Ishmaelite." The contents of ii. 6–8, 14,
15, and 18–55 appear nowhere else in the Old Testament. — "The sons
of Zerah, Zimri," &c. (6) ; "and the sons of Carmi, Achar the troubler
of Israel," &c. (7). Who was Carmi ? It is not said that he was a son of

The third chapter contains a list of the children of David, and of the descendants of his son Solomon, in the royal line of Judah, with a list of some of the descendants of Jeconiah, the last king but one.*

---

either Zerah or Zimri ; and in Joshua (vii. 1) we read of " Achan, the son of Carmi, the son of Zabdi, the son of Zerah." — " The sons of Zerah ; Zimri, and Ethan, and Heman, and Calcol, and Dara " (1 Chron. ii. 6) ; comp. 1 Kings iv. 31, which reads as follows : " He was wiser than all men, than Ethan the *Ezrahite*, and Heman, and Chalcol, and Darda, the sons of *Mahol*." — " Uri begat Bezaleel " (20); it appears to have been for the purpose of preserving the parentage of this distinguished person (comp. Ex. xxxi. 2) that the three verses ending here were written. — With 1 Chron. ii. 21 – 23, comp Numb. xxxii. 39 – 41, Deut. iii. 14, 15. — " The daughter of Caleb was Achsah " (1 Chron. ii. 49). Caleb, the contemporary of Joshua, appears to be referred to (Joshua xv. 16) ; but he is also the brother of Jerahmeel, and great-grandson of Judah (1 Chron. ii. 9, 18, 42), which would place him several generations earlier. Also, the Caleb of Joshua's time was son of Jephunneh (Numb. xiii. 6); and again, Caleb, in the last part of the chapter before us, whose son Shobal was " the father of Kirjath-jearim " (comp. ii. 18), is son of Hur (ii. 50 – 52). There is no reconciling these statements.

* With 1 Chron. iii. 1 – 4, comp. 2 Sam. iii. 2 – 5. The *Chileab* of Samuel (iii. 3) is called *Daniel* in Chronicles (iii. 1). — With iii. 5 – 9, comp. 2 Sam. v. 14 – 16. — " *Shimea*, and Shobab, and Nathan, and Solomon, four, of *Bathshua*, the daughter of *Ammiel* "(1 Chron. iii. 5). *Shimea* is in Samuel (v. 14) *Shammuah*, and Solomon's mother was *Bathsheba*, daughter of *Eliam* (2 Sam. xi. 3, xii. 24). — " Ibhar also . . . . . and Eliphelet, *nine* " (1 Chron. iii. 6 – 8). But, to make nine, Elishama and Eliphelet are named and counted twice. In the list in Samuel (v. 15, 16) each name occurs but once, and *Elishua* corresponds to the *Nogah* of Chronicles. — The list of the royal posterity of Solomon down to the captivity (1 Chron. iii. 10 – 16) accords with the history in the later portion of this book, and in that of Kings, except that Josiah's son, Johanan (15), is not mentioned elsewhere. — The passage iii. 17 – 24 has no parallel in the Old Testament. From the length of the genealogy which it contains, Geddes ("Holy Bible," &c. *ad loc.*) infers that " the period in which the Book of Chronicles, or at least this portion of it, was compiled, must have been thirteen generations after the Babylonish captivity." But no such argument can be relied upon, in the uncertainty, as to many of the names, whether they were recorded as the names of contemporaries, or of ancestors and progeny. — " The sons of Jeconiah, Assir ; Salathiel, his son," &c. (17) ; " and the sons of Pedaiah were Zerubbabel," &c. (19). But according to Matthew (i. 12) Salathiel was son of Jeconiah, and Zerubbabel son of Salathiel ; while according to Luke (iii. 27 – 31) Salathiel, Zerubbabel's father, was son, not of Jeconiah, nor of Jeconiah's son, Assir, but of Neri, and was descended from David, not through Solomon, but through Nathan.

Next we have five chapters in succession, containing
fragmentary genealogies, beginning with the patriarchs, the sons of Jacob. To a list of the sons of Judah, which has only one name (that of Pharez) in
common with the corresponding lists in the Books of
Genesis and Numbers, and in an earlier passage of
this book,* — so that one authority, at least, must be
absolutely erroneous, — succeeds a series of names of
no significance at the present day, and apparently
compiled from the most defective materials and in the
most hasty and careless manner, without system or any
attempt to explain incoherences.† An anecdote is recorded of one of the individuals named,‡ and the occu-
pations of a few of the others. § The list of the sons
of Simeon, which next follows, corresponds better with
those preserved by the more ancient authorities .|| The
account of the settlement of that tribe in the territory
of Canaan is in great part a repetition of that in the
Book of Joshua.¶ There is a relation of some particulars not recorded elsewhere. The small number of
the tribe of Simeon is referred to, with a notice, on
the other hand, of some families of the tribe distinguished for fecundity.** And there is a brief relation
of conquests made by the tribe from the Canaanites
and Amalekites, the former in the reign of Hezekiah.††

---

* Comp. 1 Chron iv. 1 with ii. 3, 4 ; Gen. xxxviii. 29, 30, xlvi. 12 ;
Numb. xxvi. 19, 20.

† iv. 2 – 23. —" Ephratah, the father of Beth-lehem " (4) ; comp. " Sal-
ma, the father of Beth-lehem " (ii. 51). — " Jered, the father of Gedor "
(18) ; comp. " Penuel, the father of Gedor " (4); also, Jered and others
are said in one part of the same verse to have been sons of Jehudijah, and,
in another, of Bithiah, a daughter of the king of Egypt.

‡ iv. 9, 10.

§ iv. 14, 21, 23.

|| iv. 24 ; comp. Gen. xlvi. 10 ; Numb. xxvi. 12, 13.

¶ Comp. iv. 28 – 33 with Josh. xix. 2 – 8. — " Ziklag . . . . . these
were their cities unto the reign of David " (1 Chron. iv. 31) ; comp. 1 Sam.
xxvii. 6.

** iv. 25 –27, 34 – 38.   †† iv. 39 – 43.

Next follow fragments of genealogies of the tribes of Reuben, Gad, and Manasseh, with brief notices of the respective places of their settlement. The writer, apparently alluding to the dying words of Jacob as recorded in Genesis,* says that Reuben is not to be reckoned as the first-born of the family, because he had by his misconduct forfeited his right to that dignity, which had been transferred to Joseph, though, after all, it had turned out that the royal line was descended from neither of these patriarchs, but 'from the stock of Judah.† He gives a list of the sons of Reuben corresponding with those in Genesis and Numbers,‡ and then, taking up the line again, apparently after an interval of about a thousand years, continues it from father to son through seven lives down to the time of one Beerah, who, he says, " was prince of the Reubenites " at the time of the Assyrian conquest.§ He names some others of the leading men of that tribe, and says that in the time of Saul, in a successful war with the Hagarites, they extended their possessions in that grazing country east of the Euphrates where their fathers were established in the time of Joshua.‖ Of the tribe of Gad, whose country bordered on that of Reuben on the eastern side of the Jordan, he records in a confused manner the names of several persons, otherwise unknown to history, who, he says, " were reckoned by genealogies in the days of Jotham, king of Judah, and in the days of Jeroboam, king of Israel." ¶ And he adds, that the Gadites, with that portion of the tribe of Manasseh who dwelt near them in the country beyond the Jordan, were allied with the tribe of Reuben

---

* Gen. xlix. 3, 4, 22 – 26.   † 1 Chron. v. 1, 2.
‡ v. 3 ; comp. Gen. xlvi. 9, Numb. xxvi. 5, 6.   § v. 4 – 6.
‖ v. 7 – 10 ; comp. Josh. xiii. 15 – 23. — " The sons of Joel ; Shemaiah his son," &c. (1 Chron. v. 4) ; comp. " Shema, the son of Joel " (8).
¶ v. 11 – 17 ; comp. Josh. xiii. 24 – 28.

in the war just before mentioned against the Hagarites; and that with a joint force, amounting to forty-
four thousand seven hundred and sixty men, "they
took away their cattle; of their camels fifty thousand,
and of sheep two hundred and fifty thousand, and of
asses two thousand, and of men an hundred thousand;
for there fell down many slain, because the war was of
God; and they dwelt in their steads until the captivity." * Seven persons, of whom nothing else is known,
are named as having been "mighty men of valor, famous men, and heads of the house of their fathers";
and of the eastern branch of the tribe of Manasseh it
is only further recorded that they extended their possessions, that "they transgressed against the God of
their fathers," and that finally, with their fellow-
citizens of Reuben and Gad, they were carried away
captive by Pul and Tilgath-Pilneser, and settled in the
Assyrian provinces, where they remained in the writer's time.†

The notices of the tribe of Levi, contained in the
sixth chapter, are more full than any others in the
series, though, besides having no pretension to com
pleteness, they are deformed by repetitions and redundancies. The lists of Levi's children, and of those of
his son Kohath, of Kohath's son Amram, and of Amram's son Aaron, are taken from Genesis and Exodus;‡
and the succession of high-priests from Eleazar, son of
Aaron, down to Jehozadak, who was exercising that
office at the time of the Chaldean invasion, mainly accords with the history in the Books of Samuel and
Kings.§ The names of the grandsons of Levi in each

---

* 1 Chron. v. 18–22. Accordingly, each warrior, on an average, after
capturing, had the charge of conducting home two or three human captives,
besides more than one camel and four or five sheep.

† v. 23–26.

‡ vi. 1–3; comp. Gen. xlvi. 11, Ex. vi. 18, 20, 23, xv. 20.

§ 1 Chron. vi. 4–15. — Between Uzzi and Ahitub the First, the compiler

of the three lines of that patriarch are repeated from
the earlier record,* and from the different branches
the lineage is traced of five persons, named Jeaterai,
Shaul, Elkanah, Abiah, and Asaiah, " whom David set
over the service of song in the house of the Lord, after
that the ark had rest," and who, after the building of
Solomon's temple, " waited on their office according
to their order." † Next we have the lineage, from
Levi down, of those who headed their respective families in the temple choir and other Levitical services,
namely, Heman descended from Levi's son Kohath,
Asaph from Gershom, and Ethan from Merari.‡ A
scrap of five verses repeats a portion of the same list of
the succession in the pontifical race which had been
given just before.§ The chapter concludes with a disjointed account of the territorial possessions of the sacerdotal family,‖ and of the three other divisions of the

of this list, having in view the lineal descent, places Zerahiah, Meraioth,
and Amariah, descendants from Uzzi and ancestors of Ahitub, while, according to the Book of Samuel, the office was during this time filled by Eli,
who was not even descended from Eleazar, but from his brother Ithamar
(comp. 6, 7 with 1 Sam. i. 9, xiv. 3, xxii. 20, 1 Chron. xxiv. 3). Also, he
makes no mention of Uriah (2 Kings xvi. 11).

    * 1 Chron. vi. 16 – 19; comp. Ex. vi. 16 – 19. The spelling Gershom
(16 *et seq.*) is peculiar.

    † vi. 20 – 32. — " Amminadab his son, Korah his son " (22). The Ko-
rah of Numb. xvi. 1 was also descended from Kohath, but his father's
name was not Amminadab, but Izhar, and no Amminadab appears in the list
of Kohath's sons in 1 Chron. vi. 18. — " The sons of *Samuel*," &c. (28).
Undeterred by the " dubio caret " of Dathe (*ad loc.*), I decline to identify
this Samuel with the famous " setter-up and putter-down of kings." It is
true that both had a son Abiah (1 Sam. viii. 2); but here the resemblance
ends : it does not appear that the latter Samuel is represented in the text as
son of Elkanah (1 Chron. vi. 26, 28) ; but if he be, it is of an Elkanah who
was son of Assir (22, 23), whereas the Elkanah of the history was son of
one Jeroham (1 Sam. i. 1).

    ‡ vi. 33 – 48. In the genealogy of Asaph only fourteen generations are
specified, and in that of Ethan, twelve, while in that of Heman, who was
their contemporary, and whose line, like theirs, is traced up to Levi, there
are twenty-one.

    § vi. 49 – 53 ; comp. 4 – 8.

    ‖ vi. 54 – 60 ; comp. Josh. xxi. 10 – 19; the Holon, Ain, and Almon of

Levitical tribe; viz. the Kohathites, Gershomites, and
Merarites.*

The seventh chapter contains some incomplete and
disconnected genealogical records of the tribes of
Issachar,† Benjamin,‡ Naphtali,§ Manasseh,|| Ephra-

Joshua (15, 16, 18) are here Hilen, Ashan, and Alemeth (58, 59, 60), and
no mention is made of the Juttah and Gibeon of the former list (Josh. 16,
17), which makes the summary "all their cities throughout their families
were *thirteen* cities" (1 Chron. vi. 60) incorrect.

* 1 Chron. vi. 61 - 81. — "Unto the sons of Kohath . . . . . out of the
half tribe of Manasseh, by lot, ten cities" (61) ; but according to Joshua
(xxi. 20 - 26) some of the ten cities were in the territories of Ephraim and
Dan ; the mistake is partly rectified below (1 Chron. vi. 66 - 70), but only
in part, for the whole number of cities in this latter passage is eight instead
of ten, the Eltekeh and Gibbethon of Joshua (xxi. 23) being omitted ; and
other diversities from the former list are, that for the Kibzaim in Ephraim
(Josh. xxi. 22) we here (vi. 68) have Jokneam, that the Aijalon and Gath-
rimmon of Dan (Josh. xxi. 24) are here ascribed (vi. 69) to Ephraim, and
that the Taanach and Gath-rimmon of Manasseh (Josh. xxi. 25) are here
called (vi. 70) Aner and Bileam. — "The cities of refuge," &c. (67) ; our
translators have here disguised the statement of the author that Gezer and
the rest, as well as Shechem, were cities of refuge, a statement contradicted
by the earlier history ; and the same is true of Hebron and the cities mentioned (57) in connection with it (comp. Josh. xx 7, xxi. 13, 21). — "Golan
in Bashan . . . . . Kirjathaim with her suburbs" (71 - 76) ; for Ashtaroth,
Kedesh, Ramoth, Anem, Hukok, Hammon, and Kirjathaim, in this passage,
the parallel passage in Joshua (xxi. 27 - 32) has Beeshterah, Kishon, Jar-
muth, Engannim, Helkath, Hammoth-dor, Kartan. — "Unto the rest
. . . . . Jazer with her suburbs" (77 - 81) ; these cities are but ten in
number, instead of twelve (comp. 63), two cities only of Zebulun, namely, Rimmon and Tabor, being comprehended in that list, while in the list in
Joshua (xxi. 34, 35) four cities of that tribe are mentioned, namely, Jokneam, Kirtah, Dimnah, and Nahalal.

† vii. 1 - 5 ; comp. Gen. xlvi. 13 ; Numb. xxvi. 23 - 25. — "The sons of
Izrahiah . . . . . five" (3) ; but the names are only four.

‡ vii. 6 - 12 (comp. Gen. xlvi. 21 ; Numb. xxvi. 38 - 41). This genealogy of Benjamin is so unmanageable, and so in contradiction to another immediately following (viii. 1 *et seq.*), that Geddes (*ad loc.*) conjectures that it
is a corruption of a genealogy of Dan, which should naturally have stood
here, but of which there is now no trace. Hushim (12) is the name of
Dan's son in Genesis. Of Dan's descendants very scanty records have been
anywhere preserved (comp. Gen. xlvi. 23 ; Numb. xxvi. 42, 43).

§ vii. 13 ; comp. Gen. xlvi. 24 ; Numb. xxvi. 48, 49.

|| vii. 14 - 19 (comp. Numb. xxvi. 29 - 34 ; xxvii. 1) ; this passage in its
present state defies translation, as the careful English reader may have

im,* and Asher,† interspersed with a few memoranda, chiefly of a census referred to the time of David.‡ The eighth chapter relates to the tribe of Benjamin. Its statements are disconnected and incoherent; § from many it is impossible to extract any sense, or any which·is not merely absurd; ‖ their repetitions do but

---

guessed from observing what the authors of our version have made of it. It has evidently come down to us in a maimed and incomplete state, and it is in vain to attempt to extract from it any representation according with that of the parallel passage. — " Ashriel, whom *she* bare " (14); who bare Ashriel ? — " Machir took to wife Huppim and Shuppim " (15), the names of men, whose sister is said in the next verse to have been Machir's wife. As I read the passage in Numbers, it speaks of Asriel, Shemida, and Hepher (Zelophe-had's father) as all sons of Gilead, and through him grandsons of Machir, Manasseh's son ; while what is intelligible of the passage now before us represents Ashriel and Zelophehad as Manasseh's own children ; and it goes on in the same sentence both to affirm and to deny that certain persons named were " sons of Gilead," and then to name the children of Shemidah, of whose own parentage it gives no information.

* 1 Chron. vii. 20 – 29. According to Numbers (xxvi. 35) Ephraim had three sons, Shuthelah, Becher, and Tahan. In this passage (20 – 22), after the words " sons of Ephraim," follow nine names, among which Shuthelah is one, and Shuthelah and ͵Tahath occur twice. If the representation was intended to be, not that these persons were sons of Ephraim, but that they were his descendants from father to son in the line of Shuthelah, then we must understand it to be related that Ephraim lived to see and bewail the misfortunes of his posterity in the seventh generation. It is impossible not to discern the hand of a writer carelessly putting together imperfect mate-rials, the import of which he did not himself understand. The statements in 21 – 27 are confirmed by no other authority. With 28, 29, compare (with-out attempting to reconcile) Josh. xvi. 5 – 10, xvii. 7 – 11.

† vii. 30 – 40. With 30, 31, comp. Gen. xlvi. 17. The contents of the rest of the passage have no parallel elsewhere.

‡ vii. 2.

§ For example ; " These are the sons of Ehud " (6) ; who was Ehud ? — " Shaharaim begat children " (8) ; who was Shaharaim ? — Who were Shimhi (21), Shashak (25), and Jehoram (27), whose sons appear to have been also sons of Elpaal (12, 18) ? — " At Gibeon dwelt the father of Gib-eon " (29) ; but Gibeon is not named among his father's sons (30, 31), nor is his father's name recorded, though it may be inferred that Ner was meant (comp. 30, 33). — Who was Mikloth (32) ?

‖ E. g. " They removed them to Manahath " (6) ; who removed whom ? — " Naaman, and Abiah, and Gera, he removed them, and begat Uzza " (7) ; who removed them, &c. ! — " Shaharaim begat children in the country of

increase the confusion,* and their inconsistencies, as
well with one another as with those of the preceding
chapter and of other parts of Scripture, are palpable
and gross.† To speak of infallible inspiration in connection with such a composition is merely monstrous.
I do not know whether in the ninth chapter the
writer means to give a list of persons who lived about
the temple, and in Jerusalem and other cities, before
or after the time of the Babylonian conquest.‡ Perhaps, in merely copying a portion of some ancient records, he had not decided this point for himself. The
statements relate chiefly to members of the tribes of
Judah and Benjamin, and to the priests, Levites, and
Nethinim.§ The chapter concludes with a repetition

Moab, after he had sent them away; Hushim and Baara were his wives"
(8).

  * Comp. 1 Chron. viii. 3, 5; 4, 5, 7; 12, 18.

  † With viii. 1, 2, comp. vii. 6; Gen. xlvi. 21; Numb. xxvi. 38–40.
— With 29, comp. 30, 31.—"Ner begat Kish, and Kish begat Saul"
(33); but according to 1 Sam. ix. 1, Kish was son of Abiel.—The genealogy in 33–40 is carried down to the twelfth generation from Saul.

  ‡ "So all Israel were reckoned by genealogies; and, behold, they were
written in the book of the Kings of Israel and Judah" (ix. 1); if so, it is
only meagre specimens of the census that are here retained. — "Who were
carried away to Babylon," &c. (ibid.); the reader hesitates how to interpret the statement, that either the kings or the people of *Israel* were "carried away to Babylon."

  § 1 Chron. ix. 2–34. — "The Nethinims" (2); this is the only instance
of the occurrence of this word, except in the books of Ezra and Nehemiah.
It designates persons employed in menial offices about the temple; comp.
Ezra viii. 20.   The idea that the origin of this class of persons is to be
found in Josh. ix. 27, 1 Kings ix. 20, 21, I suppose to be a groundless
imagination. — "In Jerusalem dwelt . . . . . of the children of Ephraim
and Manasseh" (3); the statement that members of these tribes composed
part of the population of Jerusalem is peculiar and unexplained.   The individuals specified in 4–9 (with which comp. Numb. xxvi. 20–22, 38–40)
were of the tribes of Benjamin and Judah, to which the city belonged. —
"Of the priests . . . . . very able men for the work of the service of the
house of God" (10–13); why these persons are selected for special commemoration cannot now be conjectured, and the same remark is applicable to
the names of the Levites and porters that follow. — "Azariah, the son of

of the list of descendants from Gibeon, said to be grandfather of Saul, which, instead of closing this chapter, ought, from the connection of sense, to begin the next.*˙

The account˙ of Saul's last battle, and of his death and burial, in the following chapter, is almost word for word the same with the last chapter of the First Book of Samuel.† It only adds to the narrative therein contained the following comment, in evident reference to another portion of Saul's history narrated in the same book.‡ "So Saul died for his transgression which he committed against the Lord, even against the word of the Lord, which he kept not, and also for asking counsel of one that had a familiar spirit, to inquire of it, and inquired not of the Lord; therefore he slew him, and turned the kingdom unto David, the son of Jesse." §

Hilkiah," &c. (11); comp. vi. 11-13.—"The porters were Shallum . . . . they were porters in the companies of the children of Levi" (17, 18); these *porters*, I suppose, were of the Nethinim, of which class a proper number was attached to each company of Levites, while on duty, and under its command (comp. 26).—"Whom David and Samuel the seer did ordain in their set office" (22); comp. xxvi. 1; 2 Chron. xxix. 25, 26.— "These are the singers," &c. (33); the sense is incomplete, without a list of names, which the reader naturally expects, but which he does not find.

* 1 Chron. ix. 35-44—so inartificial and careless is this compilation—is a literal duplicate, with the following exceptions, of viii. 29-40; viz. "Jehiel" (35), "Ner" (36), "and Mikloth" (37) are wanting in viii. 29-31. "Shimeam," "they," and "over against their brethren" (38), occur for "Shimeah," "these," and "over against them," in viii. 32. The words "and Ahaz" in viii. 35 are wanting in ix. 41. "Jarah" (42) and "Rephaiah" (43) are written for "Jehoadah" and "Rapha" in viii. 36, 37; and the latter passage has nothing corresponding to the last two verses of the former (viii. 39, 40).

† x. 1-12; comp. 1 Sam. xxxi. 1-13. The only variations of the slightest importance are, that in Samuel it is said that Saul's body was fastened to the wall of Bethshan (10; comp. 1 Chron. x. 10), and that his body and those of his sons were burned by the men of Jabesh-gilead before the burial of their bones (12, 13).

‡ 1 Sam. xxviii. 7-25.   § 1 Chron. x. 13, 14.

In examining the residue of the Books of Chronicles I propose generally to pass over the merely verbal deviations from the parallel passages in the Books
of Kings, of which I have given a sufficient specimen,
and to point out such only as contribute some further
illustration to the character of the composition.

The book before us contains no account of the early
portion of David's life. The eleventh chapter relates
his installation as king over all Israel, at the end of
his seven years' government over the tribe of Judah
alone, — and his conquest of "Jerusalem, which is Je-
bus"; * and recites the names of some of his "mighty"
and "valiant men," accompanied with anecdotes of a
few of their number.† The whole contents of this
chapter are substantially, and to a great extent verbally, the same with those of two passages in the
Second Book of Samuel.

The contents of the twelfth chapter are peculiar to
this book. They are a list of "the mighty men, help-
ers of the war," "that came to David to Ziklag, while

---

* 1 Chron. xi. 1 – 9 (comp. 2 Sam. v. 1 – 3, 6 – 10); the fact of Joab's commanding at the capture of Jerusalem is here first related.

† xi. 10 – 47 ; comp. 2 Sam. xxiii. 8 – 39. — " The Tachmonite . . . . .
chief among the captains . . . . . was Adino the Eznite," who "slew at
one time eight hundred " (2 Sam. xxiii. 8). To him corresponds (1 Chron.
xi. 11) "Jashobeam an Hachmonite, the chief of the captains; he lifted
up his spear against three hundred, slain by him at one time." — "Eleazar,
the son of Dodo, the Ahohite " (2 Sam. xxiii. 9), is also mentioned in
1 Chron. xi. 12. But no mention is made of " Shammah, the son of Agee,
the Hararite," to whom in the earlier history (2 Sam. xxiii. 11), and not to
Eleazar (1 Chron. xi. 13), is attributed a victory obtained over the Philistines
in a field of grain. — " An Egyptian, a goodly man ; and the Egyptian had
a spear in his hand " (2 Sam. xxiii. 21); comp. " an Egyptian, a man of
stature, five cubits high ; and in the Egyptian's hand was a spear like a
weaver's beam " (1 Chron. xi. 23) ; the compilation in Chronicles was latest,
and such legends always grow with time. — The lists of names in 2 Sam.
xxiii. 24 – 39, and 1 Chron. xi. 26 – 41, are in great part the same. There
are differences, however, which the careful reader will observe ; and the latter list is extended (41 – 47) by the addition of sixteen names.

he yet kept himself close, because of Saul," * and a
statement of "the numbers of the bands that were
ready armed to the war, and came to David to Hebron,
to turn the kingdom of Saul to him, according to the
word of the Lord." The writer extols the prowess
and military efficiency of persons named in the former
list, belonging to the tribes of Benjamin, Gad, and
Manasseh, who attached themselves to the depressed
fortunes of David in his early life,† and relates the
distrust with which he received the overtures of certain persons of Benjamin and Judah, and the assur-
ances of fidelity by which it was removed.‡ In the
muster of the troops which assembled at Hebron to
protect and solemnize the accession of David to the
royalty of all Israel, the levies of the respective tribes
are represented as extremely unequal and dispropor-
tionate, that of Judah, David's own tribe, being of less
than seven thousand men, while the comparatively
inconsiderable tribe of Zebulun sent fifty thousand.
There appeared "of the children of Levi, four thousand and six hundred," and "of the children of Benjamin, the kindred of Saul, three thousand; for hitherto the greatest part of them had kept the ward of
the house of Saul." The occasion is said to have been
one of great festivity for three days, the neighbouring
tribes having made ample provision of "bread . . . . .
and meat, meal, cakes of figs, and bunches of raisins,
and wine, and oil, and oxen, and sheep." §

---

* Comp. 1 Sam. xxvii. 1–7.

† 1 Chron. xii. 1–15; 19–22. — " They were armed with bows, ...
hurling stones " (2); comp. Judges xx. 15, 16. — " They helped them
not," &c. (19); comp. 1 Sam. xxix. 1–11. — " They helped David," &c.
(21); comp. 1 Sam. xxx.

‡ xii. 16–18.

§ xii. 23–40. — " The children of Issachar, which were men that
had understanding of the times, to know what Israel ought to do; the

The events next related, namely, the removal of the ark of the covenant from Kirjath-jearim to the house of Obed-edom,* the building of David's palace and the increase of his family at Jerusalem,† and his two victories over the Philistines in the valley of Rephaim,‡ stand in a little different order from that of their arrangement in the Book of Samuel, the removal of the ark being there placed at the end, instead of the beginning, of this series of transactions. The narrative is nearly word for word the same in the two books.§

Previous to the relation, common to both books, of the transportation of the ark with the attendance of " all Israel " from the house of Obed-edom to the new tabernacle erected for it at Jerusalem, the narrative before us introduces an account of the arrangements made by the king for a proper superintendence of the ceremony, and for the future custody of the ark, by the priests and Levites, to whose absence from their proper share in the solemnity he ascribed the recent death of Uzzah.‖ The account of the entrance of the

---

heads of them were two hundred " (32) ; the intention seems to have been to describe these leaders of Issachar as men of eminent sagacity and prudence, but interpreters, Christian as well as Jewish, have understood the sense to be that they were learned in astronomy and astrology.— " They that were nigh them, even unto Issachar, and Zebulun, and Naphtali " (40) ; these were the most northerly tribes, while Hebron, the place of rendezvous, was at the extreme south.

  * 1 Chron. xiii. 1 – 14 ; comp. 2 Sam. vi. 1 – 11.

  † xiv. 1 – 7 ; comp. 2 Sam. v. 11 – 16.

  ‡ xiv. 8 – 17 ; comp. 2 Sam. v. 17 – 25.

  § The Book of Chronicles (xiii. 1 – 4) prefixes an account of David's consultation with the people before the expedition to remove the ark. For examples of other immaterial deviations, additions, and omissions, comp. 2 Sam. vi. 1 with 1 Chron. xiii. 5 ; 2 Sam. vi. 6 with 1 Chron. xiii. 9 ; 2 Sam. v. 15, 16 with 1 Chron. xiv. 5 –7, where the names of Elpalet and of Nogah are added to the list of David's sons, and Beeliada is put for Eliada (comp. iii. 5 – 8) ; 2 Sam. v. 25 with 1 Chron. xiv. 16, 17.

  ‖ xv. 1 – 24. — With 13 comp. xiii 10 – 11 ; and with 15 comp. Ex. xxv. 14.

ark into the city of David, commemorated with music and dancing and followed by a largess to the people,* contains no mention of the altercation before related between David and his wife Michal,† and of the Divine judgment suffered by her in consequence. On the other hand, it adds to the previous narrative of the transaction some further statements respecting the arrangements for the custody and service of the tabernacle, and for the performances of vocal and instrumental music,‡ and a psalm of David's composition, delivered by him "into the hand of Asaph and his brethren," to be used by them in the installation service.§

The narrative, through the next two chapters, runs parallel with that in the Book of Samuel, with scarcely so much as any verbal differences. The incidents are, ' the proposal of David to build a temple, in the first place approved, and then, under Divine direction, dis-

---

* 1 Chron. xv. 25 – xvi 3 ; comp. 2 Sam. vi. 12 – 19.

† 2 Sam. vi. 20 – 23.

‡ 1 Chron. xvi. 4 – 6, 37 – 43. — "Zadok the priest, and his brethren the priests, before the tabernacle of the Lord, in the high place that was at Gibeon " (39) ; this is commonly interpreted to mean, that, while the ark was set up and a solemn worship instituted in its presence at Jerusalem, the tent which inclosed it was left at Gibeon, and that another national service was by David established there (comp. Vol. II. pp. 262, 263). But the words by no means require to be so interpreted. The writer may perfectly well be understood as simply saying that Zadok and those brethren of his who *had before been* priests at Gibeon during the abode of the tabernacle there ("the priests before the tabernacle . . . . . at Gibeon ") were now appointed to render the same service in the sacrifice of burnt-offerings at Jerusalem. It is of transactions at Jerusalem alone that the writer appears to be speaking (comp. xv. 29 ; xvi. 43, *et al. h. m.*), and at Jerusalem, where the ark was, there, according to various places in the context, the tabernacle was also (comp. vi. 31, 32, 48, 49, xvi. 1).

§ xvi. 7 – 36. — The first portion, viz. verses 8 – 22, is nearly word for word the same with Ps. cv. 1 – 15 ; the remainder, viz. verses 23 – 36, is mostly the same with Ps. xcvi. — "On that day David delivered first," &c. (7) ; the writer has here been understood to say that this was the first of David's hymns used in the public worship.

allowed by Nathan ; * the assurance that the work
should be executed by David's son, whose throne God
would establish for ever,† and his thankful acknowledgment of that distinction ; and his wars with the
Philistines, Moabites, Syrians, and Edomites,‡ with a
list of the principal courtiers who aided in the administration of his prosperous government.§

Omitting the account of David's care of Saul's son,
Mephibosheth, which is inserted in this place in the
other history, the narrative next proceeds to the occasion and the occurrences of the successful war waged
by David against the allied forces of Syria and Ammon, ending in the decisive defeat of the Syrian army,
and the capture and sack of the Ammonitish capital
by Joab. The passage is almost a literal transcript of
that which is preserved in the earlier book.‖

---

* 1 Chron. xvii. 1 – 10 ; comp. 2 Sam. vii. 1 – 11.

† xvii. 11 – 27 ; comp. 2 Sam. vii. 12 – 29.

‡ xviii. 1 – 13 ; comp. 2 Sam. viii. 1 – 14. — For "Gath and her
towns" (1 Chron. xviii. 1), the other copy of the passage (2 Sam. viii. 1)
reads "Methegammah." — David's measuring the Moabites "with a line,"
&c. (2 Sam. viii. 2) is not related (1 Chron. xviii. 2). — "David took
. . . . . seven thousand horsemen" (1 Chron. xviii. 4) ; "seven hundred
horsemen" (2 Sam. viii. 4). — "From Tibhath and from Chun, cities of
Hadarezer" (1 Chron. xviii. 8) ; "from Betah and from Berothai, cities of
Hadadezer" (2 Sam. viii. 8). — "He sent Hadoram his son" (1 Chron.
xviii. 10) ; "Toi sent Joram his son" (2 Sam. viii. 10). — "From Edom
and from Moab," &c. (1 Chron. xviii. 11) ; "Of Syria and of Moab" (2
Sam. viii. 12). — "Abishai, the son of Zeruiah, slew of the Edomites, in
the Valley of Salt, eighteen thousand" (1 Chron. xviii. 12) ; "David gat
him a name when he returned from smiting of the Syrians in the Valley of
Salt, being eighteen thousand men" (2 Sam. viii. 13 ; comp. Ps. lx. 1).

§ xviii. 14 – 17 ; comp. 2 Sam. viii. 15 – 18. — "Shavsha was scribe"
(1 Chron. xviii. 16) ; "Seraiah was the scribe" (2 Sam. viii. 17).

‖ xix. 1 – xx. 1 ; comp. 2 Sam. x. 1 – xi. 1. — "The children of Ammon
sent a thousand talents of silver," &c. (1 Chron. xix. 6, 7) ; for some difference of statement, especially in respect to chariots to the amazing number of
thirty-two thousand, comp. 2 Sam. x. 6. — "Shophach" (1 Chron. xix.
16, 18) ; "Shobach" (2 Sam. x. 16, 18). — "David slew of the Syrians
seven thousand chariots, and forty thousand footmen" (1 Chron. xix. 18) ;

Recording only David's proceedings in relation to the capture of Rabbah,* and passing over the sad history of his adultery with Bathsheba,† and the long train which followed of domestic and public calamities,‡ the book before us proceeds, after a hasty mention of some other wars of David and of some of his champions who obtained distinction in them,§ to the closing acts of his reign, before in his old age he associated his son Solomon with him in the administration; namely, his taking a census of the people,‖ the divinely inflicted punishment which followed that transaction,¶ and his selection of a spot on Mount

---

" David slew seven hundred chariots of the Syrians, and forty thousand horsemen " (2 Sam. x. 18).

* 1 Chron. xx. 2, 3 ; comp. 2 Sam. xii. 27–31, which adds (27–29) the circumstance that Joab reserved the actual occupation of the city for a triumph for his master.

† 2 Sam. xi. 2 – xii. 25.

‡ 2 Sam. xiii. 1 – xxiii. 39.

§ 1 Chron. xx. 4 – 8 ; comp. 2 Sam. xxi. 18 – 22. — " Gezer " and " Sippai " (1 Chron. xx. 4) for " Gob " and " Saph " (2 Sam. xxi. 18). — " Elhanan, the son of Jair, slew Lahmi, the brother of Goliath, the Gittite " (1 Chron. xx. 5) ; " Elhanan, the son of Jaare-oregim, a Bethlehemite, slew Goliath the Gittite " (2 Sam. xxi. 19).

‖ xxi. 1 – 6 ; comp. 2 Sam. xxiv. 1 – 9. — " *Satan* stood up against Israel, and provoked David to number Israel " (1 Chron. xxi. 1) ; " the anger of *the Lord* was kindled against Israel, and he moved David against them to say, ' Go, number Israel and Judah ' " (2 Sam. xxiv. 1). We have here the first indication in Scripture of that mythology of an evil spirit (answering to the Oriental *Ahriman*), learned by the Jews while at Babylon. — The one book (2 Sam. xxiv. 5 – 8) gives a more particular account of the proceedings in taking the census ; the other (1 Chron. xxi. 6) records the intentional omission of two tribes by Joab, by reason of his disgust at the measure. — " All they of Israel were a thousand thousand and an hundred thousand men that drew sword, and Judah was four hundred threescore and ten thousand men that drew sword " (1 Chron. xxi. 5) ; " there were in Israel eight hundred thousand valiant men that drew the sword, and the men of Judah were five hundred thousand men " (2 Sam. xxiv. 9).

¶ xxi. 7 – 17 ; comp. 2 Sam. xxiv. 10 – 17. — " Three years' famine " (1 Chron. xxi. 12) ; " seven years' famine " (2 Sam. xxiv. 13). — " The threshing-floor of Ornan the Jebusite " (1 Chron. xxi. 15) ; " of

Moriah for the future temple, — events, the relation of which, in substantially the same words, closes the history in the Books of Samuel.* To the statements of the other book a comment is annexed, as if it were thought necessary to justify David's course in sacrificing at "the threshing-floor of Ornan." He did so, it is said, because there he "saw that the Lord had answered him," † and he could not offer his holocaust in Jerusalem, because "the tabernacle of the Lord, which Moses had made in the wilderness," and along with it "the altar of the burnt-offering, were at that season in the high place at Gibeon," not having been yet removed to Jerusalem, according to the author of this passage, who perhaps confused the order of events.‡ Nor could David go to Gibeon to make his burnt-offering, because that place was at some distance, and the exigency was urgent. "David could not go before it to inquire of God; for he was afraid, because of the sword of the angel of God." §

Araunah the Jebusite " (2 Sam. xxiv. 16). — " David lifted up his eyes, and saw the angel of the Lord stand between the earth and the heaven, having a drawn sword," &c. (1 Chron. xxi. 16); comp. 2 Sam. xxiv. 17; the story had grown in the interval between the two records.

* 1 Chron. xxi. 18 – 30 ; comp. 2 Sam. xxiv. 18 – 25. — " The angel of the Lord commanded Gad to say to David," &c. (1 Chron. xxi. 18) ; " Gad came that day to David, and said unto him," &c. (2 Sam. xxiv. 18). — " Ornan turned back and saw the angel, and his four sons with him hid themselves " (1 Chron. xxi. 20); still the story grows (comp. 2 Sam. xxiv. 20). — " David gave to Ornan for the place six hundred shekels of gold by weight " (1 Chron. xxi. 25); " David bought the threshing-floor and the oxen for fifty shekels of silver " (2 Sam. xxiv. 24). — " David . . . . . called upon the Lord, and he answered him from heaven by fire upon the altar of burnt-offering ; and the Lord commanded the angel, and he put up his sword again into the sheath thereof " (1 Chron. xxi. 26, 27) ; all added since the time of the former compilation (comp. 2 Sam. xxiv. 25).

† Also, he was justified in so doing by the express command of the angel (1 Chron. xxi. 18).

‡ Comp. 1 Chron. xvi. 1 – 4, 2 Chron. i. 3 – 6.

§ 1 Chron. xxi. 28 – 30 ; see above, p. 19, note ‡.

With the exception of a few brief statements, the remaining eight chapters of the First Book of Chronicles have no parallel in the Books of Kings. They record the adoption of Solomon to a share in the government; the instructions given to him by his father respecting the building of the temple; the distribution of the priests, Levites, and others, for the service of the temple and other departments of the public administration; the contributions made by David and his princes for the erection and furniture of the sacred edifice; and, lastly, his death, after a reign of forty years.

Though David was forbidden himself to erect the sacred edifice, he diligently prepared materials, it is said, to speed the work which was to be executed by his son, employing foreign artificers in hewing stones, and collecting " iron in abundance for the nails for the doors of the gates, and for the joinings, and brass in abundance without weight, also cedar-trees in abundance " from Tyre and Sidon.* He told his son that he himself would fain have built a house for Jehovah, but had been forbidden because the work more fitly belonged to " a man of rest " and a time of " peace and quietness," while he had made "great wars," and "shed much blood upon the earth." † He charges his son to observe the law, that so he may be prospered in the great undertaking.‡ He acquaints him with the preparations that have been made, including the consecration of " an hundred thousand talents of gold and a thousand thousand talents of silver," a sum which has been estimated as high as twenty-five thousand

---

* 1 Chron. xxii. 1 - 5.

† xxii. 6 - 10; comp. xvii. 4 et seq., 2 Sam. vii. 5 et seq., in neither of which places, however, is this reason given.

‡ xxii. 11 - 13.

eight hundred millions of dollars; * and he charges
"all the princes of Israel," now that the Lord
had given them "rest on every side," and there
was no longer scope for military enterprise, to apply
all their energies to the aid of his son in the erection of the temple and the establishment of the national worship.†

The writer appears to describe David, after associating his son with him in the government,‡ as chiefly
employing himself with the arrangements for the national worship, designed to be celebrated at the future
temple with exact system, and on a scale of great magnificence and cost.   He had a census taken of the Levites over thirty years of age,§ and found their number to be thirty-eight thousand. Twenty-four thousand of them he appointed "to set forward the work
of the house of the Lord; and six thousand were officers and judges; moreover, four thousand were porters; and four thousand praised the Lord with the
instruments." ‖   His arrangement of them in three
divisions, agreeably to their descent respectively from
the three sons of Levi, affords occasion to the writer
to give the names and a portion of the genealogies of
several of the chief persons of the different Levitical
families.¶   Reflecting further, that the service of the

---

* 1 Chron. xxii. 14 – 16. Le Clerc's computation, however (" Comment.
in Vet. Test.," ad. loc.), reduces the sum to four thousand three hundred
millions of dollars, something more than the present national debt of England, which, it is said, all the money in the world would not pay. See also
Dathe, in 1 Chron. xxix. 7.

  † xxii. 17 – 19.

  ‡ xxiii. 1. The interesting circumstances of this transaction, as related in
1 Kings i. are all passed over here.

  § This was the age at which the Levitical attendance began, according to
the provision in Numbers iv. 3.

  ‖ xxiii. 2 – 5.

  ¶ xxiii. 6 – 23. Verses 9 and 10 appear to contradict each other.

Levites would no longer be limited, as of old, to the conveyance of the tabernacle while on the march and the care of the sacred vessels, but would extend to various offices to be discharged under the direction of the priests, and would therefore require a larger force, he ordained by a later decree another census of the tribe " from twenty years old and above." *

The priests David, assisted by a sacerdotal and Levitical conclave, distributed into twenty-four companies, under as many presidents, sixteen of these officers being descended from the house of Eleazar, son of Aaron, and eight from that of Ithamar.† In connection with this arrangement are mentioned the names of several Levites, who are said to have " cast lots over against their brethren the sons of Aaron, ... over against their younger brethren." ‡   The passage is altogether disjointed and confused; and it appears probable that the compiler, sensible of the defect of his materials, contented himself with setting it down as he found it, without pretending to be possessed of its sense.

The musicians and choristers for the public worship, to the number of two hundred and eighty-eight, are said to have been distributed into twenty-four companies of twelve persons each, each company consisting of sons and brothers of its leader, — himself a son of Asaph, Heman, or Jeduthun, — to whom was intrusted the direction of the whole.§

---

* 1 Chron. xxiii. 24 – 32 ; comp. Numb. viii. 24.

† xxiv. 1 - 19. — " According to their manner, under Aaron their father, as the Lord God of Israel had commanded him " (19) ; but we nowhere read that Aaron either received or gave directions for any such arrangement.

‡ xxiv. 20 – 31. — With 20 – 22, comp. xxiii. 16 – 18 ; with 23, comp. xxiii. 19 ; with 24, 25, comp. xxiii. 20 ; with 26 – 29, comp. xxiii. 21, 22 ; with 30, comp. xxiii. 23.   The redundances are as unmeaning as the defects, and show a writer working in the dark.

§ xxv. 1 – 31. — Of the four sons of Asaph, Asarelah (2) is called Je-

The twenty-sixth chapter is another specimen of
such incompleteness and incoherence as proceed only
from a writer not in possession of his subject. One
can scarcely avoid thinking, that, composing several
centuries after the age of David, and a long time after
the downfall of the nation, the author merely threw
together in an undigested mass such separate notices
as he was able to find of the ancestors of contemporaries of his own who were ambitious to be thus distinguished. The account of keepers of the temple gates
conveys no intelligible notion of the arrangements; it
is evidently incomplete as a mere list of those officers;
and it differs from statements of the same description
elsewhere.* In the distribution of honors among
keepers of the treasures, "officers and judges," the
same trust is assigned to different persons; immaterial
circumstances are presented with extraordinary prominence;† the whole strain, in short, wants that fulness, consistency, proportion, and compactness which
mark the work of a well-informed historian. ‡

By the twelve companies next mentioned, consisting
of twenty-four thousand men each, appears to be

---

sharelah (14); of the five (said to be "six") sons of Jeduthun, Zeri (3)
is called Izri (11); of the fourteen sons of Heman, Uzziel and Shebuel (4)
are called Azareel and Shubael (18, 20). The deficiency in the names of
the "six" sons of Jeduthun (3) is made up (17) by the name of Shimei.—
"These were the sons of Heman, the king's seer in the words of God, to
lift up the horn" (5); so wrote King James's much extolled translators;
the meaning probably is, that Heman's sons performed on the horn in the
temple service.

* 1 Chron. xxvi. 1-19; comp. ix. 14-26. — No doubt, the time for interpreting much of this has long gone by, even if the compiler understood it
himself. Our translators, after their manner where a passage is obscure,
have dashed through it pell-mell, leaving only heaps of jargon in their track.

† E. g. xxvi. 31.

‡ xxvi. 20-32; comp. 20, 22, 24, 26. — "Two thousand and seven
hundred" (32) was a large number of "brethren," or other relations, of
one man, to be sent as prefects to the trans-Jordanic tribes.

meant a succession of military guards, designed to be attendant on the royal person each for one month in the year.* The tribes, it seems, were understood to have still preserved their distinctness, for a list is given of the " princes " of them respectively,† and it is added that the aggregate number of them all was not recorded nor ascertained.‡ The chapter closes with yet another list of high officers of the court, camp, and household, and of persons intrusted with the charge of the royal exchequer, granaries, farms, vineyards, fig and olive orchards, forests, herds, flocks, asses, and camels.§

The building of the temple being the great subject upon his mind, to be disposed of before his death, David is related to have assembled at Jerusalem all the principal persons of the realm in civil or in military life, to hear his last charge to them and to his heir respecting that all-important enterprise. He told them how it had been his purpose himself to execute it, but that because of the warlike habits of his life he had been forbidden, and informed that the honor was reserved for his son Solomon, divinely selected from among his children, as himself had been among the sons of Jesse, and as the house of Jesse had been among the families of Judah, and Judah among the tribes of Israel. To Solomon Jehovah had assured him that he would be a father, and establish his king-

---

* 1 Chron. xxvii. 1 - 15. A movement of such a body of troops every month was not unattended with expense. — " The fourth captain, for the fourth month, was Asahel, the brother of Joab " (7) ; but, according to 2 Sam. ii. 23, Asahel was killed by Abner while David was as yet only king of the Judahites.

† xxvii. 16 - 22 (comp. Numb. vii. 12 - 78) ; the tribes of Gad and Asher are not mentioned.

‡ xxvii. 23, 24 ; comp. xxi. 5, 6.

§ xxvii. 25 - 34.

dom for ever, if he would but be constant to keep the
commandments and judgments of the Law.* That
obedience David exhorted first the people, and then
their young king, to render, assuring them that thus
they should secure the permanent peace and prosperity of their children, and calling him to witness that
Jehovah would be ready, if sought, to be found by
him, but if forsaken, would cast him off for ever.†
Then, in the people's presence, he delivered to·his son
the plans of the sacred edifice (communicated to himself, as he is related to have declared, by Jehovah's
"hand" upon him); schedules of his arrangements
for the services to be rendered by the priests and Levites; and, lastly, the immense treasures in precious
metals which he had amassed and dedicated to the
work, divided in suitable parcels with reference to the
uses for which they were severally destined.‡ Encouraging his son to the great undertaking by reminding him of his reasonable reliance on the Divine aid,
and the great resources of human industry, ingenuity,
and wisdom at his command,§ and bespeaking for him
the people's aid, because of his youth and inexperi-
ence, and the august purpose of the contemplated
work, he appealed to them to exercise a liberality in
some proportion to what they had witnessed in himself. ‖

The appeal was not fruitless. To the great joy of
both king and people, "the chief of the fathers and
princes of the tribes of Israel, and the captains of
thousands and of hundreds, with the rulers over the
king's work, offered willingly," bringing large contributions of gold, silver, brass, iron, and precious
stones.¶ Then " David blessed the Lord before all

---

* 1 Chron. xxviii. 1-7.   † xxviii. 8-10.   ‡ xxviii. 11-19.
§ xxviii. 20, 21.   ‖ xxix. 1-5.   ¶ xxix. 6-9.

the congregation," mingling fit expressions of a sense of ill-desert, yet confidence of a righteous purpose, with praise, thanksgiving, and supplication for the happy issue of the work, and for the lasting integrity and welfare of his people and his son.* The solemnity closed with a united prostration of the whole assembly, followed by a magnificent succession of sacrifices, and a festival at which Solomon (with Zadok for his chief adviser in sacred matters) was a second time recognized as king.†

The book concludes with recording the quiet and unresisted accession of Solomon to the throne; his enjoyment of a prosperous administration, favored both of man and God; and the death, "in a good old age, full of days, riches, and honor," of the great King David, whose acts, together with the various fortunes and misfortunes of his reign, are said to have been "written in the book of Samuel the seer, and in the book of Nathan the prophet, and in the book of Gad the seer."‡

---

* 1 Chron. xxix. 10 – 19.   † xxix. 20 – 22.

‡ xxix. 23 – 30. — Here the other narrative (1 Kings ii. 1 – iii. 1) records David's last charge to his son, including some murderous commissions which Solomon is related to have executed, after some cautious delay, and watching for opportunities; the imputed seditious plot of Adonijah, and his assassination in consequence by his brother's order; the deposition and banishment of Abiathar to his country estate; the promotion of Benaiah and Zadok; and the marriage of Solomon to an Egyptian princess.

3 *

LECTURE LV.

HISTORY FROM DAVID'S TIME TO THE CAPTIVITY.

THE SECOND BOOK OF CHRONICLES.

SOLOMON'S VISIT TO GIBEON. — ERECTION AND DEDICATION OF THE TEM-
PLE. — APPARITION OF JEHOVAH. — RETROCESSION OF CERTAIN JEWISH
CITIES BY HIRAM. — BUILDING OF OTHER CITIES, AND OF A NAVY ON
THE RED SEA. — VISIT OF THE QUEEN OF SHEBA. — SEPARATE ESTAB-
LISHMENT OF SOLOMON'S IDOLATROUS QUEEN. — HIS WISDOM, RICHES,
GREATNESS, AND DEATH. — REIGN OF REHOBOAM, AND RELATIONS OF
HIS GOVERNMENT TO THE NEW NORTHERN KINGDOM AND TO EGYPT.
— ACCOUNT OF THE REIGNS OF ABIJAH AND ASA, MORE FULL THAN
THAT IN THE BOOK OF KINGS. — MORE BRIEF ACCOUNT OF THE REIGN
OF JEHOSHAPHAT. — HIS WARS. — HIS RELIGIOUS AND CIVIL REFORMS.
— ADDITIONAL PARTICULARS OF THE REIGN OF JEHORAM. — DIVERSITIES
IN RESPECT TO THE REIGNS OF AHAZIAH AND JOASH. — EXTENDED AC-
COUNTS OF THE REIGNS OF AMAZIAH AND UZZIAH. — REIGNS OF JO-
THAM AND AHAZ, WITH RETRENCHMENTS AND ADDITIONS. — ACCESSION
OF HEZEKIAH, AND MINUTE ACCOUNT OF HIS RELIGIOUS REFORMS. —
REIGN OF MANASSEH, WITH OMISSIONS AND INSERTIONS, THE LATTER
COMPREHENDING AN ACCOUNT OF A RELIGIOUS REFORMATION IN HIS
TIME. — REIGNS OF AMON AND JOSIAH, WITH CONTRIBUTIONS OF NEW
FACTS RESPECTING THE LATTER MONARCH. — COMPENDIOUS ACCOUNT
OF THE REIGNS OF JEHOAHAZ, JEHOIAKIM, JEHOIACHIN, AND ZEDEKIAH,
AND OF EVENTS PRECEDING AND TERMINATING IN THE CAPTIVITY. —
PROCLAMATION OF CYRUS.

THE Second Book of Chronicles covers the same period as the two Books of Kings. At its beginning it
relates the visit of Solomon to Gibeon, where, after
sacrificing, he had a vision of Jehovah in a dream.*

---

* 2 Chron. i. 1-13; comp. 1 Kings iii. 2-15. — The statement of Solomon's magnificent attendance on this journey is peculiar to Chronicles (2,
3). — " Solomon . . . . . went to the high place that was at Gibeon ; for

Then, omitting the account in the earlier history of the famous instance of his judicial wisdom, the list of his great men, and the eulogy on the extent of his dominion, the affluence of his resources, the perfection of his arrangements, and the splendor of his personal accomplishments,* the narrative proceeds at once to his preparations for the great work of the temple, with only a brief reference to his military equipment, the wealth and magnificence attained under his administration, and the course of commerce in his day.†

Having first secured a hundred and fifty thousand workmen, (" strangers in the land of Israel,") and marshalled them under thirty-six hundred overseers, he wrote to the king of Tyre to inform him of his purpose, and to propose the purchase of a quantity of timber of different kinds, and the hire of " a man cunning to work " in the metals, in precious stones, and

---

there was the tabernacle . . . . . ; but the ark of God had David brought up, ... for he had pitched a tent for it at Jerusalem," &c. (3 – 5). The writer of this passage, it appears (comp. 1 Chron. xxi. 28, 29), understood that the tabernacle and great altar of burnt offerings, made in the wilderness, remained up to this time separate from the ark at Gibeon. But it does not appear that this was so understood by the author of the other history (comp. 1 Kings iii. 4), and it by no means appears that the author of either meant to approve Solomon's sacrificing at any place where the ark was not. On the contrary, the author of Chronicles implies (1 Chron. xxi. 28 – xxii. 1) that David considered himself not at liberty to do so, and the author of Kings, in introducing the narrative, makes the propensity of Solomon to offer this kind of sacrifices, in imitation of his less instructed people, an exception to the commendation which he bestows on that prince (1 Kings iii. 2 – 4), and, in his fuller account of the transaction, represents Solomon as having testified by his conduct that he understood himself to have received in the vision a rebuke for this very thing as irregular and sacrilegious (ibid. 14), for, on awaking, he made no more sacrifices at Gibeon, great and impatient as was his gratitude, but waited till he could reach the proper place for the purpose; " he came to Jerusalem, and stood before the ark of the covenant of the Lord, and offered up burnt-offerings," &c. (ibid. 15).

* 1 Kings iii. 16 – iv. 34.
† 2 Chron. i. 13 – 17.

in hangings.* The proposal was accepted, the timber
was promised, to be delivered in floats at Joppa, and
for principal artificer a Tyrian was sent, " the son of a
woman of the daughters of Dan." †
The account, in two chapters, of the building of the
temple, though not half as long as that in the other
history, is to the same effect, and to a great extent in
the same language. ‡ The two accounts of the dedication have an equal similarity, though of these, on
the contrary, that in the Book of Chronicles is somewhat the more extended. § And the two histories pro-

---

* 2 Chron. ii. 1-10, 17, 18 ; comp. 1 Kings v. 1-6. — The message
of congratulation (1 Kings v. 1) sent by Hiram (constantly called so in
Kings, but *Huram* in Chronicles) is not mentioned here ; on the other hand,
the account of Solomon's message is much more full. — " Twenty thousand
measures (*cors*) of barley " (10) ; equivalent to one hundred and sixty thousand bushels. — " Twenty thousand baths of wine " (ibid.) ; equivalent to
one hundred and fifty thousand gallons.

† ii. 11-16 ; comp. 1 Kings v. 7-18, where the correspondence is not
verbal, as in many other passages. — " Huram said, ' Blessed be Jehovah
God of Israel, that made heaven and earth,' " &c. (12) ; supposing this to
have been written by the pagan king, it is to be explained as courtesy on
his part, called out by the language of his brother monarch (6).

‡ With 2 Chron. iii. 1-4, comp. 1 Kings vi. 1-3. The height of the
main building and the breadth of the porch, given in the other account, are
here omitted, while an extraordinary statement is added (4) of the dispro-
portionate height of the porch, said to have been an hundred and twenty
cubits. — With 2 Chron. iii. 5-17, comp. 1 Kings vi. 15-28, vii. 15-22,
where the correspondence is not verbal. The " veil of blue," &c. (14), is
not mentioned in the other book, and the height of the pillars with their
capitals, instead of forty cubits (15), is there (1 Kings vii. 15, 16 ; comp. Jer.
lii. 21) stated to have been twenty-three. — With iv. 1-10, comp. 1 Kings
vii. 23-28, 38, 39, 48, 49, vi. 36, in which nothing corresponds to the important statement (1) of the building of the altar for burnt-offerings, and in
which, instead of " three thousand baths " (5), the molten sea is said to have
held two thousand (1 Kings vii. 26). — With iv. 11-v. 1, comp. 1 Kings
vii. 40-47, 50, 51. — To 1 Kings vi. 4-14, 29-vii. 12, 29-37, there is
no parallel passage in Chronicles.

§ With 2 Chron. v. 2-vi. 42, comp. 1 Kings viii. 1-53, where there is
scarcely a verbal variation, except the more circumstantial statements in 2
Chron. v. 11-13, vi. 13, and the different conclusions of Solomon's prayer in
vi. 40-42 (comp. Ps. cxxxii. 8, 9) and 1 Kings viii. 50-53. — " They

ceed together down to the end of this reign, with relations of a second appearance of Jehovah to the king,*
of the retrocession of certain Jewish cities by Hiram,†
of the building of other cities, ‡ and of a navy on the
Red Sea, § of the employment of captives on the public works, ‖ of the visit of the queen of Sheba,¶ of
the establishment of Solomon's queen, as an idolatress,
in a separate palace,** and of his great revenues, com-

brought up the ark, and the tabernacle of the congregation " (v. 5); language which seems to denote that the writer understood the tabernacle and
the ark to be together. — " Neither chose I any man to be a ruler over my
people Israel " (vi. 5); comp. Judges iii. 9; 1 Sam. ix. 16, *et al. h. m.* —
" When Solomon ·had made an end of praying, the fire came down from
heaven, ánd consumed the burnt-offering and the sacrifices ; . . . . . and
when all the children of Israel saw how the fire came down, and the glory
of the Lord upon the house, they bowed themselves with their faces to the
ground," &c. (vii. 1 - 3). Of all this marvel there is nothing whatever said
in the corresponding passage in the other book, but instead, the reader is informed (1 Kings viii. 54 - 61) of the terms in which the king " blessed all
the congregation of Israel with a loud voice." — With vii. 4 - 10, comp. 1
Kings viii. 62 - 66. The circumstance of the Levites being installed in their
office as choristers (6), and the date of the dismissal of the people from Jerusalem (10), are added, and Solomon's completion of " the king's house " is
referred to (11), though that event had not been recorded (comp. 1 Kings vii.
1 - 12). — " King Solomon offered a sacrifice of twenty-and-two thousand
oxen, and an hundred and twenty thousand sheep " (vii. 5) ; questions naturally occur to the reader respecting the time which so many sacrifices would
occupy, and the effects of their smoke and odor on the population of the city.
    * With 2 Chron. vii. 11 - 22 (which adds 13 - 15), comp. 1 Kings ix. 1 - 9.
    † viii. 1, 2 ; comp. 1 Kings ix. 10 - 14, where the dissatisfaction of Hi-
ram is said to have occasioned their restoration.
    ‡ With viii. 3 - 6, comp. 1 Kings ix. 14 - 19, containing additional matter
in 14 - 16.
    § With viii. 17, 18, comp. 1 Kings ix. 26 - 28. — " Four hundred and
fifty talents of gold " (viii. 18; comp. 1 Kings ix. 28, which reads " four
hundred and twenty talents") were, by Dr. Robinson's tables, equivalent to
about eleven millions of dollars.
    ‖ With viii. 7 - 10, comp. 1 Kings ix. 20 - 23, which differs in stating the
number of overseers at " *five* hundred and fifty."
    ¶ With ix. 1 - 9, comp. 1 Kings x. 1 - 10, which runs parallel with it al-
most word for word. — " She gave the king one hundred and twenty talents
of gold " (9), equivalent to nearly three millions of dollars.
    ** With viii. 11, which explains the reason of this arrangement, comp.
1 Kings ix. 24.

merce, enterprises, magnificence, and wealth ; * with
this important difference, however, that respecting his
uxorious apostasy to idol practices, and its disastrous
results, related in the Book of Kings,† the author of
the Chronicles is silent. The reign of Rehoboam, Solomon's son and successor, is treated in three chapters, the first of which
is derived from the same source as the corresponding one in the Book of Kings, as appears from the
sameness of language that runs through them ; ‡ the
second is principally occupied with different matter, recording transactions in Rehoboam's, or the
southern kingdom, while the other narrative employs
itself with proceedings in the territory of the revolted
tribes ; § and the third enlarges on that invasion of
Judea and capture of Jerusalem by Shishak, king of
Egypt, which the earlier history despatches in seven
verses. According to the additional statements here
furnished, Rehoboam imitated his father's example, and
built various " cities for defence in Judah," repairing

---

* With 2 Chron. viii. 12 – 16 (which adds some particulars, especially
the confirmation by Solomon of his father's arrangements for the priests,
Levites, and porters), ix. 10 – 28, comp. 1 Kings ix. 25, x. 11 – 29. The
verbal correspondence between the two passages continues almost unvaried.
— " Three hundred of gold went to one shield " (2 Chron ix. 16) ; comp.
1 Kings x. 17, which has " three pounds of gold."—" Solomon had four
thousand stalls for horses and chariots " (2 Chron. ix. 25) ; comp. 1
Kings x. 26, which reads " he had a thousand and four hundred chariots."
— With 2 Chron ix. 26, 28, compare the fuller statement in 1 Kings x. 28,
29. — With ix. 29–31, comp. 1 Kings xi. 41 – 43, where " the book of the
acts of Solomon " is referred to as authority for other incidents of that
prince's life and reign, instead of " the book of Nathan the prophet, and
the prophesy of Ahijah the Shilonite, and the visions of Iddo the seer."
† 1 Kings xi. 1 – 40.
‡ 2 Chron. x. 1 – xi. 4 (which in its patriotic indignation disdains so
much as to record that Jeroboam was made king over the rebellious tribes) ;
comp. 1 Kings xii. 1 – 24.
§ 1 Kings xii. 25 – xiv. 20.

his "strong holds," and supplying them with garrisons, munitions, and provisions, so as to make them "exceeding strong." His force was increased by the accession of priests, Levites, and other well-disposed persons from the revolted tribes, who, either suffering from the oppression of Jeroboam, or disgusted with his disorderly proceedings, "came to Jerusalem, to sacrifice unto the Lord God of their fathers," and "resorted to him out of all their coasts." "They strengthened the kingdom of Judah, and made Rehoboam, the son of Solomon, strong three years; for three years they walked in the way of David and Solomon." The royal family increased, and the king "dealt wisely, and dispersed of all his children throughout all the countries of Judah and Benjamin, unto every fenced city; and he gave them victual in abundance." Of the eighty-eight children born of his seventy-eight wives and concubines, he "made Abijah, the son of Maachah, the chief, to be ruler among his brethren; for he thought to make him king." *

But prosperity infatuated Rehoboam. "He forsook the law of the Lord, and all Israel with him"; and, as we have already been informed by the other history, "Shishak, king of Egypt, came up against Jerusalem, and took away the treasures of the house of the Lord, and the treasures of the king's house." † The present narrative adds statements of the prodigious number of the Egyptian forces, of the conquests made on their way to the capital city, of the mitigation of the threatened punishment by reason of the repen-

---

* 2 Chron. xi. 5 - 23. — "He ordained him priests for the high places" &c. (15); an apostasy from the national religion, constituting the highest possible offence in the mind of a devout Jew. — "Jerimoth, the son of David" (18); we do not find his name in the list of David's sons in 1 Chron. iii. 1 - 9.

† xii. 1, 2; comp. the fuller statement in d Kings xiv. 22 - 25; and with xii. 9 - 11, comp. the same words in 1 Kings xiv. 26 - 28.

tance of the king and nobles on the representation of Shemaiah, and of the more prosperous condition of Rehoboam's latter days.* The terminations of the two accounts of the period of Rehoboam are in part the same, though one refers the reader for further information to " the book of the Chronicles of the kings of Judah," the other asks, " The acts of Rehoboam, first and last, are they not written in the book of Shemaiah the prophet, and of Iddo the seer, concerning genealogies ? " †

The record of the three years' reign of Abijah, despatched in the former history with the briefest statements of the defective character of that prince, of the Divine forbearance to him, and of the hostile relations between him and Jeroboam,‡ is here extended through a chapter, with a narrative of the occasion and the issue of the successful war waged by the king of Judah, at the head of " an army of valiant men of war, even four hundred thousand chosen men," against Jeroboam, with his host of " eight hundred thousand chosen men, being mighty men of valor." Standing on a mountain in the territory of the principal northern tribe, Abijah is related to have made oral proclamation to its monarch and his people, remonstrating with them for their rebellion against the God-appointed representative of David, and for their lately instituted idolatrous worship of the calves and deposition and banishment of the priests and Levites, and, on the other hand, extolling the fidelity of his own adherents, the sanctity of their worship, and his and their well-founded confidence in Jehovah's favor, and cautioning the

---

* 1 Chron. xii. 3 – 8, 12.

† xii. 13 – 16 ; comp. 1 Kings xiv. 21, 29 – 31. — " Abijah, his son " (16) ; " Abijam, his son " (1 Kings xiv. 31). The same diversity is carried through the history of that prince.

‡ 1 Kings xv. 1 – 8.

adverse hosts, " O children of Israel, fight ye not against
the Lord God of your fathers, for ye shall not prosper."
By a stratagem of Jeroboam, the host of Abijah found
itself invested by the adverse army, in front and in rear.
But, nothing daunted, " they cried unto the Lord, and
the priests sounded with the trumpets; then the men of
Judah gave a shout, and as the men of Judah shouted,
it came to pass that God smote Jeroboam and all Israel before Abijah and Judah; and the children of Israel fled before Judah, and God delivered them into
their hand; and Abijah and his people slew them with
a great slaughter; so there fell down slain of Israel five
hundred thousand chosen men."   The war ended with
the crippling of Jeroboam's power, and the capture of
three towns with their dependent settlements.   " Abijah waxed mighty," and when he died left a numerous family, and a record of " the rest of his acts, and
his ways, and his sayings, written in the story of the
prophet Iddo." *

On the life and times of Asa, king of Judah, which
are despatched in the Book of Kings in sixteen verses,
the history before us is much more full.†   It records,

---

* 2 Chron. xiii. 1–22. — " His mother's name also was Michaiah the
daughter of Uriel of Gibeah " (2) ; but (xi. 20) Rehoboam " took Maachah,
the daughter of Absalom, which bare him Abijah." — " Abijah stood up
upon Mount Zemaraim," &c. (4) ; the only Zemaraim mentioned elsewhere
was in Abijah's own dominion (Josh. xviii. 22). — " A covenant of salt " (5) ;
a metaphor drawn apparently from the incorruptible and permanent nature
of that substance. — " When Rehoboam was young and tender-hearted, and
could not withstand them " (7).   The reference is to what took place after
Rehoboam ascended the throne (comp. x. 8–11); but he is said (1 Kings
xiv. 21) to have been then more than forty years old.

† Part of the matter they have in common is related in different language
(comp. xiv. 1–5 with 1 Kings xv. 9–12); part, by the similarity of phrase,
indicates that the later was copied from the earlier, or that they had a common origin (comp. xv. 16–xvi. 6, 11–14, with 1 Kings xv. 13–24). —
" There was no war [the " more " of our translators is without authority]
unto the five-and-thirtieth year of the reign of Asa " (xv. 19) ; comp. xiv. 9

in addition, that Asa took advantage of a time of long
peace to erect extensive fortifications, and equip from
his two tribes a well-provided army of five hundred
and eighty thousand men; * that, in a war with "Zerah
the Ethiopian," he obtained, by the help of Jehovah,
a decisive victory over that prince's force of a million
of soldiers, and three hundred chariots, and "carried away very much spoil"; † that, moved by the rebuke and counsel of "Azariah, the son of Oded," and
his appeals to the past experiences of the chosen race,
he "took courage, and put away the abominable idols
out of all the land of Judah and Benjamin, and out of
the cities which he had taken from Mount Ephraim,
and renewed the altar of the Lord that was before the
porch of the Lord; and he gathered all Judah and
Benjamin, and the strangers with them, out of Ephraim and Manasseh, and out of Simeon (for they fell to
him out of Israel in abundance, when they saw that
the Lord his God was with him); . . . . . and they
offered unto the Lord at the same time, of the spoil
which they had brought, seven hundred oxen, and
seven thousand sheep; and they entered into a covenant to seek the Lord God of their fathers with all
their heart, and with all their soul; that whosoever
would not seek the Lord God of Israel should be put

---

et seq.; xv. 10; 1 Kings xv. 16. — "Dan and Abel-maim, and all the store-
cities of Naphtali" (xvi. 4); "Dan, and Abel-beth-maachah, and all Cin-
neroth, with all the land of Naphtali" (1 Kings xv. 20). — "The book of
the kings of Judah and Israel" (xvi. 11); "the book of the chronicles of
the kings of Judah" (1 Kings xv. 23). — "They buried him in his own sepulchres, which he had made for himself in the city of David, and laid him
in the bed which was filled with sweet odors, and divers kinds of spices prepared by the apothecaries' art; and they made a very great burning for him"
(xvi. 14). These are additional circumstances. His body was buried, according to ancient Jewish practice; what then was the burning? Probably a
bonfire of aromatic substances. Comp. xxi. 19; Jer. xxxiv. 5.

   * 2 Chron. xiv. 6-8.   † xiv. 9-15.

to death, whether small or great, whether man or woman; and they sware unto the Lord with a loud voice,
and with shouting, and with trumpets, and with cor-
nets; and all Judah rejoiced at the oath"; * that, after
all, his proposal for an alliance with the king of Syria,
indicating a want of confidence in Jehovah, who had
given him so signal a victory over the Ethiopians,
caused the Divine displeasure to be denounced against
him by "Hanani the seer"; and that, in his resentment
against Hanani, he "put him in a prison-house," and
"oppressed some of the people the same time." †

The sketch of the thirty-five years' reign of Jehoshaphat occupies in this book about two thirds as much
space as is devoted to the same period in the Book of
Kings.   The two narratives, though pertaining to the
same time, record only in part the same events; the
one, in respect to the residue, concerning itself chiefly
with transactions in the kingdom of Judah, the other
chiefly with the affairs of the northern tribes.   Passing
over all that history in more than six chapters of the
Book of Kings, which, beginning with the accession
of Nadab and proceeding through more than fifty
years, nearly down to the death of Ahab, embraces
all the account that has been preserved of that distinguished personage Elijah,‡ the book before us sub-

---

* 2 Chron. xv. 1 - 15. — " Oded the prophet " (8) is the same person who
is called above (1) " Azariah, the son of Oded."

† xvi. 7 - 10. — " Because thou hast relied on the king of Syria, and not
relied on the Lord thy God, therefore is the host of the king of Syria escaped out of thine hand " (7). Hanani appears to be represented as saying,
that, if, instead of purchasing an alliance with Syria, Asa, trusting in Jehovah, had defied that formidable power, he would have been made victorious
over it.

‡ 1 Kings xv. 25 - xxi. 29. — Judah relied on its maintaining the divinely authorized succession and authority of the Aaronic priesthood (xiii.
9 - 13, et al. h. m.); Israel, on direct communications from Jehovah by
prophets, especially Elijah and Elisha (1 Kings xvii. 1 - 2 Kings ix. 10).

stitutes for it some comprehensive statements of the
active, patriotic, peaceful, and prosperous administration of Jehoshaphat, with a list of the principal
commanders whose merit signalized his reign. He is
said to have secured with garrisons the strongholds
of Judah, and the places conquered by his father in
the northern kingdom ; to have received a large revenue in presents; to have suppressed in Judah the
idolatrous worship in " high places and groves " ; to
have made provision for the religious instruction of
his people by an itinerant embassy of his princes,
priests, and Levites ; and, by the favor of Jehovah, not
only to have escaped all wars with " the kingdoms of
the lands that were round about," but to have received
from some of them submission and tribute.* Of the
principal officers, who at Jerusalem " waited on the
king, besides those whom the king put in the fenced
cities throughout all Judah," one is said to have commanded three hundred thousand men, another two
hundred and eighty thousand, two others each two
hundred thousand, and another a hundred and eighty
thousand, — an aggregate of a million one hundred
and sixty thousand troops, over and above those who
occupied the posts.†

The events of the alliance of Jehoshaphat with
Ahab, king of Israel, against Syria, are related in the
two histories in nearly the same terms. ‡ Then follows

---

* 2 Chron. xvii. 1– 12. — " He took away the high places and groves
out of Judah " (6) ; comp. xx. 33, 1 Kings xxii. 43, where that statement
is contradicted.

† xvii. 13 –19.

‡ xviii. 1 – 34 ; comp. 1 Kings xxii. 1 – 35. The one is merely a verbal
repetition of the other, except that the story in Chronicles refers here (1)
to Jehoshaphat's family alliance with Ahab (comp. 2 Kings viii. 16 – 18),
specifies the hospitality with which he was received by that prince (xviii. 2),
and ascribes (31, comp. 1 Kings xxii. 32) his escape from the Syrians ex-

a passage in the Book of Chronicles to which the other history has no parallel, relating some particulars of Jehoshaphat's internal administration, and of a war of his with his neighbours of Moab, Ammon, and Edom.   Awakened to his duty by the rebuke of "Jehu the son of Hanani the seer," who met him on his way home from the disasters of the ill-fated alliance with Ahab, he is said to have addressed himself with renewed diligence to reform the disorders of his government.   "He went out again through the people, from Beersheba to Mount Ephraim, and brought them back unto the Lord God of their fathers."   "He set judges in the land throughout all the fenced cities of Judah, city by city," and gave them suitable charges as to official fidelity.   Finally, he established in Jerusalem a supreme tribunal "of the Levites, and of the priests, and of the chief of the fathers of Israel," with separate presiding officers, the one the chief priest, the other "the ruler of the house of Judah," for questions relating to the ecclesiastical and to the civil administration.*

The Moabites and their allies had already penetrated into the country, before intelligence of their movements reached the king.   He immediately "proclaimed a fast throughout all Judah," and "out of all the cities of Judah they came to seek the Lord."   In the precincts of the temple, in the presence of " all Judah, ... with their little ones, their wives, and their children," Jehoshaphat offered a solemn prayer

---

pressly to Jehovah's protection ; while, on the other hand, it omits the number of the commanders of the Syrian chariots (30, comp. 1 Kings xxii. 31) and some circumstances of Ahab's death (34, comp. 1 Kings xxii. 35-40).

* 2 Chron. xix. 1-11.—" When they returned to Jerusalem " (8); for יִשְׁבוּ I presume we should read יֵשְׁבוּ, and then we shall render " and כִּי they dwelt at Jerusalem."

for direction and succour, rehearsing Jehovah's past
mercies to Israel, and exposing its present danger
from enemies whom in past time it had spared. " Then
upon Jehaziel, ... a Levite, of the sons of Asaph,
came the spirit of the Lord in the midst of the congregation." He told them where the hostile army was
encamped, and bade them resolutely march towards it
on the morrow. It would not be necessary, he said,
for them to attack it. They would have but to "stand
still, and see the salvation of the Lord." The sovereign and the people prostrated themselves and worshipped, and the Levites " stood up to praise the Lord
God of Israel with a loud voice on high." "They
rose early in the morning, and went forth into the
wilderness of Tekoa; and as they went forth, Jehoshaphat stood and said, ' Hear me, O Judah, and ye inhabitants of Jerusalem; believe in the Lord your
God, so shall ye be established; believe his prophets,
so shall ye prosper.' And when he had consulted
with the people, he appointed singers unto the Lord,
and that should praise the beauty of holiness, as they
went out before the army, and to say ' Praise the Lord,
for his mercy endureth for ever.' And when they began to sing and to praise, the Lord set ambushments
against the children of Ammon, Moab, and Mount
Seir, which were come against Judah. And they were
smitten. For the children of Ammon and Moab stood
up against the inhabitants of Mount Seir, utterly to
slay and destroy them, and when they had made an
end of the inhabitants of Seir, every one helped to destroy another."

The end was, that " when Judah came toward the
watch-tower in the wilderness," and " looked unto the
multitude," the myriads of their dreaded invaders were
but so many corses. " None escaped." Proceeding

to examine the fatal field, " they found among them in abundance both riches with the dead bodies, and precious jewels (which they stripped 'off for themselves), more than they could carry away; and they were three days in gathering of the spoil, it was so much"; after which, and after keeping a day of thanksgiving on the way, they returned in triumph home, with " Jehoshaphat in the fore-front of them," and " came to Jerusalem with psalteries, and harps, and trumpets, unto the house of the Lord." Thenceforward " the fear of God was on all the kingdoms of those countries," and " the realm of Jehoshaphat was quiet." * Well it might be, if the invaders of Israel were made to exterminate each other, after the manner described in this narrative. But what reader of it, considering whereof he affirms, will venture to maintain it to be inspired, or to be true, history? †

The conclusion of the reign of Jehoshaphat is recorded in the two histories partly in the same terms, and partly with some diversity of circumstances.‡

Passing over a portion of the history recorded in nine successive chapters of the Book of Kings and embracing the notices of the prophet Elisha, the Book of Chronicles proceeds to record the events of the reign of Jehoram, king of Judah, in a short passage, of which less than one half is paralleled in the other

---

* 2 Chron. xx. 1 – 30. — With 10, comp. Numb. xx. 21; Deut. ii. 8.

† I cannot help suspecting this to be but another *recension* of the tradition of the destruction of the Assyrians in Hezekiah's time (comp. 2 Kings xix. 14 – 37; 2 Chron. xxxii. 21.)

‡ xx. 31 – xxi. 1; comp. 1 Kings xxii. 41 – 50. — The accession of Jehoshaphat (31) wants the date from that of Ahab, given in the other book (1 Kings xxii. 41). — For a verbal difference and an omission, comp. 33 with 1 Kings xxii. 43, 44. — " The rest of the acts of Jehoshaphat, first and last, behold, they are written in the book of Jehu, the son of Hanani " (34); " in the book of the chronicles of the kings of Judah " (1 Kings xxii. 45). — With 35 – 37, comp. 2 Kings xxii. 47 – 49.

narrative. To the same account as that before given
of the duration and the character of his administration, of the reason of the Divine forbearance towards
him, and of the revolt of the Edomites and of the people of Libnah,* it is now added that he barbarously assassinated six brothers for whom their father had made
generous provision, and other principal men of the
kingdom; that he was guilty of the most high-handed
acts of idolatry; that the prophet Elijah from the
northern kingdom addressed to him a letter of reproof,
predicting for him a terrible fate; and that the prediction was fulfilled by an inroad of the Philistines
and Arabians, who sacked his palace and carried away
his wives and children, leaving him one son only, and
by a tormenting disease of the bowels, of which at the
end of two years he died.†

The two histories next relate together, in a few periods, the accession of Ahaziah, son of Jehoram, to
the throne of Judah, the evil practices into which he
was seduced by the influence of his mother's idolatrous
family, his alliance with his cousin, the king of Israel,

---

* 2 Chron. xxi. 5 - 10, 20; comp. 2 Kings viii. 17 - 24. — " The Lord
would not destroy the house of David " (7); " the Lord would not destroy
Judah " (2 Kings viii. 19). — " Jehoram went forth with his princes " (9);
" Joram went over to Zair " (2 Kings viii. 21, which also adds, " And the
people fled into their tents"). — " Because he had forsaken the Lord God of
his fathers " (10); a comment wanting in the corresponding place in Kings.
— With the more exact account of the death and burial of Jehoram in 19,
20, comp. 2 Kings viii. 23, 24.

† xxi. 1 - 4, 11 - 19. — " Jehoshaphat slept with his fathers, ...
and Jehoram, his son, reigned in his stead " (1); comp. 1 Kings xxii. 50,
2 Kings viii. 16. — " Jehoshaphat, king of Israel " (2); " the princes of
Israel " (4); but Jehoshaphat and Jehoram were kings of Judah, not of
Israel, as their whole history declares. — " There came a writing to him
from Elijah the prophet," &c. (12). But Elijah was translated, according
to the other history (2 Kings ii. 11), years before the accession of Jehoram.
Accordingly, many commentators, Jewish and Christian, have understood
that this letter was transmitted by Elijah to Jehoram from heaven.

in a war against the Syrians, and his journey to Jezreel
to visit that prince when he had been wounded in
battle.* Then, with only a brief reference to the
events which, according to the other narrative, intervened,† the history before us records with different
circumstances the death of that prince,‡ and, passing
over, as foreign to its object, the occurrences of the
reign of Jehu in Israel,§ proceeds to relate, in unison
with the earlier account, the important transactions
connected with the accession of Joash, and signalizing
his reign as one of the most memorable of those times.

In this portion of the narrative, there is, to a considerable extent, a close verbal agreement between the two
accounts, while, on the other hand, there are remarkable diversities of statement, not of the nature of contradictions, but some of them such as to show that
the two writers were looking on the subject from different positions, the one acting the part simply of a
registrar of events of high public interest, the other
disposed to lay peculiar stress on the agency of the
priests and Levites, and to present the events related
in an ecclesiastical point of view.‖ The compiler of

---

* 2 Chron. xxii. 1–6; comp. 2 Kings viii. 25–29. — "Ahaziah, his
youngest son" (1). But the only surviving son of Jehoram is said (xxi. 17)
to have been named Jehoahaz; and he is also called Azariah (xxii. 6). —
"Forty-and-two years old was Ahaziah when he began to reign" (2).
This reckoning would place his birth two years before that of his father;
comp. xxi. 20; but the parallel passage has "two-and-twenty years" (2
Kings viii. 26.

† xxii. 7; comp. 2 Kings ix. 1–26.

‡ xxii. 8, 9; comp. 2 Kings ix. 27–29, x. 13, 14. According to one
account, Ahaziah died at Megiddo of a wound received in his chariot; according to the other, he was dragged from a hiding-place in Samaria,
brought into the presence of Jehu, and there put to death.

§ 2 Kings ix. 30–x. 36.

‖ 2 Chron. xxii. 10–xxiv. 27; comp. 2 Kings xi. 1–xii. 21. — "Je-
hoshabeath" (11); "Jehosheba" (2 Kings xi. 2, which also omits to describe her as "the wife of Jehoiada, the priest"). — With xxiii. 1–3, which

the Chronicles introduces some new matter, by which
he accounts for the troubles of the Syrian invasion,
and the violent death of King Joash. He says that
after the decease of Jehoiada, the priest, at the age of
a hundred and thirty years, the weak king listened to
the solicitations of his courtiers, and permitted them
to "serve groves and idols"; and that Jehovah sent
prophets to reclaim them, but in vain; "they would
not give ear." One of them was "Zechariah, the son
of Jehoiada, the priest." Not only were they deaf to

---

names some of the persons engaged by Jehoiada in his conspiracy, and describes their proceedings, especially their assembling at Jerusalem "the Levites out of all the cities of Judah," comp. the more compendious account in
2 Kings xi. 4. — "Of the priests and of the Levites" (4) ; the other account
assigns   such distinction to these orders (comp. 2 Kings xi. 5). — "The
gate of the foundation" (5), say our translators; and "the gate of Sur"
(2 Kings xi. 6); the Hebrew being in the one place יְסוֹד, in the other סוּר.
— "Let none come into the house of the Lord, save the priests, and they
that minister of the Levites; they shall go in, for they are holy," &c. (6).
"The Levites shall compass the king round about, every man with his weapons in his hand," &c. (7). "The Levites, and all Judah," &c. (8). "Jehoiada the priest dismissed not the courses" (8). Of all these specifications
of the trusts committed to priests and Levites, there is nothing in the parallel passage (2 Kings xi. 7-9). In the same point of view, comp. 13
(where we have the addition, "also the singers with instruments of music,
and such as taught to sing praise") with 2 Kings xi. 14; also the statement, "Jehoiada appointed the offices of the house of the Lord by the hand
of the priests the Levites, whom David had distributed in the house of the
Lord, to offer the burnt-offerings of the Lord, as it is written in the law of
Moses, with rejoicing and with singing, as it was ordained by David; and
he set the porters at the gates of the house of the Lord, that none which was
unclean in any thing should enter in" (18, 19), with the simple sentence, "the
priest appointed officers over the house of the Lord" (2 Kings xi. 18). —
"Jehoiada took for him two wives, and he begat sons and daughters" (xxiv.
3); an addition to the account in the other book, and, on the other hand, a
suppression of the statement in 2 Kings xii. 3. — In the record of the early
measures, which proved abortive, "to repair the house of the Lord," the
account in Chronicles (xxiv. 4-7) is less precise than that in Kings (xii.
4-8). Different sources of the sacred revenue are specified (comp. 5 with
2 Kings xii. 4), and the e even appears a disposition to suppress a charge of
embezzlement against the Levitical order (comp. 6 with 2 Kings xii. 6-8).
— "The collection . . . . . of the congregation of Israel, for the tabernacle

his reproofs; "they conspired against him, and stoned him with stones, at the commandment of the king, in the court of the house of the Lord." His last words were, "The Lord look upon it, and require it." And it was requited when Jerusalem was spoiled by the marauding Syrian band, and Joash perished under the hands of conspirators.*

The record of the reign of Amaziah, king of Judah, in this book is substantially the same, in phrase as well as matter, with that in the earlier

---

of witness" (6; comp. 9); the writer appears to represent Joash as comparing the contribution which he had directed to that made in the wilderness for the construction of the tabernacle (Ex. xxx. 12 - 16). — With 14, comp. 2 Kings xii. 13 - 16. The verse in Chronicles omits some statements in the corresponding passage, adds one concerning burnt-offerings, and appears to contradict the other history in what is said respecting the course taken to provide the "vessels to minister, and to offer withal." — The two accounts of the Syrian war and of the death and burial of Joash are different, and partly contradictory. According to one, Hazael, king of Syria, after taking Gath, was moving towards Jerusalem, when he was bought off with a subsidy of "all the hallowed things" collected by preceding monarchs, and "all the gold that was found in the treasures of the house of the Lord and of the king's house" (2 Kings xii. 17, 18); after which Joash was put to death "in the house of Millo, which goeth down to Silla," by "Jozachar, the son of Shimeath, and Jehozabad, the son of Shomer, his servants," and was buried "with his fathers in the city of David" (xii. 20, 21). According to the other, "the host of Syria" — "a small company of men " against "a very great host," but prospered by Jehovah to execute his meditated judgment — "came to Judah and Jerusalem, and destroyed all the princes of the people from among the people, and sent all the spoil of them unto the king of Damascus" (2 Chron. xxiv. 23, 24); after which the king, "left in great diseases," was murdered in his bed by Zabad, the son of Shimeath an Ammonitess, and Jehozabad, the son of Shimrith a Moabitess," and was buried "in the city of David, but . . . . . not in the sepulchres of the kings " (xxiv. 25, 26). — " For the blood of the sons of Jehoiada the priest" (25); but we are told of the death of only one son (20, 21). — " They are written in the story of the book of the kings " (27); "are they not written in the book of the chronicles of the kings of Judah! " (2 Kings xii. 19.)

* 2 Chron. xxiv. 15 - 27. — " They buried him in the city of David, among the kings " (16); an honor that we nowhere else read of as being conferred upon any but a royal person.

history,* except that it inserts a full account of the circumstances of the war with Edom. It relates that he mustered and organized an army of "three hundred thousand choice men" of his two tribes of Judah and Benjamin, and "hired also an hundred thousand mighty men of valor out of Israel for an hundred talents of silver"; that "a man of God" remonstrated with him on this latter arrangement, on the ground that "the Lord was not with Israel," and that the king, though reluctant to lose his money, sent the Israelitish forces home, to their great displeasure, which they vented by falling upon some cities of Judah, smiting "three thousand of them," and carrying off "much spoil"; that in the sequel of the war against Idumea, for which these preparations had been made, and which proved signally successful, Amaziah "brought the gods of the children of Seir, and set them up to be his gods, and bowed down himself before them, and burned incense unto them"; that a prophet, sent to him from Jehovah, expostulated with

---

* 2 Chron. xxv. 1–4, 17–28; comp. 2 Kings xiv. 1–6, 8–20 (2 Kings xiii. as relating merely to the affairs of Israel, has of course no parallel in Chronicles). — "He did that which was right in the sight of the Lord, but not with a perfect heart" (2); a milder qualification han that in the corresponding passage (2 Kings xiv. 3, 4). — "For it came of God, that he might deliver them into the hand of their enemies, because they sought after the gods of Edom" (20; comp. 2 Kings xiv. 11); "after the time that Amaziah did turn away from following the Lord, they made a conspiracy against him in Jerusalem" (27; comp. 2 Kings xiv. 19); the insertion of such comments, pointing out providential retributions, is in the manner characteristic of this book. — "Amaziah, king of Judah, the son of Joash, the son of Jehoahaz" (23); "Amaziah, king of Judah, the son of Jehoash, the son of Ahaziah" (2 Kings xiv. 13). — "In the house of God with Obed-edom" (24; comp. 1 Chron. xxvi. 4, 8, 15); "in the house of the Lord" (2 Kings xiv. 14). — "The acts of Amaziah, first and last, behold, are they not written in the book of the kings of Judah and Israel?" (26); "are they not written in the book of the chronicles of the kings of Judah?" (2 Kings xiv. 18.) — "The city of Judah" (28); a designation found nowhere else; "the city of David" (2 Kings xiv. 20).

him for the folly as well as impiety of worshipping
gods whom himself had been able to subdue, but, being roughly answered, forbore and withdrew, with the
warning that God would take the punishment of the
royal wickedness into his own hands; a threat which
was presently fulfilled in the disastrous war with
Israel.*

The reign of Uzziah, treated in nine verses in the
Book of Kings, is in the history before us extended
over nearly three times that space, though most of
what the two have in common is related in the same
words † The additional matter celebrates his prosperity "as long as he sought the Lord," consisting in
successful wars against the Philistines, Arabians, and
Mehunims, his tribute from the Ammonites, the
spreading abroad of his name "even to the entering
in of Egypt," his buildings and fortifications of cities
and towers, his digging of wells, his interest. in herds,
in vineyards, and in husbandry, his well-marshalled and
well-equipped military force of more than three hundred and seven thousand men, "that made war with
mighty power, to help the king against the enemy,"
his "engines invented by cunning men" for the protection of Jerusalem, "to be on the towers, and upon the

---

* 2 Chron. xxv. 5 – 16 ; comp. 2 Kings xiv. 7. — "An hundred thousand
mighty men of valor out of Israel for an hundred talents of silver " (6);
something more than a dollar and a half for each mighty man.

† xxvi. 1 – 4 (which has Eloth for *Elath*, and, as also throughout, Uzziah for *Azariah*, and omits the statement that "the high places were not
removed "), 21 – 23 ; comp. 1 Kings xiv. 21, 22, xv. 2 – 8. — "The rest of
the acts of Uzziah, first and last, did Isaiah the prophet, the son of Amoz,
write " (22); if he did write them, the writing is not now extant; "the
rest of the acts of Azariah, and all that he did, are they not written in the
book of the chronicles of the kings of Judah ? " (2 Kings xv. 6.) — "They
buried him with his fathers in the field of the burial which belonged to the
kings ; for they said, ' He is a leper ' " (23) ; "they buried him with his fathers in the city of David " (2 Kings xv. 7).

bulwarks, to shoot arrows and great stones withal";
and finally, the Divine judgment by which he was
smitten with leprosy for an outrage on the preroga-
tives of the priesthood. "When he was strong, his
heart was lifted up to his destruction; for he transgressed against the Lord his God, and went into the
temple of the Lord to burn incense upon the altar of
incense." Azariah the high-priest, "and with him
fourscore priests of the Lord that were valiant men,"
forbade the sacrilege, and ordered him out of the sanctuary; and on his angrily persisting, while already he
"had a censer in his hand to burn incense, and while
he was wroth with the priests, the leprosy even rose
up in his ·forehead before the priests in the house of
the Lord, from beside the incense altar." The appalled
and disgusted priests "thrust him out from thence;
yea, himself also hasted to go out, because the Lord
had smitten him."*

The account of the reign of Jotham, son of Uzziah,
while it is partly a repetition of that in the Book of
Kings, omits some circumstances there recorded,† and
supplies the additional facts, that "on the wall of

---

* 2 Chron. xxvi. 5–20.

† xxvii. 1–3, 7–9; comp. 2 Kings xv. 32–38(which passage is preceded by a history, not paralleled in Chronicles, of the reigns of Zechariah, Shallum, Menahem, Pekahiah, and Pekah, kings of Israel, including the account
of the first Assyrian invasion ; see 2 Kings xv. 8–31). — To the statement
of Jotham's having done, like his father, "that which was right in the sight
of the Lord," the Chronicler is careful to add, "howbeit, he entered not into
the temple of the Lord " (2 ; comp. 2 Kings xv. 34), that is, as I understand, with a purpose of profanation like Uzziah's ; he passes over the prevailing religious irregularities more lightly (2 ; comp. 2 Kings xv. 35) ; he
omits to notice the movements in Jotham's time of the allied Israelites and
Syrians against Judah (2 Kings xv. 37) ; and he repeats himself as to the
king's age and the length of his reign (1 ; comp. 8). — " The rest of the
acts of Jotham . . . . . they are written in the book of the kings of Israel
and Judah " (7); " are they not written in the book of the chronicles of
the kings of Judah ? " (2 Kings xv. 36.)

Ophel he built much," that "he built cities in the mountains of Judah, and in the forests he built castles and towers," that he carried on a successful war against the Ammonites, compelling them to pay a tribute for three years, and that, on the whole, he "became mighty, because he prepared his ways before the Lord his God."*

Except in reference to one important transaction,† the reign of Ahaz, son of Jotham, is treated in the book before us more largely than in the other history.‡ The monarch's idolatrous practices are more precisely described. § Instead of the simple statement, in two periods, that the kings of Syria and Israel besieged Jerusalem without success, and that the Syrians recovered Elath, which they had lost to Judah, we read, that the Lord God "delivered Ahaz into the hand of the king of Syria, and they smote him, and carried away a great multitude of them captives"; that, aided by the personal prowess of one Zichri, the king of Israel " slew in Judah an hundred and twenty thousand in one day, which were all valiant men, because they had forsaken the Lord God of their fathers "; that "the children of Israel carried away captive of their brethren two hundred thousand, women, sons and daughters, and took also away much spoil from them"; that a prophet named Oded met the returning host, and told them that, if they had been victorious over Judah, it was because Jehovah had so decreed in consequence of Judah's sins, which

---

* 2 Chron. xxvii. 3 – 6.   † 2 Kings xvi. 10 – 16.
‡ 2 Chron. xxviii. 1 – 27 ; comp. 2 Kings xvi. 1 – 20.
§ xxviii. 1 – 4 is the same as 2 Kings xvi. 2 – 4, except in the additional statements that Ahaz " made molten images for Baalim " (2) and " burnt incense in the valley of the son of Hinnom " (3), and in the substitution of " children " for " son " (ibid.).

now they (the Israelites) were imitating by such cruelty to their brethren, and that they ought to liberate the captives and make restitution of the spoil; that "certain of the heads of the children of Ephraim" bravely sustained the representation of Oded; and that, finally, " the armed men left the captives and the spoil before the princes and all the congregation, and the men which were expressed by name rose up and took the captives, and with the spoil clothed all that were naked among them, and arrayed them, and shod them, and gave them to eat and to drink, and anointed them, and carried all the feeble of them upon asses, and brought them to Jericho, the city of palm-trees, to their brethren." * Along with the account of the embassy and subsidy sent by Ahaz to Tiglath-pileser, are related particulars of the distressing circumstances in which Judah was placed by inroads of the Edomites and Philistines, and by the not useful, but rather oppressive and dangerous, alliance of the Assyrian king.† The infatuated devotion of Ahaz to "the gods of Damascus, which smote him," is mentioned in general terms, and with an appropriate comment,‡ along with the impious desecration of "the vessels of the house of God."§ Lastly, the peculiar circumstance is recorded, that, though Ahaz was buried in Jerusalem, it was not in the place of royal sepulture. ‖

---

* 2 Chron. xxviii. 5 - 15 ; comp. 2 Kings xvi. 5, 6.

† xxviii. 16 - 21 ; comp. 2 Kings xvi. 7 - 9 (where is further mentioned the successful incursion of the Assyrians into Syria). — " Ahaz, king of Israel " (19) ; but he was king of Judah.

‡ xxviii. 22, 23, 25. — " He said, ' Because the gods of the kings of Syria help them,' " &c. (23) ; but the Syrians were not helped, according to 2 Kings xvi. 9.

§ xxviii. 24 ; comp. 2 Kings xvi. 17, 18.

‖ xxviii. 26, 27 ; comp. 2 Kings xvi. 19, 20. — " The rest of his acts, ... they are written in the book of the kings of Judah and Israel " (26) ; " are they not written in the book of the chronicles of the kings of

Without notice of the important event of the subjugation of the northern kingdom by the Assyrians,
which according to the other history took place at this
time,* the narrative records the accession of Hezekiah,†
and then proceeds with a minutely detailed account of
religious reforms instituted by that prince, of which we
learn nothing from the earlier book. We read that he
began his reign by opening and repairing the doors of
the house of the Lord, and imposing on the priests
and Levites the duty of sanctifying themselves, cleansing the holy place, and restoring the ritual service, to
the neglect of which he imputed all the recent public
calamities.‡ The work was prosecuted with diligence,
the priests removing into the court the rubbish that
had collected in the temple, and the Levites carrying
it thence and throwing it "into the brook Kidron";
and thus the temple with its furniture was put in order
in one week, and its precincts in another.§

The reinstitution of the worship was splendidly celebrated. First, in the presence of the city magistrates,
were sacrificed "seven bullocks, and seven rams, and
seven lambs, and seven he-goats, for a sin-offering for
the kingdom, and for the sanctuary, and for Judah." When, next in the order of ceremonies, "the
burnt-offering began, the song of the Lord began
also with the trumpets, and with the instruments

Judah!" (2 Kings xvi. 19.) — "They buried him in the city, even in Jerusalem; but they brought him not into the sepulchres of the kings of Israel"
(xxviii. 27). — "Ahaz . . . . . was buried with his fathers in the city of
David" (2 Kings xvi. 20).

* 2 Kings xvii.

† 2 Chron. xxix. 1, 2; comp. 2 Kings xviii. 1-3. — "His mother's
name was Abijah" (1); "his mother's name was Abi" (2 Kings xviii. 2).

‡ xxix. 3-11.

§ xxix. 12-19. — The threefold division of the Levitical tribe (12) and
of the choir of musicians (13, 14) is constantly observed; "the sons of Eli-
zaphan" (13) were a branch of the Kohathite family (comp. Numb. iii. 30).

ordained by David, king of Israel; and all the congregation worshipped, and the singers sang, and the
trumpeters sounded; and all this continued until the
burnt-offering was finished; and when they had made
an end of offering, the king and all that were present with him bowed themselves, and worshipped."
Lastly, at Hezekiah's invitation, the work of consecration being finished, the festivities of rejoicing followed, " and the congregation brought in sacrifices and
thank-offerings, and as many as were of a free heart,
burnt-offerings"; and the victims presented were so
numerous, and the priests who had sanctified themselves so few, that, contrary to strict rule, " their brethren the Levites," who " were more upright in heart to
sanctify themselves than the priests," " did help them
till the work was ended." " So the service of the
house of the Lord was set in order; and Hezekiah
rejoiced, and all the people, that God had prepared
the people; for the thing was done suddenly.* "

The next step proposed by Hezekiah and his counsellors in the reorganization of the national religious
system was to keep a solemn passover, the proper celebration of this great feast having been " of a long time "
omitted. For this purpose, letters inviting an attendance from all quarters upon that ceremony were sent
by him, not only to every part of his own dominions,
but also to such as, " escaped out of the hand of the
kings of Assyria," yet dwelt in the territory of the
northern tribes. Most of these scattered survivors
of their country's ruin received with derision the fraternal summons to resume the allegiance which their
fathers had thrown off. " Nevertheless, divers of Ash-

---

* 2 Chron. xxix. 20–36. — " They brought seven bullocks," &c. (21); the
prescribed sin-offering for the congregation was only of a single bullock
(comp. Lev. iv. 13 et seq.; Numb. xv. 23 et seq.).

er, and Manasseh, and of Zebulun, humbled themselves and came to Jerusalem," and so recovered the
forfeited favor of the God of the whole race of Jacob;
while in Hezekiah's own kingdom the proposal was
welcomed with unanimous satisfaction and alacrity.*
" There assembled at Jerusalem much people," who,
before proceeding to the object of their meeting, " arose,
and took away the altars that were in Jerusalem, and
all the altars for incense took they away, and cast them
into the brook Kidron." Though they proceeded to
execute their task as well as was permitted by their
circumstances, " the priests and the Levites were
ashamed " of the imperfect observance of so august
a ceremony; for they were killing the passover at the
wrong time, " the fourteenth day of the second month,"
when it should have been of the first; " there were
many in the congregation that were not sanctified ";
and " a multitude of the people, even many of Ephraim and Manasseh, Issachar and Zebulun, had not
cleansed themselves, yet did they eat the passover." †

Hezekiah offered a prayer for the forgiveness of this
irregularity, which the Lord accepted, " and healed the
people." Seven days, according to the provision of the
law, the feast was kept " with great gladness "; the Levites adding to the pomp and attraction of the ceremony by their daily musical performances, and the
king encouraging them to diligence in their offices
alike by his affable communications and his generous

---

* 2 Chron. xxx. 1–12. — " The king had taken counsel . . . . . to
keep the passover in the second month " (2); whereas the proper time was
the middle of the first month (Ex. xii. 18). But "they could not keep it at
that time because the priests had not sanctified themselves sufficiently, neither had the people gathered themselves together to Jerusalem " (3; comp.
xxix. 17, 34).

† xxx. 13–18. — " The altars that were in Jerusalem," &c. (14); that
is, those erected by Ahaz; comp. xxviii. 24. — " Yet did they eat the passover otherwise than it was written " (18); comp. Numb. xix. 20.

donatives.   The festival gave so much satisfaction that
there was a disposition to repeat it.   " The whole assembly took counsel to keep other seven days; and
they kept other seven days with gladness."   The pious
liberality of the king was not yet exhausted.   He
" gave to the congregation a thousand bullocks, and
seven thousand sheep; and the princes gave to the
congregation a thousand bullocks, and ten thousand
sheep; and a great number of priests sanctified themselves; and all the congregation of Judah, with the
priests and the Levites, and all the congregation that
came out of Israel, and the strangers that came out of
the land of Israel, and that dwelt in Judah, rejoiced;
so that there was great joy in Jerusalem; for since
the time of Solomon, the son of David, king of Israel,
there was not the like in Jerusalem."   And when the
priests gave their parting benediction to the assembly,
" their voice was heard, and their prayer came up to
his holy dwelling-place, even unto heaven." *

The effect of the solemnity in reviving a zeal for the
national faith was presently apparent.   " All the children of Israel returned, every man to his possession,
into their own cities."   But, before they did so, " all
Israel that were present went out to the cities of Judah, and brake the images in pieces, and cut down
the groves, and threw down the high places and the
altars out of all Judah and Benjamin, in Ephraim also
and Manasseh, until they had utterly destroyed them
all."   At Jerusalem the king reorganized the attendance of the priests and Levites upon the temple service, and settled the proportions of the contributions
for the public sacrifices, and for the maintenance of the
priests and Levites, which were to be furnished re-

---

* 2 Chron. xxx. 19 – 27. — " Since the time of Solomon," &c. (26);
when in like manner there had been a fortnight's festivity at the dedication
of the temple (comp. vii. 9).

spectively by himself and by the people of the city. His liberal plans were seconded by a liberal sympathy throughout the nation. "The children of Israel brought in abundance the first-fruits of corn, wine, and oil, and honey, and of all the increase of the field; and the tithe of all things brought they in abundantly; and the children of Israel and Judah, that dwelt in the cities of Judah, they also brought in the tithe of oxen and sheep, and the tithe of holy things which were consecrated unto the Lord their God, and laid them by heaps." Four months this contribution was making, to the great satisfaction of Hezekiah and his princes, as well as of the priests and Levites, who, he learned from the high-priest, had wanted for nothing since it began. The stores thus amassed were, by the king's command, deposited in "chambers in the house of the Lord," in the custody of suitable supervisors, while to others was committed the office of making lawful distribution of them for the supply of the priests and Levites and their families, both at Jerusalem and in the sacerdotal and Levitical cities.*

The account of the Assyrian invasion of Judea, preceded here, as well as in the other history, by a brief panegyric of Hezekiah,† begins with a quite different

---

* 2 Chron. xxxi. 1-19. — "In Ephraim also and Manasseh," &c. (1); one of the statements in this portion of the history, which are hardly to be reconciled with the condition of things in the northern kingdom as described in 2 Kings xvii. — "He appointed also the king's portion of his substance for the burnt-offerings, to wit, for the morning and evening burnt-offerings, and the burnt-offerings for the sabbaths, and for the new moons, and for the set feasts, *as it is written in the law of the Lord* (3; comp. xxx. 16); Hezekiah, then, Josiah's great-grandfather, had in his hands the written Law, — a material fact connected with the argument in Vol. III. p. 138, note, which see. — "At the commandment of Hezekiah the king, and Azariah the ruler of the house of God" (13); all the previous proceedings had been by the royal command, but the writer cannot allow it to be supposed that these appointments were made without a concurrent voice of the high-priest.

† xxxi. 20, 21; comp. 2 Kings xviii. 4-8, which adds the mention of

view of the first proceedings. The earlier narrative
represents Hezekiah as having bought off Sennacherib
from an attack upon Jerusalem by assenting to his
own terms of tribute, and as having stripped the temple of its treasures and ornaments for the purpose, as
well as his own palace.* According to the writer of
Chronicles, Hezekiah adopted the very different course
of cutting off the supplies of water, repairing and enlarging the fortifications of the city, and putting its
garrison in effective condition; and thus compelled
the Assyrians to retire.† The transactions between
Hezekiah and the lieutenants of Sennacherib, sent
from Lachish with a detachment from the Assyrian
army to Jerusalem, are here despatched in a general
outline, and with the omission of several circùmstan-
ces, in less than one quarter of the space which is devoted to them in the Book of Kings. ‡

The relation of the discomfiture of Sennacherib before Jerusalem, and of his assassination at Nineveh, is
also more brief, and abstains from a repetition of the
legend of the destruction of a hundred and eighty-
five thousand Assyrians by the angel of the Lord in
one night. § In the place of the two detailed and
peculiar accounts, in the earlier history, of the answers to Hezekiah's prayer in his sickness, and of
his imprudent frankness to the ambassadors of the
king of Babylon, with Isaiah's prediction to him of

Hezekiah's treatment of "the brazen serpent that Moses had made," and
of his successful war against the Philistines, and is less measured in its
praise of Hezekiah, not hesitating to place him above all the kings of Judah
of either earlier or later time.

* 1 Kings xviii. 13 – 16.   † 2 Chron. xxxii. 1 – 8.
‡ xxxii. 9 – 20; comp. 2 Kings xviii. 17 – xix. 34.
§ xxxii. 21 – 23 (which on the other hand adds the statements of the Divine protection and guidance permanently enjoyed by Hezekiah and his people, and the respect manifested towards him by "all nations," in bringing
tribute to him and to Jehovah); comp. 2 Kings xix. 35 – 37.

the woes which it would occasion, we read nothing here, except that, as to the one, " Hezekiah was sick to the death, and prayed unto the Lord, and he spake unto him, and he gave him a sign "; * and as to the other, that " in the business of the ambassadors of the princes of Babylon, who sent unto him to inquire of the wonder that was done in the land, God left him to try him, that he might know all that was in his heart." † It appears to be in reference to this latter transaction that the remark is made, that " his heart was lifted up; therefore there was wrath upon him, and upon Judah and Jerusalem; notwithstanding Hezekiah humbled himself for the pride of his heart, both he and the inhabitants of Jerusalem, so that the wrath of the Lord came not upon them in the days of Hezekiah." ‡ Abounding in wealth and honor, having built treasuries and storehouses, stalls, cotes, and cities, and having especially signalized his reign by the erection of an aqueduct " to the west side of the city of David," § he at length reached the end of his days, and " slept with his fathers." ‖

The first part of the record of the next reign in the Book of Chronicles runs parallel with that in the Book of Kings, after which the two authorities diverge into different matter, and again coincide in the narra-

---

* 2 Chron. xxxii. 24 ; comp. 2 Kings xx. 1 - 11.

† xxxii. 31 ; comp. 2 Kings xx. 12 - 19.   ‡ xxxii. 25, 26.

§ xxxii. 27 –30.

‖ xxxii. 32, 33 (comp. 2 Kings xx. 20, 21). — " The rest of the acts of Hezekiah, and his goodness, behold, they are written in the vision of Isaiah the prophet, the son of Amoz, and in the book of the kings of Judah and Israel " (32) ; " the rest of the acts of Hezekiah, and all his might, and how he made a pool, and a conduit, and brought water into the city, are they not written in the book of the chronicles of the kings of Judah ? " (2 Kings xx. 20.) — " Hezekiah slept with his fathers, and they buried him in the chiefest of the sepulchres of the sons of David ; and all Judah and the inhabitants of Jerusalem did him honor at his death " (33) ; " and Hezekiah slept with his fathers " (2 Kings xx. 21).

tive of Manasseh's death. After a repetition of the previous sketch of his character and of the character of
his reign,* and a reference in a single period to those
ineffectual remonstrances from the Lord which the
other book recites at length, † follows an important
portion of history, respecting which the other narrative
has preserved an extraordinary silence. In contradiction of the common opinion respecting the date of the
first deportation of a Jewish prince to Chaldea, it is
said that " the Lord brought upon them the captains of
the host of the king of Assyria, which took Manasseh
among the thorns, and bound him with fetters, and
carried him to Babylon " ; that when in his affliction
he " humbled himself greatly before the God of his
fathers," he obtained forgiveness,· and was restored to
his country and his throne; and that after his restoration he acted the part of a reformed man and of a reformer, and signalized the remainder of his reign by
acts of public spirit and piety, improving the fortifications of the metropolis, organizing the forces " in all
the fenced cities of Judah," ejecting from the temple
and from Jerusalem the statues and the altars of false
gods, repairing the altar of the Lord, and sacrificing
on it himself and encouraging the people to do the
same, though he was unable to prevent them from sacrificing also to Jehovah "in the high places."‡ And
the record of his death is accompanied with a recapitulation of this peculiar course of events. §

---

* 2 Chron. xxxiii. 1 - 9 ; comp. 2 Kings xxi. 1 - 9. The verbal identity is nearly complete ; the diversities are only such as these; viz. the
omissions in Chronicles (1, 3, 6) of the mention of the name of Manasseh's mother and of a comparison of his course to that of Ahab (2 Kings
xxi. 1, 3), and the specification (6) of " the valley of the son of Hinnom "
as the scene of the king's unnatural impiety.

† xxxiii. 10 ; comp. 2 Kings xxi. 10 - 16.   ‡ xxxiii. 11 - 17.
§ xxxiii. 18 - 20 ; comp. 2 Kings xxi. 17, 18. — " His prayer unto his

The account of the reign of Manasseh's son Amon differs in nothing from that which we have read before,* except that it contains an allusion to that reformation of Manasseh which had been mentioned in the preceding verses,† and omits to specify the name of his mother, the place of his burial, and the sources of information respecting his history. ‡

After the formal introduction to the reign of Josiah, which, like others of the sort, is in a few words, and substantially a ~~transcript from~~ the same context in the other book, § the Book of Chronicles proceeds with a *cl·* statement peculiar to it of some important transactions of Josiah's early years. From the eighth year of his reign, it is said, when he was but sixteen years old, " he began to seek after the God of David his father, and in the twelfth year he began to purge Judah and Jerusalem from the high places, and the groves, and the carved images, and the molten images." The fragments of the broken altars and images he reduced to dust, " and strewed it upon the graves of them that had sacrificed unto them, and he burnt the bones of the priests upon their altars." Nor did he confine these radical measures of reform to his own kingdom, but " so did he in the cities of Manasseh, and Ephraim,

God . . . . . before he was humbled " (18, 19) ; to most of this there is nothing equivalent in 2 Kings xxi. 17. — " The rest of the acts of Manasseh, ... behold, they are written in the book of the kings of Israel " (18) ; " his prayer also, ... behold, they are written among the sayings of the seers " (19) ; " are they not written in the book of the chronicles of the kings of Judah? " (2 Kings xxi. 17.) — " They buried him in his own house " (20) ; " in the garden of his own house, in the garden of Uzza " (2 Kings xxi. 18).

* 2 Chron. xxxiii. 21 – 25 ; comp. 2 Kings xxi. 19 – 26.

† xxxiii. 23.

‡ xxxiii. 21, 25 ; comp. 2 Kings xxi. 19, 25, 26.

§ xxxiv. 1, 2 ; comp. 2 Kings xxii. 1, 2, which furnishes the additional fact of the name of Josiah's mother.

and Simeon, even unto Naphtali," "and cut down all
the idols throughout all the land of Israel." *

It was ten years after this reform was undertaken,
when the still more interesting transactions took place
at Jerusalem of which we have already read a similar
account. A narrative, not altogether the same in
terms, but substantially equivalent as to the nature
and succession of the events, is given of the directions
issued by the king respecting his proposed repair of
the temple, and of the preliminary steps taken for
their execution ; † of the discovery by Hilkiah of the
book of the Law in the temple; of the communication
of that fact to Josiah; of his message in consequence
to Huldah the prophetess, and her reply; and of the
formal renewal by Josiah, in behalf of himself and
his people, of the covenant of obedience to Jehovah.‡

Next, despatching in a single period those proceedings of Josiah for the suppression of idolatry and its kin-

---

* 2 Chron. xxxiv. 3 – 7.

† xxxiv. 8 – 13 ; comp. 2 Kings xxii. 3 – 7. — Though there are differences of statement between these two accounts, there are no contradictions
in matters of fact. The narrative in Chronicles contributes the further facts
that two other persons were associated with Shaphan (8 ; comp. 2 Kings
xxii. 3) in the royal commission, and that it was Levites, and they (in part,
at least) selected from among the musicians, who were appointed to be overseers, " scribes, and officers, and porters " ; while, on the other hand, it for-
bears to record that, so perfect was the confidence reposed in the workmen,
" there was no reckoning with them of the money that was delivered into
their hand " (2 Kings xxii. 7).

‡ xxxiv. 14 - 32 ; comp. 2 Kings xxii. 8 - xxiii. 3, which is nearly word
for word the same. — " Abdon, the son of Micah, and Shaphan the scribe,
and Asaiah " (20) ; " Achbor, the son of Michaiah, and Shaphan the
scribe, and Asahiah " (2 Kings xxii. 12). — " Hilkiah . . . . . went to
Huldah, the prophetess " (22) ; the reader naturally wonders that Josiah
did not rather summon the prophets Jeremiah and Zephaniah to his counsels.
— " Shallum, the son of Tikvath, the son of Hasrah " (ibid.) ; " Shallum,
the son of Tikvah, the son of Harhas " (2 Kings xxii. 14). — " The priests,
and the Levites, and all the people " (30); " the priests, and the prophets,
and all the people " (2 Kings xxiii. 2). — " The king stood in his place "
(31) ; " the king stood by a pillar " (2 Kings xxiii. 3 ; comp. xi. 14).

dred impieties, in Israel as well as Judah, which in the earlier history are detailed at length,* is described in full that memorable passover at Jerusalem of which we have already read that " there was not holden such a passover, from the days of the Judges that judged Israel, nor in all the days of the kings of Israel, nor of the kings of Judah "; on which occasion it is said that the ceremonies were arranged in strict conformity to the Law, and to the written directions of David and Solomon, and that, for offerings, the king gave a largess to the people of thirty thousand lambs and kids, and three thousand bullocks, while nine persons, " rulers of the house of God," and " chiefs of the Levites," gave seventy-six hundred lambs and kids, and eight hundred oxen.† Lastly, we are told much more largely than in the Book of Kings the circumstances of the death of Josiah from a wound received in battle with the king of Egypt at Megiddo, to the effect that before the engagement Pharaoh-Necho endeavoured by an embassy to dissuade the Jewish king from the Assyrian alliance; that Josiah took the field in a disguise; that, (differently from the other history, which represents him as dying at Megiddo,) on receiving a severe wound with an arrow, he was removed by his servants from his war-chariot into another, and conveyed to Jerusalem, where he died; and that " all Judah and Jerusalem mourned for Josiah, and Jeremiah lamented for Josiah, and all the singing-men and the singing-women spake of Josiah in their lamenta-

---

* 2 Chron. xxxiv. 33; comp. 2 Kings xxiii. 4-20, 24-27.

† xxxv. 1-19; comp. 2 Kings xxiii. 21-23.—" Put the holy ark in the house," &c. (3); it had been put in at the consecration of the temple (comp. v. 7); how it had come out again, we have not been told. — " There was no passover like to that kept in Israel," &c. (18); it excelled even that celebrated under similar circumstances by Hezekiah (comp. xxx. 26).

tions to this day, and made them an ordinance in Israel." *

The rest of the history, down to the burning of Jerusalem and the deportation of the people, is told in one half the space occupied by it in the earlier narrative. In respect to the reign of Jehoahaz, Josiah's son, the record is substantially the same, though less minute.† In the short notice of the reign of Jehoiakim it is related that "against him came up Nebuchadnezzar, king of Babylon, and bound him in fetters, to carry him to Babylon; Nebuchadnezzar also carried off the vessels of the house of the Lord to Babylon, and put them in his temple at Babylon"; instead of what we have before read, that a rebellion of Jehoiakim against Nebuchadnezzar, after being his tributary three years, was followed by an invasion of bands of the Chaldees, Syrians, Moabites, and Ammonites, whom the Lord "sent against Judah to destroy it, according to the word of the Lord"; and that Jehoiakim, when he died, "slept with his fathers." ‡

---

* 2 Chron. xxxv. 20 - 27; comp. 2 Kings xxiii. 29, 30. — " Disguised himself that he might fight with him " (22); some of the ancient versions read "prepared to fight with him "; perhaps their copies had הִתְחַפֵּשׂ instead of הִתְחַזֵּק. — " He died, and was buried in one of the sepulchres of his fathers " (24); " his servants . . . . . buried him in his own sepulchre " (2 Kings xxiii. 30). — " Behold, they are written in the Lamentations " (25); whatever book may have been meant, that which has come down to us under the name of the " Lamentations of Jeremiah " contains nothing of the kind. — " His deeds, first and last, behold, they " are written in the book of the kings of Israel and Judah " (27); " are they not written in the book of the chronicles of the kings of Judah ? " (2 Kings xxiii. 28).

† xxxvi. 1 - 4; comp. 2 Kings xxiii. 30 - 34, which adds the particulars of the name of the king's mother, of his having done " evil in the sight of the Lord," of Pharaoh-Necho's having " put him in bands at Riblah in the land of Hamath," and of his death in Egypt.

‡ xxxvi. 4 - 8; comp. 2 Kings xxiii. 34 - xxiv. 6, which in addition records Jehoiakim's manner of raising the tribute-money for Pharaoh, and the name of his mother. — " The rest of the acts of Jehoiakim, and his abominations which he did, and that which was found in him, behold, they are

In the place of the circumstantial account in the Book of Kings, of the siege and capture of Jerusalem by Nebuchadnezzar in the time of Jehoiachin, and the carrying away of that prince with his people and his treasures to Babylon, the history before us simply relates, that, " when the year was expired, King Nebuchadnezzar sent and brought him to Babylon, with the goodly vessels of the house of the Lord." *

The reign of Zedekiah, and the final destruction of the city, which took place in his time, are also more briefly treated in the Book of Chronicles, one half of the space devoted to that period being occupied with a reflection on the cause of its calamities, while the other history, without any such comment, records them with some particularity.† The conclusions of the books are also different. That of Chronicles passes on to refer in a few words to the proclamation of Cyrus, fifty-two years later. That of Kings has a brief record

---

written in the book of the kings of Israel and Judah " (8) ; " are they not written in the book of the chronicles of the kings of Judah ? " (2 Kings xxiv. 5.)

* 2 Chron. xxxvi. 9, 10 ; comp. 2 Kings xxiv. 8 – 16. — " Jehoiachin was eight years old when he began to reign, and he reigned three months and ten days in Jerusalem " (9) ; " Jehoiachin was eighteen years old when he began to reign, and he reigned in Jerusalem three months ; and his mother's name was Nehushta, the daughter of Elnathan of Jerusalem " (2 Kings xxiv. 8).

† xxxvi. 10 – 19 ; comp. 2 Kings xxiv. 17 – xxv. 21. — " Nebuchadnezzar . . . . . made Zedekiah, his brother, king " (10); " the king of Babylon made Mattaniah, his father's brother, king in his stead, and changed his name to Zedekiah " (2 Kings xxiv. 17). — " Zedekiah . . . . . reigned eleven years in Jerusalem " (11); " he reigned eleven years in Jerusalem ; and his mother's name was Hamutal, the daughter of Jeremiah of Libnah " (2 Kings xxiv. 18). — " He did that which was evil in the sight of the Lord his God, and humbled not himself before Jeremiah the prophet, speaking from the mouth of the Lord " (12) ; " he did that which was evil in the sight of the Lord, according to all that Jehoiakim had done " (2 Kings xxiv. 19). — " The Lord God of their fathers sent to them by his messengers, rising up betimes, and sending " (15) ; comp. Jer. xxv. 3, 4.

6 *

of some later transactions in Judea, terminating in an
emigration to Egypt, and of the treatment experienced
by King Jehoiachin in his captivity at Babylon.*
The New Testament does not quote from the Books
of Chronicles. In one of the discourses of our Saviour,† there is a sort of allusion, not to the books,
but to a fact therein recorded.‡

---

* 2 Chron. xxxvi. 20 – 23 ; comp. 2 Kings xxv. 22 – 30. — " To fulfil
the word of the Lord by the mouth of Jeremiah, until the land had enjoyed
her Sabbaths ; for as long as she lay desolate she kept Sabbath, to fulfil
threescore and ten years " (21) ; from this, it would seem, we are to infer
that, in the opinion of the writer, the institution of the Sabbatical year
(comp. Vol. I. pp. 301 *et seq.*) had been more or less neglected for four
hundred and ninety years, a term which would run about twenty years
further back than the date of David's accession to the throne.

† Comp. Matt. xxiii. 35.

‡ 2 Chron. xxiv. 20 – 22. I say, " a sort of allusion," because part of
the statement here made does not accord with the language reported by Matthew.

LECTURE LVI.

EZRA AND NEHEMIAH.

Peculiar Structure of the Book of Ezra. — Proclamation of Cyrus. — Preparations for a Return of the Exiles to Judea. — Migration of a Party with Zerubbabel. — Celebration of the Feast of Tabernacles at Jerusalem. — Foundation of the New Temple. — Interruptions of the Work. — Singular Insertion of Matter in the Chaldee Language. — Letter of the Samaritans to the King of Persia, and his Action thereupon. — Renewal of the Work upon the Temple, with the Approbation of Darius. — Its Completion and Dedication. — Celebration of the Passover. — Chasm of Thirty-seven or Fifty-eight Years in the History. — Mission of Ezra the Scribe to Judea with Attendants. — His Authority and Instructions expressed in the Chaldee Tongue. — Inspection and Fast at the River Ahava. — Proceedings on his Arrival at Jerusalem. — Repudiation by the People of their Foreign Wives. — Authorship of the Book. — The Book of Nehemiah introduced by a Reference to Nehemiah as its Author. — Intelligence of the State of Things at Jerusalem received by Nehemiah at Shushan. — His Petition to Artaxerxes, and consequent Visit to Jerusalem. — Inspection of the Place. — Repair of the Walls and Gates. — Conspiracy of Sanballat and his Associates, and Preparations to defeat it. — Extortions of the Rulers, and Disinterestedness of Nehemiah. — His Discomfiture of the Plots of Sanballat and Geshem. — Police Arrangements. — Genealogical Register. — Celebration of the Feast of Tabernacles. — Divorce of Alien Wives. — Covenant of Future Obedience. — List of Principal Citizens of Jerusalem. — Places of Settlement of the Priests and others. — List of Companions of Zerubbabel. — Succession of High-Priests. — Catalogue of Levites, Musicians, and Porters. — Celebration of the Completion of the City Wall. — Nehemiah's Visit to Persia, and Return to Jerusalem. — Further Reforms. — Conclusion of the Book. — Considerations relating to its Authorship and Character.

THE Book of Ezra is, in respect to materials, still more heterogeneous, and in construction still more incompact, than that of Chronicles. On taking it up, the fact immediately strikes us, that it relates to two different periods of history, separated from each other by an interval of perhaps more than half a century. Sometimes, in speaking of Ezra, the writer uses the pronoun of the first person, sometimes of the third. Different parts are composed in different languages, two long passages, amounting to nearly a quarter part of the book, being written in Chaldee.

The first three chapters relate the circumstances of the return of a number of the Jews from the Babylonish provinces soon after the Persian conquest, and of their proceedings for a restoration of the temple. Cyrus, it is said, in the first year after his accession to the throne, issued a proclamation wherein he declares that it was "Jehovah, God of heaven," who had given him his dominion over "all the kingdoms of the earth," and that Jehovah had charged him "to build him an house at Jerusalem, which is in Judah." Accordingly he invited the Jewish captives to return to their native country, and called on their neighbours in the places where they were dwelling to help them "with silver, and with gold, and with goods, and with beasts." * "Then rose up the chief of the fathers of

---

* Ezra i. 1–4. The first and second verses, and part of the third, are almost literally the same with the last three verses of Chronicles. Eichhorn, who understands Ezra to have been the author of that book, supposes him to have intended at first to continue the history in the Chronicles, without interruption, with a history of the return, but, after writing the three verses in question, to have changed his mind, and left them to close that book, while he repeated them as a proper introduction to a separate treatise on the later events ("Einleitung in das A. T.," § 493). De Wette, who refers the compilation of Chronicles and of Ezra to the same person (whoever he might be), supposes those compositions to have been originally one, and separated at this place in some way which cannot now be explained (§ 196). I do not perceive that the fact presents any considerable perplexity, or that it was in any way unnatural for the author of Chronicles, on the one hand, after recording what seemed the final ruin of his nation, to overleap half a century, in order

LVI.]
EZRA.
69

Judah and Benjamin, and the priests, and the Levites, with all them whose spirit God had raised to go up to build the house of the Lord which is in Jerusalem; and all they that were about them strengthened their hands with vessels of silver, with gold, with goods, and with beasts, and with precious things, besides all that was willingly offered." The sacred vessels of Jehovah's house at Jerusalem, which Nebuchadnezzar had caused to be placed in the temples of his own gods, Cyrus directed his treasurer to bring out, and place in the hands of "Sheshbazzar, the prince of Judah." *

A list next follows of the companies of persons who attended Zerubbabel back to Jerusalem, specifying

---

to allude, in a few words, to the beginning of a better era; — nor that it was in any way singular or unsuitable for the author of Ezra, on the other hand, in undertaking to relate the later series of events, to adopt for his statement of the first in that series the words of the preceding author. — " That the word of the Lord by the mouth of Jeremiah might be fulfilled " (1); whoever may have been the writer, and whatever the degree of authority which his opinion may claim, and whatever passage of Jeremiah he may here refer to, which is by no means clear, there is no indication in his words that he ascribed to Jeremiah any supernatural foreknowledge of the transactions which took place under Cyrus. Jeremiah, like every Jew of his time, hoped that the national disasters, of which they saw the beginning, would be but temporary. Jeremiah had expressed that hope and expectation in writings which had been transmitted to the time of Cyrus, and when Cyrus manifested a favorable disposition to the Jews, the prognostics of Jeremiah were properly said to be fulfilled. To speak of nothing else, Jeremiah's magnificent language concerning a general restoration of the people was by no means *fulfilled*, in the general acceptation of that word, by the return of the inconsiderable fragment that took advantage of the permission of Cyrus. On the other hand, it deserves very special notice that, in such a connection, the author of this book has not referred to Isaiah xliv. 21 – xlv. 4, a passage which, on the common hypothesis, would have been precisely and completely to his purpose.

* Ezra i. 5 – 11. — " Sheshbazzar " (8); apparently another name of Zerubbabel, given him in captivity; comp. iii. 8, v. 14, 16. — " All the vessels of gold and of silver were five thousand and four hundred " (11); but the sum of those specified in the preceding verses is only two thousand four hundred and ninety-nine.

them severally with reference to their common ancestor, or to the parts of Judea in which they had formerly dwelt, and arranging the whole under the general heads of common Israelites, priests, Levites, singers, "children of the porters," Nethinims, and "children of Solomon's servants." * Besides these, there
were some hundreds of others, common people and
priests, who were not able to prove their genealogy,
and the latter of whom were accordingly forbidden by
Zerubbabel to associate with the priests "till there
stood up a priest with Urim and with Thummim." †

The number of "the whole congregation together"
is recorded, with the numbers of their servants, their
musicians, and their beasts of burden, and the amount
of contributions towards the erection of the temple
made by "some of the chief of the fathers, when they
came to the house of the Lord, which is at Jerusalem,"
and their companions settled about the country. The
number of the returned exiles, less than fifty thousand,
when compared with the census of a people which, in
its palmy days, is recorded to have been able to bring
more than a million and a half of warriors into the
field,‡ cannot fail to strike the careful reader as a very
imperfect accomplishment of those passages in the
prophets, if considered as supernatural predictions,

---

* Ezra ii. 1 - 58. — "The children of the province" (1); that is, of Judea, now a Persian province; comp. v. 8. — "The other Elam" (31);
comp. 7.

† ii. 59 - 63. — "The children of Barzillai" (61); comp. 2 Sam. xvii.
27, xix. 31. — "The *Tirshatha* said," &c. (63); apparently the official title
of a Persian provincial governor, and accordingly applied here to Zerubbabel; it is given to Nehemiah in Neh. viii. 9, x. 1. — "Till there stood up a
priest with Urim and with Thummim" (63); that is, as I understand, Zerubbabel resolved to leave the determination of such critical ecclesiastical
questions till a high-priest should be installed in all his pontifical dignity
(comp. Vol. I. pp. 211, 212).

‡ 1 Chron. xxi. 5.

which speak of a reëstablishment of the nation in its old domain.*

When the seventh month of the year came round, the time appointed by the Law,† the returned exiles prepared for the observance of the ancient Feast of Tabernacles. From the cities of their abode, "the people gathered themselves together as one man to Jerusalem." Under the direction of Zerubbabel and of Jeshua the high-priest, an altar for burnt-offerings was erected, upon which, through the week of the festival, and afterwards as the public ritual or private devotion dictated, were presented the legal sacrifices.‡ The next care was for the restoration of the temple, for which enterprise they had the authority of a rescript of Cyrus. Provision was made for the hire and sustenance of laborers, including the Tyrians and Sidonians who brought round cedars from Lebanon by sea; and in the second month of the second year of the reoccupation of the holy city, in the presence of Zerubbabel and Jeshua, of the priests, of the Levites (of which tribe the men over twenty years of age were to have a charge in superintending the work), and of the people at large, the foundations of the new temple were laid. "The priests in their apparel, with trumpets, and the Levites, the sons of Asaph, with cymbals," performed the parts that had been assigned them by King David in the sacred service. "They sang together by course, in praising and giving thanks unto the Lord, ... and all the people shouted

---

* Ezra ii. 64 – 70. — "The whole congregation together was forty and two thousand three hundred and threescore" (64); but the aggregate of the numbers in the preceding part of the chapter is only twenty-nine thousand eight hundred and eighteen, or something more than two thirds of this sum.

† Lev. xxiii. 24 et seq.

‡ Ezra iii. 1 – 6. — "For fear was upon them," &c. (3); rather, "though fear was upon them."

with a great shout." But others were present, who
were oppressed with different emotions. "Many of
the priests, and Levites, and chief of the fathers, who
were ancient men, that had seen the first house, when
the foundation of this house was laid before their eyes,
wept with a loud voice." *

The fourth chapter contains an account of interruptions to the prosecution of the building of the temple
which occurred in the reigns of the Persian kings
Ahasuerus † and Artaxerxes.‡ It is related that the
colonists established in the country by Esarhaddon,
after the Assyrian conquest, hearing what was going on
in Jerusalem, came to that city, and proposed to take
part in the· work, alleging that, ever since their establishment in the territory of the northern tribes,
they and their fathers had sacrificed to Jehovah. -The
rejection of their overture occasioned resentment on
their part, and " the people of the land weakened the
hands of the people of Judah, and troubled them in
building, and hired counsellors against them to frus-
trate their purpose." On the accession of another
monarch, after seven years, they persevered in their
opposition, and induced the Persian provincial officers
to write in their behalf to the king.§

---

* Ezra iii. 6 – 13. — " In the second month, began Zerubbabel, ...
and appointed the Levites," &c. (8) ; that is, as I understand, they at the
same time began the temple by laying its foundation, and by appointing the
Levites to superintend its erection. — " They sang together by course, in
praising and giving thanks unto the Lord, ' because he is good, for his mercy endureth for ever ' " (11) ; that is, probably, they sang Psalm cxxxvi.,
of which these last words are the refrain. Comp. 1 Chron. xvi. 34, 41,
2 Chron. v. 13, vii. 3, 6, xx. 21.

† Understood to be Cambyses, who came to the throne in the year 529
B. C. ; see Vol. III. p. 152.

‡ Known in profane history as Smerdis the Magian, who began to reign
in 522 B. C. ; see Vol. III. p. 153.

§ iv. 1 – 7. — " Written in the Syrian tongue, and interpreted in the Syrian tongue " (7) ; that is, as I understand, the letter was both written in

A remarkable feature of this book comes here into view. Not only is the letter to the king incorporated into the narrative in the Chaldee language, in which the original is said to have been written (a proceeding which might be accounted for, as giving a greater appearance of authenticity), but the history which immediately follows it is continued in the same language, in a passage extending through nearly two chapters.

The letter informed the king that the Jewish colonists were "building the rebellious and the bad city," and that, if allowed to persevere in their work and strengthen themselves, they would refuse to "pay toll, tribute, and custom," to the damage of the royal revenue; and declared that the writers, influenced by zeal for their master's honor, felt bound to represent that, on a search of the records of the kingdom, Jerusalem would appear to have been "a rebellious city, and hurtful unto kings and provinces," and to have "moved sedition within the same of old time," so that there was reason to fear lest, should it be fortified again, Persia would have "no portion on this side the river." * The examination instituted in consequence by the king having appeared to him to justify this representation and warning, he caused instructions to be sent "unto Rehum the chancellor, and to Shimshai the scribe," to arrest the proceedings at Jerusalem till further orders from himself; for "why should damage grow to the hurt of the kings?" Thereupon, with "their companions, they went up in haste to Jerusalem unto the Jews, and made them to cease by force and power.

---

the Chaldee character (which after the captivity was also used for the Hebrew; comp. Vol. I. p. 8), and expressed in the Chaldee dialect.

* Ezra iv. 8–16. — "The great and noble Asnappar" (10). Who was he? Perhaps Esar-haddon (comp. 2) by another name; perhaps one of his satraps.

Then ceased the work of the house of God, which is at Jerusalem." *

In the second year of Darius, encouraged by the exhortations of "the prophets, Haggai the prophet, and Zechariah, the son of Iddo," the people, under the auspices of Zerubbabel and Jeshua, renewed their labors upon the temple. Again they were interrupted and questioned · by the Persian local officers, whose opposition, however, they were enabled to parry, till there should be time for the royal pleasure to be expressed. The Persians wrote to their court, representing that, on observing that the temple at Jerusalem was rapidly rising from its ruins, they had inquired of the persons engaged in the work, by whom, and by what authority, it had been undertaken, and had been answered that the persons engaged were "servants of the God of heaven and earth," and that they were restoring a structure which a king of their nation had erected a long time before; that their ancestors had displeased their God, and had consequently been permitted to fall into the hands of Nebuchadnezzar, who had destroyed the temple, and carried away the people captive into Chaldea; that, soon after the Persian conquest of Babylon, Cyrus had issued a decree, giving permission for the temple to be rebuilt, and had restored the sacred vessels for its worship; and that it was the work, thus allowed, which was now in progress. And the prefects accordingly asked that the king would cause inquiry to be made into these alleged facts, and signify his pleasure in the matter.†

---

* Ezra iv. 17 - 24.

† v. 1 - 17. — " Then said we unto them after this manner, ' What are the names,' " &c. (4). Some of the ancient versions read, " Then said *they* unto them." The words, however, as we have them in the Chaldee, admit

Search was made, and a decree of Cyrus was found,
which directed, not only the restoration of the temple
and its furniture, but also that the expense of rebuilding the temple should be defrayed out of the royal treasury. The Persian officers were accordingly instructed
to desist from all obstruction to the Jews, and to provide them with money out of the local revenues, and
with a daily allowance of victims for their sacrifices,
and other articles needful in their worship, that so they
might "pray for the life of the king and of his sons."
Whoever should interfere with the execution of this
decree was to have his house pulled down, and to be
hung upon its timbers, and destruction was denounced
against every king and people that should dare to compass the destruction of Jehovah's house. The instructions were promptly obeyed; the work went prosperously on, and "was finished on the third day of the
month Adar, which was in the sixth year of the reign
of Darius the king." The temple was joyfully dedicated, with a proper ceremonial of sacrifices (among
which was "a sin-offering for all Israel, twelve he-
goats, according to the number of the tribes of Israel ")
and priestly and Levitical attendance, "as it is written
in the Book of Moses." * Lastly, as is related in the

---

of being rendered, " Then we told them after that manner [i. e. according
to the terms of their question] what were the names," &c.

* Ezra vi. 1 - 18. — By Achmetha (2) is probably to be understood Echa-
tana, the Median capital. Le Clerc, on slender authority, renders the word,
a *chest*, or *desk*. — " The height thereof threescore cubits, and the breadth
thereof threescore cubits " (3) ; that is, twice as high, and three times as
broad, as Solomon's temple (comp. 1 Kings vi. 2). — " The elders of the
Jews builded, ... according to the commandment of Cyrus, and Darius, and Artaxerxes king of Persia " (14).   But " the house was finished
. . . . . in the sixth year of the reign of Darius the king " (15), thirty
years before the beginning of the reign of Darius's immediate successor, and
fifty years before that of Artaxerxes Longimanus. The name of Artaxerxes, who favored the Jews, but not while their temple was building, it
would seem, must have been inserted in this passage by a later hand.

Hebrew language, to which the narrative here abruptly returns, "the children of the captivity kept the
passover upon the fourteenth day of the first month,"
associating with them in that festivity "all such as
had separated themselves unto them from the filthiness
of the heathen of the land." *

There is here a chasm in the history, extending to
"the reign of Artaxerxes, king of Persia." Who this
Artaxerxes was, whether Xerxes the First, the immediate successor of Darius, or Artaxerxes Longimanus,
who next filled the throne, is a disputed question.†
The arguments upon it on both sides appear to me
vague and inconclusive, and I see not but that it must
remain unsettled. Accordingly as we understand the
one prince or the other to be meant, the date from
which the history next proceeds, "the seventh year
of the king," is the year 478 or the year 457 before
Christ.

In that year Ezra, "a ready scribe in the law of
Moses," is related to have left Babylon for Jerusalem,
"upon the first day of the first month." A journey of
four months, "according to the good hand of his God
upon him," brought him to the holy city. He had
come under a royal safe-conduct, accompanied by "some
of the children of Israel, and of the priests," with their
attendants of different ranks. He ."had prepared his
heart to seek the law of the Lord, and to do it, and to

---

* Ezra vi. 19 - 22. — " The king of Assyria " (22) ; a title which does
not seem the most natural to apply to the Persian monarch, but which might
very properly be given to him, Assyria being one of his kingdoms.

† Josephus (" Antiq. Jud.," Lib. XI. cap. 5, § 1) understood Xerxes to
be meant. Of moderns, Michaelis (" Uebersetzung des A. T.," ad loc.) and
Jahn (" Einleitung ins A. T.," Th. II. § 57) maintain the same opinion ;
Prideaux (Book V. ad init.), Eichhorn (" Einleitung," §§ 497, 500), Bertholdt (" Einleitung," § 270), and De Wette (" Einleitung," § 195), support the opposite, with which is certainly the weight of authority.

teach in Israel statutes and judgments." * A letter had
been addressed to him by the king, of which a copy is
inserted into the narrative in the original Chaldee,
giving permission to as many of the Jews in the Persian dominions as were so disposed to accompany him
to Palestine. It recites that Ezra was "sent of the king,
and of his seven counsellors, to inquire concerning Judah and Jerusalem"; that he was " to carry the silver
and gold, which the king and his counsellors have freely offered unto the God of Israel, whose habitation is in
Jerusalem," with as much more as he could " find in
all the province of Babylon, with the free-will offering
of the people, and of the priests." With part of these
contributions he was forthwith to buy victims, to be
offered on the temple altar, and the rest he was to use
according to his own discretion and that of his associates in the trust. He was to deliver safely at their
destination the sacred vessels given him for the service of Jehovah, and with whatsoever more might be
needful for the house of his God he was to be supplied from the royal treasury. To this end, "all the
treasurers beyond the river" were charged promptly
to answer his requisitions for silver, wheat, wine, and
oil, within limited amounts, and for salt without limit,
that so there might not " be wrath against the realm
of the king and his sons." It was forbidden " to impose toll, tribute, or custom" upon " any of the priests
and Levites, singers, porters, Nethinims, or ministers
of the house of God," and Ezra was authorized to appoint magistrates and judges, learned in the law of Is-

---

* Ezra vii. 1 - 10. — The genealogy of Ezra, in 1 - 5, is the same as that of
Jehozadak in 1 Chron. vi. 4 - 14, except that in that of Ezra six names are
omitted between Meraioth and Azariah. It would appear, too, that the intention was to represent Ezra as the uncle of Jeshua, the high-priest in
Zerubbabel's time (iii. 8), though, on that supposition, the nephew appears
in public station at least sixty years earlier than the uncle.

rael, and to execute speedy judgment upon offenders,
" whether unto death, or to banishment, or to confiscation of goods, or to imprisonment." *

To this commission or decree, Ezra (now for the
first time referring to himself in the use of the first
person, which form of expression is continued through
the two following chapters) subjoins a few words of
thanksgiving to Jehovah, who had " put such a thing
as this in the king's heart." † He goes on to say that,
encouraged by such tokens of the Divine favor, he
collected for the proposed journey a company of some
fifteen hundred persons, who encamped by " the river
that runneth to Ahava." ‡ When at the end of three
days he came to inspect them, he " found there none
of the sons of Levi "; that is, none of that family beneath the rank of priests. He accordingly selected
some persons of influence and intelligence, and " sent
them with commandment unto Iddo the chief." In
due time they returned with a party of some forty Levites, and two hundred and twenty Nethinims. Then
he " proclaimed a fast there, at the river of Ahava," to
implore Divine guidance and defence; for he had spoken so confidently of the power and readiness of Jehovah to protect his true worshippers and baffle his
enemies, that he " was ashamed to require of the king
a band of soldiers and horsemen to help against the
enemy in the way." For the greater safety of the sacred utensils and other property in his charge, he selected " twelve of the chief of the priests," to whom

---

* Ezra vii. 11 - 26.   † vii. 27, 28.

‡ vii. 28 – viii. 15. — " Of the sons of Shechaniah," &c. (3); " of the
sons of Shechaniah," &c. (5); " of the sons of Shelomith," &c. (10); at
the end of each of these clauses a name appears to have been lost from the
text. — " Of the *last* sons of Adonikam " (13); apparently in distinction
from those of the same family who had been of Zerubbabel's party in the
earlier emigration; comp. ii. 13.

he delivered the whole, taking account of the vessels
and of the money by weight, to be reckoned for in the
same manner by them to "the chief of the priests and
the Levites, and chief of the fathers of Israel, at Jerusalem, in the chambers of the house of the Lord." *

The caravan "departed from the river of Ahava
on the twelfth day of the first month," and arrived at
Jerusalem by a prosperous journey. After a repose of
three days, "the silver and the gold and the vessels"
it had conveyed were counted and weighed, and the
weight recorded, under the superintendence of two
priests and two Levites. Then was celebrated a costly
sacrifice of burnt-offerings and sin-offerings. "And
they delivered the king's commissions unto the king's
lieutenants, and to the governors on this side the river; and they furthered the people, and the house of
God." †

Ezra proceeds to relate, in his own person, that the
princes presented themselves before him with a complaint that the people, including rulers, priests, and
Levites, had transgressed the law by contracting marriages with the surrounding idolaters. He heard the
statement with astonishment and horror, and, in the
presence of "every one that trembled at the words of
the God of Israel," sat mute till the hour of evening
sacrifice. Then he roused himself from his stupor,
and having rent his garments, fell upon his knees,
poured out a fervent prayer to Jehovah, confessing
and passionately bewailing the past and present per-
versity of the people, and owning them to be unworthy of a longer continuance of the forbearance and
forgiveness which, amidst so many and so gross prov-

---

* Ezra viii. 15 - 30. — " They brought us a man of understanding," &c.
(18) ; here again appears to be an omission of a name.
† viii. 31 - 36.

ocations, had never yet been withholden, and which
lately had been so signally manifested.*

The history, resuming here the mention of Ezra in
the third person, goes on to relate that, when he had
finished his prayer, accompanied with tears and other
manifestations of distress, the weeping people, " a very
great congregation of men, and women, and children,"
assembled about him, and one of them, a priest, proposed that they should seek reconciliation with God by
dismissing their foreign wives, and the children to
whom they had given birth, which Ezra accordingly,
before they dispersed, made them all swear to do.†
Ezra continued retired and fasting while proclamation
was made requiring every returned Jew to repair to
Jerusalem within three days, under penalty of excom-
munication, and confiscation of his property.‡ Within
the appointed time, " all the men of Judah and Benjamin gathered themselves together unto Jerusalem ; it
was the ninth month, and the twentieth day of the
month ; and all the people sat in the street of the
house of God, trembling because of this matter, and
for the great rain." To Ezra's · exhortation that they
should acknowledge their fault, and dissolve their un-
lawful alliances, they unanimously replied, that so it
was their purpose to do, but that, as the weather was
unfavorable, and such a business could not be immediately despatched, it would be well to appoint times
at which the persons in fault, with the elders of their

---

* Ezra ix. 1 – 15. But it is not clear how any marriages contracted by the
Jews with their unbelieving neighbours in this age could be construed as a
violation of the laws in Ex. xxxiv. 11, 12, 15, 16, Deut. vii. 1 – 4. — " To
give us a nail in his holy place " (8); that is, to *establish us;* the allusion is
to the nails driven into the ground to which were fastened the cords of tents ;
comp. Is. xxii. 23.

† x. 1 – 5. — " One of the sons of Elam " (2); comp. viii. 7.

‡ x. 6 – 8.

respective cities, should present themselves before the rulers for the observance of the necessary forms.* Two persons, assisted by two Levites, were placed in charge of the transaction, which, under the supervision of Ezra and " certain chief of the fathers," was finished in three months.† And the book concludes with a list of priests, Levites, singers, porters, and common. people, who were found chargeable with the irregularity in question.‡

This survey of the contents of the book known by the name of Ezra enables us to judge of its character, and of the probable correctness of the current opinion respecting its authorship. It appears to be a hasty and inartificial compilation. It records the events of two different periods, separated by an interval of thirty-seven or of fifty-eight years. It terminates in the most abrupt manner. Different parts of it are composed in different languages, the Chaldee being employed, not only in letters inserted, but in a long integral portion of the narrative. In the first and fourth of the four chapters of which the proceedings of Ezra are the subject, the narrator uses the pronoun of the third person; in the second and third of those chapters, the pronoun of the first person is employed, and ostensibly it is Ezra himself who is writing.

It seems impossible to regard Ezra, or any other one person, as the author of the whole book. No one composing a continuous history uses two languages alternately, or in different passages speaks of the same person as *I* and as *he*. The only reasonable questions seem to be, how many writers furnished contributions

---

* Ezra x. 9 – 14.   † x. 15 – 17.
‡ x. 18 – 44. — " Maaseiah, and Eliezer, and Jarib, and Gedaliah . . . . . offered a ram of the flock for their trespass " (18, 19) ; a proceeding which is recorded of none of the other delinquents.

to the book, and when and by whom it was put together in the form in which we now possess it.

The second chapter appears to have been a separate document. Nehemiah has the same matter, word for word, prefacing it with the introduction, "I found a register of the genealogy of them which came up at the first, and found written therein."[*] It is true that the original form of this record may have been that in which it now appears, as part of that account of the return of Zerubbabel and his companions from Babylon in which we find it incorporated in our Book of Ezra.

The passage in the Chaldee language, beginning in the fourth chapter and ending in the sixth, has unity and completeness in itself, and can hardly be otherwise regarded than as having been originally a distinct composition.

The passage beginning near the close of the seventh chapter and extending through the eighth and ninth, purports, by its use of the pronoun of the first person, to have been written by Ezra. There is no reason to doubt that such was the fact; and if so, it seems that we should ascribe to him also the preservation of the royal missive in Chaldee which immediately precedes, since with a reference to that the narrative of his own writing begins. If the following part of the book, relating as it does to transactions in which he personally took part, was his own composition, we can perceive no cause for his not continuing to speak of himself in the first person. It appears probable that the first part of the book, viz. the record in six chapters of transactions in the time of Zerubbabel, or at least a portion of it,[†] was the production of a contempo-

---

[*] Neh. vii. 5.

[†] " Then said we unto them after this manner," &c. (Ezra v. 4).

rary writer; but those transactions began fifty-eight or seventy-nine years (according to the view we may adopt of the chronology) before the arrival of Ezra in Palestine with the royal commission.

Nor was Ezra probably the compiler of the book, any more than its author in a stricter sense. We can imagine no reason why, had he been so, he should have left unnoticed (in the chasm between the sixth and seventh chapters) the events of so many years as passed between the time of Zerubbabel's government and his own, well informed as he must have been concerning them.

On the whole, no conclusion seems to approach nearer to being satisfactory than this; that the book is a compilation by some person unknown, who put together materials relating to the epochs of Zerubbabel and Ezra (among them a composition of Ezra's own), and, by way of connection between the two, himself wrote the first eleven verses of the seventh chapter.

The Book of Nehemiah begins by ascribing its own authorship, or the authorship of its first part at least, to the eminent person of that name whose actions it records; and through the first seven chapters the writer, in relating the proceedings of Nehemiah, uses the pronoun of the first person.*

He relates that, being in the palace at Shushan, "in the month Chisleu, in the twentieth year," and meet-

---

* Nehemiah was the son of a certain Hachaliah (Neh. i. 1). That he was, or was in later times supposed to have been, of a priestly family, cannot be inferred from 2 Mac. i. 18, 21, where he is not related to have offered a sacrifice himself, but to have ordered the priests to do it; nor can he have been the person of the same name who had returned to Jerusalem with Zerubbabel (Ez. ii. 2; Neh. vii. 7), for the periods of Zerubbabel's government and his own were separated by nearly a hundred years.

ing there " certain men of Judah," he made inquiries
of them concerning the condition and prospects of
those of their countrymen who had returned from
Chaldea to Jerusalem. He learned, with extreme distress, that the wall of Jerusalem was broken down, its
gates burned, and its inhabitants " in great affliction
and reproach." He " sat down and wept, and mourned certain days, and fasted, and prayed before the God
of heaven," bewailing the sins by which perverse Israel
had estranged his love, pleading his promise made to
Moses, that, when exiled and dispersed for disobedience, penitence should procure for them mercy and
restoration, and entreating that his petition in their
behalf might find favor with the king, to whom he
was attached as cupbearer.*

Four months after, Nehemiah presented himself before the king, to render his official service. Observing
a sad expression of his countenance, which had not
been worn before, Artaxerxes inquired into its cause,
and being informed that it was because of the desolate
condition of Jerusalem, the place of his " fathers' sepulchres," asked further what request he had to make.
Having encouraged himself by prayer, he presented
his petition to the king for leave to visit and rebuild
the holy city. Leave of absence for a limited time was
accordingly granted him, and, agreeably to his further

---

* Neh. i. 1 - 11. — " In the twentieth year " (1) ; that is, " the twentieth
year of Artaxerxes the king " (comp. ii. 1), which year corresponds with
the year 444 before Christ, if it was Artaxerxes Longimanus that was intended ; as it must have been, because, to mention no other reason, the
monarch here referred to reigned thirty-two years (comp. v. 14), which no
Persian king but Artaxerxes Longimanus did, except Darius Hystaspis and
Artaxerxes Mnemon, the one of whom was too early, and the other too
late, to admit of the events here recorded being referred to the time of
either. — " Shushan the palace " (i. 1); the Hebrew form of Susa, the metropolis of Persia. — " The word that thou commandedst thy servant Moses,
saying, ' If ye transgress,' " &c. (8) ; comp. Deut. iv. 25 et seq.

request, he received letters to the king's "governors beyond the river," directing them to afford him safe conduct on his way, and to provide him with timber for building. With an escort of horsemen he reached Judea, and 'delivered the letters, to the great disappointment and displeasure of "Sanballat, the Horonite, and Tobiah the servant, the Ammonite." After a stay of three days at Jerusalem, he made an examination by night of the ruinous walls of the city, accompanied by a few friends on foot, no horse (for the greater secrecy) being used by the party, except that on which he rode. Having acquainted himself by this inspection with the forlorn condition of the place, he called the chief of his countrymen together, told them of the encouragement he had received from Artaxerxes, and invited them to join him in his pious and patriotic undertaking. The proposal was welcomed, and the work entered on with alacrity, notwithstanding the ill-will of Sanballat, Tobiah, "and Geshem the Arabian," to whose remonstrances and scoffs Nehemiah did but reply, that he and his friends would prosecute the work, confiding in the favor of the God of heaven, and utterly disregarding the opposition of those who had "no portion, nor right, nor memorial, in Jerusalem." *

A detailed account is next given of the different tasks executed by different persons in the repair of the gates and walls.† Men of other cities as well as Jerusalem took part in the work,‡ and persons of every rank, from "the goldsmiths and the merchants"§ to the rulers of the half of cities,‖ and even to "Eliashib the high-priest." ¶ Nor was the help of women rejected, for "Shallum, the son of Halohesh," was assisted by his daughters.**

---

* Neh. ii. 1 – 20.   † iii. 1 – 32.   ,   ‡ iii. 2, 5, 7, et al. h. m.
§ iii. 32.   ‖ iii. 9, 12, 16 – 18.   ¶ iii. 1.   ** iii. 12.

While the building proceeded, Nehemiah heard of the rage and derision to which the adversaries were provoked while they remarked its progress; but he only prayed to Jehovah to " turn their reproach upon their own head, and give them for a prey in the land of captivity." *   At length, when the whole city was inclosed, but the wall was only raised to half its height, and the people showed some discouragement from a perception of the magnitude of the work, Nehemiah had intelligence of a conspiracy on the part of Sanballat and his confederates, to attack and demolish it.   Then Nehemiah " set a watch against them day and night," marshalling " the people after their families, with their swords, their spears, and their bows," and exciting their officers and them to their duty by reminding them of the Almighty God who would fight for them, and of the wives and children for whom they were to fight.†   This show of determination proved sufficient to disconcert the hostile plan, though Nehemiah still considered it prudent to have the builders labor with arms by their side, and to have half his servants constantly doing military duty of watch and ward, with their officers in their rear on the inner defences.   A signal was established to gather the people by sound of trumpet to any point of attack.   Orders were given for their servants, as well as themselves, to lodge within the city walls.   Nehemiah, his family, his servants, and his guards, wore their clothes day and night, " saving that every one put them off for washing"; and so all the dwellers in the city watched and labored " from the rising of the morning till the stars appeared." ‡

To the great dissatisfaction of Nehemiah, complaints

---

* Neh. iv. 1 - 5.   † iv. 6 - 14.   ‡ iv. 15 - 23.

reached him, that, when a considerable number of the
people had been compelled to contract debts for the
sustenance of their families and the payment of their
taxes, their creditors had required them to give security in their lands, vineyards, and houses, and even to
pledge their children as slaves, whom they were not
able to redeem, because their other property was
gone.* After due deliberation, he proceeded to rebuke " the nobles and the rulers " for their part in
such oppressive transactions, reminding them of his
own example, not only of entire forbearance from the
like, but of liberal contributions for the recovery of
Jewish captives who had fallen into heathen hands.

Confounded and self-condemned, they promised to restore the pledges, and relinquish every usurious claim;
and Nehemiah called the priests and imposed on them
a solemn oath to that effect, at the same time shaking
his lap, and appealing to God so to " shake out every
man from his house, and from his labor, that perform-
eth not this promise." The engagement was kept,†
and Nehemiah takes the occasion to say, that such had
been his own disinterestedness, that, during twelve
years of official service, he had not only received no
pay, either in money or in kind, as the former governors had done, nor, like them, allowed his servants to
practise authority and extortion, but that he had employed his servants as well as himself on the public
works, and kept a liberal hospitality, entertaining at
his table a hundred and fifty of the Jews and rulers,
besides those that came from the heathen that were

---

* Neh. v. 1 - 5.

† v. 6 - 13. — " I set a great assembly against them " (7); he reproved
them in a concourse of the people, whose united displeasure, added to his
own, they did not deem it prudent further to provoke. — " The hundredth
part of the money," &c. (11); a common rate of monthly interest in ancient times, as among the Romans.

about, and causing "one ox and six choice sheep" to
be prepared for him daily at his own charge, besides
fowls, "and once in ten days store of all sorts of
wine." Such had been the course which he had taken
"because the bondage was heavy upon the people,"
and for which he hoped that his God would "think
upon him for good." *

When the outer wall was all completed except the
hanging of the gates, Sanballat and Geshem, two
of the adversaries already mentioned, sent to him a
treacherous proposal for a meeting in the neighbourhood of the city. Nehemiah declined it, on account of
the urgent business which he had in hand; and four
times the invitation was repeated and refused. A fifth
time a messenger came, with an open letter, wherein
Sanballat, informing him of the currency of a rumor
that he and his people were meditating rebellion, and
that the building of the wall was but preparatory to his
causing himself to be proclaimed king, proposed again
an interview with him before the charge should be reported to the Persian court. He replied, disclaiming
any such purpose, and treating it as a calumnious invention of the writer.† The purpose which he understood to have been in contemplation was accomplished.
His companions were alarmed, and in danger of being
discouraged. But they were reassured by his own reso-
lute conduct. When a Jew, who pretended friendship,
but whom he perceived to be a hired instrument of his
enemies, prosecuting a perfidious purpose to lead him
so to act "that they might have matter for an evil report," advised him to retire and fortify himself within

---

* Neh. v. 14–19. — "Neither bought we any land" (16); that is,
using the opportunities which they had, in the distressed circumstances of
their neighbours, to possess themselves of their estates.
† vi. 1–8.

the temple, so as to be safe against assassins, he replied that it was unbecoming a man like him to flee, or so much as to go into the temple to save his life; and, trusting himself to God's care, he invoked his judgments upon the insidious arts of those " that would have put him in fear." *

The wall, with its gates, at length was finished, to the great vexation of the Samaritan and heathen neighbours of the new settlers, and the great relief of Nehemiah, whose embarrassments were increased by the interest maintained in the city, through frequent correspondence with his own companions and " the nobles of Judah," by his enemy, Tobiah, who, as well as his son, was allied by marriage with families of note.†
Having first made an arrangement of the duties of " the porters, and the singers, and the Levites " (apparently those stationed at the gates), Nehemiah placed his brother Hanani, and " Hananiah the ruler of the palace," a faithful and God-fearing man, in charge over Jerusalem, with directions to have the gates nightly closed with care, under their own inspection, and not opened in the morning till the sun was high, and to pay special attention to the stationing of the watchmen, inasmuch as, compared with the extent of the city, the inhabitants were few.‡ Proposing " to gather together the nobles, and the rulers, and the people, that they might be reckoned by genealogy," he was so fortunate as to find " a register of the genealogy of them which came up at the first," which he inserts at length

---

* Neh. vi. 9 – 14. — " Shemaiah . . . . . who was shut up " (10); for the purpose, it would seem, of communicating his own panic to Nehemiah.

† vi. 15 – 19. — " Shechaniah, the son of Arah " (18) ; comp. Ez. ii. 5. — " Meshullam, the son of Berechiah " (ibid.) ; comp. iii. 4.

‡ vii. 1 – 4. — " My brother Hanani " (2) ; comp. i. 2.

in his book, and which turns out to be the same
with that inserted in the Book of Ezra, though with
numerous variations of the text.*
Hitherto we appear to have been reading a work of

---

* Neh. vii. 5 - 73 ; comp. Ezra ii. 1 - 70. — " Azariah, Raamiah,
Nahamani, ... Mispereth, ... Nehum " (7) ; " Seraiah, Ree-
laiah, ... Mizpar, ... Rehum " (Ez. ii. 2). — " The children of
Arah," 652 (10) ; 775 (Ez. ii. 5). — " The children of Pahath-moab,"
2818 (11) ; 2812 (Ez. ii. 6). — " The children of Zattu," 845 (13) ; 945
(Ez. ii. 8). — " The children of Binnui," 648 (15) ; Bani, 642 (Ez. ii. 10).
— " The children of Bebai," 628 (16) ; 623 (Ez. ii. 11). — " The children
of Azgad," 2322 (17) ; 1222 (Ez. ii. 12). — " The children of Adonikam,"
667 (18) ; 666 (Ez. ii. 13). — " The children of Bigvai," 2067 (19) ; 2056
(Ez. ii. 14). — " The children of Adin," 655 (20) ; 454 (Ez. ii. 15). —
" The children of Hashum," 328 (22) ; 223 (Ez. ii. 19). — " The children
of Bezai," 324 (23) ; 323 (Ez. ii. 17). — " The children of Hariph," 112
(24) ; Jorah, 112 (Ez. ii. 18). — " The children of Gibeon," 95 (25) ; Gib-
bar, 95 (Ez. ii. 20). — " The men of Bethlehem and Netophah," 188 (26) ;
179 (Ez. ii. 21, 22). — " The men of Bethel and Ai," 123 (32) ; 223 (Ez.
ii. 28). — " The children of Magbish " (omitted) ; 156 (Ez. ii. 30). — " The
children of Lod, Hadid, and Ono," 721 (37) ; 725 (Ez. ii. 33). — " The
children of Senaah," 3930 (38) ; 3630 (Ez. ii. 35). — " The children of
Asaph," 148 (44) ; 128 (Ez. ii. 41). — " The porters," 138 (45) ; 139 (Ez.
ii. 42). — " Hagaba. . . . . Shalmai " (48) ; " Hagabah, Akkub, Hagab,
Shalmai " (Ez. ii. 45, 46). — " Meunim, ... Nephishesim " (52) ;
" Mehunim, ... Nephusim " (Ez. ii. 50). — " Amon " (59) ; " Ami "
(Ez. ii. 57). — " The children of Nekoda," 642 (62) ; 552 (Ez. ii. 60). —
" The whole congregation together was forty and two thousand, three hundred and threescore " (66) ; the same sum total as in Ezra (ii. 64), though
exceeding by more than eleven thousand the aggregate of the numbers
given in detail in either book. — " They had two hundred forty and five
singing men and singing women " (67) ; " two hundred singing men and
singing women " (Ez. ii. 65). — " The Tirshatha gave to the treasure a
thousand drams of gold, fifty basons, five hundred and thirty priests' garments " (70) ; of this there is nothing in the corresponding place in Ezra.
— " Some of the chief of the fathers gave to the treasure of the work
twenty thousand drams of gold, and two thousand and two hundred pounds
of silver ; and that which the rest of the people gave was twenty thousand
drams of gold, and two thousand pounds of silver, and threescore and seven
priests' garments " (71, 72) ; " some of the chief of the fathers . . . . .
gave after their ability unto the treasure of the work threescore and one
thousand drams of gold, and five thousand pounds of silver, and one hundred priests' garments " (Ez. ii 68, 69, where nothing is said of gifts of
the common people).

Nehemiah, consisting partly of a narrative of events of his own time, and partly of a transcription by him of an ancient record, of which he relates that he had occasion to make use. But from this point the pronoun of the first person ~~plural~~ ceases to be employed ⚹ till near the close of the book,* nor is there any thing else authorizing us to identify the writer of the four chapters and a half next following, with the author of those chapters which have been examined. So far from it, that there are significant indications leading to the opposite conclusion.

In the Book of Ezra, in immediate connection with the document, common to both books, which has just been remarked upon, follows a brief account of the celebration by the people, in Zerubbabel's time, of the great Feast of Tabernacles. In the Book of Nehemiah, in the same close connection, which connection is expressed even in the same language, is a more full account of a celebration of that feast, which is here said to have taken place in the time of Nehemiah, but under Ezra's superintendence.†

Ezra, it is here related, was solicited by the people assembled in "the street that was before the water gate," to produce "the book of the Law of Moses, which the Lord had commanded to Israel." He did so, and upon the first day of the seventh month, from a platform erected for the purpose, read therein aloud, "from the morning until midday, before the men and the women, and those that could understand." The people listened with devout attention, and the Levites and men of note, by whom Ezra was surrounded, "gave the sense, and caused them to understand the reading," a measure rendered necessary by the general disuse of

---

* Its use is resumed in the passage beginning at xii. 27.
† Comp. Ezra ii. 68 – iii. 1 with Neh. vii. 70 – viii. 1.

the Hebrew language during the time of their exile in
Chaldea.*   They "wept when they heard the words
of the Law"; but "Nehemiah, which is the Tirshatha,"
with Ezra and the Levites, reminded them that it was
no time for tears, for the Feast of Tabernacles, the
prescribed season for which had now arrived, was a
joyous occasion, and it became them to keep it with
grateful and generous festivity.

The next day, "the chief of the fathers of all the
people, the priests and the Levites," resorted to Ezra
to obtain further instruction.   Having received it and
made it known abroad, the people "made themselves booths, every one upon the roof of his house,
and in their courts, and in the courts of the house
of God, and in the street of the water gate, and the
street of the gate of Ephraim; and all the congregation of them that were come again out of the captivity
made booths, and sat under the booths."   "Also day
by day, from the first day unto the last day, he read
in the book of the Law of God; and they kept the
feast seven days, and on the eighth day was a solemn
assembly, according unto the manner." †   Of this celebration it is said, "since the days of Jeshua, the son
of Nun, unto that day, had not the children of Israel
done so, and there was very great gladness."   Yet in
the preceding book we have been told that that feast
had been kept within the century under circumstances
altogether similar.   Nor only this; the information
concerning the feast is represented to have been as
new to the people in the second instance as in the first.
It is impossible to overlook the probability that in the
Books of Nehemiah and Ezra we are but reading different accounts of the same transaction, which had
come into the hands of the compilers of the two books,

---

* Neh. viii. 1 - 8.   † viii. 9 - 18.

and been incorporated by them in their compositions respectively, the one referring the event to the age of Zerubbabel, the other to that of Nehemiah.

And the same observation occurs respecting the contents of the following chapter, though not with the same degree of evidence, and the common opinion of different transactions having been intended may in the latter instance be correct. We therein read that, among other reforms, took place a dissolution by the people of their idolatrous matrimonial alliances, similar to what is recorded at greater length in the last two chapters of the Book of Ezra. It is related that, keeping a solemn fast, "with sackcloth and earth upon them, the seed of Israel separated themselves from all strangers, and stood and confessed their sins, and the iniquities of their fathers; and they stood up in their place, and read in the book of the Law of the Lord their God one fourth part of the day; and another fourth part they confessed, and worshipped the Lord their God." Some of the Levites, taking the lead in the devotions of the assembly, "cried with a loud voice unto the Lord their God," and, in a long prayer, which is recorded in its place, commemorated his past dealings with the people, both of mercy and of judgment, through the successive ages of their history, bewailed their perverseness and obduracy, and professed their purpose to keep thenceforward a covenant of submission and obedience.* This covenant, committed to writing, was entered into with the solemnity of a seal by several priests, Levites, and other eminent persons, whose names are given, to the number of eighty-three, while the rest of the faithful people, of all orders, "entered into a curse, and into an oath, to walk in God's law, which was given by Moses, the servant of

---

* Neh. ix. 1 – 38.

God "; to abstain from marriage with the surrounding misbelievers; to keep holy the Sabbath, the holidays, and the sabbatical year; to forgive debts; to make an annual contribution of the third part of a shekel for the support of the temple worship; to provide fuel for the use of the altar, assigning the duty to certain persons by lot; and to bring faithfully to the sacred treasury the firstlings of their herds and flocks, and the first fruits of their fields, vineyards, and orchards, as well as the tithes, and the commutation-money for their first-born.*

At the fourth verse of the seventh chapter, immediately preceding the introduction of the list (parallel with that in the Book of Ezra) of emigrant companions of Zerubbabel, we read that "the city was large and great, but the people were few therein, and the houses were not builded." At the beginning of the eleventh chapter we are told, that "the rulers of the people dwelt at Jerusalem; the rest of the people also cast lots, to bring one of ten to dwell in Jerusalem, the holy city, and nine parts to dwell in other cities," while

---

* Neh. x. 1–39. — "Those that sealed were Nehemiah, the Tirshatha," &c. (1); the omission of the name of Ezra accords with the fragmentary character of the passage; and several of the names which follow of persons who "sealed" in Nehemiah's time (as Azariah, Pashur, Harim, Jeshua, Binnui, Parosh, Pahath-moab, Elam, Zatthu, Azgad, Bebai, Bigvai, Adin, Ater, Hashum, Bezai, Hariph, Rehum, Harim) are the names of persons whose posterity by hundreds and thousands are said to have come to Jerusalem in Zerubbabel's company, nearly a century before (comp. vii. 6 *et seq.*). — "They that had separated themselves from the people of the lands unto the Law of God" (28); that is, proselytes to Judaism from other races. — "That we would leave the seventh year, and the exaction of every debt" (31); comp. Deut. xv. 1, 2. — "The wood-offering, ... to burn upon the altar of the Lord our God, as it is written in the Law" (34); comp. Lev. vi. 12, 13. — "To bring the first-fruits," &c. (35); comp. Ex. xxiii. 19; xxxiv. 26. — "The firstborn of our sons and of our cattle, as it is written in the Law," &c. (36); comp. Ex. xiii. 12, 13; Lev. xxvii. 26; Numb. xviii. 15–17. — "The first-fruits of our dough," &c. (37); comp. Lev. xxiii. 17; Numb. xv. 19–21. — "The Levites shall bring up the tithe of the tithes," &c. (38, 39); comp. Numb. xviii. 26–31.

some "willingly offered themselves to dwell at Jerusalem," and thereby became objects of public gratitude.*
The close connection between these two statements
strengthens the presumption, arising out of circumstances which have been named, that these two verses
were originally in juxtaposition, and that the passage
beginning with the list of emigrants, and ending with
the tenth chapter, was interpolated between them in
later times. Next follows a list of " the chief of the province
that dwelt in Jerusalem," so similar in its structure,
and in many of its statements, to one which we have
already read in the First Book of Chronicles,† as to
forbid the idea of their having had an independent
origin, yet differing from that document in a large
portion of the particulars recorded.‡　The account

---

* Neh. xi. 1, 2.　　　　　　　　　† 1 Chron. ix. 1 – 17.

‡ Neh. xi. 3 – 19. — " These are the chief of the province that dwelt in
Jerusalem ; but in the cities of Judah dwelt every one in his possession in
their cities, to wit, Israel, the priests, and the Levites, and the Nethinims,
and the children of Solomon's servants " (3) ; " the first inhabitants, that
dwelt in their possessions in their cities, were the Israelites, the priests, Levites, and the Nethinims (1 Chron. ix. 2). — " At Jerusalem dwelt certain
of the children of Judah, and of the children of Benjamin " (4); " in Jerusalem dwelt of the children of Judah, and of the children of Benjamin, and
of the children of Ephraim, and Manasseh " (1 Chron. ix. 3). — " Of the
children of Judah, Athaiah, the son of Uzziah, the son of Zechariah, the
son of Amariah, the son of Shephatiah, the son of Mahalaleel, of the children
of Perez " (4) ; " Uthai, the son of Ammihud, the son of Omri, the son of
Imri, the son of Bani, of the children of Pharez, the son of Judah "
(1 Chron. ix. 4). — " Maaseiah, the son of Baruch, ... the son of
Shiloni " (5) ; " of the Shilonites, Asaiah, the firstborn, and his sons "
(1 Chron. ix. 5). — " The sons of Perez, that dwelt at Jerusalem, were four
hundred threescore and eight valiant men " (6) ; " of the sons of Zerah,
Jeuel, and their brethren, six hundred and ninety " (1 Chron. ix. 6). —
" These are the sons of Benjamin ; Sallu, the son of Meshullam, the son of
Joed, the son of Pedaiah, the son of Kolaiah, the son of Maaseiah, the son
of Ithiel, the son of Jesaiah ; and after him Gabbai, Sallai, nine hundred
twenty and eight ; and Joel, the son of Zichri, was their overseer, and Judah, the son of Senuah, was second over the city " (7 – 9); " of the sons of

next given of the places of settlement of the priests,
Levites, and Nethinims, and of the descendants from
Judah and Benjamin,* is interrupted by one or two
statements which seem to have lost their place, and

Benjamin; Sallu, the son of Meshullam, the son of Hodaviah, the son of
Hasenuah, and Ibneiah, the son of Jeroham, and Elah, the son of Uzzi, the
son of Michri, and Meshullam, the son of Shephatiah, the son of Reuel, the
son of Ibnijah, and their brethren, according to their generations, nine hundred and fifty and six" (1 Chron. ix. 7 - 9). — "Of the priests, Jedaiah,
the son of Joiarib, Jachin " (10); " of the priests, Jedaiah, and Jehoiarib,
and Jachin " (1 Chron. ix. 10). — " Seraiah, the son of Hilkiah, the son of
Meshullam, the son of Zadok, the son of Meraioth, the son of Ahitub, was
the ruler of the house of God ; and their brethren, that did the work of the
house, were eight hundred twenty and two" (11, 12); " Azariah, the son
of Hilkiah," &c. (1 Chron. ix. 11, which has nothing corresponding to the
last clause of this passage of Nehemiah). — " Adaiah, the son of Jeroham,
the son of Pelaliah, the son of Amzi, the son of Zechariah, the son of Pashur, the son of Malchiah, and his brethren, chief of the fathers, two hundred
forty and two, and Amashai, the son of Azareel, the son of Ahasai, the son
of Meshillemoth, the son of Immer" (12, 13); " Adaiah, the son of Jeroham, the son of Pashur, the son of Malchijah, and Maasiai, the son of Adiel,
the son of Jahzerah, the son of Meshullam, the son of Meshillemith, the son
of Immer" (1 Chron. ix. 12). — "And their brethren, mighty men of valor,
an hundred and twenty and eight; and their overseer was Zabdiel, the son
of one of the great men " (14) ; " and their brethren, heads of the house
of their fathers, a thousand and seven hundred and threescore ; very able
men for the work of the service of the house of God " (1 Chron. ix. 13).
— " Of the Levites, Shemaiah, ... the son of Hashabiah, the son of
Bunni" (15) ; " of the Levites, Shemaiah, ... the son of Hashabiah,
of the sons of Merari " (1 Chron. ix. 14). — " Shabbethai and Jozabad, of
the chief of the Levites, had the oversight of the outward business of the
house of God " (16); this clause has no parallel in Chronicles. — " Mattaniah, the son of Micha, the son of Zabdi, the son of Asaph, was the principal, to begin the thanksgiving in prayer ; and Bakbukiah, the second among
his brethren, and Abda, the son of Shammua, the son of Galal, the son of
Jeduthun " (17) ; " Bakbakkar, Heresh, and Galal, and Mattaniah, the son
of Micah, the son of Zichri, the son of Asaph ; and Obadiah, the son of
Shemaiah, the son of Galal, the son of Jeduthun ; and Berechiah, the son
of Asa, the son of Elkanah, that dwelt in the villages of the Netophathites "
(1 Chron. ix. 15, 16). — " All the Levites in the holy city were two hundred
fourscore and four ; moreover, the porters, Akkub, Talmon, and their brethren that kept the gates, were an hundred seventy and two " (18, 19) ; " the
porters were Shallum, and Akkub, and Talmon, and Ahiman, and their
brethren ; Shallum was the chief" (1 Chron. ix. 17).
* Neh. xi. 20, 21, 25 - 36.

are additional illustrations of the unsatisfactory character of this history.*

Turning back abruptly to nearly a century before the age of Nehemiah, the twelfth chapter opens with a list of " the priests and the Levites that went up with Zerubbabel,"† in which list it is remarkable that most of the names are the same with those of persons who had just been related to have been " sealed " with Nehemiah,‡ while others had been also mentioned as contemporary with that personage.§

Next follows a list of the succession of high-priests from Jeshua, the contemporary of Zerubbabel, to Jaddua, the contemporary of Alexander the Great, a period of two centuries.‖ This passage could not have had a place in the book much earlier than the year. 331 B. C., when Jaddua became high-priest.

" And in the days of Joiakim," the record continues, " were priests, the chief of the fathers "; and as Joiakim was son of Jeshua, so the catalogue of these chiefs of his day represents them as sons of those who had just been mentioned as chiefs in the days of his father.¶

---

* Neh. xi. 22 – 24. — " The overseer also of the Levites at Jerusalem was Uzzi," &c. (22); the subject of the condition of the Levites and others at Jerusalem appeared to have been disposed of and concluded in the passage ending two verses further back ; also comp. 15, 17, where several of the same names occur, but with a different representation. — " It was the king's commandment," &c. (23) ; that is, the command of the king of Persia, who could scarcely have been expected to take an interest in this arrangement. — " Pethahiah . . . . . was at the king's hand in all matters concerning the people " (24) ; a fact of the highest importance in the history of the time, but a fact of which we find no other trace.

† xii. 1 – 9.

‡ With xii. 1 – 5 comp. x. 2 – 8, and with xii. 8 comp. x. 9.

§ With xii. 7 comp. xi. 7, 10, and with xii. 8, 9 comp. xi. 17.

‖ xii. 10, 11.

¶ xii. 12 – 21; comp. 1 – 7 ; in the list of the chiefs of Joiakim's time there are some changes of the names of their fathers, as recited in the previous passage, as Melicu (14) for Malluch (2), Shebaniah (14) for Shecha-

The names of the chief Levites, it is said, were recorded
in the Book of the Chronicles (where, however, they
are not found) "even until the days of Johanan, the
son of Eliashib," which Johanan, if it be Jonathan,
grandson of Eliashib, that is meant, was the fourth
high-priest after Jeshua ; and the list of chief Levites
is further said to have been extended (but in what
record is not mentioned) to the time of the high-priest
Jaddua, and that of priests " to the reign of Darius the
Persian."* Last of all comes a repetition of the
names and employments of musicians and porters, of
whom we have before read, and who are now said to
have been " in the days of Joiakim, the son of Jeshua,
the son of Jozadak, and in the days of Nehemiah the
governor, and of Ezra the priest, the scribe."†

. From this unmanageable maze of incoherent *memoranda* we are extricated at the twenty-seventh verse of
the twelfth chapter, where Nehemiah's history is re-
sumed with an account of the 'rejoicings with which
he took care to celebrate the completion of the city
wall. " They sought the Levites," he says, " out of
all their places, to bring them to Jerusalem, to keep
the dedication with gladness, both with thanksgivings
and with singing, with cymbals, psalteries, and with
harps." " The sons of the singers " came together
from their country and village habitations, " and the
priests and the Levites purified themselves, and purified the people, and the gates, and the wall." Nehe-

---

niah (3), Harim (15) for Rehum (3), Meraioth (15) for Meremoth (3),
Miniamin (17) for Miamin (5), Moadiah (17) for Miadiah (5), Sallai (20) for
Sallu (7); Hattush (2) is omitted (14), and the name of the son of Minia-
min (17).

* Neh. xii. 22, 23.

† xii. 24–26. — "Mattaniah and Bakbukiah . . . . . were porters"
(25); "Mattaniah . . . . . was the principal, to begin the thanksgiving in
prayer, and Bakbukiah the second among his brethren " (xi. 17).

miah "brought up the princes of Judah upon the
wall," and marshalled two companies, one of which,
preceded by " Ezra the scribe," and attended by " certain of the priests' sons," some "with trumpets," and
others "with the musical instruments of David the
man of God," "went up by the stairs of the city of
David" to its station, while the other, followed by Nehemiah himself, proceeded by a different way.   They
met "in the house of God," "and the singers sang
loud, with Jezrahiah their overseer; also that day they
offered great sacrifices, and rejoiced; for God had made
them rejoice with great joy; the wives also and the
children rejoiced; so that the joy of Jerusalem was
heard even afar off." *   Advantage was taken of the
enthusiasm of the time, when "Judah rejoiced" at the
stately parade of the priests and Levites, to appoint
officers to collect for them the contributions which
were their right by the law of Moses, while the dispositions of singers and porters were made " according
to the commandment of David and of Solomon his
son "; and for those attendants on the temple service,
as well as for the priests and the Levites at large, the
people made provision from day to day in the time of
Nehemiah, as they had done in the time of Zerubbabel
before him.†   At the same time, the direction " that
the Ammonite and the Moabite should not come into
the congregation of God for ever " ‡ having attracted
attention in the public reading of the Law, they proceeded to expel "all the mixed multitude" from Jerusalem, or at least from the precincts of the temple.§

---

* Neh. xii. 27 – 43. — Zechariah is said (35) to have been the great-
grandson of Mattaniah, which might well be, if Mattaniah belonged (comp.
1, 8) to the time of Zerubbabel. Mattaniah's grandfather is here called
Zaccur (comp. 1 Chron. xxv. 2); in xi. 17, his name is said to have been
Zabdi.

† xii. 44 – 47.   ‡ Deut. xxiii. 3 – 5.   § Neh. xiii. 1 – 3.

Previously to these transactions the high-priest Eliashib* had become allied with Tobiah the Ammonite;† and Nehemiah, after putting the affairs of government and worship at Jerusalem in so satisfactory a train, having gone to present himself at the Persian court "in the two-and-thirtieth year of Artaxerxes," Eliashib took advantage of his absence to appropriate to the use of his friend an apartment, belonging to the temple, which had heretofore been occupied as a storehouse for the offerings contributed for the priests and their assistants. Returning to Jerusalem, and receiving information of this irregularity, Nehemiah caused the apartment to be emptied and cleansed, and restored to its former use.‡

He found that occasion had arisen in his absence for more general reforms. "The Levites and the singers" were dispersed, for want of regular provision for their support. He collected them again, rebuked the rulers for having suffered such disorder, and made suitable arrangements to prevent its repetition; services, for which he expresses his hope that God will remember him.§ The Sabbath was not kept holy. He saw men treading wine-presses, and performing other labor, on that day, and it had become a market-day in the city itself, for cultivators from the neighbouring country, and fishermen and merchants from Tyre. Having again reproved "the nobles of Judah," who should have prevented such a profanation, he directed the city gates to be closed at night-fall on the eve of the Sabbath, and not opened again till the day was over, and gave it in charge to some of his own household to see the order executed. With a view to evade the regulation, "the merchants, and sellers of all kind

---

* Neh. iii. 1.   † Comp. ii. 10; vi. 17, 18.
‡ xiii. 4 – 9.   § xiii. 10 – 14.

of ware, lodged without Jerusalem once or twice"; but being threatened by him, they desisted, and further offence was avoided by placing a guard of Levites at the gates; services for which Nehemiah again bespeaks the Divine remembrance.* He saw "Jews that had married wives of Ashdod, of Ammon, and of Moab," and heard children of Jews speaking in a corrupt tongue, half national and half foreign. This excited his righteous indignation to the highest pitch. He pointed out to the offenders the snare they had prepared for themselves, when even the wise king Solomon, the "beloved of his God," had yielded to the idolatrous seductions of "outlandish women." He "contended with them, and cursed them, and smote certain of them, and plucked off their hair, and made them swear by God" that they would not repeat the transgression.† A grandson of the high-priest, who had become "son-in-law to Sanballat, the Horonite," was banished by the faithful governor, who, having thus "cleansed" the priesthood "from all strangers, and appointed the wards of the priests and the Levites, every one in his business, and for the wood-offering, at times appointed, and for the first-fruits," concludes his history abruptly with another repetition of his characteristic prayer, "Remember me, O my God, for good." ‡

From the facts which have been observed, it appears to me that some things may be inferred with confidence respecting the authorship of the book which goes by the name of Nehemiah, while we must be content to leave others in uncertainty.

That it did not assume its entire present form till about the time of Alexander the Great is clear from the mention of Jaddua,§ who was high-priest at the

---

* Neh. xiii. 15 – 22.   † xiii. 23 – 27.   ‡ xiii. 28 – 31.   § xii. 11.

time of the Macedonian inroad into Judea.* Still, it
is not correct to infer, as has been done in all the
references to that fact which I have seen, that Jaddua
was already high-priest when that clause was inserted.
He is mentioned simply as son of Jonathan, and grandson of Joiada; and for aught that appears, though the
verse must be dated at a period after he became known,
it may have been written while his father or his grandfather occupied the high-priesthood. And were this
otherwise, still it is clearly supposable that, long after
the substantial completion of the book, this verse may
have been interpolated into it.

That the compilation was made at an indetermina-
ble, but a considerable, time after the events which it
records, appears from its general structure. It seems
to be made up in great part of disconnected materials,
which the compiler himself could not always understand, nor reconcile with each other, nor work into
a consistent narrative, nor refer respectively to their
proper periods of time.

In two long passages, one beginning the book, the
other concluding it,† the narrative is conducted in
the use of the first person of the singular number;
and I see no reason to doubt that they were written
by Nehemiah, to whom they thus expressly ascribe
themselves.‡ With another short passage, which comes
between them, but is separated from both by other matter, § they make a connected history from first to last.

---

* See Vol. III. p. 158.   † Neh. i. 1 – vii. 4 ; xii. 27 – xiii. 31.

‡ It is no objection, I think, to this view, that in one verse of the latter
passage we find Nehemiah spoken of in the third person ; "all Israel in the
days of Zerubbabel and in the days of Nehemiah gave the portions of the
singers," &c. (xii. 47). This is the way in which a writer would most
naturally speak of himself in such a connection. There would have been
a hardness in saying, "in the days of Zerubbabel and in *my* days."

§ xi. 1, 2.

The *genealogical register*, which occurs at the close
of the first of the three,* and which is declared to
have been more ancient than Nehemiah's time, may
have been incorporated into his book at a later period,
or it may have been inserted by himself. In this latter
case, it was a long parenthesis between the statement
of the smallness of the population compared with
the extent of the city,† and the statement, which in
historical sequence seems so closely connected with it,
that "the people cast lots to bring one of ten to dwell
in Jerusalem, the holy city, and nine parts to dwell in
other cities. And the people blessed all the men that
willingly offered themselves to dwell at Jerusalem." ‡
And, on the other hand, with this latter statement
naturally connects itself that with which the concluding passage begins; "and at the dedication of the
wall of Jerusalem they sought the Levites out of all
their places, to bring them to Jerusalem, to keep the
dedication."

If a treatise thus constituted was the work of Nehemiah, it must still be regarded as but a fragment,
so abrupt is its conclusion. On the supposition which
has been made, there remains a considerable part of
the present book which must have been interpolated
into it at a later period.§ The matter thus interpolated seems to consist of separate narratives, of uncertain number, but all of them, if I mistake not, relating to transactions of earlier date than the administration of Nehemiah. Coming, after Nehemiah's time,
into the hands of a person who was already in possession of Nehemiah's book, and who saw that their

---

* From vii. 5 to the middle of vii. 73.
† Neh. vii. 4.   ‡ xi. 1, 2.
§ vii. 73 (from the words "and when the seventh month came ")–x.
39; xi. 3 – xii. 26.

contents had a certain affinity with the history recorded by Nehemiah of the reëstablishment of the Jewish affairs, but who had no accurate knowledge either
of their date or of their sense, he preserved them by
an extremely unskilful insertion into Nehemiah's book;
and thus, in the compilation which resulted, and which
is now in our hands, we have occurrences of the times
of Zerubbabel and Ezra represented as taking place
midway between the first and last events of the administration of Nehemiah, who was later than either. It
is true that in one of these portions we read of the
sealing of " Nehemiah the Tirshatha," but the words
" the Tirshatha," at least, can scarcely be any thing but
a mistake of the compiler, or of some later transcriber,
who fancied there could be no other Nehemiah than
the governor of that name. To say, as the passage in
its present form imports, that the governor Nehemiah
took part in a transaction with persons * whose children came to Judea with Zerubbabel, nearly a century
before the date of that transaction,† is a mere confusion
of chronology, and contradiction of common sense.

The books which have been considered in this Lecture differ from the earlier treatises of Jewish history
in containing nothing whatever of a miraculous or extraordinary character. There is no trace in either of
them of any thing more than narrative of natural
events. Nothing is revealed or professed, requiring
or implying, in any way, or in the slightest degree,
supernatural illumination on the part of the writers.
They are fragments, not only of uninspired history,
but of very incomplete, unsatisfactory, inartificial, contradictory, and erroneous history. It is in vain to at-

---

* Neh. x. 1–19.   † vii. 7 et seq.

tempt to attach a character of superior authority to compositions like these. They will not bear the test of examination by any such standard. They are valuable if we will take them for what they are, and seek in them for important disconnected facts, or for the general tenor of a course of events, belonging to an interesting period. But a continuous trustworthy history they are not. They have no feature of resemblance to such a work as Divine inspiration might be supposed to dictate.

Neither the Book of Ezra, nor that of Nehemiah, is once quoted in the New Testament.

LECTURE LVII.

FIRST AND SECOND BOOKS OF ESDRAS.

APOCRYPHA OF THE OLD TESTAMENT. — DIFFERENT TITLES OF THE FIRST
BOOK OF ESDRAS. — ITS MATERIALS MOSTLY THE SAME AS PARTS OF
CHRONICLES, EZRA, AND NEHEMIAH. — NARRATIVE OF EVENTS PRE-
CEDING THE CAPTIVITY NEARLY IDENTICAL WITH THAT IN THE LAST
TWO CHAPTERS OF CHRONICLES. — ACCOUNT, COINCIDENT WITH THAT
IN EZRA, OF THE RETURN OF THE EXILES TO JERUSALEM, AND OF OB-
STRUCTIONS TO THE REBUILDING OF THE TEMPLE. — FEAST OF KING
DARIUS. — CONTEST OF WIT BETWEEN ZERUBBABEL AND OTHERS OF
THE KING'S BODY-GUARD. — VICTORY OF ZERUBBABEL, REWARDED BY
HIS COMMISSION TO LEAD BACK THE JEWS, AND BY OTHER BOUNTIES
TO THE NATION. — THANKSGIVING OF ZERUBBABEL, AND FESTIVAL OF
THE PEOPLE. — HISTORICAL STATEMENTS IN FOUR CHAPTERS, CORRE-
SPONDING WITH THOSE IN THE LAST NINE CHAPTERS OF EZRA, WITH
ONE TRANSPOSITION. — CLOSE OF THE BOOK, IDENTICAL WITH A PAS-
SAGE OF NEHEMIAH. — CHARACTER OF THE COMPILATION. — ORIGIN OF
THE INTERPOLATED PASSAGE. — CONCLUSIONS RELATING TO THE MA-
TERIALS OF THIS BOOK, AND OF THOSE OF EZRA AND NEHEMIAH. —
QUESTION AS TO THE COMPLETENESS OF THE FIRST BOOK OF ESDRAS,
AS NOW EXTANT. — SECOND BOOK OF ESDRAS, EXTANT IN LATIN, ARA-
BIC, AND ÆTHIOPIC. — QUESTION RESPECTING THE LANGUAGE OF THE
ORIGINAL. — REFERENCES TO IT BY CHRISTIAN FATHERS. — SUBJECT, A
SERIES OF REVELATIONS SAID TO HAVE BEEN MADE TO EZRA AT BABY-
LON. — SIMILARITY OF THE TOPICS AND STYLE TO THOSE OF PROPHETI-
CAL BOOKS. — ITS LITTLE VALUE, AND UNKNOWN ORIGIN. — QUESTION
RESPECTING THE CHARACTER OF THE COMPOSITION, CONNECTED WITH
ITS ASCRIPTION TO EZRA. — AGGADOTH OF THE JEWS. — PROPRIETY
OF THE USE OF THE NAME OF EZRA APPARENT IN ONE PASSAGE.

By the Council of Trent, in the year 1545, the
Biblical Canon was authoritatively determined for the
Catholic Church. Its list of Old Testament Scriptures, in addition to those belonging to the Canon received by Protestants, comprehended the Books of

Tobit, Judith, Wisdom, Ecclesiasticus, Baruch, the
First and Second Books of Maccabees, and those
parts of Esther and Daniel which do not exist in the
Hebrew or Chaldee language.* The First and Second
Books of Esdras and the Prayer of Manasseh, though
not included in the catalogue, still continued to be
printed in the common editions of the Vulgate Latin.
The catalogue of canonical books given by Jerome
and the Talmud, embracing only such as have been
transmitted in Hebrew and Chaldee,† is that which
has been adopted by Protestants. "All others," Jerome says, "are to be reckoned among *Apocrypha*." ‡
The books and fragments, arranged in our English
Bibles under that head, between the Old Testament
collection and the New, § are those which, though contained in the printed Vulgate, had been excluded from
the lists of Jerome and the Talmud, and rejected by the
Protestant churches at the Reformation. All of them,
except that called the Second Book of Esdras, belonged to the Alexandrine Canon of the Old Testament,
as exhibited in the Septuagint version. The word
Apocrypha ‖ is designed to indicate the distinction
which has been understood to exist between these
books and those included in the received Canon, in respect to the imputed uncertain origin, and altogether
inferior authority, of the former. Whether this distinction is capable of being sustained in the extent to
which it has been carried in current Protestant views

---

* Gallemart, "Sacrosanct. Concilium Tridentinum," pp. 8, 9.
† See Vol. I. pp. 38 – 41.
‡ " Prolog. Galeat."
§ This disposition of the books was, I believe, first made by Luther in
his translation. His collection of Apocrypha comprehends all the books
embraced under the same head in our English Bibles, except the First and
Second Books of Esdras.
‖ 'Απόκρυφος, *hidden*.

upon the subject, our observations on a portion of the canonical books have given us some preparation for deciding.

The First Book of Esdras, as we commonly call it, has been otherwise entitled the Second Book of Ezra, the canonical books of Ezra and Nehemiah being reckoned together as the First. In the Greek of the Seventy, it is placed before the canonical Book of Ezra, and takes the title of the First Book. In editions of the Vulgate, it bears the name of the Third Book of Ezra, the canonical Ezra and Nehemiah being numbered separately as the First and Second Books.* Though the Latin version was not from the hand of Jerome, but from the old Italic, he was acquainted with the book, as appears from his preface to the canonical Ezra, where he excuses himself from translating the apocryphal works under that writer's name.

The reader at once perceives this book to consist almost entirely of a collection of passages found in canonical books of the Old Testament, with an arrangement of its own (in one particular), with additions (one of them being long and important), and with some variations, particularly in respect to names and numbers. The passage occupying the third and fourth chapters and the first six verses of the fifth is peculiar to this book. The first chapter is substantially the same with the last two chapters of the Second Book of Chronicles, and the residue of the composition corresponds in like manner to the canonical

---

* Before the time of Sextus the Fifth, its place, in copies of the Vulgate, was next after Nehemiah. In the edition sanctioned by that pontiff, the Prayer of Manasseh, and the Third and Fourth Books of Esdras, were arranged at the end of the volume, after the New Testament, which place they have since retained.

book of Ezra and a small portion of that of Nehemiah.

The narrative, in the first chapter, of transactions
beginning with the famous Passover of Josiah and
ending with the Babylonish captivity, is so far identical with that in the last two chapters of the Second
Book of Chronicles as to exhibit no omission, except
the statement of the length of Jehoiakim's reign,*
very trifling variations of statement,† and no addition,
unless we consider in that light such a comment as

---

* 1 Esdras i. 39 ; comp. 2 Chron. xxxvi. 5.

† "The priests . . . . . arrayed in long garments in the temple of the
Lord " (1 Esdras i. 2) ; "he . . . . . encouraged them to the service of the
house of the Lord " (2 Chron. xxxv. 2). — "According to the magnificence
of Solomon " (5) ; "according to the writing of Solomon," &c. (2 Chron.
xxxv. 4). — "These things were given of the king's allowance, according
as he promised to the people, to the priests, and to the Levites " (7) ;
"these were of the king's substance ; and his princes gave willingly unto
the people, to the priests, and to the Levites " (2 Chron. xxxv. 7, 8). —
"Ochiel and Joram, captains over thousands " (9) ; "Jehiel and Jozabad,
chief of the Levites " (2 Chron. xxxv. 9). — "When these things were
done, the priests and Levites having the unleavened bread stood in very
comely order according to the kindreds, and according to the several dignities of the fathers before the people, to offer to the Lord, as it is written in
the book of Moses ; and thus did they in the morning " (10, 11); "the
service was prepared, and the priests stood in their place, and the Levites
in their courses, according to the king's commandment; and they killed the
passover, and the priests sprinkled the blood from their hands, and the Levites flayed them ; and they removed the burnt-offerings, that they might
give according to the divisions of the families of the people, to offer unto the
Lord, as it is written in the book of Moses ; and so they did with the oxen "
(2 Chron. xxxv. 10 - 12). — "Asaph, Zacharias, and Jeduthun, who was
of the king's retinue " (15); "Asaph, and Heman, and Jeduthun the king's
seer " (2 Chron. xxxv. 15). — "Josias did not turn back his chariot from
him, but undertook to fight with him, not regarding the words of the prophet
Jeremy, spoken by the mouth of the Lord, but joined battle with him in the
plain of Megiddo ; and the princes came against King Josias," &c. (28, 29) ;
"Josiah would not turn his face from him, but disguised himself, that he
might fight with him, and hearkened not unto the words of Necho from the
mouth of God, and came to fight in the valley of Megiddo ; and the archers
shot at King Josiah " (2 Chron. xxxv. 22, 23). — "These things are written
in the book of the stories of the kings of Judah, and every one of the acts

that "the works of Josias were upright before his
Lord, with an heart full of godliness; as to the
things that came to pass in his time, they were written in former times, concerning those that sinned,
and did wickedly against the Lord, above all people
and kingdoms, and how they grieved him exceedingly,
so that the words of the Lord rose up against Israel." *
The second chapter in like manner corresponds, in its
first fifteen verses, to the first chapter of the canonical
Ezra, and in the residue, to the last eighteen verses of
the fourth chapter of that book, the subject of the
former part of the narrative being the proclamation of
Cyrus permitting the return of the Jews to Jerusalem,
and their proceedings in consequence,† while the latter portion passes on at once to the measures con-

---

that Josiah did, and his glory, and his understanding in the law of the
Lord, and the things that he had done before, and the things now recited,
are reported in the book of the kings of Israel and Judea " (33); " behold, they are written in the Lamentations; now the rest of the acts of Josiah, and his goodness, according to that which was written in the law of
the Lord, and his deeds, first and last, behold, they are written in the book
of the kings of Israel and Judah " (2 Chron. xxxv. 25 – 27). — " The king
of Egypt also made King Joacim his brother king of Judea and Jerusalem,
and he bound Joacim and the nobles, but Zaraces his brother he apprehended, and brought him out of Egypt " (37, 38); " the king of Egypt
made Eliakim his brother king over Judah and Jerusalem, and turned his
name to Jehoiakim; and Necho took Jehoahaz his brother, and carried him
to Egypt " (2 Chron. xxxvi. 4). — " Joacim . . . . . was made king,
being eighteen years old " (43); " Jehoiachin was eight years old when he
began to reign " (2 Chron. xxxvi. 9). — " Old man nor child " (53); " old
man, or him that stooped for age " (2 Chron. xxxvi. 17). — " The vessels
of the ark of God " (54); " the treasures of the house of the Lord " (2
Chron. xxxvi. 18).

* 1 Esdras i. 23, 24.

† " The Lord of Israel, the most high Lord " (ii. 3); " The Lord God of
heaven " (Ez. i. 2). — " Sanabassar " (12, 15); " Sheshbazzar " (Ez. i.
8, 11). — " A thousand golden cups, and a thousand of silver, censers of
silver twenty-nine, vials of gold thirty, and of silver two thousand four hundred and ten, and a thousand other vessels ; so all the vessels of gold and
of silver, which were carried away, were five thousand four hundred three-

sequent on the intrigues of the Samaritan malecontents to hinder the rebuilding of the temple.*

The passage which has been mentioned as the only original one in this book relates the following story. Darius "made a great feast unto all his subjects, and unto all his household, and unto all the princes of Media and Persia, and to all the governors, and captains, and lieutenants that were under him, from India unto Ethiopia, of an hundred twenty and seven provinces." The feast being over, and the guests dispersed, Darius retired to his bed-chamber, where he slept and woke. Without any authority from him, as far as is related, three young men of his body-guard agreed together that each of them should propound a sentence, and that whichever of the three should be deemed to have uttered the wisest should receive rich presents from the king, be clothed with purple, drink from a golden vessel, sleep on gold, ride in a chariot with golden harness, wear a chain about his neck and a fine linen turban, sit next to Darius, and be called Darius's cousin. They wrote each his sentence, and placed

---

score and nine " (13, 14); " thirty chargers of gold, a thousand chargers of silver, nine-and-twenty knives, thirty basins of gold, silver basins of a second sort four hundred and ten, and other vessels a thousand; all the vessels of gold and of silver were five thousand and four hundred" (Ez. i. 9 – 11).

* With 16, 17, comp. Ez. iv. 7 – 11, where, though there is no contradiction in the facts stated, the formal difference of statement is such as to forbid the supposition that the passage in Esdras is strictly a translation from the same text as that preserved in the corresponding verses in Ezra; and the same inference is sustained by a comparison between what profess in both books to be copies of letters to and from Artaxerxes, in which there are differences of phraseology, bearing upon the question of a common original, though entirely immaterial in any other point of view. Comp. 19, 20 with Ez. iv. 13, 14, and 28 with Ez. iv. 21. — " Rathumus . . . . . removing in haste towards Jerusalem with a troop of horsemen, and a multitude of people in battle array, began to hinder the builders " (30) ; " they went up in haste to Jerusalem, unto the Jews, and made them to cease by force and power " (Ez. iv. 23).

them sealed under the royal pillow. One wrote, "Wine is the strongest"; another, "The king is the strongest"; the third, "Women are strongest"; to which proposition, as if to double his chance, he appended another, — "But, above all things, Truth beareth away the victory." *

"When the king was risen up, they took their writings, and delivered them unto him, and so he read them; and sending forth, he called all the princes of Persia and Media, and the governors, and the captains, and the lieutenants, and the chief officers, and sat him down in the royal seat of judgment, and the writings were read before them." Then the young soldiers were summoned, each to defend his thesis. The first extolled in a few sentences the great potency of wine, shown in its confusing men's judgments, banishing their sorrows and cares, exciting them to quarrels, and drowning their memories.† The second, somewhat more at length, but still briefly, set forth the power of the king, who was superior to other rulers, whether on sea or land, and could compel them to expose their lives in war, and bring the spoils to him; who in peace drew the produce of his people's labor into his treasury; and who commanded the services of multitudes, himself living in ease and luxury.‡ The third, who turned out to be Zerubbabel, spoke more fully the praises, first of woman, and then of truth. Woman, he said, ruled both kings and their subjects. Woman had brought both to life. Woman nursed the planters of vineyards, and made the garments in which men paraded their greatness. Woman was more attractive to men than any other goodly thing. For her they forsook father and mother and

---

* 1 Esdras iii. 1 – 12.   † iii. 13 – 24.   ‡ iv. 1 – 12.

country. For her they toiled and stole, and sailed over
seas and rivers, and faced the darkness and wild
beasts. For woman some had become slaves, some
had lost their reason, many had perished, and erred
and sinned. The king was great, and many realms
trembled before him. Yet a frail woman was lately
seen to take the crown from his august head, and place
it on her own, and jestingly lift her hand against him.
But, instead of resenting, the king gazed at her in
stupid admiration, laughed when she laughed, and was
fain to flatter and supplicate when she frowned.* But
though the king and princes, by their glances at each
other, seemed to confess the weight of what was said,
still there was one thing yet greater than woman, and
that was Truth. All the earth called upon it, and
heaven blessed it. Unlike wine, the king, woman, and
all things else, in truth there was no unrighteousness.
The truth was enduring and triumphant. With it
there was no fear nor favor, nor respect of persons;
truth was "the strength, kingdom, power, and majesty
of all ages."†

Having thus spoken, Zerubbabel "held his peace;
and all the people then shouted, and said, 'Great is
Truth, and mighty above all things'"; and the king
bade him sit next to himself, and be called his cousin,
and to ask whatsoever else he might desire beyond what
was "appointed in the writing." Zerubbabel seized
the opportunity to bespeak the royal favor for his afflicted nation. He reminded the king of a vow which
he had made to rebuild Jerusalem and its temple, and
restore the sacred vessels of the Jewish worship.‡
"Then Darius the king stood up and kissed him,"

---

* 1 Esdras iv. 13 – 32.   † iv. 33 – 40.
‡ iv. 41 – 46. — " To build up the temple which the *Edomites* burned"
(45); this is not the representation of the canonical books.

and granted his request; and orders were issued to
the Persian officers to convey Zerubbabel and his companions in safety on their way; to give him aid, both
by materials and labor, in the rebuilding of the city;
to abstain from intrusion into the houses of the Jews,
and hold them and their lands exempt from service
and from tribute; to compel restitution from the Edomites of Jewish villages seized by them; to make an annual contribution in money towards the rebuilding of
the temple, and the maintenance of its ritual; and
to provide by suitable allowances for the support and
equipment of the priests and Levites. "He sent away
also all the vessels from Babylon that Cyrus had set
apart; and all that Cyrus had given in commandment,
the same charged he also to be done, and sent unto
Jerusalem." All which favor was acknowledged by
Zerubbabel in praise and thanksgiving to Jehovah,
and by the people in a festival celebration, "with instruments of music and gladness, seven days." When
the party of emigrants proceeded on their way, "Darius sent with them a thousand horsemen till they had
brought them back to Jerusalem safely, and with musical instruments, tabrets, and flutes; and all their
brethren played, and he made them go up together
with them." *

Next, occupying more than one half of the book,
occurs a passage,† which is for the most part a dupli-

---

* 1 Esdras iv. 47 – v. 6. — "Jesus the son of Josedec, the son of Sa-
raias, and Joacim the son of Zorobabel, the son of Salathiel," &c. (5) ; it is
clear that the word Jesus (Jeshua) has here been lost out of the text before
Zorobabel (comp. Neh. xii. 10). Inserting this word, it would close the
sentence. With it would terminate all that is said of the priests, and the
next sentence would begin with the lineage of Zerubbabel, who not only
was not of the sacerdotal tribe, but is said in this very verse to have been of
the tribe of Judah. The simple insertion of what is supplied by the history
in Nehemiah relieves the text from a palpable self-contradiction.

† v. 7 – ix. 36.

cate of the last nine chapters of the canonical Book
of Ezra, the only difference, except such as are merely
verbal, being that which has been already referred to;
viz. that the account of the correspondence occasioned
by the Samaritan intrigues to embarrass the rebuilding of the city and temple, which in the canonical
book is represented as subsequent to the emigration of
Zerubbabel and his companions,* is in this book, by
an extraordinary arrangement, separated from its
proper connection, and made to precede Zerubbabel's
first proposal for a return.†

Of this long passage, common to the two books, the
first part contains that list of emigrants who accompanied Zerubbabel, which is also given in the
Book of Nehemiah. The differences in names and
numbers between the catalogue in Nehemiah and in
the canonical Ezra have been pointed out. Similar
differences are presented by the same catalogue in the
form now before us, when compared with either of the
two others, the diversity in respect to names being
still further increased by the Greek form required by
the language in which alone the apocryphal book has
been transmitted. As to numbers, where the two canonical authorities agree, the other sometimes agrees
with them, and sometimes differs, and in the latter
case, it sometimes gives a greater number, and sometimes a less. Where they differ, it sometimes agrees
with one, sometimes with the other, sometimes with
neither; and its differences and agreements are controlled by no rule, that I can discern. All three authorities agree that the number of " the whole congregation together " was " forty-and-two thousand three
hundred and threescore." And the same remarks re-

---

* Ezra iv. 7 – 24.   † 1 Esdras ii. 16 – 30.

specting numbers * and proper names † apply to other passages in which these occur. A sufficient specimen having been given of variations in these particulars to exhibit their nature, it seems useless to pursue the specification further.

From that verse which corresponds with the last verse of the canonical Book of Ezra, the history, without pause or interruption, proceeds to its close, with a relation of transactions of "the first day of the seventh month," recorded in the same language in a short passage of the Book of Nehemiah.‡

We thus find that the First Book of Esdras is simply the canonical Book of Ezra, in Greek, with the transposition of one passage, and the addition of three others, one of which, from the Second Book of Chronicles, is prefixed, another, not paralleled elsewhere, is inserted, and the third, from Nehemiah, is appended. The translation into Greek is free, but for the most part true, as well as graceful. The variations from the Masoretic text appear to be no greater than are easily accounted for on the same grounds as similar variations in the Septuagint version of other books; viz. those of the exercise of the translator's discretion on the one hand, and, on the other, his rendering from a text not altogether the same with that now in our hands. §

---

* With 1 Esdras viii. 32, 34, 35, 39, comp. Ez. viii. 6, 8, 9, 13.

† With viii. 29 et seq., ix. 21 et seq., and ix. 43 et seq., comp. Ez. viii. 2 et seq., x. 20 et seq., Neh. viii. 4 et seq.

‡ ix. 37 – 55; comp. Neh. vii. 73 – viii. 12. — "The priests and Levites . . . . . and the whole multitude came together with one accord into the broad place of the holy porch towards the east" (37, 38); the similarity of the language in this introduction to that in v. 47 goes to confirm the idea thrown out in the last Lecture (see above, p. 92), that in the passages of Ezra and Nehemiah corresponding to these we have a double account of the same transaction. — "Then spake *Attharates* unto Esdras" (49); a transformation into Greek of the word "Tirshatha" (comp. Neh. viii. 9).

§ It would be unprofitable to multiply examples. Occasionally there are

It is now impossible to trace the origin of that in-terpolated passage, which ostensibly explains the his-torical fact of the favor of the Persian monarch to Zerubbabel. We cannot safely argue, from its strong tincture with Hebrew idioms, that it originally existed in that language, because, even if first composed in Greek, it was no doubt composed by a Jew, and, who-ever he was, it is natural to suppose that his Greek style would be marked by Hebrew peculiarities. But as the rest of the book was made up from materials now existing in our hands in the original Hebrew and Chaldee, it appears probable that this portion also was translated from a Hebrew original, which is now lost.*

And, on the whole, it appears to result from our ex-amination of this book, and of the books of Ezra and Nehemiah, that, at a period little, if at all, anterior to that of the Macedonian conquest, there existed among the Jews disconnected narratives relating to the return of a portion of their race from the captivity at Baby-lon. Of these fragments part were composed in the Chaldee language, part in the Hebrew. Of some (namely, those indicated by the use of the pronoun of

---

trifling differences in statements of fact; as " Unto them of Sidon also and Tyre, they gave cars that they should bring cedar-trees from Libanus " (v. 55) ; " they gave . . . . . oil unto them of Zidon and to them of Tyre," &c. (Ez. iii. 7). Often the version has a paraphrastic character, similar to that which, more or less in different parts, pervades the Septuagint transla-tion (as v. 47, comp. Ezra iii. 1 ; v. 50, comp. Ez. iii. 3 ; v. 58, comp. Ez. iii. 8, 9). Sometimes an apparent difference results merely from the diffi-culty of *Grecizing* a Hebrew proper name, or the choice of a more rhetori-cal form of speech in the place of a local or idiomatic one, as " Sisinnes, the governor of Syria and Phenice " (vi. 3) ; " Tatnai, governor on this side the river" (Ez. v. 3). In some instances the representation of the apocryphal text appears to deserve the preference ; as in i. 9 (comp. 2 Chron. xxxv. 9), i. 26 – 28 (comp. 2 Chron. xxxv. 21, 22), ii. 13 (comp. Ez. i. 9, 10).

* Josephus has used the passage in full in the composition of his " An-tiquities " (Vide Lib. XI. cap. 3).

the first person) Ezra and Nehemiah were the writers; others proceeded from sources (now, at any rate) unknown; and in some instances there were different narratives of the same transaction. Different compilers took these materials in hand, and we have the result of their several labors in the three books which have now been commented upon. Sometimes they have repeated the same matter; sometimes their selection has been different; while in every instance, except the use by one of them of a passage which has the character of a fanciful fiction, they have confined themselves to materials, whether more or less authentic, such as are suitable to sober history.[*]

It has been made a question whether we now possess the compilation in its original integrity. De Wette[†] thinks it is probably only the fragment of a larger work. A writer in Eichhorn's "Allgemeine Bibliothek"[‡] argues from the concluding sentence, compared with the corresponding verse of Nehemiah,[§] that there is an abruptness in the termination, which was not exhibited in the work in its original state. The closing period is as follows:— "They understood the words wherein they were instructed, *and for the which they had been assembled.*"[||] The parallel verse in the Book of Nehemiah does not contain the latter clause; but the next following verse, which begins a

---

[*] That a considerable time must have elapsed between the events related in the Book of Esdras (at least) and the compilation of the history, might be argued from a striking anachronism in one of its statements. Zerubbabel is said (iv. 47 *et seq.*) to have received permission to go to Jerusalem in the reign of Darius (which Darius is meant is not here material), while according to Ezra the permission was given presently after the accession of Cyrus.

[†] "Lehrbuch," &c., § 298.

[‡] Band I. ss. 191 *et seq.* The treatise was afterwards inserted in Eichhorn's "Einleitung in die Schrift. Apokryph.," ss. 335 *et seq.*

[§] Neh. viii. 12.

[||] 1 Esdras ix. 55.

new paragraph, relates that the people were "gathered together." Accordingly, that paragraph, at least, the writer referred to supposes to have once followed what is now the end of the book before us. And he further suggests, that if something, agreeably to this argument, has been lost from one end of the book, so it is not unlikely that something may have been lost from the other, and that accordingly, instead of beginning, as it now does, with the eighteenth year of Josiah, a date which there appears no reason for selecting as a starting-point, it originally ran parallel with the Book of Chronicles through one earlier chapter, beginning its narrative with the first year of that monarch's reign. But the view which Bertholdt takes of the subject I regard as presenting a sufficient account of these facts. He understands the purpose of the compiler to have been to exhibit a compendious history of the temple from the last renewal of the complete ritual service in the old edifice to its full institution in the new; a plan which had the recommendation of a certain unity, and which would require the work to begin and end just where it is now seen to do.*

The Second Book of Esdras, very incongruously included in our English Apocrypha, owes its place in that collection to its having previously established itself in the editions of the Vulgate. Being there, I shall make it the subject of a few remarks.

The book has come down to us, not in Hebrew or Greek, but in a Latin text, which may be found in print at the end of the Vulgate in the common editions, in the London Polyglot,† and in Fabricius's "Codex Pseudepigraphus Veteris Testamenti." ‡ It is also extant in two versions.

---

* Bertholdt's "Historisch-kritische Einleitung," &c., § 276.
† Tom. IV. p. 29 et seq.   ‡ Tom. II. p. 193 et seq.

One of them, the Arabic (never yet printed, I suppose, and existing only in two manuscripts, in the Bodleian Library, at Oxford), dates from a period not earlier than the seventh century.* It may be conveniently compared with the older text in Whiston's " Primitive Christianity Revived," † where an English translation from the Arabic by Simon Ockley is printed side by side with the received English version from the Latin. It will be perceived that there are very material differences. The first two and the last two chapters of the Latin copy are wholly wanting from the Arabic. On the other hand, in the seventh chapter, after the thirty-fifth verse, there is in the Arabic a long insertion, amounting to about a hundred verses, relating to a future general judgment. The translator has given a very free and inexact version, even where there is no appearance of his having worked on a different text. He seems to have labored to soften the rudenesses of his original, to supply its ellipses and imperfect connections, and to furnish it with a sense where this was wanting. He has often left out a repulsive Jewish idea, and often rendered erroneously, by reason of imperfect acquaintance with Jewish opinions, manners, and forms of speech and conception.

Of the other version, the Æthiopic, Richard Laurence published at Oxford, in 1820, a Latin and English translation, made from a single manuscript, and that the work of a careless copyist. The Æthiopic version is of uncertain date, but must have been made later than the fourth century. It resembles the Arabic

---

* Lücke, "Versuch einer Vollständigen Einleitung in die Offenbarung des Johannes," s. 149. Corrodi, "Versuch einer Beleuchtung der Geschichte des Bibelkanons," Band I. s. 141, ascribes it to the thirteenth century.
† Vol. IV.

in the omission of the first two and last two chapters, and in the long insertion in the seventh chapter. It partakes of the paraphrastic character of the Arabic translation, but in a less degree.*

We do not know in what language the book was composed. That our Latin text is not the original appears in the highest degree probable, not only from its abounding in Oriental idioms, and grosser improprieties of speech, but from its often presenting combinations of words destitute of meaning, and appearing to betray the hand of a translator not himself possessed of the idea which he was undertaking to transfuse. The original may have been Chaldee or Syriac, but more probably was Greek, the work of a Hellenistic author, whose Greek style had a very strong Hebrew tinge.† A Greek "Apocalypse of Ezra" is mentioned by Nicephorus in the ninth century,‡ and that name appears in a catalogue, from an old Greek manuscript, preserved by Fabricius;§ and this may well have been the Greek original in question. It is thought, but I suppose erroneously, that there is a reference to this book in the Epistle (so called) of Barnabas.‖ If so, it is the first reference which occurs in any Christian writer. Clement of Alexandria clearly quotes from it,

---

* I take this description of the Æthiopic version, as well as remarks upon it further on, from Lücke, "Versuch," u. s. w. I have never seen Laurence's work, or either of two others which I find mentioned as having followed it, on the same subject.

† Lücke ("Versuch," u. s. w., ss. 147, 149, 150, 154) argues, very forcibly, that each of the three versions was made directly from a Greek original.

‡ Fabricius, "Codex Apoc. Nov. Test.," Tom. I. pp. 938, 952.

§ "Cod. Pseudep. Vet. Test.," Tom. II. p. 308.

‖ The supposed reference is as follows :—" Another prophet says, ' When shall these things be fulfilled?' And the Lord says, ' When wood shall lie down and stand up, and when blood shall flow from wood.'" Barnab. "Epist. Cathol.," cap. 12 ; comp. 2 Esd. v. 5. Lücke ("Versuch," s. 151) understands the reference to be to a different apocryphal writing.

about ·the year 200, and ascribes it to "the prophet Esdras." *

The book professes to be a composition of "the prophet Esdras," while a "captive in the land of the Medes, in the reign of Artaxerxes, king of the Persians," and opens with an account of his lineage, traced from Aaron, in a statement corresponding with those in the canonical Book of Ezra, and the apocryphal First of Esdras, but embracing three more names.† It purports to consist substantially of a narrative of revelations made to Ezra, while at Babylon, the form, through great part of it, being that of a dialogue between the prophet and the angel Uriel. The topics and the style are often similar to those of prophetical books in the canonical collection, particularly the Books of Daniel and Ezekiel, of which latter writer the three different manners are imitated in different parts.‡ There is a repetition of reproofs and threats, represented as being uttered by God himself, and enforced by recapitulations of the national history similar to what we have read in preceding books.§ Interspersed are exhortations to renewed obedience, and promises of a happier state of things hereafter, connected with anticipations of the Messiah's times; ‖ expostulations, on the writer's part, with Jehovah, on account of his severe dealings with his people, and vindications of them on the part of the angel; ¶ questions and answers

---

* "' Why was not the womb of my mother my grave, that I should not see the affliction of Jacob, nor the toil of the race of Israel!' saith the prophet Esdras." "Stromata," Lib. III. (" Opp.," p. 468, edit. Paris); comp. 2 Esd. v. 35.

† 2 Esd. i. 1-3 ; comp. Ez. vii. 1-5 ; 1 Esd. viii. 1, 2.

‡ The plain, ethical manner, in (e. g.) ii. 21 et seq.; the grotesquely imaginative, in x. - xii. ; the impassioned and vigorous in vi., xv., and xvi. See Vol. III. p. 463.

§ 2 Esd. i. 1-ii. 9; iii. 1-27.   ‖ ii. 10-48.   ¶ iii. 28-iv. 21.

respecting the principles of Divine Providence, and its designs for the future,* especially in the moral government of the world; † visions and dreams, explained and unexplained; ‡ and menaces of vengeance against the unbelieving nations, § from which Israel, if it be faithful, shall be delivered.||

As to any thing like a satisfactory exposition of great part of this book, even if it deserved investigation by reason of the authority of the writer, it must be given up as a hopeless undertaking. "Is it not doing him too much honor," asks Basnage, "to pretend to guess at his meaning?" ¶ Nor did antiquity always treat the work with more respect. Jerome ridicules an opponent who had quoted it in controversy,** and in his preface to the Books of Ezra and Nehemiah advises readers to take no interest in its vain dreams.††

As to the question respecting the date of this composition, I cannot but think that by the twelve kings who were to "reign after one another," and of whom the second was to "have more time than any of the twelve," ‡‡ the writer meant the Twelve Cæsars, the long-lived Augustus being the second of the series. In that case, we might refer the work to the time of Domitian, who was emperor from A. D. 81 to 96, or to the succeeding reign of Nerva, which lasted but two years.§§

---

* 2 Esdras iv. 22 – vi. 59.   † vii. 1 – ix. 37.   ‡ ix. 38 – xiv. 48.
§ xv. 1 – xvi. 39. || xvi. 40 – 78.
¶ "Histoire des Juifs," Livre VI. chap. 2, § 6.
** "Tu vigilans dormis, et dormiens scribis, et proponis mihi librum apocryphum, qui sub nomine Esdræ a te et similibus tui legitur," &c. "Epist. advers. Vigilantium" ("Opp.," Tom. IV. p. 283, edit. Martianay).
†† Ibid., Tom. I. p. 1106. This is the passage referred to above, p. 108.
‡‡ 2 Esdras xii. 14, 15.
§§ This was Lücke's opinion, when he published the first edition of his "Versuch." The second (1848) presents a different view of the intricate

In the seventh chapter, we find the following passage: — "My son Jesus shall be revealed with those
that be with him, and they that remain shall rejoice
within four hundred years; after these years shall my
son Christ die, and all men that have life."*

It would seem that this passage, if originally belonging to the work, would determine it to have proceeded from some one who was acquainted with the
name and with the death of Jesus, and who acknowledged him for the Messiah. But the name *Jesus* in
the first clause, and the whole of the last, are wanting
in the Arabic copy; and for that reason, as well as
that, while the Messiah is often mentioned in the
book, there is nothing said elsewhere to identify him
with Jesus, they must be reckoned as spurious additions from a Christian hand in later times.†

On the other hand, various phenomena of the book
seem to forbid the supposition of a Christian origin.
The idea, expressed in different parts,‡ that, except the
people of Israel, the race of men were of no value in
God's sight, could hardly have proceeded from a Chris-
tian, even an Ebionite. The representations of the
Messiah's office, throughout, have a Jewish, and not a
Christian character. And it could hardly be, that a

---

passage in the eleventh and twelfth chapters, and maintains the opinion that
the book was written in the time of the first Cæsars, before Christ's ministry.
For his argument on this subject, see " Versuch," ss. 189–210.

    * 2 Esdras vii. 28, 29.

    † On this point, see Corrodi, Band I. ss. 143, 144, and Lücke, ss. 169,
170. — On the language in v. 4, 5, quoted above (p. 121, note ‖), Basnage,
who has just very judiciously inquired, " Is it not doing him too much honor
to pretend to guess at his meaning?" makes the remark (Liv. VI. chap. 2,
§ 6): — " The author appears to have known Christianity. . . . . . It is in
vain to say that we cannot conjecture his meaning. . . . . . He alludes to
the true cross, from which the blood of Jesus Christ has flowed." The first
remark is the truly pertinent one. The comment in these last words is as
erratic as the text.

    ‡ E. g. vi. 55 – 59 ; ix. 20 – 22.

Christian writer should not have used various occasions, which occur in the course of the book, to allude to the new revelation with explicitness, if not in detail; — at all events, that, in speaking of the resurrection of the dead and the coming retribution,* he should have given no hint of the confirmation which the Gospel brought to those doctrines. Again, an earthly reign of Christ is spoken of, to continue for four hundred years; † a representation which, whether understood to relate to his first or second coming, could hardly proceed from a Christian source. In relation to the first, it is evidently not to be supposed; and though there early grew up a notion in the Church of an earthly reign of the Messiah at his second advent, to continue a thousand years, there is no trace in Christian antiquity of an expectation of a reign of four hundred, while, on the other hand, the Jews held different opinions respecting the duration of their Messiah's government, and among them this was one.‡

The book, however, has come down to these modern times through Christian hands. By those hands it was worked over, and interpolated with those references to Christian sentiment and language, which have caused some critics to refer it to a Christian origin.§ The first two and the last two chapters, which are wanting from the Arabic and Æthiopic texts, must be regarded as spurious additions. They have respectively no good connection with what follows and precedes, nor resemblance to it in matter or manner.

---

* E. g. 2 Esdras ii. 16; vii. 13 et seq.   † vii. 28.

‡ See Corrodi, " Versuch," Band I. s. 144.

§ Comp. (e. g.) 2 Esdras i. 30 with Matt. xxiii. 37; ii. 11 with Luke xvi. 9; ii. 12 with Apoc. xxii. 2; ii. 18 with Apoc. xxii. 2; ii. 40 with Apoc. iii. 4 ; ii. 42, 43 with Apoc. xiv. 1-3; xv. 8, 9 with Apoc. vi. 10; xvi. 29 et seq. with Matt. xxiv. 40, 41; xvi. 42-45 with 1 Cor. vii. 29, 30.

11 *

I have not thought it worth while to argue directly
that this book was not written by Ezra, as, besides the
evident total dissimilarity of its whole spirit and style
from the canonical book ascribed to him, there is
nothing on which to ground such an opinion, nor is it,
I suppose, entertained by any Christians of the present day. But if not his, what could the author mean
by giving it his name? Did he mean to impose his
work upon the world as a work of the ancient re-
storer of the Jewish temple and worship? So such
writers as Dr. Gray, author of the " Key to the Old
Testament," suppose, and accordingly are not sparing
of their rebukes of him for his dishonesty.

The question is just as wise as if we should ask
whether Godwin meditated a fraud on his readers in
his work entitled " St. Leon," intending to pass himself
off for the person whose autobiography, in consequence
of the form in which his inventive composition is cast,
he seems to be writing; or (to suggest an analogy
more complete, as bringing, like the book before us, an
historical character to view), it would be a question of
just as much propriety, if we should inquire whether
Lord Byron was perpetrating forgeries against Bonni-
vard, Tasso, King Saul, King Herod, and Jephthah's
daughter, when he wrote his poems founded upon the
fates of those individuals, in which, assuming their characters, he speaks for them in the first person. The truth
is, the reading and writing of works of imagination, —
works of fiction, — have been in all ages and countries
more or less a demand of the human mind. Such works
have taken different forms; and among them a favorite one has probably always been, the introduction of
a real historical character or characters, to favor the
illusion and so heighten the interest. We have no
right to presume that this would not be a want, and a

gratified want, of the Jewish mind, as much as of the mind of any other people. We have no reason to suppose that the Jews, as much as other nations, would not have, as well upon sacred themes as those of a different description, their poems and their novels, and other productions of fancy, with more or less resemblance or dissimilarity to the compositions which we describe by those names, according as the attributes and exercises of human intellect, which we have in common with them, might be more or less modified and distinguished by their and our peculiar training, our different age, social condition, temperament, habits, and knowledge. Possess such works, in fact, they did, — and those of a very marked and, as we might think it, adventurous character, agreeably to the boldness of the Oriental taste, but yet framed upon no different principles from such as we habitually recognize in our own use. They gave them the name of *Aggada*, a word which Buxtorf, in his "Talmudical Lexicon," defines, — "an agreeable and ingenious narrative, attractive to the reader's mind"; * a definition not unworthy to be introduced into our books of rhetoric, for the popular form of fictitious history current among us. The Talmud is full of such; sometimes consisting of mere invention, sometimes founded on historical facts; and when of the latter class, then of course founded on sacred history, for there is no other history of the Jews.†

---

* " Historia jucunda et subtilis, animum lectoris adtrahens."

† I translate the following remarks from Bertholdt's " Daniel " s. 41, note : — " Otho observes in his Philological Rabbinical Lexicon, that ' *Agga-doth* (אַגָּדוֹת) are historical compositions, similar to the fictions which poets sometimes invent.' But this comparison is too one-sided. There are poetical and historical *Aggadoth*. The former contain mere fiction, and are much the same with the fables of the Greeks and Romans. The latter are indeed often in great part untrue ; yet they cannot be called fiction, because they

Such a composition, on a small scale, was the narrative which we lately read in the third and fourth chapters of the First Book of Esdras. Such, on a larger scale, is the Second Book of Esdras. The author proposed to himself to embody some of the opinions, fancies, and expectations of his people and age, and some fresh from his own mind, in a specimen of a form of writing familiar to himself and them; and the result has outlived the chances of time, though its escapes have been narrow, and has struggled down to our day. He never had a thought, as far as we can judge, of imposing upon any one. He took Ezra's name for a very innocent and well authorized purpose; and the discussions by dull Christian theologians of the question whether that name was truly taken, have been all as uncalled for and senseless, as their censures of the supposed imposture have been undeserved.

The plan of the piece is not artificial, nor does the introduction of the machinery of Ezra and the angel serve for much more than a frame (so to speak), into which the author's exhortations and speculations are set. There is in parts a very copious use of Scripture language; and in others, which are more original, occasionally a great vivacity in the imagery and style. The writer appears to have imitated Daniel, as well as

always have some historical basis, though not seldom so buried under additions that it can no longer be detected, and often cannot be so much as guessed at. Every original people possesses stories of its primitive times, but none more than the Jewish, as might be expected from its freedom from mixture with other nations, and its ancient and untamable national pride. There is no person and no event of Hebrew antiquity which has not furnished occasion to the composition of such *Aggadoth*, now extant in the Talmud and other Rabbinical books, — compositions doing violence, in their adventurous character, to the taste of our times. . . . . . Most of them are, it is true, of a later age than the Aggadoth in the Book of Daniel, and in part are so extravagant and out of taste, that one would not bring them into comparison with that book. But some might well have an origin contemporary with it."

to have built, in one passage,* on the basis of that book, explaining what was understood in his own day to be the fourth kingdom therein described; namely, the Roman empire. The passage in which we perceive the most propriety in the assumption of the character of Ezra is found in the tenth chapter. The author, seeing the city and temple of his fathers, if my view of the date of the composition be correct, in the desolation in which they were left by the campaign of Titus, is reminded of Ezra's having once seen them in the same condition, when wasted by the Babylonish arms, and having lived to see them restored; and so, assuming his character, he mourns as Ezra had done over their existing condition, while he expresses his hope of witnessing too, in due time, like the ancient sage whom he personates, the dawn of a better day; — of seeing, as he represents the angel assuring him, the beauty and greatness of the building, as much as his eyes should be able to see.†

---

* 2 Esdras xi. and xii.   † x. 55.

LECTURE LVIII.

THE TIME OF THE ASMONEAN BROTHERS.

THE FIRST BOOK OF THE MACCABEES.

ORIGIN AND MEANING OF THE WORD *MACCABEE*. — FOUR BOOKS OF THE
MACCABEES. — THE FIRST, A HISTORY OF THE TIME OF THE SONS OF
MATTATHIAS. — ITS ORIGINAL LANGUAGE, AND THE TIME AND PLACE
OF ITS COMPOSITION. — ITS LITERARY CHARACTER. — ITS CONTENTS.
— INTRODUCTION TO THE REIGN OF ANTIOCHUS EPIPHANES. — HIS
VIOLENT PROCEEDINGS AT JERUSALEM. — SUCCESSFUL REVOLT OF MAT-
TATHIAS. — HIS DYING CHARGE TO HIS SONS. — VICTORIES OF JUDAS
OVER APPOLLONIUS, SERON, GORGIAS, AND LYSIAS. — PURIFICATION
AND DEDICATION OF THE TEMPLE. — FORTIFICATION OF MOUNT ZION.
— EXPLOITS OF JUDAS, SIMON, AND JONATHAN IN IDUMEA, AMMON,
GALAAD, THE PHILISTINE CITIES, AND ELSEWHERE. — TRIUMPHAL RE-
TURN OF JUDAS TO JERUSALEM. — DEATH OF ANTIOCHUS. — HEROIC
DEATH OF ELEAZAR, BROTHER OF JUDAS. — RETREAT OF JUDAS TO
JERUSALEM. — THE CITY INVESTED BY THE SYRIANS. — TREATY OF
PEACE. — ACCESSION OF DEMETRIUS TO THE THRONE OF SYRIA. —
TREACHERY OF THE JEW ALCIMUS. — HIS ELEVATION TO THE HIGH-
PRIESTHOOD. — VICTORY OF JUDAS OVER THE SYRIANS UNDER THE
COMMAND OF NICANOR. — HIS ALLIANCE WITH THE ROMANS. — DEATH
AND BURIAL OF JUDAS. — SUCCESSES OF JONATHAN AGAINST BACCHIDES.
— HIS ALLIANCE WITH ALEXANDER. — HIS DEFEAT OF THE FORCES
OF DEMETRIUS. — HIS EMBASSIES TO THE ROMANS AND LACEDÆMONI-
ANS. — HIS TREACHEROUS ARREST BY TRYPHO. — HIS DEATH, AND
BURIAL AT MODIN. — CAPTURE OF GAZA BY SIMON. — PROSPERITY OF
JUDEA UNDER HIS ADMINISTRATION. — LETTERS TO HIM FROM ROME
AND SPARTA. — HIS VICTORY OVER CENDEBEUS. — HIS ASSASSINATION
BY HIS SON-IN-LAW, PTOLEMY. — ACCESSION OF HIS SON, JOHN HYR-
CANUS, TO THE HIGH-PRIESTHOOD.

THE origin of the name *Maccabee* is uncertain. It
appears to have belonged originally to Judas, the third
of those five famous sons of Mattathias of Modin, who
acted so important a part in Jewish history in the sec-

ond century before the Christian era.*   There is a Hebrew word, signifying *a hammer*, from which the name
Maccabee is conveniently derived ; and the best modern
critics understand Judas to have been called the Maccabee, or *the hammerer*, for a like reason to that which
gave his surname to the conqueror of the Saracens,
Charles Martel.†   According to an old Jewish exposition, the word was compounded from the initial letters
of a text from the Law, adopted by the Maccabees for
a scroll upon their banners, — " Who is like unto thee,
O Lord, among the gods ? " ‡   Another scheme derived the word from a similar combination of the final
letters of the names Abraham, Isaac, and Jacob, said
to have been inscribed on the banner of the tribe of
Dan.

Josephus speaks of the Maccabees as the *Asmonean*
family, and that name has been commonly applied to
them, in both ancient and modern times.§

Four books have been called Books of the Maccabees.   That which was once known as the fourth
book, and so referred to by some of the fathers, is no
longer extant.   The first three books are found in the
Septuagint version, where they are arranged and numbered in the reversed order of the events from which
they respectively begin their narratives, — an order
probably having reference to the successive periods of
their first coming into notice, or being adopted into
collections of the sacred books.   The first and second

---

* 1 Macc. ii. 1-5 ; iii. 1.

† מַקָּבָה ; comp.1 Kings vi. 7 ; Is. xliv. 12 ; Jer. x. 4 ; Jer. l. 23.

‡ מִי כָמֹכָה בָּאֵלוֹהִים יְהֹוָה ; Ex. xv. 11.   The objection to this explanation is, that it would give כ instead of ק for the second letter of the
compounded word.

§ Josephus (" Antiq. Jud.," Lib. XII. cap. 6, § 1) calls Mattathias " the
son of John, the son of Simon, the son of Hasmonæus."   Others, deriving
the word from an Arabic root, understand it to mean a *prince*, or *great man.*

books only have a place in the Vulgate, and in the
Apocryphal collection of our English Bibles. In the
Vulgate, as in the Decree of the Council of Trent,
they are arranged at the end of the Old Testament
collection, after the prophecy of Malachi.

The first book contains a history extending over
forty years, from the beginning, in the year 175 B. C.,
of the oppressive proceedings of Antiochus Epiphanes
against the Jews, to the death of Simon, the prince
and high-priest, in 135 B. C. Thus it embraces the
events belonging to the temporary reëstablishment of
Jewish independence, after a subjection of more than
four hundred years to foreign powers.

The Greek, in which it has been transmitted to our
times, is undoubtedly a version from a Hebrew or
Chaldee original. This appears not only from the testimony of Jerome, who says that he had himself seen
a Hebrew copy,* and from the Hebrew idiom with
which it is marked throughout, but still further from
occasional indications in the phraseology that the writer
did not himself understand the sense of the original
text.

If the book was composed in Hebrew or Chaldee, a
natural inference is that its author was a Jew, not of
Egypt, but of Palestine. But who he was, or at what
precise time he lived, are questions which we are no
more able to answer than the same questions in respect
to the authors of the Books of Joshua, the Judges,
the Kings, or the Chronicles. That he lived a considerable time after that of the high-priest Simon, who
died in the year 135 B. C., may be inferred from the
way in which he speaks of the family monument
erected by Simon at Modin, which, he says, " standeth

---

* " Machabæorum primum librum, Hebraicum reperi." " Prolog. Galeat." (" Opp.," Tom. I. p. 321, edit. Martianay).

yet unto this day." * John Hyrcanus died in the year
107 B. C.; but it is probable that not only his life
had come to an end, but its whole history had been
recorded, previously to the composition of this book ;
for its concluding words are, "As concerning the rest
of the acts of John, and his wars, and worthy deeds
which he did, and the building of the walls which he
made, and his doings, behold, these are written in the
chronicles of his priesthood, from the time he was
made high-priest after his father." † On the other
hand, the book had been not only written, but translated into Greek, some considerable time previous to
the year 93 of our era; for Josephus used a copy of
it in that language in the composition of his "An-
tiquities," ‡ which work was published in that year.
On the whole, and particularly considering that the·
reign of John Hyrcanus is not treated, probably because of its being still too recent to be a fit subject
for popular history, though its events were recorded in
the " chronicles," we cannot be far from the truth in
ascribing the composition of the book to the first half
of the century before the Christian era.

The writer, though he may have placed his principal reliance on tradition for materials, appears not to
have been without written authorities. § The narrative, though not in all respects as full and precise as
could be wished, though sometimes exposing itself to
suspicion by a tone of exaggeration, and sometimes undoubtedly in error, ‖ still bears the substantial characters of credibility, and, whether judged by a standard

---

* 1 Mac. xiii. 30.   † xvi. 23, 24.

‡ Libb. XII., XIII. — In some passages Josephus transcribes from the
book, nearly word for word.

§ Comp. ix. 22.

‖ Comp. i. 6, viii. 7, which contain representations in contradiction to
those of the approved historians of the time.

having reference to its literary history or to the nature of its contents, compares by no means unfavora-
bly with books which have the advantage over it, in
having been admitted, through the application of arbitrary rules, into the authorized Protestant canon.

In a concise introduction to the main subject of his
work, the writer goes back to the Macedonian conquests. He relates that Alexander, on his death-bed,
after a reign of twelve years, " called his servants,
such as were honorable, and had been brought up
with him from his youth, and parted his kingdom with
them while he was yet alive." *   Accordingly, " after
his death, they all put crowns upon themselves ; so
did their sons after them many years ; and evils were
multiplied in the earth ; and there came out of them
a wicked root, Antiochus surnamed Epiphanes, son of
Antiochus the king, who had been an hostage at
Rome, and he reigned in the hundred and thirty and
seventh year of the kingdom of the Greeks." †

In the days of Antiochus a disposition disclosed itself in some of the Jews of Palestine to apostatize
from the law and customs of their fathers, and assim-

---

* Upon this point the writer was misinformed, if the profane historians
are to be credited, who say that when the question was put to the dying Alexander, who should succeed him, he simply replied, " The worthiest."

† 1 Mac. i. 1 - 10. — The first verse, the sense of which is disguised by
our translators, is one of those passages which show the imperfect acquaintance of the writer with foreign affairs. Ἐπάταξε τὸν Δαρεῖον βασιλέα
Περσῶν καὶ Μήδων, καὶ ἐβασίλευσεν ἀντ᾽ αὐτοῦ πρότερος ἐπὶ τὴν Ἑλλάδα.
Undoubtedly the understanding of the writer was, that Alexander, after de-
feating Darius, succeeded him as king of Greece. — " Antiochus surnamed
Epiphanes . . . . . reigned in the hundred and thirty and seventh year of the
kingdom of the Greeks " (10) ; comp. Vol. III. p. 170. The " year of the
kingdom of the Greeks " refers to what commonly bears the name of the
" era of the Seleucidæ." This chronological reckoning begins with the
time (an. 312 B. C.) when Seleucus Nicator established himself on the Syrian throne. This is the first instance of a reference by a Jewish writer to
a heathen chronology, — in other words, the first precisely stated chronological connection between Jewish and profane history.

ilate themselves to the surrounding heathen. With the royal consent, they built a gymnasium at Jerusalem, after the fashion of the Greeks; they renounced the distinguishing rite of their race, " and forsook the holy covenant." Encouraged by this movement, Antiochus, returning in the year 170 B. C. from his successful campaign in Egypt, visited Jerusalem, and - rifled the temple of its treasures, and of its precious furniture and vessels; "and when he had taken all away, he went into his own land, having made a great massacre, and spoken very proudly." The consternation and distress of the faithful Jews at these proceedings are described in the poetical strain of the ancient prophets. " The princes and elders mourned, the virgins and young men were made feeble, and the beauty of women was changed; every bridegroom took up lamentation, and she that sat in the marriage-chamber was in heaviness; the land also was moved for the inhabitants thereof, and all the house of Jacob was covered with confusion." *

Two years later, Antiochus proceeded to measures of still greater violence. He " sent his chief collector of tribute unto the cities of Judah, who came unto Jerusalem with a great multitude," and, having lulled the inhabitants into security by dishonest professions of friendship, " fell suddenly upon the city, and smote it very sore, and destroyed much people of Israel; and when he had taken the spoils of the city, he set it on fire, and pulled down the houses and walls thereof on every side; but the women and children took they captive, and possessed the cattle." The strangers erected a fort on Mount Zion, and placed a garrison therein, with an ample supply of provisions and arms.

* 1 Mac. i. 11 - 28.

In this hold they deposited the spoils of the ravaged
city, and from it they issued to commit all sorts of
outrages upon the votaries who visited the temple.
The people had to abandon their homes; "the city was
made an habitation of strangers, and became strange
to those that were born in her; . . . . . her sanctuary
was laid waste like a wilderness, her feasts were turned
into mourning, her Sabbaths into reproach, her honor
into contempt." *   The cup of the national calamity
was full, when Antiochus, in pursuance of his plan to
simplify his administration and reduce the different
provinces of his empire to the condition of a homo-
geneous people, by causing them to renounce their several peculiarities, and adopt the same Greek laws,
customs, and faith, sent to each city of the Jews his
royal command that, under pain of death, they should
abstain from circumcision and from the observance of
the temple ritual, and "profane the Sabbaths and festival days, and pollute the sanctuary and holy people,
set up altars and groves and chapels of idols, and sacrifice swine's flesh, and unclean beasts." †

His officers, assisted by apostate Jews, proceeded in
the execution of this decree, "and drove the Israelites
into secret places, even wheresoever they could flee for
succour." "They set up the abomination of desolation
upon the altar, and builded idol altars throughout the
cities of Juda on every side, and burnt incense at
the doors of their houses, and in the streets." They
tore in pieces every copy of the Law that could be
found, burned the fragments, and put the possessor to
death, making an inquisition month by month for that
purpose. On the occasion of a sacrifice upon an idol
altar which had been erected on the consecrated altar

---

* 1 Mac. i. 29 – 40.   † i. 41 - 51.

in the temple, "they put to death certain women that had caused their children to be circumcised, and hanged the infants about their necks, and rifled their houses, and slew them that had circumcised them." Under this grievous persecution, many continued faithful, and "chose rather to die, ... that they might not profane the holy covenant; so then they died." *

Among the fugitives from Jerusalem, there dwelt at the town of Modin, in the tribe of Dan, a man of priestly descent, named Mattathias. He mourned over "the blasphemies that were committed in Juda and Jerusalem;" and in token of their sorrow, he and his five sons "rent their clothes, and put on sackcloth." The Syrian officers, coming to Modin on their errand of enforcing the royal commands, addressed themselves first to Mattathias, on account of his high estimation in the place, and, by the promise of rich rewards, endeavoured to engage him to set the example of sacrificing to the heathen gods. Mattathias not only indignantly refused, but when another Jew approached to commit the impiety, put him first to death, and then the king's officer, and demolished the idol altar.† The example of his holy zeal was contagious. He fled into the mountains, accompanied by his sons. Others of his faithful countrymen took their own way into the wilderness. Thither the troops quartered at Jerusalem pursued them, and after an offer of pardon on condition of compliance, which was refused, attacked them ou a Sabbath day. Interpreting their Law as forbidding any labor even of self-defence on the

---

* 1 Mac. i. 52–64. — "The abomination of desolation" (54); that is, the abominable thing that made the temple forlorn and desolate ; understood to have been either a statue of the Greek Jupiter, or an altar for his worship.

† ii. 1–26.

12 *

Sabbath, "they answered them not, neither cast they a stone at them, nor stopped the places where they lay hid, but said, ' Let us die all in our innocency.' . . . . . So they rose up against them in battle on the Sabbath, and they slew them with their wives and children, and their cattle, to the number of a thousand people." *

When the intelligence of this massacre reached Mattathias and his party, they determined that their duty was to defend themselves, even though it should be necessary to repel an attack on the Sabbath. Being joined by numerous others, allied with them in faith and in sufferings, they went about the country, levelling the idol altars, enforcing the re-institution of the national rites, and putting oppressive foreigners and treacherous fellow-citizens to the sword or to rout. " So they recovered the Law out of the hand of the Gentiles, and out of the hand of kings, neither suffered they the sinner to triumph." †

" When the time drew near that Mattathias should die," and he assembled his sons to receive his parting benediction, he congratulated them on the success of their patriotic struggle, and exhorted them to perseverance in it to the death. He bade them remember and emulate the faithfulness and steadfastness of the founders of their nation, and of its worthies in later times, who, whether in church, in state, or in private condition, had never failed at last of honor and reward.

---

* 1 Mac. ii. 27 – 38.

† ii. 39 – 48. — " A company of Assideans " (42) ; in the Vatican edition, the words are συναγωγή 'Ιουδαίων, " a company of Jews." The word 'Ασιδαίοι, Assideans, occurs, however, elsewhere at this period of history; comp. vii. 13 ; 2 Mac. xiv. 6. Its probable derivation is from the Hebrew חָסִיד, merciful, or pious. The connections in which it is used in these books define it as a designation of those Jews who attached themselves to Judas and his brothers for the defence of the national religion.

He urged on them that the proud and threatening "words of a sinful man" were but as ordure and vermin, while the lesson of all ages was, that "none that put their trust in God shall be overcome." He advised them to place his second son, Simon, at the head of their counsels, and to intrust to the third, Judas, surnamed Maccabeus, the command of the military force, the former having already distinguished himself as "a man of counsel," and the latter as one of courage and conduct. So this sire of heroes "was gathered to his fathers; . . . . . and his sons buried him in the sepulchres of his fathers, at Modin, and all Israel made great lamentation for him." *

Assuming the post of military leader, Judas, with the help of his brothers and the support of his late father's party, "fought with cheerfulness the battle of Israel," and obtained a wide renown by brilliant successes over the Syrian oppressor, employing at the same time his power to repress defection and irregularities of conduct among his countrymen.† In a victory over Apollonius, who led "a great host out of Samaria," he slew that commander, and possessed himself of his sword, "and therewith he fought all his life long." ‡ Next, Seron, "a prince of the army of Syria," came against him, and "with him a mighty host of the ungodly." "When he came near to the going up of Beth-horon, Judas went forth to meet him with a small company." He excited the fainting courage of his companions by an eloquent appeal to them to trust in the protection of Heaven, and, making a sudden as-

---

* 1 Mac. ii. 49 – 70. — " Phinees, *our* father " (54) ; a significant appropriation of the fame of Phinehas, as ancestor of the sacerdotal line to which Mattathias and his sons belonged.

† iii. 1 – 9.

‡ iii. 10 – 12.

sault on the Syrians, killed eight hundred of them, and put the rest to flight.*

Antiochus now saw the necessity of more decisive measures. "He sent and gathered together all the forces of his realm, even a very strong army; he opened also his treasure, and gave his soldiers pay for a year." But this proceeding, coupled with the imperfect returns of revenue occasioned by his rash and severe administration, having embarrassed his finances, he determined to go in person and set them in order in his Persian provinces, leaving Lysias, "a noble man, and one of the blood royal," regent in his absence, and tutor of his son. Taking with him across the Euphrates half the military force of Syria, he committed the residue to the command of Lysias, with directions to invade Judea, "to destroy and root out the strength of Israel, and the remnant of Jerusalem, and to take away their memorial from that place, and that he should place strangers in all their quarters, and divide their land by lot." †

Lysias accordingly despatched a force into Judea of forty thousand infantry and seven thousand horse, under the command of Ptolemy, Nicanor, and Gorgias, "mighty men of the king's friends," who, proceeding on their enterprise, and joined by a band of Philistine and other allies, "came and pitched by Emmaus in the plain country"; and so irresistible seemed their array, and so desperate the affairs of the Jews, that "the merchants of the country, hearing the fame of them, took silver and gold very much, with servants, and came into the camp to buy the children of Israel for slaves." Nothing disheartened, "the congregation gathered together, that they might be ready for battle,

---

* 1 Mac. iii. 13 – 24.   † iii. 25 – 37.

and that they might pray, and ask mercy and compassion." But "Jerusalem lay void as a wilderness; there was none of her children that went in or out; the sanctuary also was trodden down, and aliens kept the strong hold; the heathen had their habitation in their place, and joy was taken from Jacob, and the pipe with the harp ceased; wherefore the Israelites assembled themselves together, and came to Maspha, over against Jerusalem." There they kept a solemn fast, presented legal offerings, and summoned to the performance of their duty those who had been bound by a vow, consulting for direction a copy of the Law, which was rendered more interesting to them by its having been profanely disfigured by the heathen. After an appropriate invocation of heavenly aid, and a scrupulous separation of persons legally exempt from military service, the multitude were marshalled by Judas under proper officers, and marched to Emmaus to give battle to the invading host. Here, having appealed to them once more by considerations of patriotism and piety suited to exalt their courage for the expected battle, he dismissed them for the night.*

Gorgias having concerted a surprise by night, with a select party of the invading force, Judas, who had intelligence of the movement, determined to take advantage of it by making, on his part, an attack on the main body of the Syrian troops, while weakened by the absence of the detachment under Gorgias. He accordingly moved from his camp, which the Syrian

---

* 1 Mac. iii. 38 – 60. — "The Israelites . . . . . came to Maspha, over against Jerusalem, for in Maspha was the place where they prayed aforetime in Israel " (46); comp. Judg. xxi. 1; 1 Sam. vii. 5. — " Such as were building houses, or had betrothed wives, or were planting vineyards, or were fearful, those he commanded that they should return, every man to his own house, according to the Law " (56); comp. Deut. xx. 5 – 8; Judg. vii. 3.

general approaching, and finding to have been abandoned, pressed into the mountains in pursuit of the
supposed fugitives. At daybreak, Judas, with three
thousand men, imperfectly armed either for attack or
defence, presented himself in front of the thoroughly
trained, equipped, and guarded hostile force. After a
short harangue, in which he reminded his followers
how Jehovah had formerly wrought deliverance for his
people, and encouraged them to hope that they would
still find him as mindful of the glory of his name,
Judas ordered the signal to be given for the assault by
sound of trumpet. The Syrians were presently put to
rout, and about three thousand of their number were
slain before the conquerors discontinued the pursuit.

The Jewish leader withheld his troops from busying
themselves about the spoil which had been won, under
the apprehension that Gorgias might return, and as-
sail them at an advantage. He had scarcely had time
to take his precaution before a portion of the party of
Gorgias was seen on the hills above, which, however,
discouraged by the fate of their comrades, whose tents
were now smoking in the plain, and seeing the array
of the Jews in preparation for a second battle, retreated hastily to their own country without attempting to strike another blow, leaving the victors to proceed in security and at leisure to rifle their magnificent camp. "They got much gold, and silver, and
blue silk, and purple of the sea, and great riches; after this they went home, and sung a song of thanksgiving, and praised the Lord in heaven ; because ♣ is
good, because his mercy endureth for ever ; thus Israel
had a great deliverance that day." *

Rousing himself from the dismay into which he had

---

* 1 Mac. iv. 1 - 25 ; comp. Ps. cxxxvi.

been thrown by the intelligence of these defeats, and by apprehension of the displeasure of his master, Lysias in the following year again invaded Judea with an army of sixty thousand selected infantry and five thousand horse. He pushed his way southward nearly to the border of Idumea, and there was met at Bethsura by Judas with ten thousand men. The Jewish hero having duly supplicated the Divine aid, " they joined battle, and there were slain of the host of Lysias about five thousand men." Lysias withdrew to Antioch, to make preparations for another renewal of the war, while Judas and his followers repaired to Jerusalem to enjoy the fruit of their great exploits in a re-institution of the worship at the temple. Struck with horror at the sight of the devastation of the sacred precincts, " the sanctuary desolate, and the altar profaned, and the gates burned up, and shrubs growing in the courts as in a forest or in one of the mountains, yea, and the priest's chambers pulled down, they rent their clothes, and made great lamentation, and cast ashes upon their heads, and fell down flat to the ground upon their faces, and blew an alarm with the trumpets, and cried towards heaven." *

But unprofitable lamentation was no employment for Judas the Maccabee. He made his dispositions for an assault by one party upon the city fortress, still occupied by the Syrians, while another was charged to re-arrange the wasted temple. The " priests of blameless conversation," to whom was assigned this latter office, bore away from the inclosure the pavement which the Gentiles had profaned, and, having consulted on the proper disposal of the altar of burnt

---

* 1 Mac. iv. 26 – 40. — " They pitched their tents at Bethsura " (29) ; comp. 2 Chron. xi. 7.

offerings, which had been defiled by impious sacrifices, concluded to break it down, and pile the stones "in a convenient place, until there should come a prophet to show what should be done with them." Having built instead a new altar on the same model, and put the sacred apartments with their adjoining courts in due order, and arranged them anew with their proper furniture and decorations according to the ancient ritual, they proceeded, "on the five-and-twentieth day of the ninth month in the hundred forty and eighth year" of the Syro-Greek era, to offer sacrifices and perform other solemn ceremonies of consecration, accompanied with festive enjoyments, "with songs, and citherns, and harps, and cymbals," and with valuable votive presents for the enriching and embellishment of the temple. This feast, prolonged through eight days, and ordained to be kept thenceforward annually for the same length of time, is the same which is referred to in the New Testament as "the Feast of the Dedication." *

To protect the city and temple from a repetition of such ravages as were thus repaired, Judas strongly fortified and garrisoned Mount Zion. He also "fortified Bethsura to preserve it, that the people might have a defence against Idumea." A war provoked by violent acts of that nation, jealous of the growing greatness of Israel, was conducted by Judas with his usual success. "He gave them a great overthrow, and abated their courage, and took their spoils," after which he proceeded to execute summary vengeance against the inhabitants of a city which had given treacherous assistance to the enemy.† Next he di-

---

* 1 Mac. iv. 41–59. — "The days of the dedication of the altar" (59); comp. John x. 22.

† iv. 60–v. 5.

rected his arms against the Ammonites, which nation, in a series of victories, he overran and subdued.* Returning to Judea, he received messages
from Gilead, where the Jews had retreated into a fortress, and from Galilee, imploring his protection against
marauding parties of their heathen neighbours, by
whom already numbers of them had been plundered
and carried into captivity or slain. After consultation
with the people, he immediately took his measures,
and leaving a proper garrison at Jerusalem, with directions to provoke no hostility in his absence, despatched his brother Simon with three thousand men
for the relief of Northern Galilee, while himself and a
younger brother, Jonathan, at the head of eight thousand, marched into the country of Galaad.

Both enterprises were successful. Simon defeated
the enemy in several battles, pursued them to the gates
of their stronghold at Ptolemais, slew three thousand
of them, and, with their spoils, and accompanied by his
rescued countrymen with their families and property,
returned in triumph to Jerusalem.† Meanwhile Judas
and Jonathan, with their forces, crossed the Jordan,
and learned from the friendly inhabitants of the country,
which they reached after three days' march, that their
brethren were still holding out in the forts of several
of the cities of Gilead, into which they had retired
for defence, and where they were threatened with an
immediate and simultaneous assault from the Syrians
by whom the cities themselves were occupied. Judas
immediately directed his course towards one of them,
and, having taken it by storm, " slew all the males with
the edge of the sword, and took all their spoils, and
burned the city with fire." Then, proceeding by night

---

* 1 Mac. v. 6 - 8.   † v. 9 - 23.

towards its citadel, which appears to have been at some distance, he came in the morning upon the Syrians, whom he found engaged in fixing scaling-ladders, and making other preparations for an assault upon the Jews within. With a single sentence of exhortation to fight that day for their brethren, he led his party in three divisions to the onset, mingling the voice of prayer to God with the notes of the trumpet. "Then the host of Timotheus, knowing that it was Maccabeus, fled from him; wherefore he smote them with a great slaughter; so that there were killed of them that day about eight thousand men." *

While Judas prosecuted his enterprise with similar success against other cities east of the Jordan, the Syrians had been collecting another large force. Being informed by his spies of the great scale of their preparations, and the place where they were posted, he proceeded to offer them battle. The Syrian commander, trusting more to the imposing numbers of his army to discourage an attack, than to their valor and conduct to repel it, told his officers that, if Judas should cross a brook that lay between the hostile parties to make an assault, they would not be able to withstand him; but that if, on coming up, he should halt on the other side, such timidity on his part would be an assurance of success against him. Judas no sooner approached the brook, than he gave orders for his whole force, without the exception of a man, to cross it after him. The Syrians, throwing away their weapons in their flight, fled in the direction of a place called Carnaim, which Judas, following close in pursuit, assaulted and took, and burned its temple, with all who had sought safety within it.†

---

* 1 Mac. v. 24 – 34.   † v. 35 – 44.

But though the country east of Jordan was overrun, it could not be secured except at too great cost. Accordingly, "Judas gathered together all the Israelites that were in the country of Galaad, from the least unto the greatest, even their wives, and their children, and their stuff, a very great host, to the end they might come into the land of Judea." Approaching a fortified city, named Ephron, through which their road lay, they asked permission of the inhabitants to pass peaceably through it; which being refused, they took it by storm, "slew all the males with the edge of the sword, and razed the city, and took the spoils thereof, and passed through the city over them that were slain." Then, recrossing the Jordan, Judas, having first halted to collect any loiterers, and put his party in suitable array, led them "up to Mount Zion with joy and gladness, where they offered burnt-offerings, because not one of them were slain until they had returned in peace." *

The tidings of the exploits of Judas and his brothers had led the officers whom, during his absence, he had left in command in Judea, to an unhappy emulation. Contrary to his orders, they had sought a battle, and had sustained in consequence a signal defeat, with a loss of "about two thousand men." The occurrence, as well as another of the same kind, when "certain priests, desirous to show their valor, were slain in battle, for that they went out to fight unadvisedly," did but exalt the repute of the sons of Mattathias, and impress the people the more with the wide difference between them and the men who "came not of the seed of those by whose hand deliverance was given unto Israel." Judas raised still higher his great

---

* 1 Mac. v. 45 – 54.

renown by victories over the Idumeans at the south and the Philistines at the west, in the course of his campaign against which latter people he took the city of Ashdod, and " pulled down their altars, and burned their carved images with fire." *

But the life of the oppressor was drawing to a close. Attracted by a representation which, during a progress " through the high countries," had been made to him of the great wealth of the Persian city Elymais, especially of treasures deposited in its temple by Alexander the Great, Antiochus " came and sought to take the city, and to spoil it." The inhabitants, having information of his movement, repulsed his attack, and he retired to Babylon, mortified and desponding. In this condition intelligence reached him of the disastrous state of his affairs in Judea. Sick with grief and disappointment, he took to his bed, persuaded that he was never to rise from it. Continuing to fail, he in the hearing of his friends reproached himself with his cruelties to the Jews, and robbery of their temple, as the cause for which his trouble had come upon him, and for which he was to " perish through great grief in a strange land." At length, having committed his regalia to one of his courtiers, named Philip, and appointed him regent of his kingdom and tutor of his son, " King Antiochus died there in the hundred forty and ninth year." His last arrangements appear to have been disregarded; for Lysias, being in possession of the young king's person, assumed the reins of government as his guardian, giving him at the same time the surname of Eupator.†

The Syrians, who, in the recent troubles with the Idumeans and Philistines, had been able to retain

---

* 1 Mac. v. 55 – 68.   † vi. 1 – 17.

possession of the fortress on Mount Zion, continuing
to annoy the Jews in the precincts of the temple, and
to push their encroachments upon their city, it became
an object of the first importance to Judas to dislodge
them.   While his preparations were going on, a party
of them managed to leave the fortress, and, having
been joined by some treacherous Jews, presented themselves before the young king, soliciting an immediate
reinforcement for the besieged garrison; whereupon
he raised an army, to the number of "an hundred
thousand footmen, and twenty thousand horsemen,
and two-and-thirty elephants exercised in battle," the
troops being partly his subjects, and partly foreign
mercenaries.   He directed his march to the south, and
attacked the fortress of Bethsura, which made a vigorous sally, burned his military engines, and defended
itself successfully against an assault of several days'
continuance.*

Moving to the relief of that place, Judas fell in
with the enemy, at a place called Bathzacharias.   And
now for a time his course of hitherto almost unbroken
good fortune was checked.   Exciting the elephants by
showing them "the blood of grapes and mulberries,"
the Syrians disposed these formidable animals in different parts of their army, each guarded by a force of a
thousand infantry in complete armour and five hundred
horse of the best description, and each bearing on
his back a wooden tower "with two-and-thirty strong
men that fought upon them, besides the Indian that
ruled him."   As the vast array displayed its ranks on
the hills, and passed down into the valley to the onset, "the sun shone upon the shields of gold and
brass, the mountains glistered therewith, and shined

---

* 1 Mac. vi. 18 – 31.

13 *

like lamps of fire," and, the blaze of their approach dazzling the eyes that watched it, "they marched in safety and in order," the sound of their heavy tread, and "the rattling of the harness," increasing the terror of their advance. The Jews waged the unequal contest with honorable constancy. "There were slain of the king's army six hundred men," and the day was illustrated by one great act of self-devoting courage on the part of one of the Asmonean brotherhood. Eleazar, fourth son of Mattathias, inferring from the superior size and gorgeous trappings of one of the elephants that he bore the royal person, forced his way sword in hand through the Syrians, "slaying on the right hand and on the left, so that they were divided from him on both sides; which done, he crept under the elephant, and thrust him under, and slew him; whereupon the elephant fell down upon him, and there he died." *

The Jews were compelled to retire before a force so disproportioned to their own. Following them to Jerusalem, "the king pitched his tents against Judea and against Mount Sion," having in the mean time received the submission of the garrison at Bethsura (which had been compelled by famine to surrender), and occupied the place with his own troops. The same fate was barely escaped by that of the temple at Jerusalem, which, having long held out against a vigorous siege, was at length about to yield, the "vessels being without victuals," and the force being much reduced by the desertion of numbers, who, pinched by the scarcity of food, had found means of retreat, when relief came in an unexpected way. Information reached Lysias, that Philip was approaching at the

---

* 1 Mac. vi. 32 – 46.

head of an army to claim the regency of the kingdom and the guardianship of the young king, assigned to him by the last will of Antiochus. Desirous to lose no time in fortifying himself against this new enemy, Lysias represented to the king and his officers, that, as their strength was daily wasting, and their supplies falling short, while the place besieged was still strong, and other affairs required attention, it was the part of prudence to make terms with the Jews, and remove the occasion of quarrel, by allowing them to "live after their laws, as they did before." On these terms the Jews capitulated, and "went out of the strong hold." The engagement, though ratified by an oath, was not honestly kept on the part of the king; he "entered into Mount Zion; but when he saw the strength of the place, he brake his oath that he had made, and gave commandment to pull down the wall round about." He then hastened to Antioch, his capital, of which Philip, during these proceedings, had possessed himself; "so he fought against him, and took the city by force." *

The face of affairs is now changed by the appearance on the scene of the rightful heir of the throne of Syria. Demetrius, son of Seleucus,† leaving Rome with a few followers, and making a successful descent on the kingdom of his fathers, established himself in

---

* 1 Mac. vi. 47–63. — "They had no victuals there to endure the siege, it being a year of rest to the land" (49) ; "their vessels being without victuals, for that it was the seventh year, and they in Judea that were delivered from the Gentiles had eaten up the residue of the store" (53) ; either we are to infer from these texts that the peculiar institution of the Sabbatical year (Vol. I. p. 301) was now observed, or else, which is more probable, we are to interpret them as a glorification by the writer of the extraordinary piety of his people at that age.

† Comp. Vol. III. p. 170.

"a city of the sea-coast." * A party of his troops
made Antiochus and Lysias prisoners, and conducted
them to him. He refused to see them; they were put
to death; and "Demetrius was set upon the throne of
his kingdom." †

Certain "wicked and ungodly men of Israel," with
Alcimus at their head, an intriguer who was ambitious of the high-priesthood, excited the new king
against Judas and his party, by representations of their
having put to death or driven into exile all Jews who
were in the Syrian interest. At the solicitation of
these persons, Demetrius sent Bacchides, "a great man
in the kingdom, and faithful to the king," and with
him Alcimus (raised to the dignity of high-priest), at
the head of "a great power," to "take vengeance of
the children of Israel." Arrived in Judea, "they sent
messengers to Judas and his brethren with peaceable
words deceitfully." Their friendly professions, belied by
the military preparations, found no credit with Judas,
though they imposed upon many, and, among them,
persons of consideration. "The Assideans," who are
said to have been "the first among the children of
Israel that sought peace of them," too easily believing
that, as "a priest of the seed of Aaron" had come with
the army, no wrong could be intended, paid dear for
their credulity; Alcimus, having entrapped them into
his power, put to death thirty of them in one day.
This perfidious act having caused desertions from the
ranks, and created universal distrust, indignation,
and complaint among the people, Bacchides withdrew his troops from Jerusalem, and, having vented
his rage by further executions, transferred his com-

---

* Josephus ("Antiq.," Lib. XII. cap. 10, § 1) says that its name was
Tripolis.
† 1 Mac. vii. 1–4.

mand to Alcimus, and went to make his report to the king.*

The pretensions of Alcimus to the high-priesthood were not without support on the part of malecontents among his own countrymen, who, adding to the disasters of foreign invasion the excesses of civil conflict, "did much hurt in Israel." Bacchides having retired, Judas was again in motion. "He went out into all the coasts of Judea round about, and took vengeance of them that had revolted from him, so that they durst no more go forth into the country." Pressed hard by his patriotic countrymen, Alcimus in his turn withdrew to the king of Syria, "and said all the worst of them that he could." Demetrius next "sent Nicanor, one of his honorable princes, a man that bare deadly hate unto Israel, with commandment to destroy the people." Nicanor, coming to Jerusalem with a formidable force, resorted a second time to the usual device of treachery. He attempted to lull Judas into security "with friendly words," and an interview was held, which Judas, informed meanwhile of his purpose to seize his person, refused to repeat. Resuming a hostile attitude, the two armies met near a place called Capharsalama, where the Syrians were defeated, with the loss of about five thousand men, and retreated again to their hold in Jerusalem.†

Here, when some priests and others approached him

---

* 1 Mac. vii. 5-20. — "Who ruled beyond the flood" (8); that is, I suppose, who was satrap of some territory beyond the Euphrates. — "The Assideans were the first among the children of Israel" (13); see above, p. 138, note †. I understand the historian to say that that portion of the Jews who were attached to the Asmonean family were yet so remote from any partisan feeling that they were even the foremost to think favorably of a descendant of Aaron, to believe the false pledges of Alcimus, and so fall into the snare that he spread.

† vii. 21 - 32.

with friendly demonstrations, and would have shown him "the burnt sacrifice that was offered for the king," he treated them with insult and outrage, and swore that he would burn the temple, if Judas and his followers were not given up to him. The priests returned to the temple, and with tears prayed to Jehovah to avenge himself on the blasphemers of his name. Nicanor again left Jerusalem, and encamped about twelve miles further north, at Beth-horon, where he received a reinforcement from Syria. Judas followed him with three thousand men, and having offered a prayer that the fate of the Assyrians of old, of whom the angel smote a hundred and eighty-five thousand, might be that of the enemy before him, he attacked and utterly routed them, killing their general at the first onset, and pursuing them a day's journey towards the north. They were harrassed on their flight by the inhabitants of the region, who " came forth out of all the towns of Judea round about, and closed them in; so that they, turning back upon them that pursued them, were all slain with the sword, and not one of them was left. Afterward they took the spoils, and the prey, and smote off Nicanor's head, and his right hand, which he stretched out so proudly, and brought them away, and hanged them up towards Jerusalem." This great victory was commemorated by a festival, which it was determined to repeat thenceforward every year; and "the land of Judah was in rest a little while." *

Looking about for some alliance with which to strengthen his exposed position, Judas turned towards

---

* 1 Mac. vii. 33 — 50. — "There were slain of Nicanor's side about five thousand men" (32); Josephus ("Antiq. Jud.," Lib. XII. cap. 10, § 4) makes the victory to have been with Nicanor; but the sense of the Greek is here clearly the other way.

a people, which, great part as it had been playing in
the world's affairs, had, through the imperfect means
of communication of those ancient times, just begun
to be heard of in the distant province of Judea. He
" had heard of the fame of the Romans, that they were
mighty and valiant men, and such as would lovingly
accept all that joined themselves unto them, and make
a league of amity with all that came unto them; and
that they were men of great valor." He had been
told further of their conquests in Gaul, and in Spain,
with its mines of silver and gold; of the " policy and
patience " by which they had become masters of many
distant kings and countries; of their victories over
Philip, over Perseus of Macedonia, over Antiochus
of Syria, from whom they had taken India, Media,
Lydia, and other provinces, and over the Peloponne-
sians, whom they had made their servants. He was
informed " how they destroyed and brought under
their dominion all other kingdoms and isles that at
any time resisted them, but with their friends, and
such as relied upon them, they kept amity "; that
though they took and gave crowns, they wore none,
nor were " clothed in purple, to be magnified thereby,"
but that in their senate-house " three hundred and
twenty men sat in council daily, consulting always for
the people, to the end they might be well ordered;
and that they committed their government to one man
every year, who ruled over all their country, and
that all were obedient to that one, and that there was
neither envy nor emulation amongst them." *

To this formidable power Judas sent an embassy,
soliciting " a league of amity and confederacy," and

---

* 1 Mac. viii. 1-16. — The Roman character described in the thirteenth
and fourteenth verses is precisely Virgil's

" Parcere subjectis et debellare superbos."

succour against the king of Syria.   It was "a very great journey"; and this was the beginning of the relations between Judea and Rome.

The Roman Senate received the overture favorably, and returned an answer, engraven on tablets of brass, containing the terms of their agreement with the ambassadors for a defensive alliance, to last during the pleasure of both parties.   And the Jews were informed that the Senate had sent a remonstrance to Demetrius against his treatment of their allies, and that, if the annoyance was continued, they would repress it by force.*

But, probably on account of their distance, this alliance seems little to have availed the Jews.   When tidings reached Demetrius of the defeat and death of Nicanor, he despatched Bacchides and Alcimus with another army, who, having taken on their way a city named Mesaloth, where they massacred "much people," and having halted awhile before Jerusalem, "moved and went to Berea, with twenty thousand footmen, and two thousand horsemen."   Here they confronted Judas, with a party of only three thousand choice troops.   Alarmed by such a disparity of force, numbers deserted, so that Judas at last saw himself at the head of only eight hundred men.   Overwhelmed with anxiety as he was for the issue of so unequal a strife, and discouraged further by the wish of the few faithful men who still remained with him to retreat and rally their friends, so as to go into the conflict in greater force and with a less desperate prospect, he endeavoured to sustain in them a courage superior to circumstances, like his own, saying, "God forbid that I should do this thing, and flee away from

---

* 1 Mac. viii. 17 – 32.

them; if our time be come, let us die manfully for our brethren, and let us not stain our honor." *

A battle followed, and lasted a whole day. The troops of Bacchides were marshalled in two divisions. Of these Judas, with his best troops, attacked the stronger, which was commanded by Bacchides in person, defeated it, and drove it from the field. But in the pursuit he was himself assailed by the other division, and there ensued " a sore battle," in which Judas fell, and his followers were put to flight. His brothers, Jonathan and Simon, secured his body, and buried it " in the sepulchre of his fathers at Modin. Moreover, they bewailed him, and all Israel made great lamentation for him, and mourned many days, saying, ' How is the valiant man fallen that delivered Israel!' " And the historian adds his testimony that the recorded exploits of the departed champion fall short, in number and excellence, of the full sum of those which won him his illustrious renown.†

After the death of Judas, the party opposed to him, and in league with the Syrians, " began to put forth their heads in all the coasts of Israel," and, availing themselves of the discontents occasioned by a prevailing scarcity of food to increase their influence, and aided by the favor of Bacchides, they made themselves " lords of the country." The severities practised at their instigation against the adherents of Judas, occasioning " a great affliction in Israel, the like whereof was not since the time that a prophet was not seen among them," led to another struggle to throw off the Syrian yoke. Learning that the patriotic party had arranged with Jonathan, youngest brother of Judas,

---

* 1 Mac. ix. 1 - 10. — Berea (4), according to Josephus, is the same with the *Bezeth* of vii. 19.

† ix. 11 - 22.

to assume the military command, Bacchides " sought
for to slay him," whereupon Jonathan and Simon
" fled into the wilderness of Thecoe," and encamped.
Bacchides pursued, and came up with them on a Sab-
bath-day, the river Jordan dividing the two armies.*
Jonathan meanwhile had had a skirmish with some of
the people of the neighbouring city of Medaba, who,
when Judas, in order to disencumber the movements
of his army, had sent some of their effects to a neighbouring friendly city for safe-keeping, had seized upon
the property, and captured its guard.   Not long after,
intelligence came to the Jewish leaders, that those
same persons had " made a great marriage," and would
soon approach, bringing the princely bride in a pom-
pous procession to her new home.   The Jews waylaid
the caravan, and when the bridegroom and his friends,
with music and arms, came out to meet it, " made a
slaughter of them in such sort as many fell down
dead, and the remnant fled into the mountain, and
they took all their spoils." †
   Surrounded by the Jordan, a marsh, and a wood, with
the enemy in front, and so cut off from the possibil-
ity of retreat, Jonathan found himself without other
resource than to hazard the issue of a battle.   The
Jews, having been so far successful as to put to death
a thousand of the enemy, retreated by swimming over
the river, which the Syrians, disabled by their loss, did
not venture to cross in pursuit.   Bacchides returned
to Jerusalem, which he fortified and garrisoned strong-

* 1 Mac. ix. 23 – 34. — "The wilderness of Thecoe" (33) ; comp.
2 Chron. xi. 6, xx. 20.
† ix. 35 – 43. — " Jonathan sent his brother " (35); " the children of
Jambri . . . . . took John " (36); " they had avenged fully the blood of
their brother " (42) ; this captain of the escort, who was captured and slain,
Josephus (" Antiq. Jud.," Lib. XIII. cap. 1, § 2) understood to have been
John, the eldest of the Asmonean brothers (comp. 1 Mac. ii. 2).

ly, as well as other strongholds in different parts of the country, while, to secure his master's interests still further, "he took the chief men's sons in the country for hostages, and put them into the tower at Jerusalem to be kept." On the death of Alcimus, who, in the midst of some sacrilegious operations upon the temple buildings, had been arrested by a paralysis, which had deprived him of speech, and of which he had lingered "with great torment," Bacchides returned to Syria, and "the land of Judea was in rest two years." *

The quiet was disturbed by a plot of some recreant Jews to induce Bacchides to return into Palestine and seize Jonathan and his company, whom they observed to be living "at ease and without care." He listened to the overture, and "came with a great host." But the conspiracy had already been detected and punished by the execution of fifty "of the men of the country that were authors of that mischief." Jonathan and Simon withdrew their followers to a place called "Bethbasi, which is in the wilderness," which they fortified, and to which the invaders soon laid siege. Leaving Simon to defend it, Jonathan took with him a party, and made an attack on a division of the enemy outside, immediately followed up by 'his brother by an assault upon Bacchides, in which he "burned up the engines of war," and "afflicted him sore." . Incensed at the officious friends who had exposed him to such vexation, Bacchides "slew many of them, and purposed to return into his own country." Jonathan watched the auspicious moment. His pro-

---

* 1 Mac. ix. 44 – 57. — "Alcimus died at that time," &c. (56). Josephus says, on the contrary ("Antiq. Jud.," Lib. XII. cap. 10, § 6), that Alcimus died in the time of Judas, and was succeeded by him in the high-priesthood.

posal for peace and a surrender of prisoners was gladly
entertained by the perplexed and disappointed Syrian.
" He returned and went his way into his own land,
neither came he any more into their borders.   Thus
the sword ceased from Israel; but Jonathan dwelt at
Machmas, and began to govern the people, and he destroyed the ungodly men out of Israel." *

The politics of Judea became involved in a compe-
tition for the Syrian throne.   Alexander, who claimed
to be a son of Antiochus Ephiphanes, had set up pretensions to it, and now held his court at the city of
Ptolemais.   Demetrius, besides mustering " an exceeding great host," thought he should do well to quiet
the ancient grudges of Jonathan the Jew, to whom he
despatched letters for that purpose, with instructions
for the release of the Jewish hostages whom his officers still held, and with authority to Jonathan to provide men and arms for his assistance.   Jonathan repaired to Jerusalem, received the hostages and delivered them to their parents, renewed the city walls and
repaired the fortifications of Mount Zion, but forbore
to declare himself as to his future course.   Concerned
for the authority which he had received from Syria,
and for the reserve which they saw him practise, " the
strangers that were in the fortresses which Bacchides
had built fled away, insomuch as every man left his
place and went into his own country; only at Bethsura certain of those that had forsaken the law and
the commandments remained still; for it was their
place of refuge." †

---

* 1 Mac. ix. 58 – 73. — " They took of the men of the country . . . . .
and slew them " (61); Josephus, erroneously, as I think, understood the
historian as saying that Bacchides put to death these fifty men, in resentment of the failure of his treachery. — " Bethbasi, which is in the wilderness " (62); Josephus calls the place *Bethalaga*. — " Jonathan dwelt at
Machmas " (73); that is, I suppose, Michmash (comp. 1 Sam. xiii. 5).

† x. 1 – 14.

Alexander, informed of these transactions of Demetrius, tried the same policy, and with better success.
Satisfied of the importance of conciliating Jonathan by
what had been " told him of the battles and noble acts
which he and his brethren had done, and of the pains
that they had endured," he resolved to try the effect
of the most liberal advances.   " He sent him a purple
robe and a crown of gold," and named him high-priest,
a dignity which Jonathan assumed at the next Feast
of Tabernacles,* after which he proceeded diligently
to recruit men and provide arms.   Demetrius, alarmed
by his equivocal movements, wrote again with promises much more liberal, coupled with flattering commendation, scarcely earned, for past loyalty.   He offered a perpetual release, extending to all Judea, Galilee, and Samaria, from various tributes, customs,
crown-taxes, halves, thirds, and tithes ; to give up his
fortification at Jerusalem to the high-priest ; to set at
liberty Jewish captives in every part of his dominions,
with full restitution of their cattle ; to recognize all
the festival days of the Law as " days of immunity and
freedom " for all his Jewish subjects ; to receive into his
armies thirty thousand Jews, with pay equal to that
of the native troops ; to raise others of the nation to
posts of military and civil trust in his realm, and commit to them the sole administration of the affairs of
Judea according to their own laws; to annex Samaria
to the · southern government ; to give Ptolemais and
its precincts (now occupied by Alexander) " as a free
gift to the sanctuary at Jerusalem, for the necessary
expenses of the sanctuary "; to make an annual donative of fifteen thousand shekels for the same use, besides such sums as should prove to be still due from

---

* The Asmonean family was descended from Aaron. 1 Mac. ii. 1;
comp. 1 Chron. xxiv. 7.

14 *

officers in arrears, and besides a sum equivalent to the amounts which had in past years been wrongfully embezzled from the priests' revenues; to allow privilege of sanctuary to the temple, extending even to the release of debts due to the king, and dispensation for offences against him; and finally, to make contributions from the royal exchequer for the repair of the decayed "works of the sanctuary," and of the walls and fortifications of Jerusalem and other Jewish cities.*

These promises, especially taken in connection with the past oppressions and perfidy of Demetrius, appeared too generous to be sincere. The Jews preferred the more promptly offered alliance of Alexander, to which they afterwards steadfastly adhered. Having been successful against Demetrius, in a battle in which that prince was slain, Alexander solicited and obtained Cleopatra, the daughter of Ptolemy, king of Egypt, in marriage. The nuptials were celebrated with royal pomp, and "a league of amity" was formed between the monarchs.† Jonathan had on this occasion been invited by Alexander to Ptolemais, where he was honorably and cordially received by the two kings and their retainers. Some complaints brought against him by "certain pestilent fellows of Israel, men of a wicked life," were contemptuously dismissed; and, to the confusion of his traducers, Alexander directed that he should change his dress for royal purple; that he should sit by his own side; and that the Syrian princes should attend him through the city, and make proclamation forbidding all persons to bring any charge against him. "So the king honored him, and wrote him amongst his chief friends, and made him a duke, and partaker of his dominion. Afterward Jon-

---

* 1 Mac. x. 15 – 45.   † x. 46 – 58.

athan returned to Jerusalem with peace and gladness." *

Demetrius, son of the late king of that name, coming from the island of Crete to push his pretensions
to the throne, Alexander, alarmed, retired to his capital city, Antioch. Apollonius, commander for Demetrius in Palestine, having sent an insolent defiance to
the Jews to try the issue of a battle, Jonathan marched from Jerusalem with ten thousand men, and, being
joined by his brother Simon, proceeded towards the
sea-coast, where he laid siege to and took the city of
Joppa, occupied by the party of Demetrius. Hereupon
Apollonius took the field with " a great host," including three thousand cavalry, and, Jonathan moving
southerly along the coast, they met under the walls of
Azotus, or Ashdod. Apollonius had placed a thousand horse in ambush, which disposition being known
to Jonathan, he took his measures accordingly. His
party standing firm against the assault, the enemy's
cavalry, on which the chief reliance was placed, were
at length spent with fatigue, and, Simon coming up
with his reinforcement, were driven with the rest of
the Syrian force into Ashdod, where they sought refuge in the temple of Dagon. Jonathan sacked the
city, with others in the neighbourhood, then set it on
fire and consumed it, with its temple, and all that it
contained. " Thus there were burned and slain with
the sword wellnigh eight thousand men." Jonathan
still pursuing his march southerly, the citizens of Ascalon threw open their gates to him with a cordial
welcome. Thence he returned, bearing the spoils of
his illustrious campaign, to Jerusalem. And " when
King Alexander heard these things, he honored Jona-

---

* 1 Mac. x. 59 - 66.

than yet more, and sent him a buckle of gold, as
the use is to be given to such as are of the king's
blood; he gave him also Accaron, with the borders
thereof, in possession." *

This was the last of the prosperity of Alexander.
The king of Egypt, having "gathered together a great
host, like the sand that lieth upon the sea-shore, and
many ships," came into the dominions of his son-in-
law, with friendly professions, but with a treacherous
purpose. As he entered, one after another, the cities
in which Alexander had given orders for his courteous
reception, "he set in every one of them a garrison of
soldiers to keep it." When he came to Ashdod, pains
were taken to excite his displeasure against Jonathan,
by showing him the ruins of the late battle, and the
heaps of disfigured remains of those who had been
burned and slain. "But the king held his peace."
Jonathan went to meet him at Joppa, and was favorably received; then, having accompanied him for
some distance, he "returned again to Jerusalem." †

"Having gotten the dominion of the cities by the
sea, unto Seleucia upon the sea-coasts," King Ptolemy,
pretending the excuse of an injury meditated against
him by Alexander, proposed and concluded an alliance
with Demetrius, to whom, taking her from Alexander, he gave his daughter in marriage. He then proceeded to Antioch, where he was solemnly crowned
king of Asia Minor and Egypt. Informed of these
transactions, Alexander, who was absent in Cilicia,
engaged in quelling a revolt, returned and offered battle to the Egyptians. He was defeated, and withdrew into Arabia, where he was put to death by one
Zabdiel, and his head sent to Ptolemy. Ptolemy him-

---

* 1 Mac. x. 67–89.   † xi. 1–7.

self died three days afterwards. In the midst of such changes, Demetrius held the reins with a feeble hand; parties were arrayed and embroiled, they knew not how; disorder ruled; "and they that were in the strongholds were slain one of another." *

The king, having been informed by some evil-disposed Jews that Jonathan had taken measures towards a forcible possession of " the tower that was in Jerusalem," sent to him in displeasure to discontinue his operations, and come to him immediately to Ptolemais. Careless of the danger to which he exposed himself, Jonathan repaired thither, with "silver and gold, and raiment, and divers presents besides," to propitiate Demetrius, leaving it, however, in strict charge to the elders and priests who had the direction of affairs in his absence, to prosecute with vigor the siege of the tower. Notwithstanding further intrigues to his prejudice, "the king entreated him as his predecessors had done before, and promoted him in the sight of all his friends, and confirmed him in the high-priesthood, and in all the honors that he had before, and gave him preeminence among his chief friends." Jonathan offered a subsidy of three hundred talents, in consideration of which he obtained from Demetrius a definition of boundaries for Judea and its dependent governments in Samaria, with a release from certain imposts, ratified by a letter to the provincial superintendent, in which the provision was declared irrevocable, and directions were given to communicate it to Jonathan, and set it up upon the holy mount in a conspicuous place.†

Demetrius, seeing " that the land was quiet before him, and that no resistance was made against him,"

---

* 1 Mac. xi. 8 – 19.   † xi. 20– 37.

committed the great error of dismissing his native
Syrian troops, and retaining only foreign mercenaries
in his service. For this course of action, "all the
forces of his fathers hated him." Aiming to take
advantage of the disaffection, "one Trypho, that had
been of Alexander's part before," betook himself to a
person, "that brought up Antiochus, the young son
of Alexander, and lay sore upon him to deliver him
this young Antiochus, that he might reign in his father's
stead." While he was urging this business, Jonathan had applied to Demetrius for the removal of some
of his people from certain fortresses whence they an-
noyed the Israelites, which request was granted, with
the promise of still further favors, on the condition
of his sending a reinforcement to the king in his en-
feebled condition. Jonathan accordingly, to his great
satisfaction, "sent him three thousand strong men
unto Antioch." They arrived in time to rescue him
from extreme danger. "They that were of the city
gathered themselves together into the midst of the
city, to the number of an hundred and twenty thousand men, and would have slain the king." Attempting to escape, but finding all the thoroughfares obstructed by the rebels, "he called to the Jews for
help, who came unto him all at once, and, dispersing
themselves through the city, slew that day in the city
to the number of an hundred thousand; also they set
fire on the city, and gat many spoils that day, and delivered the king." After this struggle, the courage of
the revolters gave way; they surrendered their arms,
and sued for pardon, which was granted; the Jewish
army was honorably dismissed with rich booty; "King
Demetrius sat on the throne of his kingdom, and the
land was quiet before him."*

---

* 1 Mac. xi. 38-52.

The professed friendship of Demetrius for Jonathan
was insincere, or, at all events, transient. He "troubled him sore," and estranged him, little knowing how
soon he was to need again the help which had lately
proved so serviceable. Trypho had the young Antiochus crowned, and, the Syrian troops who had been
so rashly dismissed gathering around him, he defeated
Demetrius, and, with the help of the captured elephants, took the city of Antioch. Antiochus wrote
to Jonathan, confirming him in his appointments and
dignities, sending him rich presents, and investing his
brother Simon also with an important command. Jonathan took the field, "and all the forces of Syria gathered themselves unto him." Ascalon opened its gates
to welcome him. Gaza at first refused him admission,
but, when he had burned and plundered some of its suburbs, capitulated, and placed in his hands some youths
of the chief families as hostages, whom he sent to
Jerusalem, designing himself to go to Damascus. But
hearing that Demetrius had sent to Galilee "a great
power, purposing to remove him out of the country," he repaired to that province, relinquishing the
command in the south to his brother Simon, who,
after a long blockade, took the strong city of Bethsura, and occupied it with a garrison of his own
troops. Encountering his enemy in a plain, Jonathan
found himself assailed at the same time by a force
which lay in ambush in the mountains in his rear.
His followers all fled except two, named Mattathias
and Judas, "the captains of the host." Jonathan,
having "rent his clothes, and cast earth upon his head,
and prayed," attacked the enemy, and put them to
flight; an example which rallied his scattered troops,
and brought them back to another onset. Victory
now declared fully in his favor, and, having driven

the enemy back to their camp, with the loss of " about three thousand men," Jonathan returned once more to Jerusalem.*

Perceiving a favorable opportunity to strengthen himself by foreign alliances, Jonathan sent an embassy to Rome, which was favorably received, "for to confirm and renew the friendship" which had been established by his brother. He also wrote to the Lacedæmonians in the name of the nation, reminding them that a king of theirs, named Darius (a Spartan king unknown in any other history), had "in times past" sent to the Jewish high-priest Onias a friendly embassy and letters, which were favorably received; proposing to renew the friendship, albeit not driven thereto by any necessity, inasmuch as they had "the holy books of Scripture" in their hands to comfort them; declaring that the Jews rejoiced in the reputation of the Spartans, and remembered them in sacrifices and prayers on festivals "and other convenient days"; referring briefly to the "great troubles and wars on every side," which, by "help from Heaven," they had been able to dispose of, without being troublesome to their confederates and friends, and finally proposing a renewal of the ancient relations of brotherhood through the ambassadors sent to Rome, who would take Lacedæmon on their way. Of the ancient letter herein referred to, a copy is annexed. With characteristic Lacedæmonian brevity, but in other respects fashioned with singular faithfulness by the Jewish mould, it recognized the Spartans and Jews as of the same race, "brethren," "of the stock of Abraham," as it was "found in writing"; and it invited a correspondence, with the profession of fraternity in strictly Jewish

---

* 1 Mac. xi. 53 – 74.

phrase, — "Your cattle and goods are ours, and ours are yours." The careful reader needs not to have pointed out the violation of historical probability in the transaction itself, and still more in the topics and phraseology of the alleged correspondence.*

Learning that the party of Demetrius were making greater efforts than ever before to overwhelm him with overpowering numbers, Jonathan anticipated the movement by going out to meet them as far as " the land of Amathis," where he learned from his spies that they were projecting a night attack. He made preparations accordingly, of which they being in turn informed, they were seized with a panic, and decamped in the darkness, leaving their watch-fires burning. Returning from an ineffectual pursuit, Jonathan attacked and spoiled an Arabian tribe, " and, removing thence, came to Damascus, and so passed through all the country," while Simon pursued his operations in the south and occupied Joppa with a garrison, having learned that there was a plan to surrender it to Demetrius. Both the brothers then employed a short respite from the hazards of the field in constructing and repairing fortifications, those of Jerusalem being newly arranged by Jonathan, so as to separate them from that part of the city which was frequented for purposes of trade.†

Trypho, who was scheming against the throne and life of his young ward, fearing opposition from Jonathan, resolved on his destruction first. Jonathan, who had warning of his purpose, met him at the head of

---

* 1 Mac. xii. 1 – 23. — "This is the copy of the letters which Oniares sent; 'Areus, king of the Lacedæmonians,'" &c. (19, 20); comp. 7, where the Spartan king is called Darius.

† xii. 24 – 38. — "The land of Amathis" (25); probably Hamath is intended; comp. Numb. xiii. 21; 2 Kings xviii. 34.

forty thousand men. Unable to cope with such a
force, Trypho resorted to artifice. He received the
Jewish prince with flattering distinction, made him
presents, and, kindly expostulating with him for the
jealousy which he had manifested, induced him to dis-
miss all his followers except a thousand men, and accompany him to Ptolemais, with the promise that that
city and others should be intrusted to his command,
in the fulfilment of a purpose which Trypho declared
to have been the cause of his present expedition. No
sooner had Jonathan and his party entered the city,
than the gates were closed upon them, and his attendants were all put to the sword. Trypho immediately
followed up the blow, by sending an expedition against
the forces left by Jonathan in Galilee. These, however, proved to be roused rather than dispirited by the
intelligence of their leader's fate, and the Syrians,
seeing no prospect of a successful attack, retired;
"whereupon they all came into the land of Judea
peaceably, and there they bewailed Jonathan, and them
that were with him." *

The disaster of their chief distressed and alarmed the
Jews, in the same degree that it elated and encouraged their enemies. Simon, the only survivor (except
Jonathan) of the heroic brotherhood, repaired to Jerusalem. His courageous exhortations revived the
drooping spirits of the people, and with one consent he
was chosen their leader. He hastened to put the fortifications of the capital city in good order; sent a
party to occupy Joppa; and proceeded to meet Trypho, who, accompanied by Jonathan as a prisoner, was
advancing from Ptolemais. Trypho sent him a message, that Jonathan was detained solely on account of

---

* 1 Mac. xii. 39 - 52. — Here Josephus ("Antiq. Jud.," Lib. XIII. cap.
6, *ad calc.*) ceases to follow the narrative in this book.

arrears due from him to the royal treasury, and that he should be released on the payment by Simon of a hundred talents, and the placing of two of Jonathan's sons in Trypho's hands as hostages, to secure his refraining from any act of vengeance. Simon sent the money and the children, not because he gave any credit to the proposal, but to shield himself from the imputation of causing his brother's death by his refusal. As he expected, Jonathan was still detained, and after a time was put to death. As soon as the withdrawal of Trypho permitted, Simon, who had been harrassing him by constant pursuit, had the remains of his brother disinterred from the grave beyond Jordan, and, amidst great lamentations of the people, reburied "in Modin, the city of his fathers." There he erected a monument faced with hewn stone, and "set up seven pyramids, one against another, for his father, and his mother, and his four brethren," and surrounded them with a colonnade, carved with military and naval emblems and trophies, "that they might be seen of all that sail on the sea." *

At length Trypho executed his long-cherished purpose of putting the young Antiochus to death, and usurping his crown. For protection against his violence, — for "all that Trypho did was to spoil," — Simon, besides strengthening and victualling the Jewish posts, sent an embassy, with presents, to bespeak the good-will of King Demetrius. Demetrius answered with the most friendly professions, confirming the immunities previously granted, the treaties of earlier time, and the possession of fortresses built by the Jews, forgiving past irregularities, releasing the payment of taxes, and inviting Jews to the Syrian court.

---

* 1 Mac. xii. 53 – xiii. 30.

The transaction came to be considered as a sort of era of Jewish independence, so that "then the people of Israel began to write in their instruments and contracts, ' In the first year of Simon the high-priest, the governor and leader of the Jews.' " *

The people of Gaza, besieged and finally stormed by the troops of Simon, were treated by him with a clemency which appears to have distinguished him from his equally valiant brothers. On their submission, he contented himself with dispossessing them of their dwellings, which, after cleansing from idolatrous pollutions, he distributed among his own followers, at the same time strengthening the fortifications of the place, and erecting within it a dwelling for himself. The hostile party within the tower of Jerusalem being blockaded there by him, and finally reduced by famine, he accepted their submission, "and when he had put them out from thence, he cleansed the tower from pollutions, and entered into it the three and twentieth day of the second month, in the hundred seventy and first year, with thanksgiving, and branches of palm-trees, and with harps, and cymbals, and with viols, and hymns, and songs, because there was destroyed a great enemy out of Israel; he ordained also that that day should be kept every year with gladness." He strengthened the fortification on Mount Moriah, and established himself therein; and seeing that "John his son was a valiant man, he made him captain of all the hosts; and he dwelt in Gazara." †

Demetrius, in an expedition in which he had hoped to obtain assistance from the Medes against Trypho, fell into their hands, and was detained by them a prisoner. Judea meanwhile prospered, and "was quiet all

---

* 1 Mac. xiii. 31 – 42.   † xiii. 43 – 53.

the days of Simon," on whom and whose administration the historian takes occasion at this point to pronounce an elaborate panegyric, applauding him for all the qualities which can illustrate a just, wise, patriotic, gracious, and religious prince, qualities which in his case were attended with a good fortune not less extraordinary.*

At Sparta and Rome, the intelligence of Jonathan's death had been received with sorrow. The Romans, hearing that Simon had succeeded, wrote to him a letter on brazen tablets, renewing the engagements into which they had entered with his brothers ; and he in return " sent Numenius to Rome with a great shield of gold of a thousand pound weight, to confirm the league." And the Spartans, always slow in their movements, except in war, replied in friendly terms to the communications made three years before by Numenius and Antipater.† The Jews, attaching much importance to these foreign relations, and feeling their own confidence in their ruler increased by seeing to what an extent he had excited that sentiment even in the people of distant regions, resolved to honor him with a costly and enduring memorial of their reverence and gratitude. They accordingly directed the preparation of " tables of brass, which they set upon pillars in Mount Sion," inscribed with the record of a sort of epitome of his achievements and deserts, in peace and war, with passing allusions to those of others of the glorious Maccabean family. The inscription also recited the decree of the people, appointing Simon " to be high-priest, and captain and governor of the Jews and priests, and to defend them all," and his acceptance of those trusts. And it was further directed that " copies

---

* 1 Mac. xiv. 1 – 15.   † xiv. 16 – 24.

thereof should be laid up in the treasury, to the end
that Simon and his sons might have them." *

The son of Demetrius, named Antiochus, who, during his father's detention in Persia, had succeeded to
the administration of his affairs, " sent letters from
the isles of the sea " to Simon, informing him that he
had collected forces for the purpose of sustaining the
claims of his house, and reëstablishing the ancient order of things, against the usurpation from which the
kingdom was suffering ; confirming the grants of foreign monarchs to the Jews, and adding to them among
others the right of coining money ; and promising still
greater favors, when affairs should be settled, to the
high-priest, the nation, and the temple. Landing in
his paternal dominions, the force of Antiochus was
greatly increased by desertions from that of Trypho, so
that, when the usurper fled before him " unto Dora,
which lieth by the sea-side," he besieged him there at
the head of " an hundred and twenty thousand men of
war, and eight thousand horsemen," at the same time
blockading the port with a naval armament.†

Meanwhile the Jewish ambassadors to Rome had
brought back a circular letter from the Consul Lucius,
addressed to Ptolemy, king of Egypt, and to the rulers
of various Asiatic realms and provinces, commanding
them to observe peace with the Jews, as allies of the
Roman people, and to deliver up to Simon the high-
priest, for punishment, all "pestilent fellows " who had

---

* 1 Mac. xiv. 25 – 49. — " The Jews and priests were well pleased that
Simon should be their governor and high-priest *for ever, until there should
arise a* [or, *the*] *faithful prophet* " (41) ; comp. iv. 46 ; also, Vol. I. pp.
463, 464. Does the decree constituting Simon " governor and high-priest
for ever, until," &c., mean that the dignity was to be hereditary in Simon's
family (comp. 49), till the expected Messiah should come to supersede
them ? In point of fact, his line succeeded.

† xv. 1 – 14.

fled from their country for objects unfriendly to him. Apparently with a view to avail himself of the favorable moment of this communication to strengthen his interest with Antiochus, Simon "sent him two thousand chosen men to aid him; silver also, and gold, and much armour." But that prince, now at the height of his fortunes, was elated, capricious, and exacting. "He would not receive them, but brake all the covenants which he had made with him afore, and became strange unto him"; and he sent a messenger to Simon to complain of his having "done great hurt in the land, and got the dominion of many places," and especially of his retaining possession of "Joppe and Gazara, with the tower in Jerusalem," and to threaten him with war unless he should surrender the cities which he occupied, with the revenues collected from them, or make a commutation by the payment of a thousand talents.*

"Athenobius, the king's friend," having come to Jerusalem and made known his errand, could not disguise his amazement, "when he saw the glory of Simon, and the cupboard of gold and silver plate, and his great attendance." Simon explained that this magnificence was no result of robbery and wrong, but fairly furnished from means belonging to the national inheritance, at length recovered, after being long unrighteously withheld. As to the principal military posts reclaimed, Simon replied that, though his people had suffered great harm from them while in hostile hands, he would give a hundred talents for them, to avoid a controversy. The courtier made no answer, "but returned in a rage to the king, and made report unto him of these speeches, and of the glory of Si-

---

* 1 Mac. xv.   15–31.

mon, and of all that he had seen; whereupon the king was exceeding wroth." *

Trypho having managed to escape by sea from the place where he was invested, was pursued by Antiochus in person, who left one Cendebeus in command, with orders, among other things, to invade the interior country of Judea. Simon, being informed of the proceedings of Cendebeus in execution of his trust, summoned to him his two eldest sons, John and Judas, and, having reminded them of the public services of his family, told them that he had grown too old for the labors of the field, which now ought to be assumed by them; and to that end he placed them in command of " twenty thousand men of war with horsemen," invoking for them the blessing of Heaven. Proceeding, with this force, on the expedition, they fell in near Modin with the troops of the Syrian prefect, " a mighty great host, both of footmen and horsemen." Simon, seeing his followers reluctant to cross a brook which separated the two armies, himself passed over first. They followed; he arranged his order of battle; " the holy trumpets " sounded; and the Syrians were put to flight, with the loss of many of their number. Judas, Simon's son, was wounded, but John pursued the fugitives to a stronghold lately built by Antiochus's command; then, having burned Ashdod, where many of them had sought a refuge, and put about two thousand men to the sword, " he returned into the land of Judea in peace." †

Simon's long and glorious life was brought to a violent end by a treacherous member of his family. One Ptolemy, who had married his daughter, and been advanced and enriched by his favor, and who now com-

---

* 1 Mac. xv. 32 – 36.   † xv. 37 – xvi. 10.

manded "in the plain of Jericho," "thought to get the country to himself, and thereupon consulted deceitfully against Simon and his sons to destroy them." In a progress which Simon was making through the different parts of the country, "taking care for the good ordering of them," he came to Jericho, attended by his sons, Mattathias and Judas. Ptolemy invited them to an entertainment, at which, when they had drunk freely, he, with the assistance of men whom he had concealed in the apartment, got possession of their weapons, and assassinated them with some of their attendants. He then sent to apply to Antiochus for a reinforcement, with the aid of which he proposed to subdue the country to his rule. Other messengers he despatched in different directions; to the tribunes, with promises of reward if they would join his standard; others to Jerusalem, to secure the city and temple for the king; and others "to Gazara, to kill John," whom that prince, however, forewarned of his danger, seized and put to death.

Here the history closes; referring the reader for information "concerning the rest of the acts of John [Hyrcanus], and his wars, and worthy deeds which he did, and the building of the walls which he made, and his doings," to "the chronicles of his priesthood, from the time he was made high-priest after his father."

LECTURE LIX.

SECOND AND THIRD BOOKS OF THE MACCABEES.

The Second Book an Abridgment, by an Unknown Writer, of a
Larger Work by one Jason. — The Abridgment, and probably the
Original Work, composed in Greek. — Two Letters from the Jews
in Palestine to their Compatriots in Egypt. — Their Contents.
— Their Spurious Character. — Prologue to the Abridgment.
— Mission of Heliodorus, the Syrian Treasurer, to Jerusalem.
— His Supernatural Expulsion from the Temple. — Intrigues of
Jason against his Brother the High-priest. — His Introduction
among his Countrymen of Heathen Usages. — Visit of Antiochus
Epiphanes to Jerusalem. — Accession of Menelaus to the High-
Priesthood. — Murder of Onias avenged by Antiochus. — Outrages of Menelaus. — Contest bewteen him and Jason. — Violent
Proceedings of Antiochus at Jerusalem. — Sufferings and Heroism of Certain Jews. — Rising of Judas the Maccabee. — His Victories over Nicanor, Timotheus, and Bacchides. — Death of Antiochus. — Purification and Dedication of the Temple. — Accession of Antiochus Eupator. — Further Successes of Judas, partly
obtained by Supernatural Aid. — His Treaty with Lysias. — Renewal of the War. — Exploits of Judas against Timotheus, Lysias, Gorgias, and King Antiochus. — Another Treaty of Peace.
— Accession of Demetrius Soter. — Intrigues of Alcimus. — Establishment and Rupture of Friendly Relations between Judas
and Nicanor. — Defeat and Death of Nicanor. — Third Book of
the Maccabees, originally composed in Greek, by an Egyptian
Jew. — Its Subject a Fabulous Account of a Deliverance of
the Jews in Egypt from a Persecution of Ptolemy Philopator.

The author of the Second Book of the Maccabees
explains the occasion and design of his work, or of
part of his work, as follows: —

"As concerning Judas Maccabeus and his brethren,
and the purification of the great temple, and the dedication of the altar, and the wars against Antiochus

Epiphanes and Eupator his son, and the manifest signs
that came from heaven unto those that behaved themselves manfully to their honor for Judaism; so that,
being but a few, they overcame the whole country, and
chased barbarous multitudes, and recovered again the
temple renowned all the world over, and freed the
city, and upheld the laws which were going down, the
Lord being gracious unto them with all favor; all
these things, I say, being declared by Jason of Cyrene
in five books, we will assay to abridge in one volume." *

Concerning Jason of Cyrene or his writings, we have
no information from any other source. We do not
know the time when he lived. Of course he was later
than the year 161 before Christ, since his history included the events of that year.† Cyrene, on the African coast, opposite to the Peloponnesus, was a resort
of numerous Jews, whose position, pursuits, and social
affinities connected them with their countrymen in
Egypt rather than with those in Palestine.

Nor do we know any thing of the name, or history,
or any thing with exactness concerning the time, of
the person who thus undertook to abridge Jason's
work. If the book came from his hands in the form
in which it has descended to us, it is certain that he
lived later than the year 124 B. C., since he professes
to relate a transaction of that year. ‡ It is decidedly
probable that we should place him many years later
than this. The errors in dates and the intermixture of
legendary tales indicate that, between the period treated
of and the composition of the history, there had been

---

* 2 Mac. ii. 19 – 23.
† Or later than the year 164 B. C., if Bertholdt's hypothesis be correct;
see below, p. 203, note †.
‡ i. 10.

considerable time for the true dates to be forgotten, and for legends to be invented and become current. Probably we should not be far from the truth in assigning the composition of the book to about the middle of the century before the Christian era.

It was undoubtedly written in the Greek language. Jerome asserts this for a fact, and adds that the structure of the style confirms it.* The style is so purely Greek, after the Alexandrine fashion, as to preclude the idea of its being a translation from any other original. Eichhorn † and Bertholdt ‡ go so far as to argue, from the purity of Greek style in the abridgment, that Jason's work which is abridged must have been also in Greek. But though the conclusion is on all accounts highly probable, this argument in its favor seems little worthy of reliance. Finally, that the author was not a Jew of Palestine appears probable from his thinking it necessary to qualify the temple at Jerusalem as "the great temple." § The errors in chronology and geography likewise lead to the same conclusion. A resident of the country would have been likely to be better acquainted with both.

Prefixed to the abridgment of Jason's work is an introduction explaining the writer's purpose and plan in making it. ‖ And prefixed to this introduction are two letters, represented as having been written at different times, by the Jews in Judea to their brethren in Egypt.

The first of these letters is short. In it "the Jews that be at Jerusalem and in the land of Judea," after

---

* "Maccabæorum primum librum Hebraicum reperi; secundus Græcus est, quod ex ipsâ quoque phrasi probari potest." (Prolog. Galeat.)

† "Einleitung in die Apok. Schrift. des Alt. Test.," s. 260.

‡ "Historisch-kritische Einleitung," u. s. w., Th. III. s. 1071.

§ 2 Mac. ii. 19; xiv. 13.   ‖ ii. 19 – 32.

the customary salutation, express their wish that God
may be gracious to their Egyptian brethren, remember in their favor his covenant with their fathers, give
them a heart to serve him steadfastly and cheerfully,
acquaint them with his law, send them peace, hear
their prayers, and be their constant friend in trouble.
They say that to their fraternal good wishes they unite
their prayers. They refer to their having written a
similar letter " what time as Demetrius reigned, in the
hundred threescore and ninth year," when they were
"in the extremity of trouble." They declare that
then they offered sacrifices, "and lighted the lamps,
and set forth the loaves," and " prayed unto the Lord,
and were heard." And the missive closes with the exhortation, " Now see that ye keep the Feast of Tabernacles in the month of Casleu." *   By this is meant
the feast established to commemorate the re-dedication
of the temple in the time of Judas the Maccabee.†
The Feast of Tabernacles, properly so called, was celebrated in the month Tisri.‡

It is plain that this letter did not belong to the
abridgment from the work of Jason of Cyrene, for,
as it professes to have been written later than the
year 169 of the era of the Seleucidæ, its place would
then have been at the end of the book, which only
comes down to the year 149 of that era, instead of
standing, where we find it, at the beginning. It is by
no means probable that the composition is what it
purports to be, a genuine letter from the Jews of Palestine to those of Egypt. It appears rather to be the
fiction of a person imperfectly acquainted with the
history of the time referred to. It can hardly be said
that the Jews were " in the extremity of trouble " at
the period specified, during the reign of Demetrius

---

* 2 Mac. i. 1–9.   † Comp. i. 18; x. 5, 6.   ‡ Comp. Lev. xxiii. 34.

Nicator; nor is there an air of probability in the
construction of the letter itself, considered as being,
what it represents itself, a communication from the
body of Jews in Palestine to their Egyptian brethren.
In a certain character of its style, Bertholdt supposed
himself to discern indications of its having been composed originally in the Hebrew language.*

And the same opinion he expresses, though less
confidently, respecting the second letter, there being
nothing to determine, as to either, whether a translation
existed previously to the compilation of the book before us, or whether the translation was made for that
purpose. The latter missive professes to have been
sent " in the hundred fourscore and eighth year," by
" the people that were at Jerusalem and in Judea,
and the council, and Judas, ... unto Aristobulus,
king Ptolemeus's master, who was of the stock of the
anointed priests, and to the Jews that were in Egypt ";
and with the same purpose as the former, that of recommending to the persons addressed the observance
of the Feast of Dedication. The writers refer to the
deliverance of their nation consequent upon the death
of Antiochus, which event they relate to have taken
place under circumstances entirely different from those
detailed in the account in the First Book. They say
that when the Syrians had been driven from the holy
city, their king, retiring into Persia, was entrapped
there into the temple of a certain goddess named
Nanea; " for Antiochus, as though he would marry
her, came into the place, and his friends that were
with him, to receive money in name of a dowry ";
and that, being shut in, he was stoned to death by
her priests from an opening in the roof.†

* " Hist. Einleit.," Th. III. s. 1072.
† 2 Mac. i. 10 – 17 ; comp. 1 Mac. vi. 3 – 16, where the representation is,
that Antiochus died of grief at Babylon.

The letter, making known the purpose of the writers " to keep the purification of the temple," proceeds
to recommend the same observance to those to whom
it is addressed. And it appears to represent the festival as being kept partly in commemoration of another
event, of which we have no information in any other
part of Scripture, and which is here related as follows;
namely, that at the time of the captivity, which is
called a captivity in *Persia*, some priests took the fire
from the altar, and hid it away from the knowledge
of all men in a dry place under ground; that, on the
return from the captivity, Nehemiah sent some of the
descendants of those priests to search for it, who returned to say that they could find nothing but muddy
water; that he commanded a quantity of the water to
be brought, and poured over a sacrifice which had
been prepared; that, the sun shining out from a cloud,
the wood which had been thus drenched burst into a
spontaneous blaze; that, the priests having " sung
psalms of thanksgiving" while the sacrifice was consumed, with prayers with and for the people, and for
the punishment of their oppressors, " Neemias commanded the water that was left to be poured on the
great stones," and " when this was done, there was kindled a flame, but it was consumed by the light that
shined from the altar"; that the king of Persia, hearing of what had taken place, directed that the spot
where the water was found should be inclosed and
kept sacred; that he further distributed largesses on
the occasion; and that Nehemiah called the inflamma-
ble water by the name of *Naphthar*, which others cor-
rupted into *Nephi*.*

The letter proceeds to state, as facts " also found in

---

* 2 Mac. i. 18–36. —" Jonathan beginning " (23); comp. Neh. xii.
11, 14, 35.

the records," that, at the time of the captivity, the
prophet Jeremiah commanded the exiles to take with
them fire kindled from the altar at the temple, at the
same time charging them to keep the Law, and especially to abstain from the idolatrous usages of the
nation among whom they were to sojourn; that the
same prophet, following a Divine direction, caused the
tabernacle and the ark to be carried along with him as
on his sad way to banishment he was passing by Mount
Pisgah, from the top of which Moses, emerging from
the wilderness at the head of the people eight centuries before, had extended his rejoicing view over the
promised land; that " when Jeremy came thither, he
found an hollow cave, wherein he laid the tabernacle,
and the ark, and the altar of incense, and so stopped
the door"; that his followers afterwards sought in
vain for the place, and that he blamed them for the
attempt, telling them that it must remain unknown
till God should " gather his people again together,
and receive them unto mercy," at which time, he said,
the glory of Jehovah should appear, and he should
take visible possession of his temple, manifesting himself in the cloud in which he was seen by Moses at the
consecration of the tabernacle,* and in which at Solomon's dedication of the temple he filled the sacred
courts,† when that great monarch kept the dedication
festival for eight days, and when his sin-offerings, directed by the Law to be consumed, were gloriously
consumed by fire from heaven,‡ as that of Aaron before the tabernacle had been in ancient times.§

The second letter further declares, that " the same
things also were reported in the writings and com-

---

* Ex. xl. 34, 35.   † 1 Kings viii. 10, 11.
‡ 2 Chron. vii. 1.   § Lev. ix. 22 – 24.

mentaries of Neemias " (though there is no trace of
them in what has come down to us under his name);
" and how he, founding a library, gathered together
the acts of the kings, and the prophets, and of David,
and the epistles of the kings concerning the holy gifts,"
and that " in like manner also Judas gathered together
all those things that were lost by reason of the war,"
which things were still in the possession of the Jerusalem Jews, and were at the service of those of Egypt,
if they would " send some to fetch them." And, finally, the writers advise the Jews of Egypt to imitate
their example in keeping the Feast of the Purification, and express the hope that God, who had chosen
their people, and given them " an heritage, and the
kingdom, and the priesthood, and the sanctuary," and
who had lately delivered them out of great troubles,
and permitted his holy dwelling-place at Jerusalem to
be purified for his reoccupation, would crown his mercies by gathering all the children of Jacob again, " out
of every land under heaven, into the holy place." *

It is impossible that this pretended letter should be
authentic. Independently of the legendary tone which
characterizes it throughout, the mention of the fathers'
being " led into Persia " at the time of the captivity is
an error into which no Jewish " council " † could have
fallen. " Aristobulus, king Ptolemeus's master," is a
fabulous character.‡ Judas, represented as one of the
writers in the year 188 of the Seleucidan era, can be
no other than Judas the Maccabee; § but no fact in
the history of those times is more unquestionable, than
that he had fallen in battle thirty-six years before this
date.‖

---

* 2 Mac. ii. 1-18.   † i. 10; comp. 19.   ‡ i. 10.
§ Ibid.; comp. ii. 14.   ‖ 1 Mac. ix. 3, 18.

16 *

Nor is it likely that this letter made a part of the original compilation. More probably it was brought into its present place by some later hand. Without it, the work, consisting of an abridgment of Jason's larger treatise, not only has completeness as a narrative, but it is furnished with its formal introduction and close; * and the compiler would hardly have presented in the same history contradictory accounts of the death of one of the principal personages in it, at least without some intimation that he observed the inconsistency derived from his different sources of information.† It is true that the passage next following the letter is introduced with the connecting particle which our translators have rendered " now." ‡ But this proves nothing. The use of that particle at the beginning of a discourse belongs to the Hebrew-Greek, or *Hellenistic* style. And if this were not so, there is not the slightest difficulty in supposing that the same person, whoever he was, that prefixed this prefatory matter to the abridgment from Jason's work, inserted this word by way of completing the union.

The considerations that have been presented render it highly probable that the work originally consisted only of the abstract from Jason's history, with its pre-lude and close, and that the two fictitious letters which begin the book were afterwards added by a later hand. The author of the compendium, having announced his plan in the passage quoted at the beginning of this Lecture, says that he desires to relieve the patience of the reader from the tediousness, and his memory from the burden, of a variety of details. He adds, that in executing, with a view to " the pleasuring of many,"

---

* 2 Mac. ii. 19–32; xv. 37–39.   † i. 14–16; comp. ix. 3–28.
‡ ii. 19. Τὰ δὲ κατὰ τὸν 'Ιούδαν, κ. τ. λ.

what to himself is "a matter of sweat and watching," it will be impossible for him "to stand upon every point, and go over things at large, and to be curious in particulars." He must "use brevity," and will accordingly dilate no more upon his scheme, remembering "that it is a foolish thing to make a long prologue, and to be short in the story itself." *

The abridgment embraces a history of fifteen years, beginning with the year 176 B. C., the last year of Seleucus Philopator. At that time, we are told, all things were prospering at the holy city under the godly high-priesthood of Onias the Third ; † "the laws were kept very well," kings sent presents to the temple, and Seleucus "bare all the costs belonging to the service of the sacrifices." But one Simon, a Benjamite, governor of the temple, on some difference with Onias, repaired to Apollonius, the Syrian governor, and informed him that there were "infinite sums of money" in the treasury at Jerusalem, "which did not pertain to the account of the sacrifices." This being reported by Apollonius to the king, he sent Heliodorus, his treasurer, to Jerusalem, to seize the money. Arriving there, ostensibly in the course of a tour of inspection of that portion of his master's dominions, Heliodorus inquired of the high-priest, by whom he had been courteously received, whether the representation which had been made was true, at the same time avowing the object of his visit. Onias replied, "that there was such money laid up for the relief of widows and fatherless children ; and that some of it belonged to Hircanus, son of Tobias, a man of great dignity, and not as that wicked Simon ·had misinformed ; the sum whereof in all was four hundred talents of

---

* 2 Mac. ii. 19 – 32.   † See Vol. III. p. 170.

silver, and two hundred of gold; and that it was altogether impossible that such wrongs should be done
unto them that had committed it to the holiness of
the place, and to the majesty and inviolable sanctity
of the temple, honored over all the world." *

The persistence of Heliodorus in his demand spread
a universal consternation and distress through the
city. The priests, robed in their sacred vestments,
prostrated themselves before the altar. "Whoso had
looked the high-priest in the face, it would have
wounded his heart," so changed was he by "the in-
ward agony of his mind." The people "ran flocking
out of their houses to the general supplication." The
women, girt with sackcloth, thronged the street, the
maidens came to the doors and windows, all calling
passionately "upon the Almighty Lord, to keep the
things committed of trust safe and sure, for those that
had committed them." †

Jehovah heard his people, and glorified his dwelling-place. As Heliodorus with his guards came into
the treasury, "there appeared unto them an horse with
a terrible rider upon him, and adorned with a very
fair covering; and he ran fiercely, and smote at Heliodorus with his forefeet; and it seemed that he that
sat upon the horse had complete harness of gold;
moreover, two other young men appeared before
him, notable in strength, excellent in beauty, and
comely in apparel, who stood by him on either side,
and scourged him continually, and gave him many
sore stripes." He fell in a swoon, and, lying "speech-
less without all hope of life," was taken up and carried away in a litter by his friends. At the suggestion of some of them, and at the same time to quiet

---

* 2 Mac. iii. 1 – 12.   † iii. 13 – 22.

any suspicion on the king's part (well or ill founded) that this was a scene gotten up by the Jews, Onias determined to offer a solemn sacrifice for the restoration of the health of Heliodorus; and while he was engaged in doing so, the same apparition presented itself again to Heliodorus, charging him to be grateful to Onias, for whose sake it was that Jehovah intended to spare his life, and to publish abroad that it was " the mighty power of God " which had discomfited his impious attempt. When, having " offered sacrifices unto the Lord, and made great vows unto him that had saved his life, and saluted Onias," the baffled treasurer returned to the king, and was consulted by him as to the selection of a person to repeat the experiment, Heliodorus replied from the fulness of his heart, " If thou hast any enemy or traitor, send him thither, and thou shalt receive him well scourged, if he escape with his life; for in that place, no doubt, there is an especial power of God; for he that dwelleth in heaven hath his eye on that place, and defendeth it, and he beateth and destroyeth them that come to hurt it." *

Simon, persevering in his intrigues against Onias, countenanced the suspicion that had been propagated of his having arranged the stratagem by which Heliodorus had been driven from the temple, and denounced him as a traitor. Onias, seeing that the royal governor Apollonius espoused hotly the cause of Simon, one of whose faction had even gone to the length of committing murders, determined to represent the state of things in person to the king, " not to be an accuser of his countrymen, but seeking the good of all, both public and private." †   Seleucus was by this time dead;

---

* 2 Mac. iii. 23 – 40.

† iv. 1 – 6. — From ii. 20, in which no reigns except those of Antiochus Epiphanes and Antiochus Eupator are mentioned as being included in Ja-

Antiochus Epiphanes had succeeded; and Onias found the royal ear closed against him by the intrigues of his own brother Jason, who was aspiring to supplant him in the office of high-priest, and who, by large pecuniary subsidies, accomplished the object of his ambition.*

Jason's policy was to abolish the peculiarities of his nation, and amalgamate them with their Syro-Greek masters. To this end he set up a gymnasium within Jerusalem; he arranged with the king to have its inhabitants legally styled *Antiochians*, and he imposed on them a Greek fashion of dress. The priests themselves "had no courage to serve any more at the altar," but scandalously addicted themselves to Greek customs, to the great displeasure of Jehovah, who in due time punished them by the instrumentality of those "unto whom they desired to be like in all things." † On the occurrence of certain games kept every fifth year in honor of Hercules at Tyre, and at this time attended by the king, Jason sent a con-

---

son's history, Bertholdt argues ("Einleitung," Th. III. s. 1066) that the abridgment from that work must be considered as beginning with the fourth chapter, and that the third, relating to the time of Seleucus, must be supposed to be derived from some other written source, or from oral traditions. But the reasoning is inconclusive, for the description of Jason's work in ii. 19 - 23 by no means excludes the supposition of its having covered more ground than that of the two reigns specified. And Eichhorn, by an inversion of the argument, infers that Jason's history comprehended the four reigns, from the fact that what is here called an abridgment of his work actually has that extent. ("Einleitung in die Apok. Schrift.," s. 259.)

* 2 Mac. iv. 7, 8.

† iv. 9 - 17. — With 9, comp. 1 Mac. i. 14, 15. — "John, the father of Eupolemus, who went ambassador to Rome," &c. (11). Here an embassy to Rome, headed by John, is said to have accomplished a certain object, subsequently frustrated by Jason, who became high-priest in or about the year 173 B. C. But in a passage of the other history, where the son of this John is said to have been sent ambassador to Rome twelve years later, the Romans appear to be spoken of as a people with whom the Jews had up to that time had no relations (1 Mac. viii. 1 - 16).

tribution of three hundred drachms of silver, which he directed to be expended in sacrifices to the pagan god, though the bearers diverted it to another use.*

Antiochus, being informed by the ambassador whom he had sent into Egypt to attend the coronation of Ptolemy Philometor, that his friendly professions were distrusted by the governors of that kingdom, went to Joppa to inspect its defences, and on his return thence visited Jerusalem, where he was magnificently entertained. Notwithstanding this, when, three years afterwards, Jason sent Menelaus, brother of that Simon who had occasioned the distractions in the time of Onias, " to bear the money unto the king, and to put him in mind of certain necessary matters," Menelaus, by his politic address, and by the promise of a higher price, in his turn obtained the high-priesthood, and coming back to Judea, " with the fury of a cruel tyrant, and the rage of a savage beast," Jason " was compelled to flee into the country of the Ammonites." † Menelaus, failing to execute his extravagant promise of money, was summoned to present himself, with the officer to whom it should have been paid, before the king, who, being just then called away hastily to suppress an insurrection which had broken out in Asia Minor, the profligate high-priest took the opportunity to bribe Andronicus, who was left in charge of the government in the king's absence, with " certain vessels of gold " stolen by him out of the temple, while he raised money by selling others in the markets of Tyre and the neighbouring cities. Onias, the deposed high-priest, charged him with the theft, and then retired, for fear of his vengeance, into a sanctuary, from which, at the instance of Menelaus, Andro-

---

* 2 Mac. iv. 18 – 20.   † iv. 21 – 26.

nicus, by false oaths, persuaded him to emerge, and immediately put him to death. The outrage excited the warmest indignation, not only on the part of Jews, but of "many also of other nations." Even Antiochus, when informed of it, "was heartily sorry, and moved to pity, and wept, because of the sober and modest behaviour of him that was dead"; and whether really influenced by this act, or using it as a popular pretence, "forthwith he took away Andronicus his purple, and rent off his clothes, and, leading him through the whole city unto that very place where he had committed impiety against Onias, there slew he the cursed murderer." *

Lysimachus, brother of Menelaus, clothed with his authority during his absence from the city, was, with his privity, guilty of such thefts and sacrileges as greatly incensed the people, who threatened him with violence. Lysimachus armed against them a force of three thousand men, "one Auranus being the leader, a man far gone in years, and no less in folly." An outbreak being provoked by their rashness, Lysimachus was "killed beside the treasury" and his followers were put to flight. Menelaus, being convicted before the king at Tyre for his agency in these transactions, with difficulty averted his displeasure, by the mediation of one Ptolemy, a favorite courtier, whom he bribed; and the royal vengeance fell, instead, upon them "that followed the matter for the city, and for the people, and for the holy vessels." "Those poor men, who, if they had told their cause, yea, before the Scythians, should have been judged innocent, them he condemned to death." The people of Tyre, indignant at the injustice, gave them honorable burial; but, "through the covetousness of them that were in pow-

* 2 Mac. iv. 27 – 38.

er, Menelaus remained still in authority, increasing in malice, and being a great traitor to the citizens." *

The fifth, sixth, and seventh chapters relate to the same period of time as the first two chapters of the First Book of the Maccabees. Like that passage, they describe the oppressive proceedings of Antiochus Epiphanes, previous to the organized resistance of Judas the Maccabee and his friends; but the record is in different language, and for the most part with a specification of different incidents, so as to afford no indication that either book was in the hands of the author of the other when he wrote.

According to the account now before us, while Antiochus was preparing for a second expedition to Egypt, there were, for nearly forty days, apparitions at Jerusalem of embattled horsemen, splendidly armed, contending in the air. A false rumor being spread of the death of the king, Jason, the lately deposed high-priest, at the head of a thousand men, assembled and took the city, drove Menelaus into the citadel, and put to death many of the inhabitants. He was at length, however, compelled again to have recourse to a flight into the country of the Ammonites, where he was no longer favorably received, and, becoming a fugitive from one country to another, he at last died at Lacedæmon, whither he had retired, "thinking there to find succour by reason of his kindred." †

The king, hearing of the disturbance at Jerusalem, and regarding or pretending to regard it as a national revolt, marched from Egypt in high displeasure, and,.

---

* 2 Mac. iv. 39 – 50. — " Ptolemee, the son of Dorymenes " (45); comp. 1 Mac. iii. 38.

† v. 1 – 10 ; comp. 1 Mac. i. 16 – 19, which passage, instead of the movement of Jason, relates the successes of Antiochus during the same time in Egypt.

having taken the city, commanded an indiscriminate massacre, without regard to sex or age; "and there were destroyed, within the space of three whole days, fourscore thousand, whereof forty thousand were slain in the conflict; and no fewer sold than slain." Guided by the perfidious high-priest Menelaus, Antiochus next "presumed to go into the most holy temple of all the world," where he seized "the holy vessels with polluted hands," and gave away "the things that were dedicated by other kings to the augmentation, and glory, and honor of the place," Jehovah granting him impunity, and not dealing with him as with Heliodorus, because "the Lord was angry for a while for the sins of them that dwelt in the city," though he designed in due time to be reconciled to them, and to "set up with all glory" the place of their solemnities. With a spoil from the temple amounting to "a thousand and eight hundred talents," and so demented with pride that he thought he could "make the land navigable, and the sea passable by foot," Antiochus departed for his capital, leaving Menelaus and others of his creatures in Judea, "to vex the nation" in his stead. One of them, whom he had placed in command of "an army of two-and-twenty thousand, commanding him to slay all those that were in their best age, and to sell the women and the younger sort," came to Jerusalem with friendly professions, and, conducting himself peaceably till the Sabbath, took advantage of the religious celebration of that day, and "slew great numbers. But Judas Maccabeus, with nine others, or thereabout, withdrew himself into the wilderness, and lived in the mountains after the manner of beasts, with his company, who fed on herbs continually, lest they should be partakers of the pollution." *

* 2 Mac. v. 11 - 27; comp. 1 Mac. i. 20 - ii. 70, in which passage the

Persevering in his purpose " to compel the Jews to depart from the laws of their fathers, and not to live after the laws of God," Antiochus sent an officer with orders " to pollute the temple in Jerusalem, and to call it the temple of Jupiter Olympius, and that in Gari-zim, of Jupiter the Defender of Strangers." The holy precincts became a scene of the grossest riot and de-bauchery. The altar was covered with objects of prof-anation. It was punishable " for a man to keep Sab-bath-days, or ancient feasts, or to profess himself at all to be a Jew." In Judea and in the provinces Jews were compelled to eat, on each monthly return of the king's birthday, of the victims of pagan sacrifices, to walk in idolatrous processions, and, under pain of death, to conform themselves to heathen customs.* Two women, for circumcising their children, were, with their infants, thrown headlong from the walls. A party who had retired into caves, to keep the Sabbath in secret, being discovered, were burned to death, cru-elties, the recital of which, the writer takes occasion to remark, should not discourage the reader, but rath-er lead him to recognize the just and merciful admin-istration of Jehovah, who chastens only that he may restore.† And then he goes on to describe at length the heroic conduct of " Eleazar, one of the principal scribes, an aged man, and of a well-favored counte-nance," who, scorning to resort to an artifice for safe-ty, was scourged to death for refusing to eat swine's flesh, and who continued to the last exhorting the

---

account (in chap. i.) of the excesses of Antiochus is more full, and ap-parently from a writer better informed ; in the narrative in the second book, we read nothing of Mattathias, father of the Maccabean brothers (1 Mac. ii. 1 - 5); its account of the massacre at Jerusalem on the Sabbath (2 Mac. v. 25 - 27) is probably another version of those in 1 Mac. i. 29 - 32, ii. 31 - 38, blended together. — With v. 24, comp. 1 Mac. i. 29, 30, iii. 10.

* 2 Mac. vi. 1 - 9. † vi. 10 - 17.

by-standers to practise a similar constancy; and of a
mother and her seven sons, who, "not accepting deliverance," were for the same cause successively murdered before each other's eyes with still more cruel
tortures, each of the youths, as his turn came, sustained in his sufferings by the courageous exhortations
of their mother, and each, on his part, sustaining those
who were to follow by his courageous example, till, full
of pride and of gratitude for the piety of her offspring,
"last of all, after the sons, the mother died." *

By private communications with his friends in the
several towns, Judas the Maccabee collected a force of
some six thousand faithful men, with whom, having
first devoutly "called upon the Lord," and frequently
taking advantage of the night for his enterprises, "he
came at unawares, and burned up towns and cities,
and got into his hands the most commodious places,
and overcame and put to flight no small number of his
enemies." † Concerned at the tidings of Judas's progress, the governor of Jerusalem applied for succour
to Ptolemy, his immediate superior, who accordingly
despatched Nicanor and Gorgias, with twenty thousand men, "to root out the whole generation of the
Jews." Nicanor flattered himself with the hope of
taking Jewish prisoners in such numbers, that, being
sold for slaves, they would pay a tribute of two thousand talents, due from his sovereign to the Romans,
and he accordingly sent notices to the seaports that he

---

* 2 Mac. vi. 18 – vii. 42. — To the accounts of martyrdoms in these two
chapters (which are in a style of genuine pathos) there is nothing corresponding in the First Book. Scattered through them are various recognitions of
a belief in a future state at the age of the history, or at least of its author.
Comp. vii. 9, 11, 14, 23, 36.

† viii. 1 – 7; comp. 1 Mac. iii. 1 – 9, which in different language also
makes a general statement of the success of Judas's operations; to 1 Mac.
iii. 10 – 37 there is nothing in this book which corresponds.

should presently have slaves to sell at the rate of ninety for a talent.

The alarm of Nicanor's approach, conveyed to the camp of Judas, caused many to desert his standard and secrete themselves, while others sold the remnants of their property and betook themselves to prayer. Undismayed, he addressed himself to communicate his own courage to his diminished band of six thousand followers. He reminded them of the barbarous oppression from which they were seeking redress; of the power of the great God, who would fight on their side; of the deliverance that had been wrought for them when a hundred and eighty-five thousand Assyrian invaders perished in a night; and how at Babylon eight thousand Jews, embarrassed rather than aided by four thousand " perplexed " Macedonians, had destroyed a force of " an hundred and twenty thousand, because of the help that they had from Heaven." Dividing his force into four columns of equal numbers, led respectively by himself and three of his brothers, he advanced upon Nicanor; " and, by the help of the Almighty, they slew above nine thousand of their enemies, and wounded and maimed the most part of Nicanor's host, and so put all to flight, and took their money that came to buy them, and pursued them far."

The pursuit was not, however, pushed as it would otherwise have been, because the battle was fought on the day before the Sabbath, which they desired to keep with holy ceremony, " yielding exceeding praise and thanks to the Lord, who had preserved them unto that day, which was the beginning of mercy distilling upon them. And after the Sabbath, when they had given part of the spoils to the maimed, and the widows and orphans, the residue they divided among them-

17 *

selves and their servants." Then they joined in supplication to "the merciful Lord to be reconciled with
his servants for ever."* The defeat of other commanders, Timotheus and Bacchides, accompanied by
a great slaughter of their army, the conquest of
strongholds, and the capture of rich booty, and followed by the death of Philarches and Callisthenes,
two notorious enemies of the Jewish race, and the dis-
graceful flight of Nicanor to Antioch, alone and in
disguise, crowned for Judas the triumphs of this campaign.†

King Antiochus, driven by the inhabitants from the
Persian Persepolis, which he had attempted to hold,
and to plunder its temple, came to Ecbatana, where
"news was brought him what had happened unto Nicanor and Timotheus." Maddened with passions exasperated by his own recent mortification, he bade his
charioteer drive him with all haste to Jerusalem, that
he might "make it a common burying-place of the
Jews ; but the Lord God Almighty, the God of Israel,
smote him with an incurable and invisible plague ;
for, as soon as he had spoken these words, a pain of
the bowels that was remediless came upon him, and
sore torments of the inner parts." For a while he
abated nothing of his plans of vengeance, though the

---

* 2 Mac. viii. 8 - 29 ; comp. 1 Mac. iii. 38 - iv. 35, where different incidents of this war are related, and Gorgias and Lysias, not Nicanor, are
represented as the commanders actively engaged. — " Ptolemeus, the governor of Celosyria and Phenice, ... choosing Nicanor, ... sent
him with no fewer than twenty thousand, ... and with him he joined
also Gorgias " (2 Mac. viii. 8, 9) ; " Lysias chose Ptolemee the son of
Dorymenes, and Nicanor, and Gorgias, ... and with them he sent
forty thousand footmen, and seven thousand horsemen " (1 Mac. iii. 38,
39). — With 18, comp. Ps. xx. 7. — " He appointed Eleazar to read the
holy book " (23) ; comp. 1 Mac. iii. 48.

† viii. 30 - 36 ; comp. 1 Mac. v., where a much more detailed account is
given of operations against Timotheus during the life of Antiochus Epiphanes.

distressing and noisome disease, aggravated by "a sore fall" from his chariot, was rapidly approaching its fatal close. At length, becoming intolerable to himself as well as to his attendants, his proud spirit was subdued. He professed his submission to the Divine power, and vowed that he would give liberty to the holy city, make its inhabitants "equals with the citizens of Athens," restore to the temple its rifled treasures, enrich it with new gifts, and defray the cost of its sacrifices; that he would even "become a Jew himself, and go through all the world that was inhabited and declare the power of God. But for all this his pains would not cease." As a last act he wrote a flattering letter to the Jews, expressing his anxiety for their welfare, thanking them for their past good-will, and bespeaking in return for the benefits he had rendered them their loyal affection for his son and successor. And "thus the murderer and blasphemer, having suffered most grievously, as he entreated other men, so died he a miserable death in a strange country in the mountains." Philip, his foster-brother, to whom was committed the charge of his body, "fearing the son of Antiochus," or rather, probably, fearing Lysias, who now had the young prince under his control, "went into Egypt to Ptolemeus Philometor." *

It was after the death of Antiochus, according to the representation here made, that "Maccabeus and his company, the Lord guiding them, recovered the temple and the city," purified the sacred precincts from the pollutions of the heathen, consecrated them anew

---

* 2 Mac. ix. 1-29; comp. i. 13-17, 1 Mac. vi. 1-16, passages in which accounts are given of the death of Antiochus, differing radically both from this and from each other.

with sacrifices, prayers, and the ritual of the Feast of
Tabernacles, and instituted the Feast of Dedication to
commemorate those important transactions.*

Antiochus Eupator, succeeding to his father's throne,
"set one Lysias over the affairs of his realm, and appointed him chief governor of Celosyria and Phenice."
Ptolemy Macro, who had formerly commanded for the
king of Egypt in Cyprus, and who, by betraying it to
Antiochus Epiphanes, had established himself in the
favor of that prince, was thus superseded in his government, and, stung with the insults that followed
upon his downfall, soon after terminated his life by
poison.　The lenity which had of late been practised
by Ptolemy towards the Jews had been matter of reproach against him, and other counsels now prevailed.
"When Gorgias was governor of the holds, he hired
soldiers and nourished war continually with the Jews."
Some posts on the southern border, occupied by Idumeans, having given especial annoyance, Judas resolved to assault them, which he did with success, after
having, with his followers, "made supplication," "and
killed no fewer than twenty thousand," giving the enemy no quarter.　A force of nine thousand having
found a refuge in two strong fortresses, Judas left his
brother to besiege them, while he should repair to
other places more in need of his presence.　Some of
Simon's followers proving treacherous, and accepting a
bribe to permit a portion of the beleaguered party to
escape, Judas, having instituted a proper investigation,
"slew those that were found traitors, and immediately
took the two castles, and, having good success with his

---

* 2 Mac. x. 1–9; comp. 1 Mac. iv. 36–59, where these proceedings are
related to have been had previously to the death of Antiochus (comp. 1 Mac.
vi. 5–16).　With 2 Mac. x. 3, 4, comp. i. 20–29.

weapons in all things he took in hand, he slew in the
two holds more than twenty thousand." *

Timotheus, whom the Jews had formerly defeated,
again invaded their country with " a great multitude
of foreign forces, and horses out of Asia not a few."
After solemn penitential prayer at the temple, Judas
drew his troops out of the city to meet them. The
battle began at sunrise, the one side confiding in their
own virtue and in God, the other in a brutal fury.
When it was at its height, " there appeared unto the
enemies from heaven five comely men upon horses,
with bridles of gold, and two of them led the Jews,
and took Maccabeus betwixt them, and covered him
on every side with their weapons, and kept him safe,
but shot arrows and lightnings against the enemies,"
who were consequently defeated, with the loss " of
footmen twenty thousand and five hundred, and six
hundred horsemen." Timotheus " fled into a very
strong hold, called Gazara," where the Jews besieged
him four days. On the fifth, twenty young men, in-
furiated by the insolent language of his soldiers, by a
desperate onset cleared a part of the wall of its de-
fenders. " Others, likewise ascending after them, while
they were busied with them that were within, burned
the towers, and, kindling fires, burned the blasphemers alive ; and others broke open the gates, and, having received in the rest of the army, took the city."
Timotheus, dragged from a hiding-place, was put to
death, with his brother, and another person, who, for
what reason we know not, was of note enough to be

---

* 2 Mac. x. 10 - 23. — " He set *one* Lysias over the affairs of his realm "
(11) ; but according to the other account Lysias had been the principal
mover in public affairs during the preceding reign ; comp. 1 Mac. iii. 32,
38, iv. 28, 35. — " Ptolemeus, that was called Macron " (12) ; apparently
the person before mentioned in iv. 45, viii. 8. — With 15 - 17, comp. 1
Mac. v. 3 - 5, and with 19, comp. 1 Mac. v. 55, 56.

named in the history.   And the Jews, in acknowledgment of their victory, " praised the Lord with psalms
and thanksgiving." *

Provoked by these disasters, Lysias, the regent for
the young king, himself took the field, with a force of
eighty thousand infantry, besides cavalry and eighty
elephants.   Designing to occupy Jerusalem, so as " to
make a gain of the temple, ... and to set the
high-priesthood to sale every year," he laid siege to
Bethsura, described in this place as " a strong town,
but distant from Jerusalem about five furlongs."   The
people, struck at first with consternation and grief,
were encouraged by the exhortations of Judas, and
when " at Jerusalem there appeared before them on
horseback one in white clothing, shaking his armour
of gold, then they praised the merciful God all together, and took heart, insomuch that they were ready, not
only to fight with men, but with most cruel beasts,
and to pierce through walls of iron ; . . . . . and giving a charge upon their enemies like lions, they slew
eleven thousand footmen and sixteen hundred horsemen, and put all the other to flight."   Whereupon
Lysias, reflecting whàt ill-fortune he had had against
the Jews, and how potently God helped them, determined to persuade the king to make peace with them
on reasonable terms.   " Maccabeus consented to àll
that Lysias desired, being careful of the common
good."   With the approbation of " Quintus Memmius
and Titus Manlius, ambassadors of the Romans," who,
it appears, were consulted (as they claimed to be still
further should further measures be proposed), it was
agreed that the Jews should have possession of their

---

* 2 Mac. x. 24 - 38. — " Timotheus, whom the Jews had overcome before " (24) ; comp. 1 Mac. v. 6 - 43 ; 2 Mac. viii. 30 - 32.

temple, and "live according to the customs of their forefathers." And "when these covenants were made, Lysias went unto the king, and the Jews were about their husbandry." *

Several of the Syrian governors, neglecting the provisions of the recent treaty, continued to give disturbance to the Jews. Two hundred persons, men, women, and children, having been treacherously drowned at Joppa from boats into which they had been courteously invited, Judas placed himself at the head of a party, "and burned the haven by night, and set the boats on fire, and those that fled thither he slew." Leaving the inhabitants in alarm lest he should return for yet more terrible vengeance, he proceeded to inflict a similar punishment upon the Jamnites, who, he heard, were meditating a similar crime; and "the light of the fire was seen at Jerusalem, two hundred and forty furlongs off." Marching against Timotheus, he fell in with five thousand Arabians, accompanied by five hundred horsemen; and, a battle ensuing, the Arabians were defeated, and sued for peace, which was granted them on generous terms. †

---

* 2 Mac. xi. 1 - xii. 1. — " Bethsura, ... distant from Jerusalem about five furlongs " (5) ; the Bethsura at which in the earlier book a battle is related to have taken place between Lysias and Judas, in the lifetime of Antiochus Epiphanes, appears to have been on the southern border of the Holy Land (comp. 1 Mac. iv. 29, vi. 31). — " This hundred and eight and fortieth year " (38) ; these words are conclusive as to the spuriousness of the letter. No Roman ambassadors would have dated by the era of the Seleucidæ.

† xii. 2 - 12 — Bertholdt, adopting a suggestion of Grotius (" Hug. Grot. Annott." ad loc. 2 Mac. xii. 2), maintains the opinion that the abridgment from the work of Jason ends with the close of the eleventh chapter. (" Einleitung," Th. III. ss. 1063 - 1070.) He argues this from the continuation of the history of Timotheus (xii. 2 et seq.), understood by him to be the same person whose death had been already related (x. 37, viii. 30, 32, 1 Mac. vi. 37), and from characteristic differences in the compositions respectively, such as the more frequent interspersing of chronological references in the latter part, and, on the other hand, the absence from it of those moral reflections which abound in the other. And, pursuing this idea

The next exploit of Judas was at a city called Caspis, " inhabited by people of various countries," which
he took by assault; and his followers, provoked by irri-
tating language with which they had been defied,
" made unspeakable slaughters, insomuch that a lake
two furlongs broad, near adjoining thereto, being filled
full, was seen running with blood." Having proceeded to a distance of nearly a hundred miles in fruitless
pursuit of Timotheus, a party of them fell upon a garrison of ten thousand men whom that commander had
left behind, and put them to the sword. At length
Judas overtook him and his army of an hundred and
twenty thousand infantry, and twenty-five hundred
horse. Informed of the approach of the Jewish force,
" he sent the women and children, and the other bag-
gage, unto a fortress called Carnion," where they might
await in security the issue of the approaching battle.
At the first sight of the van of Judas's army, the
enemy were seized with consternation, turned their
weapons on one another, and fled in every direction.
Thirty thousand of them fell that day. Timotheus,
himself taken prisoner, was released, in consideration
of his promise to set at liberty his own Jewish captives. At the temple of Atargatis, at Carnion, Judas
put to death twenty-five thousand persons.*

---

as to the earlier part of the book, he proposes the opinion, that the abridgment from Jason's treatise began with the fourth chapter, thus making one
half of the book due to another source. For the events recorded in the third
chapter, immediately after the prologue, took place in the reign of Seleucus
Philopator, while the description of Jason's work does not inform us that he
wrote of any transactions earlier than the time of Antiochus Epiphanes (ii.
19 – 23), and the story in the third chapter has so much of a mythical character, as to make it probable that it was derived from oral tradition. But
see above, p 189, note †.

* 2 Mac. xii. 13 – 26. — " The name of it was Caspis " (13); " thence
went he and took Casphon " (1 Mac. v. 36). — " The Jews that are called
Tubieni " (17) ; " our brethren that were in the places of Toby " (1 Mac.
v. 13 ; comp. Judg. xi. 3, 5). — " Maccabeus marched forth to Carnion,

Proceeding from Carnion to Ephron, "a strong city wherein Lysias abode, and a great multitude of divers nations," the Jews "won the city, and slew twenty and five thousand of them that were within." At "Scythopolis, which lieth six hundred furlongs from Jerusalem," being informed by the Jewish inhabitants that they had been treated with sympathy and kindness, they offered no violence, but, expressing their gratitude for the good treatment extended to their compatriots, and their hope of its continuance, they returned to Jerusalem, to celebrate the Feast of Pentecost.*

That duty performed, they marched to meet Gorgias, who was advancing from Idumea with the inconsiderable force of three thousand foot, and four hundred cavalry. In the action which followed, though the Jews suffered a small loss, the advantage, after their commander had prayed, and "sung psalms with a loud voice," was on their side, and the adverse leader narrowly escaped capture. Having kept the Sabbath in a neighbouring city, they returned to the field of battle to bury their dead, when "under the coats of every one that was slain they found things consecrated to the idols of the Jamnites; . . . . . then every man saw that this was the cause wherefore they were slain." The people "betook themselves unto prayer . . . . . that the sin committed might wholly be put out of remembrance"; and "that noble Judas,"

---

and to the temple of Atargatis," &c. (26) ; "the heathen . . . . . fled unto the temple that was at Carnaim ; but they took the city, and burned the temple with all that were therein " (1 Mac. v. 43, 44). In the passages from which these verses are respectively taken, the writers seem to have had in view the same succession of events ; — the more, as both immediately go on to relate the capture of Ephron, and the conflicts with Gorgias. But in the previous book all these transactions are represented as having occurred before the death of Antiochus Epiphanes.

* 2 Mac. xii. 27 – 31.

making a collection among his troops of a sum of
money, "sent it to Jerusalem to offer a sin-offering,"
and profited by the occasion to exhort his people " to
keep themselves from sin, forsomuch as they saw before their eyes the things that came to pass for the
sins of those that were slain." *

The young king now undertook a more formidable
invasion of Judea, attended by "Lysias his protector,
and ruler of his affairs, having either of them a Grecian power of footmen an hundred and ten thousand,
and horsemen five thousand and three hundred, and
elephants two-and-twenty, and three hundred chariots
armed with hooks." The pseudo-high-priest, Menelaus,
who had been the occasion of so much disturbance in
the preceding reign, was also in his train; but some
criminal practices of his having been brought to light
through the agency of Lysias, he was by the royal
command smothered in a heap of ashes fifty cubits
high; "for, insomuch as he had committed many sins
about the altar, whose fire and ashes were holy, he received his death in ashes."

Apprised of the sanguinary intentions of the king
and his advisers, Judas summoned the people to "call
upon the Lord night and day" for his protection.
They accordingly "besought the merciful Lord with
weeping and fasting, and lying flat upon the ground
three days long." Having, in consultation with the
elders, "determined, before the king's host should enter into Judea, and get the city, to go forth and try

---

* 2 Mac. xii. 32 – 45. — "In that he was mindful of the resurrection (for
if he had not hoped that they that were slain should have risen again, it had
been superfluous and vain to pray for the dead), and also in that he perceived
that there was great favor laid up for those that died godly (it was an holy
and good thought)" (43 – 45); — an interesting indication of a state of
opinion existing in the writer's time, and, according to him, in the earlier
time of which he records the history.

the matter in fight by the help of the Lord," and having "committed all to the Creator of the world, and exhorted his soldiers to fight manfully, even unto death, for the laws, the temple, the city, the country, and the commonwealth, he camped by Modin," his native city. Here, "with the most valiant and choice young men, he went into the king's tent by night, and slew in the camp about four thousand men, and the chiefest of the elephants, with all that were upon him." *

"When the king had taken a taste of the manliness of the Jews, he went about to take the holds by policy, and marched towards Bethsura, which was a stronghold of the Jews; but he was put to flight, failed, and lost of his men," though subsequently, by means of information from a treacherous agent in the Jewish camp, who was detected and imprisoned, he was enabled to make a composition with the garrison. Venturing on another battle with Judas, he was worsted. At this juncture, hearing that his presence was rendered necessary at Antioch by the infidelity of the officer left in command there, he hastened to make a peace. He "submitted himself, and sware to all

---

* 2 Mac. xiii. 1 – 17. — "In the hundred forty and ninth year" (1); "in the hundred and fiftieth year" (1 Mac. vi. 20). Both books date events by the era of the Seleucidæ, or *of Contracts*, beginning at the foundation of the Greek-Syrian kingdom by Seleucus Nicator, 312 B. C. But the Second Book gives to the same events a date one year earlier. This has been generally regarded as an essential discrepance. But, according to Bertholdt ("Einleitung," Th. III. a. 1079), such a difference of chronological computation existed among the ancients, some counting from a year earlier than others, in consequence of an uncertainty, to this extent, respecting the time of the establishment of the Syrian empire, or rather on the question whether it was to be regarded as coincident with Nicator's first or second capture of Babylon. — "An hundred and ten thousand," &c. (2); comp. 1 Mac. vi. 30. — In the passage in the earlier book relating to this expedition, there is nothing parallel to the account of the death of Menelaus, or of the night attack on the Syrian camp (3 – 17).

equal conditions, agreed with them, and offered sacrifice, honored the temple, and dealt kindly with the
place, and accepted well of Maccabeus, made him
principal governor from Ptolemais unto the Gerrhe-
nians." The citizens of Ptolemais, dissatisfied with
the terms of the pacification, were with difficulty reconciled by the representations of Lysias.*

After the successful struggle of Demetrius Soter for
the crown of Syria, which in due time became known
to Judas, the apostate high-priest Alcimus came to
that prince with presents, and, being consulted by him
respecting the present state and dispositions of the
Jews, declared himself compelled by duty to his nation to say that the Assidean party among them was
bent on sedition and disturbance, and that, as long as
Judas lived, it was " not possible that the state should
be quiet." Other malicious representations to the
same effect confirmed the king's displeasure ; " and
forthwith calling Nicanor, who had been master of the
elephants, and making him governor over Judea, he
sent him forth, commanding him to slay Judas, and to
scatter them that were with him, and to make Alcimus high-priest of the great temple." Men, lately fugitives from Judea, flocked to his standard ; the Jews,
alarmed by the formidable force with which he was
approaching, proceeded to renew their courage by
prayer ; and Nicanor, distrusting the prudence of a
battle with such men, though he had obtained some
partial success against Simon, preferred to attempt a
settlement by negotiation. Judas, with the approbation of his followers, accepted his proposal for a con-

---

* 2 Mac. xiii. 18 – 26. — These transactions are related with much more
detail in 1 Mac. vi. 30 – 63. Grotius (" Annott." ad xiii. 1) thinks that this
chapter goes over the same ground as the two preceding, with additions
and omissions.

ference, taking due precautions at the same time against any treachery which might be meditated. In the sequel Nicanor dismissed his numerous followers, established himself peaceably at Jerusalem, and formed an intimate friendship with Judas, who, at his solicitation, "married, was quiet, and took part of this life." *

Exasperated at this state of things, so different from what was desirable for the objects of his own ambition, Alcimus charged Nicanor to the king with being "not well affected towards the state"; and Demetrius, "in a rage," expressed his displeasure at the treaty, and directed that Judas should be sent "prisoner in all haste unto Antioch." The unwonted reserve and austerity of Nicanor, who, however mortified by this turn of affairs, perceived that "there was no dealing against the king," escaped not the notice of Judas; and, with a company of followers, he withdrew from Jerusalem. Nicanor came to the temple, and called upon the priests there to surrender him, threatening with an oath, that, if it were not done, the temple and altar should be levelled with the ground, and a temple to Bacchus erected in their place. The priests resorted to prayer as their only protection. Nicanor, in a frenzy of vengeance, sent five hundred soldiers to seize "one Razis, one of the elders of Jerusalem, a lover of his countrymen, and a man of very good report, who for his kindness was called a father of the Jews."

---

* 2 Mac. xiv. 1-25; compare 1 Mac. vii. 1-29, where are related (8-25) transactions previous to the expedition of Nicanor, and the purposes of that courtier are differently represented (26-29) as having been treacherous from the beginning. — "After three years" (1) Judas was informed of an event which had taken place after the expiration of two years (comp. xiii. 1 with xiv. 4). — "The haven of Tripolis" (1); "a city of the sea-coast" (1 Mac. vii. 1). — "The heathen that had fled out of Judea from Judas" (14); comp. 1 Mac. ii. 44.

18 *

He, "choosing rather to die manfully, than to come
into the hands of the wicked, to be abused otherwise
than beseemed his noble birth," perished horribly by
his own hand, first piercing himself with his sword,
then casting himself from a wall, then, from the top
of a steep rock, " calling upon the Lord of life and
spirit to restore him " the parts of his body, which,
while life enough remained, he threw about upon the
crowd.*

Following Judas to " the strong places about Samaria," Nicanor prepared to attack him there on the Sabbath day, replying with insolent pride to the remonstrances of the Jews, whom he had compelled to serve
in his army, against such a desecration of the day.
The Jewish leader, having " ever sure confidence that
the Lord would help him," addressed his followers,
" comforting them out of the Law and the prophets,"
reminding them of " the falsehood of the heathen, and
the breach of oaths," and appealing to past deliver-
ances as so many pledges of similar manifestations of
Divine love in future.   " Thus he armed every one of
them, not so much with defence of shields and spears,
as with comfortable and good words."   He further related to them a dream, in which he had seen the venerable high-priest Onias praying for the people, and
his prayer answered by an apparition of the prophet
Jeremiah, who " gave to Judas a sword of gold, and,
in giving it, spake thus : ' Take this holy sword, a gift
from God, with the which thou shalt wound the adversaries.' "   Thus excited, and anxious even more for
the safety of the temple than for that of their own
families and friends, who on their part were thinking
less of themselves than of what was passing in the

---

* 2 Mac. xiv. 26 – 46 ; comp. 1 Mac. vii. 30 – 38.

field where the battle of Israel was to be fought, the
followers of Judas were impatient for the coming conflict. The armies at length, in complete preparation,
stood line opposed to line; Judas briefly appealed to
Jehovah for such a deliverance as had been wrought
in the time of Sennacherib; "then Nicanor and they
that were with him came forward with trumpets and
songs, but Judas and his company encountered the enemies with invocation and prayer." Victory declared
for the right. Nicanor fell, with thirty five thousand
of his troops. The conquerors shouted, and praised
their Almighty deliverer in their native tongue. By
Judas's command, the head, hand, and shoulder of Nicanor were cut off, and conveyed to Jerusalem to be
exposed at the temple, and his tongue was thrown "by
pieces" to the birds of prey. An annual festival was
appointed to be held, the day before the Feast of
Purim, in commemoration of this rescue, "and from
that time forth the Hebrews had the city in their
power."

"And here," concludes the writer, "will I make an
end. And if I have done well, and as is fitting the
story, it is that which I desired; but if slenderly and
meanly, it is that which I could attain unto. For as
it is hurtful to drink wine or water alone; and as wine
mingled with water is pleasant, and delighteth the
taste; even so speech finely framed delighteth the
ears of them that read the story. And here shall be
an end."*

---

* 2 Mac. xv. 1-39 (comp. 1 Mac. vii. 39-50). — "To celebrate the
thirteenth day of the twelfth month" (36; comp. 1 Mac. vii. 49). Josephus
says ("Antiq.," Lib. XII. cap. 10, § 5) that the commemoration continued
to be observed in his day. A festival of the same sort on a subsequent
occasion is related to have been instituted by Simon (1 Mac. xiii. 52); but
I do not know that there is any later record of its observance. Josephus
does not mention it. — "If I have done well," &c. (38); whether an acci-

The Third Book of the Maccabees demands but a passing notice, and this only on account of its being a specimen of a kind of composition much in favor with the Jews, and exhibited in other books which have obtained more credit and consideration than itself. It is contained in many of the manuscripts, and generally in the printed editions, of the Alexandrine or Septuagint collection; and there is extant of it a Syriac version, or rather paraphrase (for the resemblance is far from being exact in form, or even in matter), probably a production of the third century. It has no place in the Vulgate version, and never acquired authority in the Western Church. The internal evidence leaves no doubt that the book in Greek is an original work, and not a translation from the Hebrew or Chaldee. It is written in a rather inflated, but flowing and easy, Greek style. Its fashion of thought and representation belongs to the Alexandrine school; and both from that circumstance, and from the locality where the scene of the events related in it is laid, there can be little question that it was written by a Jew of Egypt. The first notice of it is believed to be found in the "Apostolical Canons"* (a work commonly ascribed to the end of the third century); after which time it is occasionally referred to by the Greek fathers. To how much earlier a period we are to ascribe its composition, is a question which there are no means to determine. There is no appearance that Josephus knew any thing of it.

The book has no historical value. It has been improperly termed a "Book of the Maccabees," as the period of which it professes to treat was prior to the

---

dental coincidence or not, this turn of phrase is the same as that in the last period but one of the Oration of Æschines on the Crown.

* Can. LXXXV. "Ss. Patr. Opp.," &c., edit. Cotelier, Tom. I. p. 453.

time when that name came into use, and to the men
who bore it. The story related in it is briefly as
follows.

Ptolemy Philopator, returning to Egypt from his
successful campaign against Antiochus the Great, took
Jerusalem in his way.* Here he presented an offering at the temple, and, struck by the magnificence
with which he saw himself there surrounded, determined that he would enter the Holy of Holies. Persisting in that purpose, notwithstanding the expostulations of the high-priest and the distress of the people, he was miraculously stunned, and stricken to the
ground.† He returned home breathing vengeance,
and resolved to wreak it on that portion of the people
which was most completely in his power. He accordingly issued an edict depriving the numerous Jews of
Alexandria of the great privileges which they had
hitherto enjoyed as equal citizens of that place, unless
they would violate their integrity by taking part in
the religious ceremonies observed in honor of Bacchus.‡

Some of the unfortunate Jews yielded. The greater
number refused. Incensed at their contumacy, the
king gave orders for all the Jews in Egypt, men,
women, and children, to be brought in chains to the
great hippodrome at Alexandria, where they remained
several days in the open air. The master of the king's
elephants was directed to intoxicate those animals,
that they might be more furious when let loose on the
devoted victims. On the appointed day Ptolemy took
his place in state, with his courtiers and the bloodthirsty multitudes of his people surrounding him.§

* See Vol. III. p. 167.   † 3 Mac. i. 1 – ii. 24.
‡ ii. 25 – iii. 30.   § iv. 1 – v. 51.

While his wretched countrymen were expecting their fate, Eleazar, an aged priest, offered a prayer for their deliverance.* No sooner had he finished it, than two angels descended from heaven, and, unseen by the Jews, but visible to the Egyptians and the elephants, lifted their majestic forms in the space between the parties. The terrible animals, frightened by the vision, turned back masterless upon the Egyptian troops and people, spreading wide carnage in their ranks.† The alarmed and conscience-stricken king gave orders that the Jews should be relieved from their chains, and that liberal supplies of provisions should be furnished to them. They kept the occasion as a high religious festival, and resolved that it should be so kept annually by their posterity; and before they separated, Ptolemy issued • in their favor a decree, commanding all his subjects, as they feared the displeasure of God, to refrain from doing them any injury. He also re- stored their confiscated property, and gave them per- mission to put to death any of their countrymen who, under his own command and threat, had been induced to violate their national law ; a privilege of which they availed themselves freely.‡

Inserted in the Latin translation by Rufinus, about the year 400, of the treatise of Josephus against Api- on, there is found a story so analogous to this, as to justify the conclusion that one was derived from the other, or that the two had a common source. It is as follows.§

"Ptolemy, surnamed Physcon, after the death of his brother Ptolemy Philometor, left Cyrene with the purpose of getting rid of Cleopatra and the late king's

---

* 3 Mac. vi. 1 – 15.   † vi. 16 – 21.
‡ vi. 22 – vii. 23.   § "Cont. Apion.," Lib. II. § 5.

sons, and establishing himself upon the throne; upon which Onias took command against him on Cleopatra's side, and in that emergency faithfully executed his trust. And God manifested his approbation of this loyalty. For when Ptolemy Physcon . . . . . had exposed all the Jews in the city, stripped and bound, with their wives and children, to the rage of drunken elephants, those animals, taking no notice of the intended victims, rushed upon the king's friends, of whom they killed many. After which there was seen by Ptolemy a terrible apparition, charging him to do that people no harm. And his favorite concubine, called by some Ithaca, by others Irene, interceding in their behalf, he granted her suit, and repented of his purpose. And with good reason the Jews of Alexandria celebrate that day on which they obtained from God this conspicuous deliverance."

The first two Books of the Maccabees, reckoned as one, are included in Origen's catalogue of Jewish canonical writings; * and the fact of their being comprehended in the Septuagint version determines their estimation among the Egyptian Jews. They also belonged to the Canon established by the Council of Carthage, in the year 397.†

In two instances, the Second Book of the Maccabees is probably referred to in the Epistle to the Hebrews.‡

The Third Book of the Maccabees suggests to the

---

* See Vol. I. p. 35.

† Ibid. p. 38.

‡ With Heb. xi. 35, comp. 2 Mac. vi. 19, 28, in all which texts the word τύμπανον and its derivative have a very peculiar use. With Heb. xi. 38, comp. 2 Mac. v. 27; also 1 Mac. i. 53, ii. 31. Perhaps in Heb. xi. 35, in the words " not accepting deliverance," there is an allusion to 2 Mac. vi. 30.

attentive reader the similar subjects, and the similar treatment of them, in the canonical books of Esther and Daniel.

The First and Second Books, in their tone of representation, bear a general similarity to older historical treatises, which have enjoyed a higher estimation. Like those earlier histories,• they relate marvellous events, and ascribe them to Divine interposition. In their materials they are both defective and redundant. The Second Book sometimes gives more than one account of the same transaction, and it sometimes contradicts itself in different statements. It bears a relation to the First Book much resembling that of the Books of Chronicles to those of Samuel and Kings; relating to periods and transactions partly the same and partly different; now confirming, more or less, the statements of the earlier authority, and now contradicting it; and tinged still more than the former with the character of legend and fiction. In a separate study, and in a comparison together, of the two Books of the Maccabees, I find much to bring into question their separate, and, still more, their joint, credibility. But I find nothing of the sort which does not equally, or more, affect the circumstantial credibility of the Books of Samuel, Kings, and Chronicles.

LECTURE LX.

THE BOOK OF JOB.

ARGUMENT OF THE BOOK. — PROSPERITY OF JOB. — JEHOVAH'S PERMIS-
SION TO SATAN TO AFFLICT HIM. — SATAN'S PROCEEDINGS THEREUPON,
AND JOB'S PIOUS SUBMISSION. — SATAN'S REPETITION OF THE AT-
TEMPT, WITH NO BETTER SUCCESS. — VISIT OF JOB'S THREE FRIENDS. —
COLLOQUY BETWEEN JOB AND THEM ON THE PRINCIPLES OF THE DIVINE
GOVERNMENT. — DISCOURSE OF ELIHU. — INTERVENTION OF JEHOVAH. —
HUMBLE DEPORTMENT OF JOB. — RESTORATION AND INCREASE OF HIS
PROSPERITY. — CHARACTER OF THE WORK. — DEFECTIVE EXECUTION
OF THE COMMON VERSION. — PROPER METHOD OF INTERPRETATION. —
ANALYSIS OF THE SEVERAL DISCOURSES. — OLD AND NEW TESTAMENT
REFERENCES TO JOB. — SUBJECT OF THE BOOK, THE PROBLEM OF PROVI-
DENCE AND RETRIBUTION. — THE AUTHOR INCOMPETENT TO ITS SOLU-
TION. — SCENE OF THE POEM. — QUESTION RESPECTING THE AUTHOR
AND HIS TIME. — UNSATISFACTORY ARGUMENTS FOR A MODERN ORIGIN.
— THE WRITER'S FAMILIARITY WITH ARABIA AND EGYPT. — ABSENCE
OF ALL REFERENCE TO JEWISH PECULIARITIES. — PROBABILITY THAT
MOSES WAS THE WRITER OF THE BOOK. — ALLEGED SPURIOUSNESS OF
SOME PARTS. — NEW TESTAMENT QUOTATION FROM IT.

I HAVE followed the track of the Jewish history
to the latest period to which it is brought down in the
Biblical writings, Canonical or Apocryphal. This has
been done, both because of the convenience of presenting in a continuous series the narrative contained
in the Hagiographical and Apocryphal books, and because, in ascertaining the dates of the composition
of other writings embraced in those collections, it is
sometimes necessary to refer to different periods of
that history, from the earliest to the latest. Proceeding to the consideration of other writings belonging

to those divisions of Scripture, I am to remark first on
the Book of Job, which I think was probably the
earliest of the works classed by the Jews under the
head of *Hagiographa*, and perhaps the earliest in the
Old Testament collection.

The *argument* of the book is briefly as follows: —

In the country of Uz, there lived a good man, named
Job. He was the richest of all the Eastern people,
having "seven thousand sheep, three thousand camels,
five hundred yoke of oxen, five hundred she-asses, and
a great number of servants." It was the practice in
his family for each son to make an entertainment on
his birthday, and invite his brothers and sisters; at
the conclusion of which their father was used to offer
a burnt-offering for each one, as an atonement for any
sins they might have committed.*

One day "the sons of God came to present themselves before Jehovah." Addressing one of them, who
is called Satan, or *the adversary*, God asked him whence
he came. He said, he came from wandering up and
down in the earth. Jehovah asked him, if he had
taken notice of that upright and good man, his servant
Job. Satan replied, that it was no wonder that Job
reverenced God, for God had prospered him in every
thing; but that his piety was not equal to the trial of
a reverse of fortune. Jehovah gave Satan permission
to make the experiment, with only the restriction that
Job's person must not be touched; and Satan took his
departure.†

Accordingly, one day when the family holiday was
celebrating at the house of the oldest son, a message
came to Job that a party of Sabeans had stolen all
his oxen and asses, and put to death all his servants

---

* Job i. 1 – 5.   † i. 6 – 12.

who were at work with them, except the messenger.
Scarcely were these tidings told, when further intelligence was brought, that his sheep and the shepherds
with them had been consumed by lightning.   Immediately came the further news, that three companies of
marauders from Chaldea had driven away his camels,
and killed their keepers.   And hardly had this been
heard, when there came the most melancholy information of all, that a whirlwind had prostrated the
house where all his children were assembled, and
buried them in its ruins.   "Naked came I forth from
my mother's womb, and naked shall I return thither,"
said the bereaved man, tearing his clothes, and throwing himself on the ground in the agony of his sorrow.
But his spirit of pious submission to the Divine will
was not yet broken.   "Jehovah gave," he added, "and
Jehovah hath taken away; blessed be the name of
Jehovah." *

There came another day when the sons of God
presented themselves before Jehovah; and Satan, addressed by Jehovah with the same question as before,
as to where he had been, returned the same reply.
Jehovah rejoined by repeating the second inquiry
made on the former occasion, namely, whether Satan
had observed the character of Job; adding, that the
trial which he had now been made to pass through
had but exhibited his goodness in a brighter light.
Satan answered, that a man might be patient of affliction which only fell upon his circumstances, however
heavily; but that if it should be brought nearer, and
made to touch his person, Job's language would be
different.   Jehovah bade Satan make the experiment,
without other restriction than that Job's life must be

---

* Job i. 13 – 22.

spared. The adversary went away, and smote Job
with a loathsome leprosy, covering his body "from
the sole of his foot to his crown; and he took a pot-
sherd to scrape himself withal, and sat down among
the ashes." Still he rebuked the petulance of his wife,
and said, "'Shall we receive good at the hand of God,
and shall we not receive evil?' In all this Job sinned
not with his lips." *

A severer trial of his equanimity than all the past
was, however, yet to come. Three friends of his, hearing of his misfortunes, "agreed to come to mourn
with him, and to comfort him." They approached him
with every suitable demonstration of affectionate sympathy, and "sat down with him upon the ground
seven days and seven nights, and none spake a word
to him." † At the end of the week, Job broke the
silence, and gave vent to his grief and disgust in language which excited their displeasure. One of them
replied; Job rejoined; another resumed the censure
against him; and a long colloquy took place on the
principles of the Divine government of men; the three
friends, in the same order in which they are first
named, each speaking three times at length, except
Zophar, who spoke but twice, and each being answered
in his turn by Job. The conference having proceeded
thus far, another person is introduced, to treat the
same high theme with great fulness, and with more
discretion than any of those with whom Job has hitherto disputed. Last of all, Jehovah interposes, and,
speaking out of a whirlwind, magnifies his attributes,
and shows how rash and vain a thing it is for a being
so impotent and ignorant as man to undertake to unriddle the mysteries of his sway. Job expresses his

---

* Job ii. 1 – 10.   † ii. 11 – 13.

convictions and his penitence.* Jehovah rebukes the
three friends for their reprehensible language, and
directs them to sacrifice a burnt-offering of seven bullocks and seven rams by way of expiation, and to engage Job's intercession in their behalf, that so they
may be forgiven. "And Jehovah had regard to the
prayer of Job; and Jehovah restored the prosperity
of Job, when he had prayed for his friends, and Jehovah gave him twice as much as he had before." His
relations and former acquaintance visited him with
condolence, congratulations, and presents. "Jehovah
blessed the latter end of Job more than the beginning;
for he had fourteen thousand sheep, six thousand camels, a thousand yoke of oxen, and a thousand she-
asses; he had also seven sons, and three daughters."
The latter, named Jemima, Kezia, and Kerenhap-
puch, were the most distinguished beauties of the
East; and their patrimony was made equal to that of
their brothers. "And Job lived after this a hundred
and forty years, and saw his sons, and his sons' sons,
even four generations; then Job died, being old, and
satisfied with days." †

The work is thus seen to consist of an introduction,
a close, and, occupying much more space than the
other two parts, a discussion of a great question of religious philosophy. It is an elaborate didactic poem, in
the form, not unusual in modern times, of a colloquy
between parties who present different views. It is a
work of great vigor and beauty. Its author was a
man of genius and of various knowledge. The translation of it, in King James's version, is on the whole
worse than that of any other book; so bad, as to be
much of it altogether unintelligible, and to indicate

---

* Job iii. 1 – xlii. 6.   † xlii. 7 – 17.

that the translators, perceiving their incapacity to discern the sense of their author, were fain, verse after verse, if not page after page, to put down words evidently without meaning, under the pretence of rendering him into English. But of late the book has been carefully studied and illustrated; and in the excellent version in which Dr. Noyes has incorporated the results of his own erudite inquiries, as well as those of earlier scholars, the unlearned reader may consult it with high satisfaction.

The genius of the author was so adventurous, the coloring of his sentiments is so highly imaginative, and so free a use is made of all the artifices of poetical diction, that it is in vain to think of tracing a logical argument through each of the several discourses, or even of showing that a uniform strain of opinion and sentiment pervades them respectively. We discern clearly enough the general idea designed to be enforced by the successive speakers. But it would be too much to expect that, in the treatment of such a problem as he had proposed to himself, and clothing his thoughts too in a poetical garb, the writer should have been able to present a consistent and compact sequence of reasoning, and to avoid all irrelevant matter. And to proceed on such a supposition is to embarrass one's self greatly in attempting to illustrate his sense. We must allow for abrupt transitions, where the language of strong emotion is in different places introduced; for chasms and obscurities in the argument, occasioned by the writer's imperfect grasp of his great subject; for rhetorical amplification, due to the copiousness of the poetical vein.

The first discourse of Job is but a passionate burst of impatient complaint. He curses the day of his birth. He asks why he was made to survive that hour, and not permitted at once to find shelter from the ills of life in the peaceful grave; why it is, that death is denied to those who would welcome it as the most precious boon.*

Eliphaz breaks the silence by which the friends had hitherto expressed their sympathy, by reproving the sufferer for thus vehemently repining at affliction, which he ought to regard as God's rebuke for his sins. He must speak, he says, though at the hazard of giving offence, and administer to Job the admonition which Job himself had been used to address. If God had brought distress upon him, it was simply because God saw that he deserved it. It was in vain for him to confide in the supposed uprightness of his ways; for when was such a thing known as that the innocent perished, or that the righteous was cut off? The experience of the speaker had made manifest, his "thoughts in visions of the night" had confirmed the truth, that a pure God discerned frailty in all that he had made, and that a just God, in his Providence, would send trouble only on the wicked, and cause all their prosperity to be transient. He advises Job not to strive with the Almighty, but contritely, and at the same time hopefully, to seek a renewal of his favor by repenting of the sins which must needs have provoked such retribution.†

In his reply, Job excuses himself for the passionate warmth of his complaints, by appealing to the extreme severity of his sufferings. He complains of the harshness of friends, from whom he had a right to expect different treatment. His petulance had been blamed; but was it right to deal so sternly with the rash words of a despairing man, which were but wind?

---

* Job iii. 1 - 26.　　　　　† iv. 1 - v. 27.

He might reasonably look for compassion, and tender-
ness, and a fair judgment, for his sufferings were
great, and there was no prospect of relief for him in
the future. And even if he had sinned, as was alleged, had his sins been so distinguished above
others that he merited to be distinguished above them
in misfortune ? *

Bildad, another of the friends, next enforces the
doctrine of Eliphaz, in a manner still more peremp-
tory. He asks the disconsolate Job how he dares to
assume such a tone. He tells him that the death of
his children had been owing to their transgressions,
and that, if he would have his own prosperity restored,
the way for him was, not to murmur, but to reform.
God would never " cast away an upright man," nor, on
the other hand, would he "strengthen the hands of
evil-doers." That such was the order of God's righteous government, he declares to be a lesson of all human experience ; and he exhorts Job to recognize it,
and act accordingly.†

To this Job answers, that it is true enough that,
judged by the standard of God's perfect purity, there
is no man but will fall short; and that, at all events,
it would be futile and rash to contest any thing with
him, because of his resistless power. If comparatively he were ever so innocent, he says, he would not
think of maintaining his innocence, but would simply
cast himself on the mercy of his judge. That would
be the way to conciliate the favor of one who had
shown himself austere and absolute, and who, he
would boldly declare, in the distributions of life, dealt
alike with all men, whether better or worse. After a
repetition of these ideas, he returns to his strain of

---

* Job vi. 1 – vii. 21.   † viii. 1 – 22.

complaint. He asks what pleasure it can be to God to exert his arbitrary power in distressing him thus, and why he should have cared to create him for so terrible a doom. And, finally, he begs for a little interval of ease and repose, before he shall take his departure for " the land of darkness, and the shadow of death." *

Zophar follows, in the same strain as the other friends, except that he administers still more unsparing and rude reproof. He says that a babbler ought to be answered, and a mocker put to shame, and that bold lies should not escape contradiction. As to Job's pretensions to purity, and to being made to suffer beyond his desert, he says that if God would but speak, it would be seen how baseless they were, and that it was only because God had exercised much forgiveness, that the retribution was not even heavier. God's infinite wisdom, so different from the pretended wisdom of man, he declares to be capable of discerning transgressions which escape even the consciousness of the perpetrator; and he advises Job to abandon the unprofitable idea of self-vindication, and by confession and reformation to seek a renewal of the prosperity which on that condition God would be willing to restore.†

The next discourse of Job is longer and less cohe-

---

* Job ix. 1 – x. 22.

† xi. 1 – 20. — " Deeper than *hell* " (8). Our translators, in their double use of this Hebrew word, have confounded two things altogether different ; viz. the nether world, in which, according to ancient opinion, the shades of all the dead were congregated, and the place or state of future retribution for the wicked. The former is of course the sense in the present instance. The Hebrew word שְׁאוֹל, rendered *hell* in this place, never has the other meaning. Comp. x. 21, 22, xxvi. 6 ; Gen. xxxvii. 35, xlii. 38 ; Numb. xvi. 30 ; Ps. vi. 5, xvi. 10, xviii. 5, lv. 15, cxvi. 3 ; Prov. ix. 18 ; Is. v. 14, xiv. 9 *et seq.*, xxxviii. 10, 18 ; Ez. xxxi. 16 *et seq.*, xxxii. 21 *et seq.* See also Campbell's " Four Gospels," &c., Diss. VI. part 2.

rent than the foregoing. He derides the pretensions of his friends to a wisdom superior to his own, and declares that it was their prosperity, contrasted with his wretchedness, that emboldened them to treat him as they had done. He reasserts his opinion, that, in the distributions of Providence, there is no discrimination having reference to the characters of men. Enlarging on the unrestricted sovereignty and power of God, he says that they could say nothing on that doctrine that was new; that the very beasts, fowls, and fishes gave instruction in it; that all experience enforced it; and that he was as well acquainted with it as themselves.* But as to their hasty judgment that his sufferings were a retribution for sins, he denies its equity; he appeals from the sentence; he wishes he could argue the question before God himself, rather than before presumptuous and hypocritical men, who, pretending zeal for his honor, and an immaculate character of their own, could be so uncharitable to their friend. Could he be permitted to do so, and for that purpose would God but withdraw his terrible hand from him, and make known the offences with which he was charged, he would proceed to maintain his cause with a confidence that he should be found innocent.† Then, resuming the strain of lamentation over his cruel fate, he asks why, feeble and unresisting as he is, God should thus wreak upon him his almighty vengeance. As at best man's life is short and unhappy, he prays that some rest may be granted him before the close of his determined days. Then he wishes that that time had come for him, which must come at last for all, and that from the tempest of wrath which had burst upon him he could be hidden

---

* Job. xii. 1 – xiii. 2. † xiii. 3 – 23.

at once in the grave, to sleep the dreamless sleep, and know no more for ever of earthly things.*

The second series of discourses on the part of the friends begins with a more vehement strain of censure on the part of Eliphaz. He condemns the confidence with which Job had protested his innocence, as manifesting irreverence towards God, distrust of his justice and of his readiness to hear prayer, and a presumptuous estimate of his own consequence and merits. And then he reaffirms the doctrine, as sustained by the testimony of all past experience, that Providence never suffers the wicked to escape signal punishment, and that accordingly such afflictions as those of Job must be taken for evidence of signal ill desert.†

Job turns upon Eliphaz with increased resentment, and says he has heard enough from pretended friends, who, professing to have come to offer comfort, have but embittered his distress by their causeless animadversions, showing a spirit so different from what he would have displayed, had their positions been reversed. But, passing presently from this topic, he relapses into his common strain of complaint. Neither speech nor silence, he says, gives him any relief. God's anger is tearing him in pieces. Yet he is conscious of no wickedness that should have brought him to such extremity. His friends insult him, and take his guilt for granted. He wishes that, before it is too late, and he goes the way which cannot be retraced, he could argue his case before God, whose justice

---

* Job xiii. 24 – xiv. 22. — " If a man die, can he live again! " &c. (xiv. 14). This is clearly, in an interrogative form, Job's expression of disbelief in any life after the present. If there were another life, he says, if it were with man as it is with a tree, of which there is hope that, if cut down, it will sprout again (comp. 7 – 12), then he might bear affliction which now he finds insupportable.

† xv. 1 – 35. — With 14 – 16, comp. iv. 17 – 19.

could not fail to acquit him. It is because his revilers
are infatuated, that he receives such wrong at their
hands; but that wrong will be visited upon their own
children. Innocence will vindicate itself, and the
righteous man will be secure and strong. But though
this is true as the general issue of God's providence,
a different disposal seems to have been made for him;
and he desires not that his friends should argue longer,
or remain longer with him, for he despairs of finding
wisdom enough among them to lead to conviction of
the truth, and his own example will not illustrate it,
for he sees that his days are at an end, and that all his
hopes are presently to go with him into the grave.*

The second discourse of Bildad, of nearly the same
length with the first, differs from it in the omission of
the topic of encouragement to Job to confess and forsake his sins so as to obtain forgiveness.† Like the
former, after reproving the afflicted man for the bold
tone of his self-justification, it enforces at some length
the settled opinion of the three collocutors, that such
sufferings as have been visited on their friend can only
be regarded as tokens of God's displeasure at his
wickedness.‡

Job's next reply is simply a bitter protest against
the hard treatment which he experiences at the hands
both of God and man. God, he says, has stripped him
of his glory, and taken the crown from his head. His
acquaintance are estranged, and he is an object of disgust to his wife and servants. Fainting under the
hand of God, it might be supposed that his friends
would have pity on him, and that, even supposing he
had erred, they would not wish to triumph over him
in his distress. But no; ten times have they reviled

---

* Job. xvi. 1 – xvii. 16.   † Comp. viii. 5 – 7, 20 – 22.   ‡ xviii. 1 – 21.

him, and they break him in pieces with their abuse. He wishes that his words, which they find so blame- worthy, were all written down, for he is persuaded that then they would at last be fairly weighed, and better justice would be done him. He will not yet give up the hope that a just God, though for a sea- son estranged and averse, will yet, before he is wholly wasted away, be manifested as his vindicator, and as his avenger upon those who have indulged themselves in such malignant accusations against him.*

Zophar enlarges again on the single supposed prin- ciple of God's moral government, which makes the substance of the argument of the three friends. His zeal, he says, impels him, and his intelligence enables him, to reply to the injurious representations of Job; and then he goes on to repeat with his own illustra- tions the idea that, from the very beginning of human things, " the triumphing of the wicked hath been short,

---

* Job xix. 1 - 29.

> "I know that my Vindicator liveth,
> And will stand up at length on the earth;
> And although with my skin this body be wasted away,
> Yet in my flesh shall I see God." (25, 26.)

This, in conformity with the best commentators, is the rendering of Dr. Noyes. In the lofty poetical phraseology which pervades the book, Job ex- presses his confidence in his innocence by declaring that, wasted as he is, he is satisfied that, before his last hour comes, God will somehow reveal himself as his vindicator, and not allow him to depart weighed down by such cruel aspersions. (Comp. xvi. 19.) The singular interpretation which has been put upon this passage, as if it indicated Job's belief of a future life, is contradicted by various direct declarations of his persuasion that the grave is the goal of all human concerns. (Comp. vii. 7 - 10, xiv. 7 - 14, 18 - 21, xvii. 16.) The knowledge of that doctrine would have solved the problem of the book, and superseded all the discussion therein contained. Had the writer been acquainted with it, he would of course have introduced it into the concluding discourse of Jehovah, as the proper determination of the controversy which had been carried on; but in that discourse no trace of it appears. The Jewish commentators are at great pains to find some inti- mation of a future life in the Old Testament; but it is said that no one of them has ever adduced this passage in that connection.

and the joy of the impious but for a moment"; that
"in the fulness of his abundance he shall be brought
low, and every kind of misery shall come upon him";
that "such is the portion of the wicked man from
God, and the inheritance decreed to him by the Almighty." *

In the heat of discussion, as not seldom happens,
Job is driven still further from his opponents; so far
as even to appear to assert that, in respect to the dispensations of life, the wicked are particularly favored.
Give me but your attention, he says, before you deride
further, and I will dispense with the sympathy which
it seems you have not to bestow; and be not intoler-
ant of my warmth, when there is so much in what I
see of men's conduct and condition to excite it. Bad
men, even such as openly disclaim all knowledge of
Jehovah, and all desire to serve him, spend their days
in prosperity, and end them in peace. It is seldom that
they are swept away " as stubble before the wind," and
if it be true that trouble sometimes overtakes their
children after their death, it is nothing to the offender
himself; for he knows not of it in the dust which receives the fortunate and the wretched to the same in-
sensibility and repose. Nor is all this true of one part
of God's earth alone; but any traveller in distant
countries will testify that there also " the wicked is
spared in the day of destruction," and " is borne with
honor to the grave." †

In his third turn of speaking, Eliphaz insists yet
more directly and positively than had been done before,
that it was Job's crimes that had brought on him
his calamities. Beginning with what appears to be a
perversion of Job's argument, he asks whether Job sup-

---

* Job xx. 1 - 29.   † xxi. 1 - 34.

poses that the wisdom and goodness of which he appears inclined to boast can do the Almighty any good,
or whether he expects by his bold pretensions to deter
the Almighty from judging and punishing him. Then
he appeals to him whether his iniquities have not been
great and numberless; charges him directly with various specific sins; and says that it is idle to suppose
that they have escaped God's notice, because "dark
clouds are a veil to him, and he cannot see." He
asks Job whether he proposes himself to pursue that
"old way" of wicked men, which, judging from his
comments on it, he seems to think so safe, but which
in fact leads to ruinous consequences that excite the
derision of the righteous. Finally he urges that the
only way for Job to find returning peace and prosperity is through reconciliation to God by repentance.*

Job repeats his complaint of the great hardship of
having no opportunity for self-vindication. If God
were but a judge whom he could find, address, and
argue with, he does not doubt, he says, that he should
be able to clear himself, and find deliverance; for he
has not neglected God's precepts, but treasured up his
words, and kept his way. But he cannot find God
by going backward or forward, to the right hand or
the left, and, as things are, God seems to be implacable
and inflexible in his terrific purposes of wrath towards
him; while from the same cause, namely, that "the
condition of men" is "hidden from the Almighty,"
the wicked run a long course of success. They remove landmarks; they steal flocks; they oppress the
poor, who cry to God unregarded, and drive them to
utter destitution; avoiding the light of day, they commit deeds of impurity and blood in the darkness; yet

---

* Job xxii. 1 - 30.

at length they lie down in a peaceful grave; " they
are brought low, and die, like all others; cut off, like
ripened ears of corn." *

In reply, Bildad merely extols in a very few words
the majesty and holiness of God, and rebukes the
arrogance of " the son of man, a reptile," who would
presume to call himself pure in his sight.†

The discussion between the parties hitherto engaged
is concluded by a discourse of Job, much longer than
any of the preceding. After a contemptuous allusion
to the small contribution made by Bildad towards the
illustration of the subject in controversy, he proceeds
in the first place to pursue in vigorous terms the topic
of God's power and greatness.‡   Then, in a more
moderate strain than he has hitherto employed, he
goes on to say that, though he cannot disingenuously
declare that his friends have treated him justly, or
that he is the guilty man they have pretended, still he
will admit that there is much truth in what they have
advanced concerning the danger of a wicked course.
Nothing worse can be imprecated on an enemy than
the sinner's doom; for the sinner can have no hope in
God, and, in the common course of things, however
he may be seen to prosper, his prosperity will be but
transient.   He may have many children, but they will
die by violence; he may heap up silver, but the innocent will share it.   He will be pierced by God's arrows, and banished by men's contempt. And the result of the whole is, that that wisdom which is so hard
to be found, and for which the vast enterprise and
skill of man, so successful in other researches, often
seek in vain, is the most desirable and precious of all
things, so that " gold and crystal are not to be com-

---

* Job. xxiii. 1 – xxiv. 25.　　† xxv. 1 – 6.　　‡ xxvi. 1 – 14.

pared with it, nor shall silver be weighed out as the price thereof"; and that this wisdom, which only the all-seeing eye of God is able to discern in its secret re-tirements, is synonymous with a devout fear of the Lord in the heart, and a careful departure from evil in the life.*

Reverting to the present misery of his own condi-tion, Job next dwells on the vivid contrast between it and the time when God was his guardian, and held a light for him to walk by; when he communed with God, sitting in his tent, surrounded by his children; when, in his walks abroad, the young and the old, princes and nobles, paid him reverence; when the poor and forsaken, the fatherless and widow, passed him with benedictions; when men waited humbly and anxiously for his counsel, were cheered by his sympa-thy, and prided themselves upon his notice.† Now, he says, he is jeered at by young people, to whose fathers he would not have given so much as a place among his watch-dogs. Worthless vagabonds, with-out a crust to keep them from famishing, or a shelter from the weather, make him the by-word of their odious disdain. Meanwhile bodily suffering racks him. His bones are pierced with pain, and his sinews have no rest. His skin is parched, and he burns with fever. It is to no purpose that in his agony he cries to God. God is inexorable, God will show to him no such pity as he was himself used to manifest to the unhappy.‡ His life has provoked no such vengeance.

---

* Job xxvii. 1 - xxviii. 28.

" This is the portion of the wicked man from God,
    The inheritance which oppressors receive from the Almighty," &c.
                                                        — xxvii. 13.
A repetition of the words of Zophar (xx. 29); as if Job had said, so far I agree to what Zophar has declared.

† xxix. 1 - 25.   ‡ xxx. 1 - 31.

By no impurity has he displeased that God who sees
the ways and numbers all the steps of men, and who
appoints ruin for the workers of iniquity. He has
never "walked with falsehood," nor allowed his heart
to covet what his eye observed. He has never refused
justice to the humblest suitor or dependant. He has
fed and clothed the destitute, and befriended and pro-
tected the fatherless and widow. He has not been
elated or perverted by his great prosperity; he has
rendered no idolatrous service; he has felt no malignant pleasure in the misfortunes of enemies and ri-
vals; he has kept a hospitable house, and a bosom un-
burdened by unacknowledged sin; he has paid honorably the price of his land, and the wages of its cultivators. If it had been otherwise, it would be right that
contempt should follow him, and that he should con-
demn himself to perpetual seclusion. But as it has
been thus, he fears no accusation. He would triumph
in any charge, and wear it as an ornament in public
view, — so conspicuously, when examined, would his
innocence appear. Could he find the way to the Almighty's tribunal, he would approach it with the lofty
step of a princely confidence.*

Thus "the words of Job are ended," and Zophar,
whose turn for speaking has come, finds nothing to
reply, as Bildad, the next preceding speaker, had found
very little,† and even Eliphaz had been more brief
than before.‡ The idea of the author seems to have
been to represent Job as gradually getting the better

---

* Job xxxi. 1-40.
   "If I have beheld the sun in his splendor,
      Or the moon advancing in brightness,
      And my heart have been secretly enticed," &c. (26, 27.)
No other worship than that of the heavenly bodies is referred to. It was
probably the most ancient form of idolatry.
† xxv.   ‡ xxii.

of his antagonists, who could but repeat the same thought, and driving them from their ground.

Under these circumstances, a third collocutor is introduced, who, seeing the other disputants silenced, thinks it time to interpose with his views. When the " three men had ceased to answer Job, because he was righteous in his own eyes, then was kindled the wrath of Elihu, the son of Barachel, the Buzite, of the family of Ram; against Job was his wrath kindled, because he had pronounced himself righteous, rather than God; against his three friends also was his wrath kindled, because they had not found an answer, and yet had condemned Job."

Elihu says, that, being but a young man, he had hitherto sat by only as a listener, refraining from any expression of his own thoughts, because he regarded it as the prerogative of age to teach wisdom; but that, as it was, after all, the inspiration of the Almighty that gave understanding, and the aged were not always intelligent, he was resolved to declare his opinion. He says he has listened attentively to all their arguments; and that none of them has confuted Job, or has a right to plume himself on having been victor in the discussion; but that, on the contrary, Job has reduced them to silence. He says that, not having been addressed by Job, he does not propose directly to answer him, — at all events, to answer him with such speeches as theirs; but that he finds his mind full to overflowing with the theme, and therefore he will speak upon it frankly, without unworthy flattery of any man.*

Job had complained that he had not a fair chance to make good his cause, so heavily did a sense of the

---

* Job xxxii. 1- 22.

greatness and terribleness of his Divine Judge rest upon and distress him.* Elihu calls upon him to set
forth his reasons calmly and fearlessly before one ani-
mated by upright intentions, one formed of clay like
himself, one whose terror cannot dismay, nor his hand
be heavy, like God's. This premised, he finds fault
with Job for so boldly asserting his innocence, and implying that God, who afflicted him, was unjust. He
declares that God is greater than man, and cannot
properly be called by him to "account of any of his
doings"; that, however, in his dealings with men, he
addresses them for gracious purposes; that he admonishes and chastises them to correct their pride, and
save them from destruction; and that, if they have the
wisdom rightly to interpret and profit by the lesson,
they will be "delivered from going down to the grave,"
and their eyes will "behold the light." Such, he insists, is a common method of God's providence. Thus
does he deal "time after time with man." If Job has
any thing to object to this, let him say it, and he will
have a candid and friendly hearing. If not, let him
listen, and be instructed further.†

Job, Elihu continues, was greatly to blame for adopting the impious language of evil-doers, and alleging
that "a man profiteth nothing by delighting himself in
God." Far from the truth is this. "For what a man
hath done" will the just God "requite him, and render
to every one according to his deeds." As he "hath
created the whole world," so he will rightly administer
·it. Were he hostile to man, every trace of man's existence would be presently swept away. It is rash to
cast reproaches on earthly sovereigns; how much
more to reproach him whose workmanship all men

---

* Job ix. 34, 35; xiii. 21 – 28.   † xxxiii. 1 – 33.

are, and who cares for them all alike, rich and poor,
prince and peasant; whose vengeance no evil-doer,
however great or however crafty, can resist or elude;
whose ear of compassion is reached by the cry of
the humblest sufferer. Instead of complaint, the
Divine chastisements should be received with submission; with prayers that they may be made to impart their designed instruction; and with promises of
amendment. Let Job gainsay this, if he can. Let
men of understanding consider the case, and pronounce
whether Job's murmurs have not been unwise.* Job
had seemed to pretend that he was "more righteous
than God," and that, while he had rendered to God
every duty, God had been wanting in duty to him;
but how could he place the Supreme under any obligation, or affect him by any act? Job had represented the oppressed as being left without succour.
But why were they not succoured? Because they did
not pray for redress aright. "God will not hear the
vain supplication," still less the cry of those who do
not own him. Therefore it is that, as Job insists, violent men are not presently visited in God's anger, nor
relief sent to the sufferers, whom they oppress. But
to those who will but confidingly wait for it, a sure
justice will at length be done.†

The rest of the harangue is more discursive than
argumentative. It exhibits, in a diffuse strain, the
speaker's views concerning various attributes of God.
Premising that he intends to traverse a wide range of
remark, he declares that God is not a despiser of any
thing, but is as excellent in wisdom as in might; that
"he suffereth not the wicked to prosper, but rendereth

---

* Job xxxiv. 1 – 37.

† xxxv. 1 – 16. — " When thou sayest, 'I cannot see him'"(14); comp.
xxiii. 8, 9.

justice to the oppressed"; that he establishes and
exalts the good, like kings; admonishes them of their
errors by allowing them to fall into trouble; and when
they "return from iniquity," and "obey and serve
him," reinstates them in all their past prosperity. He
says that early death is the doom of "the corrupt in
heart," who "cry not to God, when he bindeth them";
but that, on the contrary, it is his delight to give deliverance and abundance to the poor; that with him
"guilt and punishment follow each other," — punishment which no rich ransom can avert, so that it is not
safe to indulge in passionate repining. God is so
great, that none can dictate to him his course, or
should venture to charge it with any fault. Rather
his greatness should be reverently admired and extolled, — that incomprehensible and everlasting greatness which the clouds, collecting and dispersing the
rain, the irradiated atmosphere, the rayless sea, the
lightning launched from his hands, all the agencies
which he employs for feeding or for punishing the
nations, attest and proclaim.*

"My heart trembleth," continues the speaker, "and
is moved out of its place," when I hear the thunder,
and see the lightning, of his storms. When I watch the
snow and rain, that, driving the beasts to shelter, and
interrupting the labor of husbandmen, compel them
to acknowledge his presence; when his cold winds
blow, and his ice stops the course of rivers, when his
clouds "descend in rain, and his lightning scattereth
the mists," I discern in all these changes of nature the
instruments of his wise purposes of judgment or of
mercy. Let Job consider them, and, comparing his
own ignorance and impotence with the infinite wis-

---

* Job. xxxvi. 1 - 33.

dom and power of God, own how great and dangerous is the presumption of undertaking to pass judgment on his ways. Man cannot bear to look up to the sky on a cloudless day. How much less able is he to gaze on the majesty of God. We cannot explore him. Of himself he gives no account. To fear him, not to judge him, is true wisdom.*

Elihu having ceased, Jehovah, before whom Job had repeatedly expressed his wish to plead his cause, interposes in the controversy. He " spake to Job out of the whirlwind," and in a long discourse, consisting almost wholly of questions, exposed to him the folly of undertaking to criticize the Divine government, when he was not able to control, or even to comprehend, the most common phenomena of nature. Who art thou, says Jehovah, who presumest, in thy ignorance, to prate about my dispensations? Come forward, and prepare to answer some questions. Thou who art so wise as to revise God's proceedings, relate the process of the creation of the earth. Tell how the seas were restrained and bounded. Thou whose years and whose knowledge run back to the beginning of things, explain whence and how comes the light, which brings out the forms and hues of objects, and makes " all things stand forth as in rich apparel." Show the way to the dwelling-place of darkness, " the gates of the shadow of death." Describe, if thou hast visited them, " the storehouses of the snow," " the treasury of hail." Who directs the course of " the east wind," of " the glittering thunderbolt," of the fructifying rain, which falls in untrodden wildernesses? Who distils the drops of dew? Who makes the land white with frost, and with ice bridges the waters as if they were

* Job xxxvii. 1 - 24.

paved with stone? Canst thou regulate, or dost thou understand, the courses or the influences of the heavenly bodies? Canst thou muster and discharge the clouds when the earth is dry, and compel the lightnings to do thy bidding? Canst thou hunt for the wild beast, or cater for the bird of prey? Dost thou know the laws of increase of the inhabitants of the forest? Canst thou catch the wild ass in his desert mountain-range, or tame and use the strong but unmanageable buffalo? Who takes care of the young of the ostrich, neglected by the stupid and wayward mother bird? Didst thou give strength, swiftness, and courage to the war-horse? Didst thou implant the instincts of the eagle and the hawk? — Is the presumption of thy rash censures yet enough exposed, or " will the censurer of the Almighty yet contend with him? will the reprover of God yet answer?" *

The appeal was conclusive. Job was confounded and shamed. He could only reply, —

> " Behold, I am vile! what can I answer thee!
> I will lay my hand upon my mouth.
> Once have I spoken, but I will not speak again ;
> Yea, twice, but I will say no more." — xl. 4, 5.

To enforce and illustrate further the reasonableness and rectitude of this sentiment of humility on the part of man in respect to the character and dispensations of the Almighty, Jehovah is finally represented as appealing to his power displayed in the creation of the river-horse † and the crocodile. Having first responded to Job's lowly acknowledgment of error by declaring that when he has a mighty arm or a voice of thunder like God's, when he is able to array himself

---

* Job xxxviii. 1 – xl. 2.

† Others understand by *Behemoth*, the elephant. The subject is fully treated in the " Natural History of the Bible " (ad verb.) by our learned countryman, Dr. Harris.

in divine splendor and glory, and in the exercise of
a divine sovereignty to "look upon every proud one,
and bring him low, yea, break the wicked in pieces,"
then it will be time for him to set his own righteousness against God's, and have it confessed that his own
right hand can save him, — the discourse proceeds to
its close with a copious description of those two formidable animals, expressed in a gorgeous strain of poetry.   If the strength of such monsters can defy all
human force, much more, it is implied, their creation
infers a power with which Job, or any man, should
shrink from contending.*

Job's expression of meek submission and repentance
concludes the whole colloquy; —

> " Then Job answered Jehovah, and said :
> " I know that thou canst do every thing,
> And that no purpose of thine can be hindered.
> Who is he, that darkeneth thy counsels by words without knowledge?
> Thus have I uttered what I understood not ;
> Things too wonderful for me, which I knew not.
> Hear thou then, I beseech thee, and I will speak ;
> I will ask thee, and do thou instruct me.
> I have heard of thee by the hearing of the ear,
> But now mine eye seeth thee ;
> Wherefore I abhor myself,
> And repent in dust and ashes." — xlii. 1 – 6.†

The discussion finished, Jehovah is represented as
addressing Eliphaz, signifying his displeasure against
him and his two friends for speaking wrongly concerning himself, and directing them, in expiation of
their offence, to present a burnt-offering of seven
bullocks and seven rams, after which he would listen
to Job's prayer for their forgiveness.   Lastly, the issue

---

* Job xl. 3 – xli. 34. — With xl. 7 comp. xxxviii. 2. — " Though *the
Jordan* rush against his mouth " (23) ; an evidence of the writer's acquaintance with one feature of the geography of Palestine.

† With xlii. 3, comp. xxxviii. 2.

of the transaction is related in the restitution of the prosperity of the sufferer, after his successful intercession for his uncharitable friends. " Jehovah gave him twice as much as he had before." His relatives "and all his former acquaintances," each with a present of a piece of money and an earring, assembled to enjoy anew the ancient welcome of his generous hospitality, and offer their sympathy and congratulations. The former number of his flocks and herds was doubled, and he had as many sons and as many daughters as before. His daughters, who are named, were the unrivalled beauties of the land, and they shared in his wealth equally with their brothers. He lived a hundred and forty years longer, and saw his family multiply to the fourth generation. " Then Job died, being old, and satisfied with days." *

I cannot imagine it to be necessary at this day to argue the question whether the Book of Job is a true history. To suppose it to be so is to suppose that several long discourses, in the highest style of poetry, were actually pronounced, some of them by a man in a dismal state, not only of misfortune, but of sickness, and one of them by the Deity himself speaking from a whirlwind, and that they were written down with the accuracy of a reporter of our modern debates. Let any reasonable reader look over the prose passages

---

* Job xlii. 7 - 17. — " Take therefore seven bullocks and seven rams " (8); the same was the solemn sacrifice of the soothsayer, Balaam (comp. Numb. xxiii. 1). — " Ye have not spoken concerning me that which is right, as hath my servant Job " (xlii. 8). What was it that Job had spoken so much better than his friends ? Is the reference to the general strain of his discourses, as is commonly understood ? I think not, but to his last reply in xlii. 2 - 6. He had abandoned his former ground, and expressed submission and penitence, which his friends had not done. — "A piece of money " (11); קְשִׂיטָה ; all the ancient versions with which I am acquainted render the word a sheep or lamb; a translation which accords better with the opinion of those who refer the composition to a date anterior to the general use of coin.

at the beginning and close, and ask himself what he
is asserting when he affirms them to be a recital of
real transactions.   The whole structure of the work
bears the impress of fictitious narrative.   The possessions of Job are described in round numbers, by thousands and half thousands.*   When the time of restitution comes, they are doubled, while the number of
children is the same as before, so as to double the patrimony of each.†   Job lived after his troubles just
twice the age of man.‡   His name, according to the
best interpretation, is significant of his lot.§   There
are three colloquies between him and his friends, each
consisting of three dialogues, except the last, from
which the last speaker appears to have withdrawn,
discomfited.   In the earliest Jewish notice of the book
which has reached us, it is spoken of as a fable.‖

To this view of the character of the book, which it
might seem perfectly safe to assume (had not the fact
proved otherwise) would be the view of every judicious
reader, no valid objection can be drawn from references to it in other parts of the Bible.   James writes
in his Epistle,¶ " Ye have heard of the patience of
Job "; but if he had also written, " Ye have heard
of the benevolence of the good Samaritan," no reader
would have felt surprised, or considered himself authorized to infer that James regarded the good Samaritan
as an historical person.   And the same remark holds
good of the texts in which Ezekiel mentions Job along
with Noah.**   So in a discourse of our Lord, the beg-
gar Lazarus is represented as in the bosom of Abra-

---

* Job i. 3.   † xlii. 12.   ‡ xlii. 16.

§ אִיּוֹב, the persecuted.

‖ אִיּוֹב לֹא הָיָה וְלֹא נִבְרָא אֶלָּא מָשָׁל הָיָה, " Job was never created ; these
things are a parable."   Babylonish Talmud, " Bava Bathra " (Tom. VIII.
Fol. 16, p. 1, five lines from the foot).

¶ v. 11.   ** Ezek. xiv. 14, 20.

ham; * but no one scruples to distinguish between
the real existence of the father of the faithful, and
the fictitious one of the creation of a parable.   Or
even if a different construction were put upon the
language of Ezekiel and James, it would only authorize the inference that they understood some worthy of
the name of Job to have lived in ancient times; it
would by no means bear out the conclusion that they
understood every thing, or any thing, to be historically
true, which is related in the book called by his name.

The theme of the book is the question, why it is that,
under the government of a righteous God, the good
sometimes suffer, — a question which presents no perplexity, now that Christianity has brought life and immortality to light, but which, before the revelation
through Jesus of the retributions of another world,
was a perpetual riddle to the wise.† The friends deny the fact, and insist that God's distributions of weal
and woe are judicial, and that the sufferer must needs
have been a sinner, though his transgressions may have
been unknown to men. Job with equal pertinacity insists, that he is conscious of having deserved none of his
troubles, and that, on the whole, under God's government, the righteous and the sinner fare alike. Elihu,
represented as a young man, expresses in an ambitious
style his dissatisfaction with both views alike, while his
own vague and excursive rhetoric, seeming to clothe
sentiments alternately according with the one and the
other, contributes nothing material to the solution of
the enigma. At length, Jehovah interposes, and ends
the controversy, not by solving it, but by showing its
unprofitableness. He does not vindicate his justice by
explaining the principles of his government, and show-

---

* Luke xvi. 23.

† Comp. Ps. xxxvii. and lxxiii., which also treat of the problem of the
want of apparent correspondence between condition and desert.

ing that it is not in caprice or cruelty, but in justice
and mercy, that he sends afflictions. He only pro-
claims that power of his, with which it would be pre-
posterous for man to contend, and of the exertion of
which it is insolent for him to complain.

I think that those critics go too far who undertake to extract a definite lesson from the book, such
as that " character is not to be inferred from external
condition," * " that God sends calamities upon good
men, who have suffered themselves to be somewhat
arrogant in prosperity, in order that they may be ad-
monished thereby and return to a proper course of life,
and afterwards regain their prosperous condition"; †
" that the common doctrine of retribution is unfounded"; ‡ or that, " having a due respect to the
corruption, infirmity, and ignorance of human nature,
as well as to the infinite wisdom and majesty of God,
men are to reject all confidence in their own strength,
in their own righteousness, and to preserve on all occasions an unwavering and unsullied faith." §   The
truth is, the author was unable to extract for the benefit of his readers any such definite moral from the
problem he discussed; for it mastered him. He " finds
no end, in wandering mazes lost." He starts a great
question, treats it at much length, makes no progress
towards its solution, and after all concludes, in effect,
that it is useless to discuss the mystery, because it is
inscrutable, and that it is presumptuous and dangerous to refer to it in a complaining tone.‖   Whatev-

---

* Noyes's "Amended Version," &c. Introd. p. iv.
† Expositors referred to by Jahn, "Einleitung," Band II. § 191.
‡ De Wette, " Einleitung," § 286.
§ Lowth's " Lectures on Hebrew Poetry," Lect. XXXII. p. 467.
‖ Bishop Warburton's peculiar theory of the book is in the truest vein of
that erratic schemer. He supposes it to have been written after the return
from the captivity, and that its design was to symbolize the national troubles

er of direct practical moral is enforced by the book must be deduced from the passage at the close, where are related the censures passed on the friends for their uncharitable judgment of Job, and the rewards bestowed on him on account of his repenting of the unsubmissive language into which he had been betrayed.

By "the land of Uz," in which the scene of the poem is laid, appears to have been intended a district of Idumea, — that country lying between Palestine on the north, and Arabia and Egypt on the south and west, so well known through the whole period of ancient Jewish history as the territory of the descendants of Esau. In the Lamentations of Jeremiah is a mention of Uz, which seems to determine for it this geographical position.* Eliphaz was a "Temanite" and Elihu a "Buzite";† and *Tema* and *Buz* are mentioned by the same author in connection with Uz and Idumea.‡ Zophar was a "Naamathite"; and *Naamah* occurs in the same connection in the description of the southern boundary of Canaan, in the Book of Joshua.§

The book does not declare who was its author, nor have we any credible historical information on that point. He must have been a person to whom the Hebrew tongue was vernacular, for the purity, copiousness and elegance of his Hebrew style — and that, too, the Hebrew style of poetry — absolutely repel

at that period. By the three friends he understands to be represented San-ballat, Tobiah, and Geshem (comp. Neh. ii. 19), and by Job's wife the idolatrous women (comp. Ezra ix. 1, 2) with whom the Jews had contracted marriages (comp. "Divine Legation of Moses," Lib. VI. § 2).

* Lam. iv. 21 ; comp. Gen. xxxvi. 9, 15, 28.

† Job ii. 11, xxxii. 2.

‡ Jer. xxv. 20, 21, 23 ; comp. Gen. xxxvi. 9, 11, Jer. xlix. 7, 20, Ezek. xxv. 12, 13, Amos i. 11, 12, Obad. 8, 9.

§ Job ii. 11 ; Josh. xv. 41, comp. 21.

the supposition that the work was a translation from any other language.

The time when he wrote is the next question that occurs. It seems to me that the opinion of those critics has no small probability, who regard the book as the oldest in the Biblical collection, and accordingly, as far as we know, the most ancient book in existence.

In favor of a modern origin, two arguments have been presented. Some supposed Chaldee forms of language have been referred to, as indicating a date for the composition as late as the time when the Jews came into political relations with Babylon; but I believe no *Chaldaisms* have been pointed out which are not equally well accounted for as *Arabisms*, which latter forms of speech betoken a very early, instead of a modern, origin.

And a similar argument has been drawn from the mention of *Satan* in the introduction,* erroneously supposed to be that great Evil Spirit of whom the Jews knew nothing till, at the time of the captivity, they adopted some superstitions of the Chaldeans. Such an inference rests on a mere confusion of ideas, growing out of an accidental similarity of terms. The *Satan* of the first two chapters of Job is by no means the *Ahriman*, the Prince of Darkness, the Devil, the Satan, of the Oriental mythology, afterwards transferred to the mythology of the Jews, and from them to that of the Christians. Job's Satan is a "sociable spirit," one of "the sons of God," who on a day of high ceremony comes to present himself among his associate splendors "before the Lord," and with whom the Lord holds gracious discourse. *Satan* was not originally a proper name. It only became so by a particular appropria-

---

* Job i. 6, 7, 8, 9, &c.

tion to a new idea of foreign origin, just as the Hebrew was going out of use as a spoken language.
Satan is a generic word, signifying *an adversary*, and
repeatedly rendered by that English word in the common version of the Old Testament; and the "son of
God" spoken of in the passage in question is called a
Satan, simply in his character of *the adversary* of Job.
The writer, whoever he was, was well acquainted
with the scenery and natural objects of Arabia and
Egypt, for these furnish the *commonplaces* of his poetical imagery.* He appears also to have at least heard
of the river Jordan; † but there is no such reference
to the geography or natural history of Palestine as
would indicate him to have been an inhabitant, or even
a visitor, of that country.

One fact, taken in connection with those which have
been mentioned, is very remarkable. While the purity
and freedom of the language and style incontestably
prove the work to have been the composition of a native
Hebrew, and no translation from a foreign original,
there is no other indication from beginning to end of its
having been written by a Jew. It is stamped with
none of those peculiarities of the Jewish mind which
were formed by the Law of Moses. It contains no
reference to the Jewish ritual or history.‡ It alludes

---

* For full illustrations of this point see Eichhorn's "Einleitung," §§ 641,
642. — "Arabian deserts, fountains dried up, marching hordes and caravan-
seras, bands of robbers, inhabitants of caverns, lions and wild asses, ...
the leviathan and behemoth," &c. Herder's *Oriental Dialogues*, pp. 206,
207.

† Job xl. 23.

‡ This material point has been brought into question, as the necessity
of the argument required ; — with what success, let the reader judge from
the following instances, as specious, I believe, as any that have been produced. Warburton thought he found references to the Law in xvii. 5, xxi.
19, xxii. 6, xxiv. 7, 9, 10 (comp. Deut. xxiv. 12, 13), xxxi. 28; to
the miracles in Egypt, in ix. 7, 9, xxvi. 12, xxxviii. 15; and to events in

to no king, no priests, no tabernacle, no temple.   The all-pervading Jewish idea of the *royalty* of God is never presented.   It is not enough to say, in answer to this remark, that the scene is laid, not in Judea, but in a foreign country.   We seem to know enough of Jewish habits of thought, to make it matter of surprise that no traces of them should appear in a long and sustained composition like this, from a Hebrew source.

At what time could a Jew have lived, writing his mother tongue in perfect purity, and with extraordinary force, and yet capable of writing as if absolutely ignorant of the national ritual and history?   I think, only before a Jewish Law and a Jewish nation existed. And in accordance with this theory of the high antiquity of the book is the fact, that, while the Hebrew language changed but little during the ten centuries over which the Old Testament collection extends, we seem to find indications of its most ancient form in the phraseology of this composition.   It is observed that several expressions occur in it, which are scarcely or never to be found elsewhere, except in the Pentateuch; that, on the other hand, forms of speech, found in the later books, but not in the Pentateuch, are rarely or never found in the Book of Job; and that, finally, it has some words peculiar to itself, which appear to have gone into disuse before the later Old Testament books were written.*

In the earliest Jewish mention of the book that has come down to our times, it is ascribed to Moses as its author; † and this opinion prevailed with the Greek

---

the later history, in xxxiii. 15 – 26 (comp. 2 Kings xx.), xxxvi. 8 – 12 (comp. 2 Chron. xxxiii. 11 - 13), xxxiv. 20 (comp. 2 Kings xix. 35).   Is this any thing but very stupid trifling?

* For examples under each of these heads, see Jahn, " Einleitung," Band II. § 199.

† מֹשֶׁה כָּתַב כְּפַרוֹ וְאִיּוֹב, Babylonish Talmud, " Bava Bathra " (Tom.

and Syrian fathers. The opinion of writers in an age
so recent, as compared with that of the production of
the work, carries with it but little historical authority.
And yet, in the absence of better proof, I am strongly
inclined to give it attention, and to suppose that Moses
wrote the book during his sojourn in Midian, between
the time of his flight from Egypt and his summons to
return thither for his people's deliverance.

The facts of the case accord well with that view.
In his solitude, and in the mood of mind incident to
his circumstances, it was natural that the great problem discussed in the Book of Job should present itself to his thoughts, while, as yet unenlightened by
any revelation, he possessed no advantages for its solution, beyond other men. His place of exile was
near the country of Idumea, where the scene of the
Book of Job is placed. He was living in the midst
of Arabian scenery and manners; and he had lived,
till he was forty years of age, in the midst of those of
Egypt; to both of which the book abundantly refers.
Respecting Palestine, where Moses had never been, it
is silent, except that it once refers to one great feature
of the geography of that country, the River Jordan,
an object so considerable in connection with the former
abode of his fathers, that Moses could not be supposed
to be uninformed of it. The word *Jehovah*, the proper
name of the Supreme Being, occurs repeatedly in the
prose parts, and once, perhaps, in the poetry.* Moses
was acquainted with the name, for it had been known

VIII. Fol. 15, p. 2, fourth line from the foot). For other evidences of this
ancient Jewish opinion, see Wolf, " Biblioth. Heb.," Vol. II. p. 102.

* Besides the instances in the introduction and the close, see xxxviii. 1,
xl. 6, xlii. 1. The only instance of the appearance of the word in the poetical part is in xii. 9, where its genuineness has been denied, on satisfactory
critical grounds. See Eichhorn, " Einleitung," § 644, note e.

to his ancestors, Abraham, Isaac, and Jacob; but it is
to be presumed that it would not be in so familiar and
constant use with him as with a writer subsequent to
the period when Jehovah, under that name, gave the
people a law, and adopted them for his own. And
supposing the book to have been a production, ante-
cedently to the Law, of the great lawgiver, Moses, we
have an explanation of the fact, otherwise extremely
perplexing, that a work, having nothing whatever to
do with Jewish religion, politics, morals, history, manners, or any other national interest or subject, should
have been adopted with such a welcome, preserved
with such care, and regarded with such veneration, by
that people. A work attributed to the great founder
and lawgiver would have peculiar claims to estimation and reverence.

If to this opinion the objection occurs, that, had the
work proceeded from Moses, it might have been expected that a uniform Jewish tradition would have
placed that fact beyond doubt, it is to be remembered,
on the other hand, that, in the early times, at least,
the Jews were not readers, and that this book, considering its subject, was very likely to be preserved only
in the hands of the curious and learned; that the
other writings of Moses were mainly important to his
countrymen, and maintained their free circulation
among them, as memorials of history, and documents
of law, while the Book of Job, being neither the one
nor the other, might be left comparatively out of view;
and that it may even have suffered a degree of neglect from being regarded as at most only a vague speculation of the great legislator while as yet in a semi-
heathen state.

If we could know that Moses wrote the book, and
that he wrote it under the circumstances at which I

have hinted, we should have further light upon its design.   He was in Midian as an exile from Egypt,
where he had left his wretched countrymen oppressed
by cruel taskmasters.   The once brilliant fortunes of
his race were changed for degradation and despair.
The hand of sorrow, and, as it seemed, the avenging
hand of God, was heavy upon them.   Why was it
thus with them ?   What had they done to merit such
a visitation?   To his patriotic feelings, made more
tender by absence from his fellow-sufferers, and by
compassion for their lot, it seemed that they had not
provoked, by any gross ill-desert, such a grievous chas-
tisement from God.   Why, then, had it been permitted
to come upon them?   How was it consistent with
God's righteousness, that he should so severely afflict
the innocent?

This is the problem with which the mind of Moses,
under the circumstances related in the history, must
be supposed to have been exercised in the solitude of
his sojourn near to the land of Uz.   And this is the
problem — stated, it is true, with reference to an individual, and not to a nation, but in its principles the
same — which is discussed in the Book of Job.   It
is altogether consonant with probability, that Moses,
musing on this subject under the circumstances described, should throw his thoughts into this form, and
that, in that concluding discourse of Jehovah, in which
are exposed the folly and rashness of presuming to
question or to explain his proceedings, it was the purpose of Moses to quiet the discontents of his countrymen, — those chosen of Jehovah, whom Jehovah
seemed now to have cast off, — by enforcing on them
a lesson of unmurmuring submission to the Divine
will, and quickening the hope of a future exaltation,
through the restored favor of God, to a prosperity
even greater than the past.

Some parts of the book have, with more or less
confidence, been discarded by different critics as spurious; as the prose introduction and conclusion, the
whole discourse of Elihu, and a considerable part of
the last long discourse of Job,* which is thought to
contain matter discordant with his views elsewhere
expressed. In my opinion, there are not only no plausible critical grounds for eliminating either of these
passages, but their rejection would mar the integrity
of the composition, disturb its *lucid order*, confuse that
skilful development of character, for which, among
its other beauties, it is distinguished, and efface the
traces of that *naturalness*, which, in such a poem, is
the highest attainment of art.

The suspicion against these passages as spurious
has, I apprehend, arisen from a desire to simplify the
scheme and design of the book in regard to its inculcation of a moral. A definite moral having been assumed as the object of the writing, whatever appeared
to lend no aid to its inculcation came under a doubt
as to its genuineness. But a rule which assumes that
a book so ancient as this must have been composed
agreeably to the principles of a strict logic, will bear
no examination. It is entirely inapplicable to the
case. Even in the much more recent parables of the
New Testament, we often find matter which does not
aid in the enforcement of the main lesson intended to
be taught. If the half-maddened sufferer, Job, seems
to admit in one place what he had denied in another,
this may not show the consistency of the skilful rea-
soner, but it does show the clear perceptions of the
poet and the student of human nature. If Elihu appears to mingle some vanity and loquacity with his

---

* Job xxvii. 11 - xxviii. 28. — Eichhorn (" Allgemeine Bibliothek,"
Band II. ss. 613 - 616) refers xxvii. 13 - 23 to Zophar.

wisdom, he does but sustain the character in which
the author introduced him, of an earnest, but inexperienced youth. If to one critic it seems that, "for
the completeness of the poem, one might wish the
historical passages away," * another, of at least equal
discernment, expresses the opinion, that "without the
prologue the whole would be without beginning or
end, without plan or completeness," and that "the
epilogue gives to the whole the appropriate finish."†
The New Testament quotes this book but once.‡

---

* De Wette's " Einleitung," § 289.

† Eichhorn's " Einleitung," Band III. § 644. — The question runs much
into detail, and there is no medium between merely adverting to it, and
treating it at considerable length, which I forbear to do, because it seems to
me that a mere unsubstantial and indefensible theory as to a particular kind
of necessary unity of plan in the book has led to inferences which there are
no good critical reasons to support. The student may find it treated by
Eichhorn, Bertholdt, De Wette, Jahn (very briefly), and in most other modern Introductions and Commentaries.

‡ 1 Cor. iii. 19 ; comp. Job v. 13. — James iv. 10 and 1 Peter v. 6 may
allude to Job xxii. 29.

LECTURE LXI.

THE PSALTER.

The Lyric the Earliest Form of Poetry. — Early Hebrew Odes. — King David a Master and a Patron of Poetry and Music. — High Antiquity of a Portion of the Psalms. — The Psalter a Collection of the Writings of various Authors. — Mostly written during the Period of the Jewish Monarchy. — Credit due to the Titles. — Meaning of several Words occurring in them. — Meaning of the Word *Selah*. — Division of the Psalter into Five Books. — Redundancies and Deficiencies. — Peculiarity of Arrangement in the Septuagint and Vulgate Versions. — Classification as to Contents and Character. — Great Value of these Poems, arising from their Antiquity, and from the Information they impart concerning the Culture of the Chosen People. — Remarkable Contrast between the Intellectual Backwardness and Religious Proficiency of the Jews, and the Intellectual Cultivation and Religious Imbecility of other Ancient Nations. — References in the Psalms to the expected Messiah. — Origin and Growth of the Jewish Conception of that Personage. — Different Conceptions of the Messiah current in the Northern Kingdom. — Ideas of the Future Greatness of the Nation entertained by the Egyptian Jews.

The books which we now approach throw more light than those hitherto examined on the culture of the Jewish mind, and the influence of the national, religious, and other institutions on private life and character. The materials furnished by the Later Prophets for information and judgment upon this subject are not so ample, besides relating to times less ancient, and to times, during the decay of the civil state, less suited to develop and manifest a distinctive national character.

The Book of Psalms is a collection of a hundred
and fifty poems of unequal length,-from two verses, as
the hundred and seventeenth, to nearly two hundred,
as the hundred and nineteenth. Some are of a didactic character; * several are strictly in the elegiac
strain ; † the Psalms which are occupied with a recital
of historical facts, and others, are referred by Lowth
to the class of *idyls*.‡ But most of them are, strictly
speaking, *lyrics;* that is, they are songs, odes, or
hymns. And, with few exceptions, all of them have
more or less of a lyrical form and character.

Putting out of view those rhythmical sentences in
which laws were embodied in ancient times for the mere
purpose of fixing them in the memory, and which there
would be no propriety in calling by the name of poetry,
it is natural to suppose that the lyric has been with all
nations the earliest form of poetical composition. The
ode, though it admits of great art in its construction,
is also susceptible of the most perfect simplicity; indeed, its highest art consists in a successful imitation
of spontaneous feeling. It requires no skilful adjust-
ment of parts. Its great charm being its fervor and
enthusiasm, it aims at an effect which would be destroyed by any appearance of elaborate arrangement.
Its great law is to be or to appear unstudied. The
emotions of the heart prompt it, and its excellence is in
unconsciously following and expressing them. When
the feelings have kindled the imagination, the material
for poetry is supplied ; musical numbers are the appropriate clothing in which poetical conceptions are manifested. It is to be presumed that the poet will first

---

* Vide Pss. xxxiii., l., lxxiii., cxix.
† Vide Pss. xxxix., xlii., xliii.
‡ " Lectures on the Sacred Poetry of the Hebrews," pp. 401–410 ; comp.
Pss. lxxviii., cv. – cvii., cxxxvi.

avail himself of that form of his art which is the
most impulsive and the least artificial. It may be
added, that wherever instrumental music has preceded
and suggested poetry, the musical accompaniment
has necessarily given to the poetry its form; and that
form is the lyric.

A few specimens survive of lyric poetry referred to
early periods of the Jewish history. The dying directions of Jacob,* and, in a later age, of Moses,† as
they have been transmitted to us, have the appearance
of being cast in this form. On the passage of the
Red Sea, the Israelites are related to have sung a triumphal hymn, with a chorus and a musical accompaniment; ‡ and something of the same sort seems to
have attended the removals of the ark in the wilderness.§ Deborah and Barak are said to have celebrated
with song their victory over Jabin and the Canaanites.||
Hannah, the mother of Samuel, expressed her gratitude in a psalm.¶ "The Book of Jasher," referred to
as existing at a very early age, appears to have been
a collection of lyric poems.** The "schools of the
prophets," first mentioned in the time of Samuel,††
and probably enough instituted by him as an instrument for the civilization of the people, whatever else
their discipline may have embraced, appear to have
instructed their pupils in the art of minstrelsy in both
its branches, that of music and that of verse.

That the genius of David was developed by instruction in a "school of the prophets" does not appear. It is quite as likely that nature, the discipline
of life, and the general culture of the time, were his
only teachers. But, however his art was acquired, he

---

* Gen. xlix. 1 - 27.   † Deut. xxxiii. 1 - 29.   ‡ Ex. xv. 1 - 21.
§ Numb. x. 35, 36. || Judges v. 1 - 31.   ¶ 1 Sam. ii. 1 - 10.
** Josh. x. 13; 2 Sam. i. 18.   †† 1 Sam. x. 5, 10.

22 *

is related to have attained such skill in it, while yet
a youth, as to lead to his selection from the whole nation, as capable of soothing the frenzy of the king.
The history has preserved his pathetic "lamentation
over Saul and over Jonathan his son." * When, after
his recognition as king of the twelve tribes, and his
establishment of the ark and tabernacle at Jerusalem,
he proceeded to arrange the national worship with circumstances of due magnificence, the musical part of
the ritual claimed his especial care. He delivered a
"psalm, to thank the Lord, into the hand of Asaph
and his brethren," and appointed "Heman and Jeduthun, and the rest that were chosen, who were expressed by name, to give thanks to the Lord, because
his mercy endureth for ever; and with them Heman
and Jeduthun, with trumpets and cymbals for those
that should make a sound, and with musical instruments of God."† And at a later period still of his
reign, there were instituted twenty-four classes of
choristers for the tabernacle, consisting of twelve musicians each,‡ an arrangement which appears to have
been revived by Hezekiah, and again by Josiah, at the
restoration of the worship in their respective reigns.§

With the exception of the Pentateuch, the Books
of Joshua and Judges, and that of Job (if my conjecture concerning the date of the latter is correct),
a large number of the Psalms are more ancient than
any other Hebrew composition now extant. Some of
them were composed for use in the public worship;
much the larger portion, however, with no such design. Though they are frequently called "the Psalms

---

* 2 Sam. i. 17–27.

† 1 Chron. xvi. 7, 41, 42. Comp. Pss. xxiv., cxviii., cxxxvi., which appear to have been composed for this use.

‡ 1 Chron. xxv. 1–31.   § 2 Chron. xxix. 25, 28, 30; xxxv. 15.

of David," and have been so called from very ancient times, every one knows that a large portion of them cannot have been his production. The freedom with which this title has been used, even in connections which preclude a literal interpretation of it, surprises a reader of the present day. The Septuagint version, for example, has the following inscriptions: "A Song of David, when the temple was rebuilt after the exile";* "A Song of David by Jeremiah"; † "A Song of David by Haggai and Zechariah"; ‡ "A Song of David by the sons of Jonadab."§

To more than three quarters of the Psalms inscriptions are prefixed, most of them containing, with or without addition, the name of the supposed author. To Moses,‖ Heman,¶ and Ethan ** are thus referred one Psalm each; to Solomon, two; †† to "the sons of Korah," eleven; ‡‡ to Asaph, twelve; §§ and to David, seventy-four. It is probable, from the contents, that several of those which are anonymous were also David's productions. Besides those of which he was the author, almost all were written between his time and that of the captivity; that is, between six hundred and a thousand years before the Christian era. A few have been thought, but without decisive grounds, to belong to a period as late as that of the Maccabees.‖‖ Of the whole collection, none are in a higher style of poetry than those ascribed to Asaph and the sons of Korah.

That the originals of such poems should often, at least, bear inscriptions with their author's names, which

---

* Ps. xcvi.   † cxxxvii.   ‡ cxxxviii.
§ lxx.   ‖ xc.   ¶ lxxxviii.
** lxxxix.   †† lxxii. and cxxvii.
‡‡ xlii., xliv.–xlix., lxxxiv., lxxxv., lxxxviii.
§§ l., lxxiii.–lxxxiii.   ‖‖ E. g. xliv., lx., lxxiv., xciv., ci., cxviii.

would afterwards be retained in copies, is what we
might expect from the nature of the case, and accords
with what we find to have been the practice of other
sacred writers.* In one case, a poem embraced in the
collection is also found inserted in the history with the
same title,† indicating that the title was probably an
original part of the composition. That some of the
inscriptions now in our copies were already ancient at
the time when the Septuagint version was made appears from this, that the authors of that version,
through ignorance of the meaning of some of their
.terms, have left them untranslated, merely expressing
the Hebrew word in Greek letters.‡ On the other
hand, their genuineness is liable to the following
weighty objections. The old versions more recent than
the Septuagint sometimes omit in whole or in part the
inscriptions preserved in the Hebrew, and sometimes
exhibit inscriptions of an altogether different tenor.
The want of uniformity manifest in the prefixing of
titles to only a portion of the Psalms, is a striking
fact. But what is most important is, that in not a few
the contents either contradict the inscription, or at
least give it no confirmation. On the whole, it appears safe to conclude, that, while some of the inscriptions are original and authentic, others were added by
later hands. To which of these classes a given inscription belongs must be determined, so far as it may
be determinable at all, by considerations belonging to
the particular case.

Along with the name of the author, the inscription

---

* Ex. xv. 1; Deut. xxxi. 30; xxxii. 44; xxxiii. 1; Judges v. 1; and the
Later Prophets, *passim*.

† Ps. xviii. 1; comp. 2 Sam. xxii. 1.

‡ Perhaps, however, this curious fact may be otherwise explained by the
position of the translators, as Egyptian Jews.

to a Psalm sometimes states its occasion and subject. Also, there occur in these titles several words whose meaning has long been the subject of critical inquiry, without any satisfactory result. Our translators, in their ignorance, have generally adopted the method of merely representing them in English letters. Most of them, it is likely, were directions to musical perform-ers. They are the following.

*Aijeleth Shahar.** The words mean, *hind of the morning.* "To us," says Gesenius, "these words seem to be the name of some other poem or song, to the measure of which this Psalm was to be sung or chanted." †

Alamoth.‡ The word means, *young women.* In this application it is probably to be understood as denoting, "with the female voice"; that is, to be sung in *treble* or *soprano.*§

Al-taschith.‖ This is a combination of two familiar words, which signify literally, *do not lose* or *destroy.*¶ It would be natural to consider them as descriptive of the subject of two of the Psalms in which they occur,** deliverance from enemies being therein invoked. But in the two other cases the phrase is not susceptible of the same explanation. Gesenius †† interprets it as "the first words or name of a song to the melody of which these Psalms were to be sung."‡‡ I suggest yet a different view. Wherever the phrase occurs, it is in connection with the address, "To the chief mu-sician." The piece then was *sent* by its author to a musical performer. Was not *Al-taschith* simply a cau-

---

* עַל־אַיֶּלֶת הַשַּׁחַר; Ps. xxii.   † Lex. *ad loc.*   ‡ עֲלָמוֹת; Ps. xlvi.
§ Gesen. Lex. *ad loc.*   ‖ אַל־תַּשְׁחֵת; Pss. lvii., lviii., lix., lxxv.
¶ Comp. 1 Sam. xxvi. 9, where the same words occur.
** Pss. lvii. and lix.   †† Lex. *ad verb.* שָׁחַת.
‡‡ As we should say, "To the tune of ' When first the sun o'er ocean glowed.' "

tion to the messenger respecting its safe conveyance,
(like "with care" or "with speed" upon a modern
letter or parcel), or a request to the receiver to preserve it for further use?

Gittith.* According to one exposition, this word denotes *a musical instrument,* so called, 1. from its being
manufactured at Gath,† or, 2. from its resemblance in
shape to a wine-press (in Hebrew *Gittoth*), or to its
being used in the festivities of the vintage.‡ Others
understand the word as signifying that the Psalms to
which it was prefixed had some association with the
city of Gath, as having been there composed by David,
or as having relation to events of his residence there.§
But this latter interpretation is not corroborated by
any thing in the contents of the poems.

Jeduthun.‖ The proper name of one of the chant-
ers in David's time.¶ If either of the Psalms to
which it is prefixed requires to be referred to a later
period than that of David, it is natural to understand
the word Jeduthun as being applied to the descendants of that distinguished person, agreeably to a well-
known Hebrew use.**

Jonath-elem-rechokim.†† Gesenius ‡‡ renders the
words, *the silent dove among strangers ;* De Wette,§§
the dove of the distant terebinth-trees. Both explain
them as a reference to the words of some other song,
in the same tune.

Leannoth ‖‖ it appears singular that our translators
did not render into English. It is a well-known word,

---

* גִּתִּית ; Pss. viii., lxxxi., lxxxiv.   † Comp. 2 Sam. vi. 10.
‡ Comp. Is. xvi. 10 ; Jer. xlviii. 33.   § 1 Sam. xxi. 10 *et seq.*
‖ יְדוּתוּן ; Pss. xxxix., lxii., lxxvii.
¶ 1 Chron. xvi. 41, 42 ; comp. xxv. 1, 3.
** Isaiah xi. 13 ; comp. Ps. xxxix. 1 ; xliv. 1.
†† יוֹנַת אֵלֶם רְחֹקִים ; Ps. lvi.   ‡‡ *Ad verb.* אֵלֶם.
§§ " Uebersetzung," u. s. w., *ad loc.*   ‖‖ לְעַנּוֹת ; Ps. lxxxviii.

consisting of a verb and prefix, signifying *to reply, to respond;* and, in this connection, can only mean that the Psalm is so constructed as for the choristers to respond in alternate strains.

Mahalath, from the connections in which it appears, may be safely interpreted as the name of some musical instrument. No more precise definition of the word can be ascertained.*

Mangaloth.† This is the plural of a noun signifying *a step* or *ascent;* and by our translators is rendered *degrees.* The *songs of degrees,* says Gesenius,‡ were "probably so called from a certain number or rhythm obvious in several of them, by which the sense, as it were, *ascends* by degrees or steps, the first or last words of a preceding clause being often repeated at the beginning of the succeeding one.§ . . . . . On slight grounds, also, some refer the name to the argument of the Psalms, and translate *songs of ascent,* or *pilgrim songs,* supposing them to have been sung by the Israelites while returning from exile ‖ or on their annual journeys to Jerusalem; but this would apply to only two of them,¶ while the others are wholly different." Others, with still less probability, understand them to be designated as hymns sung by choirs standing on the *steps* of the temple.

Maschil would, from its etymology, seem to signify, *a didactic Psalm.*** But if so, it was used with great

---

* מָחֲלַת; Pss. liii. and lxxxviii. Gesenius (*ad verb.*) defines it *a stringed instrument, lute, guitar;* but I see not on what authority. Others, on the contrary, would have it to be a wind instrument, deriving it from חָלַל, *he pierced.*

† מַעֲלוֹת; Pss. cxx.–cxxxiv.   ‡ Lex. *ad verb.*

§ E. g. cxxi. 1–5; cxxiv. 1–5.   ‖ Comp. Ez. vii. 6, 7.

¶ Pss. cxxii. and cxxvi.

** מַשְׂכִּיל (Ps. xxxii. and twelve others), from שָׂכַל, *he was wise.* Michaelis (~~Supplem. ad Lex. Hebraic.~~) derives the word from an Arabic root, signifying *he fastened* or *restricted.*

freedom of application; since, of the thirteen Psalms to which it is prefixed, only one, the thirty-second, appears peculiarly to deserve that appellation.

The word *Menatzeah*, occurring in a prefix to more than one third part of the Psalms,* is always rendered by our translators, *the chief musician.* In this version they are probably correct.† Other renderings, however, have had their advocates. That of the Septuagint, which is followed by the Vulgate,‡ is very peculiar. Literally rendered into English, it signifies, *to the end.* What meaning the authors of those versions intended thus to express, is quite uncertain. According to one interpretation, the phrase *to the end* is to be understood as equivalent to *perpetually*,§ and is used in this connection to distinguish some Psalms which might be used in the religious worship of every day, from others which were appropriated to the ritual of the Sabbath or other festivals. According to other explanations, less plausible, it meant that the Psalms thus distinguished should be sung *with a loud voice,* or *with care,* or *earnestness.*‖ Possibly by *the chief musician* we are to understand David, designated as the author of these Psalms by a descriptive name, as Solomon was called " Koheleth," or *the preacher.*

Michtam.¶ This word has been differently understood as meaning, — 1. *Golden,*** and so intended to designate the peculiar excellence of the poems which it prefaces, or their having been inscribed in some

---

* לַמְנַצֵּחַ; Ps. iv. and fifty-two others.

† Comp. 2 Chron. ii. 2, 18, xxxiv. 13, where the same word is properly translated *overseers.*

‡ Εἰς τὸ τέλος, Sept. *In finem,* Vulg.

§ Comp. Luke xviii. 5.

‖ Quasi *forte, con espressione;* in 1 Chron. xv. 21, לְנַצֵּחַ is rendered *to excel.*

¶ מִכְתָּם; Pss. xvi., lvi. - lx.   ** From כֶּתֶם, *gold.*

public place in letters 'of gold; but they do not appear
to deserve such a distinction. 2. *Hidden,** and thus intimating that the Psalms were written by David while
in exile; but besides being extremely far-fetched, this
explanation supposes a fact hardly consistent with the
language in two at least of the poems in question.†
3. *Sculptured*, or *engraved*, ‡ as on some monumental
tablet; but there appears nothing in their contents
specially destining them to such a use, and the length
of some renders it improbable. 4. Simply, *a writing;*
a meaning very suitable and satisfactory, though the
etymology by which it is obtained is not obvious.§
The rendering in the version of Aquila is peculiar.
For the unmeaning phrase of our translators, *Michtam of David*, he has, " of the humble and sincere
David."   His text appears to have exhibited the same
letters as ours, but he understood them to constitute
two words.‖

Mismor; commonly understood as simply *a Psalm.*¶
But Lowth would give the word a more specific meaning.   " I suppose *Mismor*," he says, " to denote *measure*, or *numbers*, what the Greeks call ῥυθμόν.   It may
also be more immediately referred to the former and
original sense of the root, as signifying a poem *cut
into short sentences*, and *pruned* from every luxuriancy
of expression, which is a distinguishing characteristic
of the Hebrew poetry."**

---

* From כֶּתֶם (Jer. ii. 22).   † Pss. lviii., lx.

‡ From another conjectural meaning of כֶּתֶם, derived from a Syriac root.

§ From the common verb כָּתַב, *he wrote*, the labial ב being supposed to
be changed for מ.   With מִכְתָּם לְדָוִד, thus supposed to mean *a writing of
David*, compare מִכְתָּב לְחִזְקִיָּהוּ (Is. xxxviii. 9), rendered *the writing of
Hezekiah*.

‖ מַךְ, from מָכַךְ, *he was humble*, and the well-known adjective תָּם.

¶ מִזְמוֹר, from זָמַר, *he sang*, Piel of זָמַר, *he cut*, or *pruned*.   The word
is prefixed to numerous Psalms.

** "Lectures on the Sacred Poetry of the Hebrews," p. 46, note.

Muth-labben * defies the skill of the interpreters. The ancient versions render it with extraordinary diversities of sense.†

From its etymology *Neginoth* is inferred, with a high degree of probability, to denote stringed instruments, played with the touch, like the guitar and harp.‡

Nehiloth occurs but once. Its etymology in like manner indicates it to denote a wind instrument, like a pipe, flute, or organ.§ Here again the Septuagint and Vulgate versions coincide in a peculiar translation, importing " for her who obtains an inheritance "; by which they probably intended to describe the Psalm as being a prayer for the Israelitish people, which had obtained an inheritance in Canaan. They appear to have also had recourse to etymology for a definition, and to have derived the word from a different root. ||

Sheminith ¶ appears, from the connection in which it occurs in a passage in the history,** to have meant an instrument of music. The probable derivation of the word from the Hebrew numeral corresponding to eight, indicates its particular meaning to have been *a lyre with eight strings*, or possibly *an octave flute*.

---

* מוּת לַבֵּן ; Ps. ix.

† Gesenius (" Lex." *ad verb.* עַלְמוּת) proposes to render עַל מוּת as equivalent to עַל עֲלָמוֹת, and says that " perhaps it should be so read." But this is very unsatisfactory, besides providing no explanation of the לַבֵּן. Dathe (" Psalmi," *ad loc.*) cuts the knot by assuming that *Muth-labben* was the name of a musical instrument.

‡ נְגִנוֹת ; Pss. iv., vi., liv., lv., lxvii., lxxvi. Comp. 1 Sam. xvi. 23; Is. xxxviii. 20. The verb in the Piel form (נִגֵּן) occurs in 1 Sam. xvi. 16, 17, 18; 2 Kings iii. 15; Ps. xxxiii. 3; Is. xxiii. 16.

§ נְחִילָה (Ps. v.), apparently a derivative from חָלַל, *he bored*.

|| Their rendering is ὑπὲρ τῆς κληρονομούσης, pro eâ quæ hereditatem consequitur; *quasi* from נָחַל, *he possessed* or *inherited*.

¶ שְׁמִינִית ; Pss. vi., xii.. ** 1 Chron. xv. 21.

Shiggaion is found but once.* There is no guide to
its meaning except etymology. Some, deriving it from
a Hebrew verb which signifies *to wander*, understand
it to denote an ode in a free, excursive, erratic strain; †
others, tracing it to a root now lost in the Hebrew, but
retained in the Arabic, render it *a threnody*, an ode
expressive of anxiety and grief; a meaning less con-
gruous with the contents of the Psalm to which it is
prefixed, than to the connection in which it appears in
the prophecy of Habakkuk.

Shoshannim; ‡ "a musical instrument," says Gesenius, "probably so called from its resemblance to a lily;
to the common lily several kinds of trumpets and pipes
may be said to have a resemblance; . . . . . the name
of *cymbal* was at a later period sometimes given to this
flower." § Sometimes the word occurs with an addition,
as *Shoshannim-Eduth*, ‖ the meaning of which is still
more obscure. The best conjecture appears to me that
which explains it to mean a song *for the harp*, a sense
obtained by reference to a similar word extant in the
Arabic, which is constantly used in the Arabic version
of the Old Testament to express that Hebrew word
which our translators render *harp*.

Another untranslated word appears seventy-one
times in the version of the Psalms, as well as elsewhere, ¶ which, though not occurring in inscriptions,
may not unsuitably be considered in this place. Some
commentators understand *Selah* to be a single uncom-
pounded word,** and to indicate a musical *pause*, or

---

* Ps. vii. ; comp. Habak. iii. 1. † שִׁגָּיוֹן, *quasi* from שָׁגָה, *he wandered.*

‡ שֹׁשַׁנִּים ; Pss. xlv., lx., lxix., lxxx.

§ "Lex." *ad verb;* שׁוּשַׁן is the Hebrew for *lily.*

‖ Pss. lx., lxxx.   ¶ Hab. iii. 3, 9, 13.

** סֶלָה, from a supposed root סָלָה, equivalent to שָׁלָה (which signifies *he
rested*), the sibilants in Hebrew being often thus interchanged.

rest of the vocal music, while the instruments played an interlude or symphony. This interpretation, which appears the most probable, is supported by the Septuagint and Syriac translations of the term, by the place which it occupies in the Psalms, which is commonly at the close of a section or *strophe*, and by a particular text where it occurs in a more full expression,* which it appears should be rendered (*vice versâ*) "instrumental music, pause." Others, on another etymological ground, understand it as a different musical direction, equivalent to the modern *crescendo* or *forte*;† while yet others, more artificially, regard it as a word compounded, in the way of abbreviation, of the initial letters of three words, and signifying *repeat, da capo,*‡ or *let the whole join in chorus.* § A common notion that it denotes affirmation or emphasis, like "Amen!" or "Consider that!" has no foundation.

In imitation, probably, of the Pentateuch, the Psalter is divided into five books, the separation being marked by a doxology at the end of each section, except the last.‖ As to the questions by whom the collection was made and thus arranged, we have no historical information. It seems probable, from the note at the close of the second book, "The prayers of David, the son of Jesse, are ended," that the first two books once constituted a separate collection, consisting, in the opinion of the person who affixed that note, of poems of David's composition; and yet, in the present titles, one of them is referred to Asaph,¶ and several (according to the most approved translation) to "the

---

* "Higgaion, Selah." Ps. ix. 16.   † From כָּלָה, *he lifted up, he raised.*

‡ סֹב לְמַעֲלָה הַשִׁיר, i. e. *go back, singer.*

§ סִימָן לְכֹל חָיִם.

‖ Ps. xli. 13; lxxii. 18–20; lxxxix. 52; cvi. 48.   ¶ Ps. l.

sons of Korah." * Of the seventeen Psalms in the third book, the titles refer ten to Asaph,† four to "the sons of Korah," ‡ and one each to David,§ Heman the Ezrahite, ‖ and Ethan the Ezrahite.¶ Of the seventeen Psalms in the fourth book, three only have inscriptions with the names of their authors, one being ascribed to Moses ** and two to David.†† The contents of the last book are mostly anonymous; one Psalm, however, is ascribed to Solomon, ‡‡ and fifteen to David. §§

That the collection was not made with critical care may be inferred from the repetitions which it presents. The fifty-third Psalm is a duplicate of the fourteenth, and the seventieth consists of the last five verses of the fortieth. ‖‖ While the collection is thus redundant on the one hand, it appears to be defective on the other, even in respect to the productions of its principal author. It omits two poems which are preserved as David's in the history. ¶¶ The eighteenth Psalm is preserved in the history, in a copy with some different readings.***

In the Septuagint and Vulgate versions, the ninth and tenth Psalms of the Hebrew text, and in like manner the one hundred and fourteenth and one hundred and fifteenth, are united as one poem. On the other

---

* Pss. xlii., xliv. – xlix.　　　　　† lxxiv. – lxxxiii.

‡ lxxxiv., lxxxv., lxxxvii., lxxxviii.　　§ lxxxvi.

‖ lxxxviii.　　　　　¶ lxxxix.

** xc.　　　　†† ci., ciii.　　　　　　‡‡ cxxvii.

§§ cviii. – cx., cxxii., cxxiv., cxxxi., cxxxiii., cxxxviii. – cxlv.

‖‖ Also, comp. lvii. 5 – 11 with cviii. 1 – 5, and lx. 5 – 12 with cviii. 6 – 13.

¶¶ 2 Sam. i. 17 – 27 ; xxiii. 1 – 7.

*** 2 Sam. xxii. For instances of diversity of reading, see Ps. xviii. 2 (comp. 2 Sam. xxii. 3) ; 10 (comp. 2 Sam. xxii. 11) ; 12 (comp. 2 Sam. xxii. 13) ; 15 (comp. 2 Sam. xxii. 16) ; 42 (comp. 2 Sam. xxii. 43). It would be useless to multiply them. Dathe plausibly remarks upon them (" Lib. Hist. V. T.," *ad loc.*), that, as the readings in both places give a good sense, we are rather to attribute them to two different copies proceeding from the author, than to errors of transcribers.

hand, the one hundred and sixteenth and one hundred
and forty-seventh are each divided into two. These
circumstances of course occasion a difference of numer-
ation between the Hebrew text and those versions, in
all the Psalms except the first nine and the last three.
The versions also give an apocryphal Psalm as the one
hundred and fifty-first.*

In respect to their contents and character, De Wette †
classes the Psalms as follows, viz. : —

I. Hymns in praise of Jehovah ; — 1. As God of nature and of man. ‡ 2. As God of nature and national
God. § 3. As national God. || 4. As Saviour and
friend, (1.) of Israel ; ¶ (2.) of individuals.**

II. National Psalms, referring to the ancient national history, and the people's relation to Jehovah.††

III. Psalms of Zion and of the Temple. ‡‡

IV. Psalms relating to the King of the Jews. §§

V. Psalms, containing complaints in affliction, and
prayers for relief; — 1. Personal. |||| 2. National.¶¶
3. Personal and national united.*** 4. Reflections

---

* The junction or division of single passages, so as to cause them to
belong to one or more psalms, appears to have been somewhat arbitrary,
and in several instances is represented differently in different manuscripts and
versions. Some manuscripts, for instance, make only one psalm of the seventieth and seventy-first. Others divide the hundred and eighteenth into
three, beginning respectively at the first, fifth, and twenty-sixth verses. See
Eichhorn, " Einleit. ins A. T.," Band III. s. 500.

† " Commentar über die Psalmen," Einleit., ss. 4, 5.

‡ E. g. Pss. viii., civ., cxlv.

§ xix., xxix., xxxiii., lxv., xciii., cxxxv., cxxxvi., cxlvii.

|| xlvii., lxvi., lxvii., lxxv.

¶ xlvi. – xlviii., lxxv., lxxvi.

** xviii., xxx., cxxxviii.

†† lxxviii., cv., cvi., cxiv.

‡‡ xv., xxiv., lxviii., lxxxi., lxxxvii., cxxxii., cxxxiv., cxxxv.

§§ ii., xx., xxi., xlv., lxxii., cx.

|||| vii., xxii., lv., lvi., cix.

¶¶ xliv., lxxiv., lxxix., lxxx., cxxxvii.

*** lxix., lxxvii., cii.

on the wickedness of the world.* 5. Didactic Psalms on the retributions of life.† 6. Thanksgivings for deliverance. ‡

VI. Religious and moral Psalms;—1. Odes to Jehovah. § 2. Expressions of religious conviction, hope, confidence, &c. ‖ 3. Expressions of religious experience, resolutions, &c. ¶ 4. Development of religious or moral ideas.** 5. Poems of religious doctrine.†† 6. Proverbs in an alphabetical series. ‡‡

With the exception of the Pentateuch, the Book of Psalms is the most important and valuable book in the Old Testament collection.

Many of the Psalms are of an earlier date than any works of classical literature which have come down to our day. All the interest which belongs to compositions derived from a remote age, and from an immature stage of civilization, attaches to them in the highest degree.

They convey the best information which we possess concerning that remarkable nation, whom, before sending Christianity, God distinguished by the revelation of a system of faith and worship. In the Scriptural books containing a history of the ages which followed, we have an account, partially authentic, of the national condition and fortunes; but only information extremely imperfect concerning what is more desirable to be known, the state of mental, moral, and religious culture among the people, and their habits of thought and feeling in general. To fill this chasm, the Psalms contribute very material aid. They express the views and feelings of their writers, and to some extent they

---

* Pss. x., xii., xiv., xxxvi.   † xxxvii., xlix., lxxiii.
‡ xxxiv., xl.   § xc., cxxxix.
‖ xxiii., xci., cxxi., cxxvii., cxxviii.   ¶ xlii., xliii., ci., cxxxi.
** i., cxxxiii.   †† xxxii., l.   ‡‡ cxix.

refer to and imply the views and feelings of others, on
various matters of judgment, speculation, and experience, and on various occasions of excitement, personal
and public. Thus, while the historical books present
a view, such as it is, of the Hebrew commonwealth,
the Psalms, much more than they, and more than any
other book, acquaint us with the condition of the Hebrew mind, under its divinely ordained training before
the advent of Jesus; with the effect exerted upon it
by the Mosaic revelation; and, in general, with its degree of intellectual and moral proficiency.

Here a fact of the greatest curiosity and interest is
brought to light, which would be vastly more clear
and striking even than it now is, if, instead of being
familiar with these poems from early years, we should
take them up for the first time in the maturity of our
powers of perception and judgment, and when in possession of the knowledge necessary to prepare us for a
comparison of them with other ancient writings. If
for a short time, just after the establishment of the
monarchy, the Jews appear to have had a considerable share in the imperfect civilization of the age, this
was but a bright spot in the generally gloomy track
of their history. With the partial exception of that
short period, their national annals, from first to last,
represent them as in an unsettled and troubled state,
altogether unpropitious to the successful cultivation of
the arts of peace, to social improvement, to intellectual
development, to the growth of science, letters, taste,
art, humanity. In the times of national independence, what record is there of any Jewish mathema-
tician, inventor, orator, artist? What proof of the
existence, among the people at large, of any degree of
that expansion and refinement of mind, which, as
far as merely human instrumentality can have the

effect, appear to afford the proper preparation for just and elevated views of God and of religious truth? On the contrary, in respect to all great subjects of thought and exercises of intellect, except one, nothing is more certain than that the culture of the Jewish mind was low, its capacity and comprehension mean, its conceptions tame and narrow.

While the Jew occupied this humble position in respect to much of what belongs to the dignity and grace of human nature, other nations had attained a high degree of general culture. Building on the basis of a more ancient civilization, the Greek and Roman mind had been exercised with singular success in the speculations of philosophy, the investigations of science, the refinements of literature, the embellishments of art. While as to the elegances of mental culture the Jewish annals are a blank, Greek and Roman sciences paved the way to whatever improvements have since superseded them, and Greek and Roman history, eloquence, poetry, architecture, sculpture, have not been surpassed, if ever equalled.

This is one contrast. There is another, which, considered in connection with it, is manifestly of the most extraordinary character. The Greek and Roman, much as they understood of other things, knew little of God, and of the service acceptable to him! The Jew, knowing little of other things, was a proficient in the knowledge of God and duty.

A more remarkable fact than that here brought to view can scarcely claim our attention. So far as the human mind, unenlightened by direct supernatural revelation, was capable of attaining, by its own investigations, to the knowledge of religious truth, that knowledge, it would seem, should have been attained by the nations of classical antiquity. But, in truth, it was not attained, either by the people at large, or so much as by individual men of rare sagacity. Even the fundamental truths of God's unity, and of the moral perfection of the Divine nature, had only here and there disclosed themselves, and that in dim outline, to the solitary musings of some philosophic mind. That moral excellence, a pure and righteous life, kind and devout affections, were the way to conciliate the Divine favor, was a truth still less, if possible, perceived. That "obedience was better than sacrifice, and to hearken than the fat of rams," was a grand truth which the humblest Jew understood, but which was not understood by the most acute and accomplished heathen.[*]

In short, knowledge of the greatest moment, pertaining to the highest subjects of thought, was not possessed by the most enlightened nations of antiquity. It was possessed by the otherwise unenlightened nation of the Jews. A fact so remarkable seems absolutely to preclude every explanation except one. How is it possible to imagine that this came to pass, except through a direct revelation to that people?

So accordant are the representations in the Psalms respecting the perfections of God, the relations he sustains towards man, and the service due and acceptable to him, with the representations on those subjects since communicated by Christianity, that Christians of every age have found in that book the best manual for their own devotions and edification. The language in which, ages ago, the singers of Israel expressed gratitude, confidence, resignation, contrition, — in short, the various moods of the pious mind, — is

---

[*] See the author's "Lowell Lectures on the Evidences of Christianity," Vol. I. pp. 74-89.

found eminently to suit the wants and experiences of the believer of the present day. And, next to the Gospels, the Psalter is to him the most indispensable of books.

Yet there is one great exception. After all that has been said by interpreters to the end of explaining in a less obnoxious sense the language expressive of vindictive and ferocious anger which occasionally occurs, it must be owned that there are passages indicating a state of feeling towards enemies, such as the gentle and forgiving spirit of Christianity absolutely disowns and condemns. The fact is so. The temper which Jesus inculcated on his followers when he taught them to forgive as they hoped to be forgiven, was not that which dictated the imprecations in the hundred and ninth and hundred and thirty-seventh Psalms. What then? The wonder is not that a religious system, confessedly and necessarily imperfect,* as being designed to operate in the first instance on a low condition of moral and spiritual culture, had but an imperfect effect on the character of its votaries, and fell short of making them eminent saints. The wonder is, on the contrary, that it accomplished so much for their religious instruction, edification, and improvement, as we see clear proof that it did accomplish, in the writings they have left.

There is another point of view in which the Book of Psalms possesses a strong interest for the Christian reader. For different purposes, it is frequently quoted — sixty or seventy times — in the books of the New Testament. In a few of these quotations, — though not nearly as often as is commonly supposed,

---

* "Moses, because of the hardness of your hearts, suffered you," &c. (Mat. xix. 8); "The Law was our schoolmaster, to bring us unto Christ" (Gal. iii. 24).

— the writer of the Psalm is represented as having intended to refer to the expected Messiah; and there are, I think, other Psalms, not quoted in the New Testament, in which a similar reference was also designed.

In a former Lecture, I presented briefly my view concerning the origin and growth of the Jewish notion in respect to that great personage, called in later times the *Messiah* (or *anointed*).* An ancient tradition, which had descended to the time of Moses, and been incorporated by him into his collection of fragments of primitive history, had represented Abraham, Isaac, and Jacob, the patriarchs of the Jewish race, as having received a Divine promise that in their posterity "all the families of the earth" should be blessed; † and Moses had himself received authority to reveal to his people that God had said to him, "I will raise them up a prophet from among their brethren like unto thee, and will put my words in his mouth, and he shall speak unto them all that I shall command him."‡ This was the primitive idea which the Jews of later ages amplified and distorted into the conception of their warlike and (in a worldly sense) magnificent Messiah. The promise of Moses in its true sense referred to Jesus, that Saviour who eighteen centuries ago did appear among the Jews, a prophet (or teacher) like Moses, to speak the words which God "put in his mouth," and, by thus publishing Divine truth, to be a blessing to "all the families of the earth." So St. Peter correctly explained the record of the ancient lawgiver, when he told the assembly in Solomon's porch, "Moses truly said unto

* Vol. II. pp. 377 – 386.　　　† Gen. xii. 3 ; xxvi. 4 ; xxviii. 14.
‡ Deut. xviii. 18.

the fathers, 'A prophet shall the Lord your God raise up unto you of your brethren, like unto me; him shall ye hear in all things whatsoever he shall say unto you.' . . . . . Ye are the children of the prophets, and of the covenant which God made with our fathers, saying unto Abraham, 'And in thy seed shall all the kindreds of the earth be blessed.'"* These are Peter's quotations from old Scripture. Then follows his application of them: God has now fulfilled that ancient promise. He has "raised up" the "prophet," the *teacher*, like unto Moses. "His son Jesus" is that predicted teacher. He has sent him to "bless" you, agreeably to his recorded promise to the patriarchs of the race. But to bless you, how? To bless you as a teacher, a spiritual teacher. To bless you in the way that Moses indicated, by means of instructions suited to "turn away every one of you from his iniquities."

But though this, of a religious teacher, was, as St. Peter declares, the primitive Mosaic idea of the Messiah who was to come, that idea, as early as the earliest time when again in the history it presents itself to view, had become much disguised in the popular conception. Nor was this unnatural. The ambition of national splendor and aggrandizement grew up as spontaneously in Judea as elsewhere, and Moses himself had encouraged its people to hope for the permanency of their institutions and the extension of their power. Without wholly losing sight of the character of their great expected countryman as a religious reformer, it was easy for them to merge that character in the more complex one of a mighty and beneficent prince, at the same time extending the true faith and worship by the success of his arms, and sustaining them among his own subjects by a wise ad-

---

* Acts iii. 22 – 26.

ministration. When David came to the throne of Israel, with his high personal qualities and his fair prospect of establishing a prosperous and permanent dynasty, no one can wonder that he, and his courtiers, and his people generally, should readily embrace that idea, and that the vague words of Moses should take a more definite form in the expectation of a splendid prince of David's line.

That form and explanation accordingly they did take, as, I think, we shall presently see, in Psalms belonging to the early period of the monarchy. The lineage of David occupied the throne of the southern kingdom down to the time of the Babylonian conquest, a period of nearly five hundred years, during which time the same expectation of an illustrious scion from the royal stock appears to have prevailed, an expectation of which in previous Lectures we have seen numerous traces in the writings of the prophets of successive ages. Nor did the expectation cease with the capture of the holy city. On the contrary, it was excited to new strength after that catastrophe, as we shall see when we come to examine the Book of Daniel. Though the temple was in ruins, and the country a waste, the royal line was not extinct, nor was there any necessity to abandon the hope of its revival. Nor was that hope ever more confident than when, after Judea had been successively overrun by Chaldean, Persian, Greek, and Roman, the people said of Jesus (with evident reference to Moses's words), " This is of a truth that *prophet* that should come into the world," and then, following out the ancient popular misconception of the promised prophet's character, would have taken him " by force to make him a king." *

---

* John vi. 14, 15.

But the history of opinions concerning the Messiah is not uniform. I have stated only that which, owing to natural causes, became established among the Jews of the southern kingdom, and subsequently among that portion of them who returned to the Holy Land after the decree of Cyrus.

While the Jews of the southern kingdom, after the separation in Rehoboam's age, continued to identify their expected Messiah — that is, the imaginary character compounded of the *prophet* predicted by Moses and of unfounded conceptions of their own*— with a personage who was to spring from the lineage of their own kings, which was the. lineage of David and of Judah, the people of the ten northern tribes as naturally fell, by the operation of the same cause, into a different opinion. In the northern kingdom Ephraim was the predominating tribe, as Judah was in the southern; and from that tribe Jeroboam, the founder of the Israelitish dynasty, appears to have descended. Accordingly, as in the Jewish kingdom the expected prince was looked for among the descendants of David, and so of Judah, in the Israelitish kingdom it was thought that he would spring from the stock of Ephraim. This I take to be the solution of the idea of two Messiahs, one a son of Judah, the other a son of Ephraim, which occasionally appears in the later Jewish writings. The people of the two kingdoms having different ideas of the origin of the expected prince, the writers of subsequent times adopted both, though, as might be expected from the circumstances, the greater prominence was given to the idea of the Messiah from the Judahite stock.*

---

* " Thy two Saviours, who shall deliver thee, Messiah, the son of David, and Messiah, the son of Ephraim, resemble Moses and Aaron," says the Targum on Cant. iv. 5; vii. 3. (See Walton's Polyglott, *ad loc.*) For

There were settlements of the Jews in Egypt immediately after the Babylonian conquest of Palestine;
that is, nearly six hundred years before the Christian
era.* At Alexandria, in that kingdom, two hundred
and fifty years later, a large Jewish colony was established by Alexander the Great, which increased and
flourished under the government of the Græco-Egyp-
tian kings. The Alexandrine Jews, from their Greek
connections, adopted habits of speculation and criticism altogether different from those of their countrymen in Palestine. After their fashion, they became
philosophers and rhetoricians. They extolled and
studied Pythagoras and Plato. They labored to *Hel-
lenize* their faith, and to this end had recourse to ingenious interpretations of its documents. We have traces
of their notion of the character of the future glorious
age of their nation in the Book of Wisdom, composed
by one of their number,† and in the copious works of
Philo, their principal writer.‡ Neither has any reference to any expected *person*, who was to put a better
face on Jewish affairs, though the latter treats largely of
a future moral government, a reign of truth and righteousness, to be established through the instrumentality
of the Jewish nation. If they lost sight, as much as
the Jews of Palestine, of the original Mosaic notion
of another divinely commissioned teacher to come in
the fulness of time, they did not substitute for it, or
make it subordinate to, the idea of a king and hero.

This, I repeat it, the Jews of Palestine did, through
their whole history, from the establishment of the

---

numerous specimens of the same language, see Bertholdt's "Christologia
Judæorum," § 17, notes.

* Jer. xliii., xliv.

† See Wisdom, iii. 7, 8; v. 15 - 23.

‡ "Philon. Opp."(edit. Mangey), Tom. I. p. 647; II. pp. 424-427, 435, 436.

monarchy. It was not only at the time of the birth of Jesus, as has been often erroneously represented, that they were looking for the great deliverer to appear. They were expecting him with anxious desire through the whole period of their national depression. It was not only in respect to John the Baptist that they raised the question, whether he was the prince " that should come," or whether they were to " look for another." That question arose in respect to any remarkable champion of the nation who appeared during the afflicted ages.

Of this notion of the *Messiah* we have seen abundant traces in the writings of the Later Prophets. Other traces of it are also found, in a few instances, in the book before us. And some of these, referable to the time of David, are, of course, the earliest which exist.

The two subjects which I have proposed in the latter part of this Lecture are both so important, as to demand further consideration.

LECTURE LXII.

THEOLOGY, DEVOTION, AND MORALITY OF THE PSALMS.

The Mosaic Law the Religious Teacher of the Psalmists. — Their Knowledge of the Divine Unity, — Eternity, — Immutableness, — Omnipresence, — Omniscience, — Omnipotence, — Providence, — Moral Government, — Parental Character. — Their Conception of the proper Character and Expressions of a Devout Spirit. — Their Just View of the Afflictive Dispensations of Providence. — Their Sense of the Superiority of Moral over Ceremonial Obedience. — Imperfection of their System of Morals. — Importance ascribed by them to Worship of God in Prayer, and Ritual Observances. — Recognitions of the Mosaic Institutions of Sacrifices and Consecrated Days. — References to the Ancient History, as related in the Books of Moses.

In my last Lecture, I called attention to the extraordinary and profoundly interesting fact of the correctness of the views entertained by the writers of the Psalms concerning the nature and attributes of the Supreme Being, and the service due to him from men. In the present Lecture I am further to illustrate that topic, by merely bringing together some passages which will be recognized as fair specimens of the uniform tone of the book in relation to these subjects.

In reading them, we cannot fail to observe with admiration what a fruitful germ of correct, comprehensive, and profitable thought the Mosaic revelation had proved.   The Psalmists, as far as we know, had no advantages over the rest of men for religious speculation and improvement, except what they possessed as Jews ; that is, except what was afforded them by the

writings and the institutions of Moses. But his law
they made their study; it opened their eyes, and in
it they beheld wondrous things.* Building on that
basis, following out the trains of thought which that
elementary doctrine suggested and involved, they
attained to views of God and of the service due to
him, — they passed through religious frames and experiences of every variety, — such as make the expression of their convictions and emotions correspond,
with wonderful exactness, to those of the devout mind
at the present day, and cause them to be the intimate
companion of the Christian in all the moods of his self-
communion, and through all the changes of his life.

"He that cometh to God must believe that he is,
and that he is a rewarder of them that diligently seek
him." The foundation of all religion lies in just views
of the Divine being, character, and government.

According to the theology of the Psalms, God is
one, and reigns with undivided sway.

> "Our God is in the heavens;
> He doth whatever he pleaseth.
> But their idols are silver and gold,
> The work of men's hands;
> They have mouths, but they speak not;
> Eyes have they, but they see not;
> They have ears, but they hear not;
> Noses have they, but they smell not.
> They have hands, but they handle not;
> They have feet, but they walk not;
> Nor do they speak with their throats.
> They that make them are like them;
> And so is every one that trusteth in them.
> But let Israel trust in Jehovah!
> He is their help and their shield."—cxv. 3-9.

He is eternal and unchangeable.

> "Of old hast thou laid the foundations of the earth,
> And the heavens are the work of thy hands;

---

* Ps. cxix. 18.

They shall perish, but thou shalt endure ;
Yea, all of them shall wax old like a garment ;
Thou shalt change them as a vesture, and they shall be changed ;
But thou art for ever the same ;
Thy years shall have no end ! " — cii. 25 - 27.

He is omnipresent and omniscient.

" O Lord, thou hast searched me and known me.
Thou knowest my resting and my rising ;
Thou understandest my thoughts from afar.
Thou seest my path and my lying down,
And art acquainted with all my ways !
Before the word is upon my tongue,
Behold, O Lord, thou knowest it altogether !
Thou inclosest me behind and before,
And layest thine hand upon me !
Such knowledge is too wonderful for me ;
It is high, I cannot attain to it !
Whither shall I go from thy spirit,
And whither shall I flee from thy presence ?
If I ascend into heaven, thou art there !
If I make my bed in Hades, behold, thou art there !
Should I take the wings of the morning,
And dwell in the remotest parts of the sea,
Even there shall thy hand lead me,
And thy right hand shall hold me !
If I say, Surely the darkness shall conceal me ;
Even the night shall be light about me.
Yea, the darkness hideth not from thee,
But the night shineth as the day ;
The darkness and the light are both alike to thee ! " — cxxxix. 1 - 12.

" Be instructed, ye most stupid of mankind ;
O, when, ye fools, will ye be wise !
He that planted the ear, shall he not hear !
He that formed the eye, shall he not see !
He that chastiseth nations, shall not he punish !
He that teacheth man knowledge, shall not he know !
Jehovah knoweth the thoughts of men." — xciv. 8 - 11.

He is almighty.

" By the word of the Lord were the heavens made,
And all the hosts of them by the breath of his mouth.
He gathereth the waters of the sea, as a heap ;
˒ He layeth up the deep in storehouses.
Let all the earth revere Jehovah ;
Let all the inhabitants of the world stand in awe of him !

For he spake, and it was done;
He commanded, and it stood fast."—xxxiii. 6-9.

" By wonderful deeds dost thou answer us in thy goodness,
O God, our saviour!
Who art the confidence of all the ends of the earth,
And of the most distant seas!
    " Thou makest fast the mountains by thy power,
Being girded ,with strength!
Thou stillest the roar of the sea,
The roar of its waves,
And the tumult of the people.
The remotest inhabitants of the earth are awed by thy wonderful works."
                                                   lxv. 5-8.

" I know that Jehovah is great;
That our Lord is above all gods.
All that Jehovah pleaseth, that he doth,
In heaven and upon earth,
In the sea, and in all deeps.
He causeth the clouds to ascend from the ends of the earth;
He maketh lightnings with rain;
He bringeth the wind from his storehouses."—cxxxv. 5-7.

" He covereth himself with light as with a garment;
He spreadeth out the heavens like a curtain;
He buildeth his chambers on the waters; ,
He maketh the clouds his chariot;
He rideth upon the wings of the wind.
He maketh the winds his messengers,
The flaming lightnings his ministers.
    " He established the earth on its foundations;
It shall not be removed for ever."—civ. 2-5.

He extends a constant providence over his creation.

" He covereth the heavens with clouds;
He prepareth rain for the earth;
He causeth grass to grow upon the mountains;
He giveth to the wild beast his food,
And to the young ravens, that cry to him."—cxlvii. 8, 9.

" He maketh peace in thy borders,
And satisfieth thee with the finest of the wheat.
He sendeth forth his word to the earth;
His command runneth very swiftly.
He giveth snow like wool,
And scattereth the hoar-frost like ashes.

He casteth forth his ice like morsels ;
Who can stand before his cold ?
He sendeth his word and melteth them ;
He maketh his wind to rise, and the waters flow." — cxlvii. 14 – 18.

He exercises a just moral government.

"Jehovah is in his holy palace ;
Jehovah's throne is in heaven ;
His eyes behold, his eyelids prove the children of men. ·
Jehovah trieth the righteous ;
But the wicked, and the lover of violence, his soul hateth.
Upon the wicked he will rain lightning ;
Fire and brimstone and a burning wind shall be the portion of their cup.
For Jehovah is righteous ; he loveth righteousness ;
His countenance doth behold the upright." — xi. 4 – 7.

"The Lord is gracious in all his ways,
And merciful in all his works.
The Lord is nigh to all that call upon him ;
To all that call upon him in truth.
He fulfilleth the desire of them that fear him ;
He heareth their cry, and helpeth them.
The Lord preserveth all that love him ;
But all the wicked he will destroy." — cxlv. 17 – 20.

His goodness to men is bountiful, tender, patient, forgiving, parental.

" Bless the Lord, O my soul,
And all that is within me, bless his holy name !
Bless the Lord, O my soul,
And forget not all his benefits !
Who forgiveth all thine iniquities ;
Who healeth all thy diseases ;
Who redeemeth thy life from the grave ;
Who crowneth thee with kindness and mercy !
Who satisfieth thine old age with good,
So that thy youth is renewed like the eagle's.
" The Lord executeth justice
And equity for all the oppressed.
He made known his ways to Moses ;
His mighty deeds to the children of Israel.
The Lord is merciful and kind ;
Slow to anger and rich in mercy.
He doth not.chide for ever,
Nor is his displeasure everlasting.

He hath not dealt with us according to our sins,
Nor requited us according to our iniquities.
As high as are the heavens above the earth,
So great is his mercy to them that revere him.
As far as the east is from the west,
So far hath he removed our transgressions from us.
Even as a father pitieth his children,
So the Lord pitieth them that revere him.
For he knoweth our frame,
He remembereth that we are dust." — ciii. 1-14.

" I lift up mine eyes to the hills;
Whence cometh my help?
My help cometh from Jehovah,
Who made heaven and earth.
He will not suffer thy foot to stumble;
Thy guardian doth not slumber.
Behold! the guardian of Israel
Doth neither slumber nor sleep.
Jehovah is thy guardian;
Jehovah is thy shade at thy right hand.
The sun shall not smite thee by day,
Nor the moon by night.
Jehovah will defend thee from all evil;
He will preserve thy life.
Jehovah will defend thee, when thou goest out, and when thou comest in,
Now and for ever! " — cxxi. 1-8.

" The Lord is my shepherd; I shall not want.
He maketh me to lie down in green pastures;
He leadeth me beside the still waters.
He reviveth my spirit;
He leadeth me in the right paths,
For his name's sake.
When I walk through the darkest valley
I fear no evil, for thou art with me;
Thy crook and thy staff, they comfort me.
Thou preparest a table before me,
In the presence of mine enemies.
Thou anointest my head with oil;
My cup runneth over.
Surely goodness and mercy shall follow me all the days of my life,
And I shall dwell in the house of the Lord for ever." — xxiii. 1-6.

Here is a perfect outline of a true system of theology. There is nothing resembling it in the writings
of heathen antiquity. With such views of the Divine

character and administration, nothing was wanting to an effective religious belief, except the great doctrine, first brought to light by Christianity, of a future life and retribution.

The piety, or devotional temper, of the Psalmists, corresponds to the just and affecting conceptions entertained by them of the Divine attributes. Piety is made up of reverence and love, and of that cheerful submission and trust which are their natural fruit. What Christian ever gave to these sentiments more fervent and genuine expression than is found in those numerous strains of the Jewish Psalter, of which the following are but a familiar specimen?

> " I will bless the Lord at all times ;
> His praise shall be continually in my mouth.
> In the Lord doth my soul boast ;
> Let the afflicted hear, and rejoice !
> O, magnify the Lord with me,
> And let us exalt his name together!
>   " I sought the Lord, and he heard me,
> And delivered me from all my fears.
> Look up to him, and ye shall have light;
> Your faces shall never be ashamed.
> This afflicted man cried, and Jehovah heard,
> And saved him from all his troubles.
> The angels of Jehovah encamp around those who fear him,
> And deliver them.
> O, taste, and see, how good is the Lord !
> Happy the man who trusteth in him !
> O, fear the Lord, ye his servants !
> For to those who fear him, there shall be no want.
> Young lions want and suffer hunger ;
> But they who fear the Lord want no good thing." — xxxiv. 1 – 10.

> " O God, thou art my God ! earnestly do I seek thee !
> My soul thirsteth, my flesh longeth for thee,
> In a dry, thirsty land, where is no water !
> Thus I look toward thee in thy sanctuary,
> To behold thy power and thy glory !
> For thy goodness is better than life ;
> Therefore my lips shall praise thee !

So will I bless thee, while I live ;
With thy name will I lift up my hands !
My soul shall be satisfied as with marrow and fatness,
And with joyful lips my mouth shall praise thee ;
When I think of thee upon my bed,
And meditate on thee in the night-watches ;
For thou art my help,
And in the shadow of thy wings I rejoice ;
My soul cleaveth to thee ;
Thy right hand holdeth me up." — lxiii. 1 – 8.

"He who sitteth under the protection of the Most High
Dwelleth in the shadow of the Almighty.
I say to Jehovah, Thou art my refuge and my fortress,
My God, in whom I trust.
He will deliver thee from the snare of the fowler,
And from the destructive pestilence ;
He will cover thee with his feathers,
And under his wings shalt thou be secure ;
His truth shall be thy shield and buckler.
Thou needest not dread the terror of the night,
Nor the arrow that flieth by day ;
Nor the pestilence that walketh in darkness,
Nor the plague that wasteth at noonday.
A thousand shall fall by thy side,
And ten thousand on thy right hand,
But no harm shall come nigh thee.
Thou shalt only behold with ʹthine eyes,
And see the recompense of the wicked.
Because thou hast made Jehovah thy refuge,
And the Most High thy shelter,
No evil shall befall thee,
Nor any plague come near thy dwelling.
For he shall give his angels charge over thee,
To guard thee in all thy ways.
They shall bear thee up in their hands,
Lest thou dash thy foot against a stone.
Thou shalt tread upon the lion and the adder ;
The young lion and the dragon shalt thou trample under foot.
' Because he loveth me, I will deliver him ;
I will protect him, because he acknowledgeth my name.
When he calleth upon me, I will answer him ;
I will be with him in trouble ;
I will deliver him and bring him to honor.
With long life will I satisfy him,
And show him my protection.' " — xci. 1 – 16..

To the wise interpretation of this devout spirit, the
afflictive dispensations of Providence ceased to be a
mystery. Their sanctifying efficacy, their gracious
instrumentality in the purification and elevation of the
character, became known.

> "It is good for me that I have been afflicted,
> That I might learn thy statutes.
> Better to me is the commandment of thy mouth
> Than thousands of gold and silver.
> " Thy hands have made and fashioned me ;
> Give me understanding, that I may learn thy commandments !
> They who fear thee shall see me and rejoice,
> Because I trust in thy promise.
> I know, O Lord, that thy judgments are right,
> And that in faithfulness thou hast afflicted me.
> O, let thy goodness be my consolation,
> According to thy promise to thy servant !
> Let thy compassion come to me, that I may live !
> For thy law is my delight." — cxix. 71 - 77.

And even the great perplexity of the want of correspondence between earthly condition and desert,
though it had not that adequate solution which only
the knowledge of a retribution in a future life can
supply, was not allowed to disturb the believer's trust
in that divine goodness which it seemed to contradict.

> " Truly God is good to Israel,
> To those who are pure in heart.
> Yet my feet almost gave way ;
> My steps had wellnigh slipped ;
> For I was envious of the profane,
> When I saw the prosperity of the wicked.
> " For they have no pains to the day of their death ;
> Their bodies are in full health.
> They have not the woes of other men,
> Neither are they smitten like other men.
> Therefore pride encircleth their neck, as a collar ;
> Violence covereth them, as a garment.
> From their bosom issueth their iniquity ;
> The designs of their hearts burst forth.
> They mock, and speak of malicious oppression ;
> Their words are haughty ;

They stretch forth their mouth to the heavens,
And their tongue goeth through the earth;
Therefore his people walk in their ways,
And there drink from full fountains.
And they say, 'How doth God know?
How can there be knowledge with the Most High?'
Behold these ungodly men!
They are ever prosperous; they heap up riches.
    "Verily I have cleansed my heart in vain;
In vain have I washed my hands in innocence.
For every day have I been smitten;
Every morn have I been chastened.

                .   .   .   .   .

    "When my heart was embittered with envy,
And my bosom vexed with indignation;
Then I was stupid, and without understanding;
I was like one of the brutes before thee.
Yet am I ever under thy care;
By my right hand thou dost hold me up.
Thou wilt guide me with thy counsel,
And at last receive me with glory.
Whom have I in heaven but thee,
And whom on earth do I love in comparison with thee?
Though my flesh and my heart fail,
God is the strength of heart, and my portion for ever."

                                    lxxiii. 1-26.

The devout spirit has two appropriate expressions; — one, in worship; the other, in virtuous conduct, in a sober, righteous, and beneficent life. False religions have fully recognized only the former; they have established no intimate connection between religion and morality. The Jewish religion, as understood by the Psalmists, recognized both; but, as distinctly as justly, gave the preference to the former, as being less equivocal, and more important by reason of its tendency to a fulfilment of God's benevolent designs for the happiness of his children. In their view, that course of conduct, on the part of any man, which was most suitable to secure his own permanent happiness and the happiness of others, — consisting in the discharge of the personal and social duties, was at once the most

desirable manifestation and the surest evidence of his
fear and love of God.

Their morality was the morality of natural conscience
and of the law of Moses. A good life, according as,
with this degree of illumination, they understood that
life, was with them the most becoming homage to
God, and the most availing recommendation to his
favor.

> " Lord, who shall abide at thy tabernacle,
> Who shall dwell upon thy holy hill?
>   " He that walketh uprightly, and doth righteousness,
> And speaketh the truth from his heart;
> He that slandereth not with his tongue;
> That doth no injury to his neighbor;
> And uttereth no reproach against his neighbor.
> He in whose eyes the worthless are contemptible;
> But who honoreth them that fear the Lord;
> He that sweareth to his neighbor, and changeth not;
> He that lendeth not his money for interest,
> Nor accepteth a gift against the innocent;
> He that doth these things shall never fall." — xv. 1 - 5.

> " Come, ye children, listen to me!
> I will teach you the fear of the Lord.
> Who is he that loveth life,
> And desireth many days, in which he may see good?
> Guard well thy tongue from evil,
> And thy lips from speaking guile.
> Depart from evil and do good;
> Seek peace and pursue it.
>   " The eyes of the Lord are upon the righteous,
> And his ears are open to their cry.
> But the face of the Lord is against evil-doers,
> To cut off their remembrance from the earth.
> The righteous cry, and the Lord heareth,
> And delivereth them from all their troubles.
> The Lord is near to them that are of a broken heart,
> And saveth such as are of a contrite spirit.
> Many are the afflictions of the righteous;
> But the Lord delivereth him from them all.
> He guardeth all his bones;
> Not one of them shall be broken.
> Adversity destroyeth the wicked,
> And they who hate the righteous suffer for it.

Jehovah redeemeth the life of his servants,
And none that put their trust in him will repent of it."

xxxiv. 11 – 22.

" He calleth to the heavens on high,
And to the earth, while he judgeth his people.
' Gather together my worshippers before me,
Who have made a covenant with me by sacrifice!'
(And the heavens shall declare his righteousness,
For it is God himself, that is judge.)
"' Hear, O my people, and I will speak;
O Israel, and I will admonish thee!
For I am God, thine own God.
I reprove thee not on account of thy sacrifices;
For thy burnt-offerings are ever before me.
I will accept no bullock from thy house,
Nor he-goat from thy folds;
For mine are all the beasts of the forest,
And the cattle upon a thousand hills.
I know all the birds of the mountains,
And the wild beasts of the field are before me.
If I were hungry, I would not apply to thee;
For the world is mine, and all that is therein.
Do I eat the flesh of bulls,
Or drink the blood of goats?
Offer to God thanksgiving,
And pay thy vows to the Most High!
And call upon me in the day of trouble,
I will deliver thee, and thou shalt glorify me!'
" And to the wicked God saith,
' To what purpose dost thou talk of my statutes!
And why hast thou my laws upon thy lips!
Thou, that hatest instruction
And castest my words behind thee!
When thou seest a thief, thou art pleased with him,
And hast fellowship with adulterers.
Thou lettest loose thy mouth to evil,
And thy tongue frameth deceit,
Thou sittest and speakest against thy brother;
Thou slanderest thine own mother's son.
These things hast thou done, and I kept silence;
Hence thou thoughtest that I was altogether like thyself;
But I will reprove thee, and set them in order before thee.
Mark this, ye that forget God,
Lest I tear you in pieces, and none deliver you!
"' Whoso offereth praise honoreth me;
And to him who hath regard to his ways
Will I show the salvation which is from God.'" — l. 4 – 23.

25 *

" I will sing of goodness and justice ;
To thee, O Lord, will I sing !
I will have regard to the way of uprightness ;
When thou shalt come to me,
I shall walk within my house with an upright heart.
I will set no wicked thing before mine eyes ;
I hate the conduct of transgressors ;
It shall not cleave to me.
The perverse in heart shall be far from me ;
I will not favor a wicked person.
The secret slanderer I will cut off ;
Him that hath a haughty look, and a proud heart, I will not endure.
Mine eyes shall seek the faithful of the land to dwell with me ;
He that walketh in the way of uprightness shall serve me.
He who practiseth deceit shall not dwell in my house ;
He who telleth lies shall not remain in my sight.
Every morning will I destroy the wicked of the land,
That I may cut off from the city of Jehovah all evil-doers."
                                                    ci. 1 – 8.

" Praise ye the Lord !
Happy the man, who feareth the Lord ;
Who taketh delight in his commandments.
His posterity shall be mighty on the earth ;
The race of the righteous shall be blessed.
Wealth and riches shall be in his house ;
His righteousness shall endure for ever.
To the righteous shall arise light out of darkness ;
He is gracious, and full of compassion and righteousness.
Happy the man who hath pity and lendeth ;
He shall sustain his cause in judgment ;
Yea, he shall never stumble ;
The memory of the righteous shall be everlasting.
He is not afraid of evil tidings ;
His heart is firm, trusting in the Lord.
His heart is firm ; he hath no fear,
Till he see his desire upon his enemies.
He hath scattered blessings ; he hath given to the poor ;
His goodness shall endure for ever ;
He shall be exalted to honor.
The wicked shall see and be grieved ;
He shall gnash with his teeth and melt away ;
The hope of the wicked shall perish." — cxii. 1 – 10.

" Happy are they whose ways are pure ;
Who walk in the law of the Lord.
Happy they who observe his ordinances,
And seek him with the whole heart ; .

Who also do no iniquity,
But walk in his ways.
Thou hast commanded us to keep thy precepts diligently.
O that my ways were directed to keep thy statutes!
Then only shall I not be ashamed,
When I have respect to all thy commandments.
Then shall I praise thee with an upright heart,
When I shall have learned thy righteous laws." — cxix. 1-7.

And from beginning to end of the long Psalm from which the last extract is taken, and which might almost stand for a system of ethics, is set forth, with abundant variety of expression, the great truth that the obedience of a virtuous life is the most acceptable religious service.

In some particulars the idea of a virtuous disposition and conduct was erroneous and imperfect, derived, as it was, from the sources of a perverted natural conscience and the incomplete system of Moses. The Jewish Psalmists had not arrived at the knowledge of those excellent graces of humility, forgiveness of injuries, and universal love, taught and exemplified in a later age by Him for whose instructions their Law was but a "schoolmaster" to prepare the minds of men. They had not learned his lesson, to love their enemies, to bless those that cursed them, to do good to those that hated them, and pray for those who despitefully used them and persecuted them. Their system of morality admitted of such shocking maledictions as the following.

" Set thou a wicked man over him,
And let an adversary stand at his right hand!
When he is judged, may he be condemned,
And may his prayer be accounted a crime!
May his days be few,
And another take his office!
May his children be fatherless,
And his wife a widow!
May his children be vagabonds and beggars
And seek their bread far from their desolate abodes!

May a creditor seize on all that he hath,
And may a stranger plunder his substance!
May there be none to show him compassion,
And none to pity his orphans!
May his posterity be cut off;
In the next generation may his name be blotted out!
May the iniquities of his fathers be remembered by Jehovah,
And may the sin of his mother never be blotted out!
May they lie before the Lord continually;
And may he cut off their memory from the earth!
Because he remembered not to show pity,
But persecuted the afflicted and the destitute,
And sought the death of the broken-hearted.
As he loved cursing, let it come upon him;
As he delighted not in blessing, let it be far from him!
May he be clothed with cursing as with a garment;
May it enter like water into his bowels,
And like oil into his bones!
May it be to him like the robe that covereth him;
Like the girdle with which he is constantly girded!
May this be from Jehovah the recompense of mine adversaries,
And of them that speak evil against me!" — cix. 6 - 20.*

But according to the measure of their understanding of the nature of moral excellence, they clearly apprehended and earnestly set forth its power, above all other things, to recommend to the approbation and favor of God.

On the other hand, they did not overlook the obligation, nor undervalue the use of worship, as a homage suitable to be paid to the Divine Being, and to quicken, while it expresses, the emotions of the pious heart. Nature prompts the utterance of our feelings in significant acts and speech. To him who has some right views of the relation in which he stands to God, and of God's constant universal presence and readiness to hear, the language of praise and prayer is spontaneous. The correct views entertained by the Psalmists of prayer and its appropriate topics and spirit are

---

* See also lxix. 20 - 28; cxxxvii. 7 - 9; cxl. 9, 10; cxliii. 12.

apparent from their writings. Many of those poems are acts of private devotion; hymns of adoration, thanksgiving, confession, supplication, and intercession.

Many others are sacred songs, with or without choruses,* designed to be used in the public worship of the tabernacle and temple,† as that worship was arranged by the magnificent taste of David,‡ and afterwards reinstituted and improved by some of his successors.§

In the books of the Law, we find no mention of music, either vocal or instrumental, as making part of the appointed ritual.‖ The public worship instituted by Moses consisted of sacrifices.¶ As pious votaries of the religion of Moses, familiar with its provisions, nurtured under its discipline, ambitious to discharge its obligations, and having their whole train of religious thought associated with impressions derived from its solemn services, the Psalmists recognized this form of homage to the Deity.

> " May Jehovah hear thee in the day of trouble;
> May the name of the God of Jacob defend thee!
> May he send thee help from his sanctuary,
> And strengthen thee out of Zion!
> May he have regard to all thine offerings,
> And accept thy burnt sacrifice! " — xx. 1 - 3.

> " With a willing heart will I sacrifice to thee ;
> I will praise thy glorious name, O Jehovah!
> For thou hast delivered me from all trouble." — liv. 6, 7.

> " I will go into thy house with burnt-offerings ;
> I will pay thee my vows ;

---

* E. g. Pss. cvii. ; cxviii. 1 - 4, 29 ; cxxxvi.   † E. g. Pss. cxlvi. - cl.
‡ 1 Chron. xv. 16 - 28 ; xxv. 1 - 8.
§ 2 Chron. xxix. 25 - 30 ; xxxv. 15 ; Neh. vii. 1 ; xi. 22, 23.
‖ Numb. x. 10 can scarcely be considered an exception to this remark.
¶ See Vol. I. pp. 237 - 255.

The vows which my lips uttered;
Which my mouth promised in my trouble.
Burnt sacrifices of fatlings will I offer to thee with incense;
Rams, bullocks, and goats will I sacrifice to thee." — lxvi. 13 – 15.

"Jehovah is God, he hath shone upon us;
Bind the sacrifice with cords to the horns of the altar!
Thou art my God, and I will praise thee;
Thou art my God, and I will exalt thee!" — cxviii. 27, 28.

"I cry to thee, O Lord! make haste unto me!
Give ear to my voice when I cry unto thee!
Let my prayer come before thee as incense,
And the lifting up of my hands as the evening sacrifice!" — cxli. 1, 2.

It is true that in two or three places, where the object is to set forth the superiority of moral to ritual obedience as a homage acceptable to God, the legal worship is referred to in terms which, literally taken, appear to be disparaging.

"In sacrifice and oblation thou hast no pleasure;
So thou hast instructed me;
Burnt-offering and sin-offering thou requirest not.
Therefore said I, Lo, I come
To do what in the written volume is prescribed to me.
O my God, to do thy will is my delight;
And thy law dwelleth in my heart!" — xl. 6 – 8.

"O Lord! open thou my lips,
That my mouth may show forth thy praise!
For thou desirest not sacrifice, else would I give it;
Thou delightest not in burnt-offerings.
The sacrifice which God loveth is a broken spirit;
A broken and contrite heart, O God, thou wilt not despise!"

li. 15 – 17.

But the meaning of these strong statements, expressed in a familiar form of Scripture language, simply is, that, compared with a right state of the heart and a right course of conduct, ceremonial homage is of inferior value, and that independent of them it is of no avail.*

---

* Comp. Gen. xlv. 8; Ex. xvi. 8; Hos. vi. 6.

That this is the whole meaning of the passage last quoted is made perfectly evident by the context itself. For the words which immediately follow are these.

" Do good to Zion according to thy mercy;
 Build up the walls of Jerusalem!
 Then shalt thou be pleased with just sacrifices;
 With burnt-offerings perfectly complete ;
 Then shall bullocks be offered upon thine altar." — li. 18, 19.

This view of the subject is fully developed in part of another Psalm, from which I have before quoted.

"Our God cometh, and will not be silent;
 Before him is devouring fire,
 And around him a raging tempest.
 He calleth to the heavens on high,
 And to the earth, while he judgeth his people.
 ' Gather together my worshippers before me,
 Who have made a covenant with me by sacrifice!'
 (And the heavens shall declare his righteousness,
 For it is God himself that is judge.)
   " ' Hear, O my people, and I will speak !
 O Israel, and I will admonish thee !
 For I am God, thine own God.
 I reprove thee not on account of thy sacrifices ;
 For thy burnt-offerings are ever before me.
 I will accept no bullock from thy house,
 Nor he-goat from thy folds ;
 For mine are all the beasts of the forest,
 And the cattle upon a thousand hills.
 I know all the birds of the mountains,'
 And the wild beasts of the field are before me.
 If I were hungry, I would not apply to thee ;
 For the world is mine, and all that is therein.
 Do I eat the flesh of bulls,
 Or drink the blood of goats?
 Offer to God thanksgiving,
 And pay thy vows to the Most High !
 And call upon me in the day of trouble,
 I will deliver thee, and thou shalt glorify me ! ' " — l. 3 – 15.

Here Jehovah is represented describing his people as those "who have made a covenant with him by sacrifice." And he says that what he reproves them for is not any neglect in offering sacrifices. In that kind of service they abound; " their burnt-offerings are ever before him." But this is not what he cares most for. He is not dependent upon their offerings of beasts, as from their exalted idea of the merit of such donations they might seem to suppose. He does not feed on the flesh of bulls, or the blood of goats. And if he did, he could supply himself, for the game in the thickets, the herds on the hills, the birds of the mountains, and the wild animals of the desert, all belong to him. But what he desires more is what they alone can render, — the offering of submissive vows and a genuine gratitude.

> " I am poor, and sorrowful ;
> May thine aid, O God, set me on high !
> Then will I praise the name of God in a song ;
> I will give glory to him with thanksgiving.
> More pleasing shall this be to Jehovah,
> Than a full-horned and full-hoofed bullock." — lxix. 29 – 31.

Here again is expressed the same sentiment; — not that " a full-horned and full-hoofed bullock," a prescribed offering of the Mosaic ritual, would not be " pleasing to Jehovah," but that that state and habit of a grateful heart, which the offering was intended to express, had in themselves more power to please him.

The following lines are a specimen of another kind of reference to the legal ritual : —

> " Sing joyfully to God, our strength !
> Sing with gladness to the God of Jacob !
> Raise a song, and strike the timbrel,
> The sweet-sounding harp, and the psaltery !
> Blow the trumpet at the new moon ;
> At the full moon, also, our festal day !
> For this is a statute for Israel,
> A law of the God of Jacob ;
> He appointed it as a memorial in Joseph,
> When he went out of the land of Egypt,
> Where he heard a language which he knew not." * — lxxxi. 1 - 5.

---

* Comp. Numb. x. 10; xxviii. 14.

If, in such passages as these, we have a recognition of the national ritual as it was prescribed by Moses in the Law, it is also interesting to find in several of the Psalms recognitions of the national history, as that is related to us in the books which have come down to us as the work of the founder of the Jewish state. Sometimes these appear in mere passing allusions to single events.* Sometimes there is a sort of orderly abridgment of the national history, from the earliest period to that of the Exodus, and establishment in Canaan.† In the seventy-eighth Psalm the history is brought down to the time of the accession of David, and in the hundred and sixth, to that of the captivity: —

"Praise ye the Lord!
O, give thanks to the Lord, for he is good;
For his mercy endureth for ever!
Who can utter the mighty deeds of Jehovah?
Who can show forth all his praise?
Happy are they who regard justice;
Who practise righteousness at all times!
   "Remember me, O Lord, with the favor promised to thy people;
Visit me with thy saving help!
That I may see the prosperity of thy chosen,
That I may rejoice in the joy of thy people;
That I may glory with thine inheritance!
   "We have sinned with our fathers;
We have committed iniquity; we have done wickedly.
Our fathers in Egypt did not regard thy wonders;
They remembered not thy numerous benefits;
But rebelled at the sea, the Red Sea.
Yet he saved them for his own name's sake,
That he might make known his mighty power.
He rebuked the Red Sea, and it was dried up,
And he led them through the deep as through a desert.

---

* As in Ps. lxxxi. 6 - 10 (comp. Ex. i. 11, xiv. 19, xvii. 7, xx. 2, 3); lxxxiii. 9 - 11 (comp. Numb. xxxi. 7, Judges iv. 21, 23, vii. 25, viii. 21); xcv. 8 - 11 (comp. Ex. xvii. 7, Numb. xiv. 22); cxxxv. 9 - 11 (comp. Ex. xii. 29, Numb. xxi. 21 - 35, Josh. xii. 7 - 24).

† As in Pss. cv., cxxxvi.

He saved them from the hand of him that hated them,
And delivered them from the hand of the enemy.
The waters covered their enemies;
There was not one of them left.
Then believed they his words,
And sang his praise.
But they soon forgot his deeds,
And waited not for his counsel.
They gave way to appetite in the wilderness,
And tempted God in the desert;
And he gave them their request,
But sent upon them a plague.
  " They also envied Moses in the camp,
And Aaron, the holy one of Jehovah.
Then the earth opened, and swallowed up Dathan,
And covered the company of Abiram,
And a fire was kindled in their company;
The flames burned up the wicked.
  " They made a calf in Horeb,
And worshipped a molten image;
Thay changed their God of glory
Into the image of a grass-eating ox.
They forgot God, their saviour,
Who had done such great things in Egypt,
Such wonders in the land of Ham,
Such terrible things by the Red Sea.
Then he thought of destroying them;
Had not Moses, his chosen, stood before him in the breach,
To turn away his wrath, that he might not destroy them.
  " They also despised the pleasant land,
And believed not his word;
But murmured in their tents,
And would not listen to the voice of Jehovah.
Then he lifted up his hand against them,
And swore that he would make them fall in the wilderness;
That he would disperse their descendants among the nations,
And scatter them in the lands.
  " They also devoted themselves to the worship of Baal-peor,
And ate sacrifices offered to lifeless idols.
Thus they provoked his anger by their practices,
And a plague broke in upon them.
Then stood up Phinehas, and avenged the crime,
And the plague was stayed.
And this was counted to him for righteousness,
To all generations for ever.
  " They provoked him also at the waters of Meribah,
And Moses suffered on their account.

For they irritated his spirit,
So that he spake inconsiderately with his lips.
  " They did not destroy the nations,   .
As Jehovah had commanded them.
They mingled themselves with the heathen,
And learned their practices.
They even worshipped their idols,
And thus they became to them a snare.
Their sons and their daughters they sacrificed to demons,
And shed the blood of the innocent,
The blood of their own sons and daughters,
Whom they sacrificed to the idols of Canaan;
And the land was contaminated with blood.
Thus they polluted themselves with their works,
And defiled themselves with their inventions.
  " Then burnt the anger of Jehovah against his people,
So that he abhorred his own inheritance.
And he gave them into the hand of the nations ;
And they that hated them ruled over them.
Their enemies oppressed them,
And under their hands were they humbled.
Many times did he deliver them,
But they provoked him by their conduct,
And they were brought low for their iniquities.
Yet, when he heard their cries,
He regarded their affliction ;
He remembered his covenant with them,
And relented according to the greatness of his mercy,
And caused them to find pity
Amongst all that carried them captive.
  " Save us, O Jehovah, our God, and gather us from among the nations,
That we may give thanks to thy holy name,
And glory in thy praise !

  " Blessed be Jehovah, the God of Israel,
From everlasting to everlasting !
And let all the people say, Amen !
Praise ye the Lord ! " — cvi. 1 - 48.

LECTURE LXIII.

MESSIANIC PSALMS, AND PSALMS QUOTED IN THE NEW TESTAMENT.

Question respecting Supernatural Predictions relating to Jesus, in the Psalms. — Comments on the Eighty-fifth Psalm, — the Eighty-seventh, — the Sixty-eighth, — the Eighty-ninth, — the Hundred and Thirty-second, — the Seventy-second, — the Forty-fifth, — the Hundred and Tenth, — the Second, — the Sixteenth. — Of these Ten Psalms, only Five quoted from in the New Testament. — Numerous Quotations from other Psalms. — Illustrations of the Sense in which they are made, from the Seventy-eighth Psalm, — the Twenty-second, — the Forty-first, — the Sixty-ninth, — the Hundred and Ninth. — List of Passages quoted from the Psalms in the New Testament.

According to the prevailing opinion, many of the Psalms contain indications of a supernatural knowledge, on the part of their authors, respecting Jesus of Nazareth, the Messiah, the Saviour of men. I find no proof of this assumed fact. I believe that in a small number of these poems, some eight or ten out of the hundred and fifty, there are references to the person, or government, or both, of that heroic ruler whom, from an early age, the Jews expected to appear among them, to exalt the race of Jacob and be a blessing to all nations. In these instances we find only traces of the opinion which prevailed among the people at an early time, and was handed down through their successive generations; — an opinion erroneous in great part, though having for its basis and rudiment the promise made through Moses of a *prophet*, or teacher, whom God designed in good time to send. That any one of the Psalmists has alluded to the coming Christ in a way to show that he was supernaturally inspired with any knowledge concerning that personage, or even had any views concerning him superior to the erroneous ones current in his age among the people at large, I take to be an utterly unauthorized belief.

The contents of the eighty-fifth Psalm convey much more information than is usual respecting the date of the composition. From the first verses it appears to have been written by one of the captives returned from the exile in Babylon. The last verses describe the prosperity which the pious and patriotic men, who were undertaking to rebuild the Jewish institutions out of their recent ruins, encouraged themselves to hope for.

" O Lord, thou hast been favorable to thy land ;
Thou hast brought back the captives of Jacob ;
Thou didst forgive the iniquity of thy people,
And cover all their sins.
Thou didst take away all thy displeasure,
And abate the fierceness of thy wrath.
" Restore us, O God, our Saviour,
And let thine anger towards us cease !
Wilt thou be angry with us for ever !
Wilt thou continue thy wrath from generation to generation !
Wilt thou not revive us again,
That thy people may rejoice in thee !
Show us thy compassion, O Jehovah,
And grant us thy powerful aid !
" I will hear what God Jehovah saith !
Truly he speaketh peace to his people, and to his servants ;
Only let them not turn again to folly !
Yea, his aid is near to them that fear him,
That glory may dwell in our land.
Mercy and truth shall meet together,
Righteousness and peace shall kiss each other ;
Truth shall spring out of the earth ;
Righteousness shall look down from heaven.
Yea, Jehovah will give prosperity,

26 *

And our land shall yield her increase.
Righteousness shall walk before him,
And keep her steps in the way." — lxxxv. 1 – 13.

But not only was Judea to be happy and glorious
in itself. It was to be greatly illustrious among the
nations. Pilgrims were to resort to it from the most
distant foreign lands, and somehow all the excellence
and delights of the world, all power, luxury, and gay-
ety, wherever diffused, were to have their origin from
the seat of Jewish royalty. Such is the representation
of the eighty-seventh Psalm, the date of which is
immaterial; nor is there any thing to determine it, except that the poem must have been written after Mount
Zion was occupied by David, and after the relations of
the Jews with foreign nations were considerably extended.

" Her foundations are upon the holy mountains;
Jehovah loveth the gates of Zion
More than all the dwellings of Jacob.
Glorious things are said of thee,
O city of God!
'I name Egypt and Babylon amongst my worshippers;
Behold! Philistia, Tyre, and Ethiopia,
They also were born there.'
And of Zion it shall be said,
'Men of every nation were born there,
And the Most High hath established her.'
Jehovah, when he numbereth the nations, shall write,
'These were born there!'
Singers as well as dancers, —
All my springs are in thee!" — lxxxvii. 1 – 7.

The same is the representation of part of the sixty-
eighth Psalm.

" God has ordained thy strength, O Israel!
Show forth thy might, O God, thou who hast wrought for us!
Because of thy temple in Jerusalem
Shall kings bring presents to thee.
Rebuke the wild beast of the reeds,
The multitude of bulls with the calves of the nations,
So that they shall cast themselves down with masses of silver;

Scatter thou the nations that delight in war!
Princes shall come from Egypt;
Ethiopia shall hasten with outstretched hands to God." — lxviii. 28 - 31.

But under what auspices, through what instrumentality, was such national greatness to be attained?. This brings us to that conception of the royal Messiah, the conquering and beneficent descendant of David, which prevailed in the nation from David's own time, which in all times of national depression was cherished with peculiar tenacity and fondness, which Jesus during his earthly ministry labored so constantly to correct, and which to this day the erring nation clings to. God has long ago sent, and Christians have welcomed, the "prophet" whom he promised through Moses. The Jews still vainly look for that martial prince, erroneously described by ancient writers of their nation. The eighty-ninth Psalm, which — it is true, on no grounds of positive proof, but yet not without a degree of internal probability — has been attributed to David's descendant, Hezekiah, develops this whole subject with an explicitness that leaves nothing to be desired. It begins as follows: —

" Of the mercies of Jehovah I will ever sing;
With my mouth will I make known thy faithfulness to all generations!
For I know that thy mercy endureth for ever;
Thou hast established thy truth like the heavens.
' I have made a covenant with my chosen;
I have sworn to David, my servant;
Thy family will I establish for ever,
And thy throne will I uphold from generation to generation.' *
The heavens shall praise thy wonders, O Jehovah,
And the assembly of the holy ones thy truth." — lxxxix. 1 - 5.

Next follow several stanzas in which are extolled that power, consistency, and graciousness of Jehovah which might be securely relied upon for the fulfilment of the purpose which the writer conceives him to have

---

* See p. 309, note.

formed, and accordingly, in poetical language, represents him to have solemnly expressed. Then the poem returns to the topic with which it began, the great mercy which God designs for his people, however at present afflicted, through the instrumentality of an offspring from David's race.

" Happy the people that know the trumpet's sound !
They walk, O Jehovah, in the light of thy countenance ;
In thy name they daily rejoice,
And in thy goodness they glory.
For thou art the glory of their strength ;
Yea, through thy favor we lift up our heads !
For Jehovah is our shield,
And the Holy One of Israel our king.
Once thou spakest in a vision to thy holy one,
And saidst : ' I have laid help on one that is mighty ;
I have exalted one, chosen from the people ;
I have found David, my servant ;
With my holy oil have I anointed him.
With him shall my hand be firm,
And my arm shall support him.
The enemy shall not have power over him,
Nor shall the unrighteous man oppress him.
For I will beat down his foes before him,
And overthrow them that hate him.
My faithfulness and mercy shall be with him,
And through my name shall his head be exalted.
I will extend his hand to the sea,
And his right hand to the rivers.
He shall say to me, " Thou art my father,
My God, and the rock of my salvation ! "
I will also make him my first-born,
Highest of the kings of the earth.
My mercy I will continue to him for ever ;
My covenant with him shall be steadfast.
I will make his family to endure for ever ;
And his throne shall be as lasting as the heavens.[*]
Should his children forsake my law,
And walk not in my statutes,
Should they break my commandments,
And observe not my precepts,
I will punish their transgressions with a rod,
And their iniquity with stripes.

---

* See p. 309, note.

But my kindness will I not withdraw from him,
Nor suffer my faithfulness to fail.
I will not break my covenant,
Nor alter what hath gone from my lips.
Once have I sworn in my holiness ;
Shall I then prove false unto David?
His family shall endure for ever,
And his throne as the sun before me.*
It shall be established for ever like the moon ;
Like the faithful witness in the sky.'
   " But now thou forsakest, and abhorrest,
And art angry with thine anointed.
Thou hast made void the covenant with thy servant;
Thou hast cast his crown to the ground.
Thou hast broken down all his hedges ;
Thou hast brought his strongholds to ruin.
All who pass by plunder him ;
He is a reproach to his neighbors.
Thou hast lifted up the right hand of his enemies ;
Thou hast made all his adversaries to rejoice.
Thou hast even turned the edge of his sword,
And made him unable to stand in battle.
Thou hast brought his glory to an end,
And hast cast down his throne to the ground.
Thou hast shortened the days of his youth :
Thou hast covered him with shame.
   " How long, O Jehovah, wilt thou utterly hide thyself?
How long shall thine anger burn like fire?
Remember how short is my life ;
To what frailty thou hast created all men !
What man liveth, and seeth not death ?
Who can deliver himself from the power of the grave !
Where, Lord, is thy former kindness,
Which thou didst swear to David by thy truth?
Remember, O Lord, the reproach of thy servants,
How I bear in my bosom the taunts of many people,
With which thine enemies have reproached me, O Jehovah,
With which they have reproached the footsteps of thine anointed !

   " Praised be Jehovah for ever !
Amen and amen ! " — lxxxix. 15 – 52.

---

* Comp. 2 Samuel vii. 12 – 16, where we read as follows : —
   " And when thy days be fulfilled, and thou shalt sleep with thy fathers,
I will set up thy seed after thee, which shall proceed out of thy bowels, and
I will establish his kingdom.   He shall build an house for my name, and I
will establish the throne of his kingdom for ever.   I will be his father, and

The same is the leading idea of the hundred and thirty-second Psalm, supposed, not without probability, to have been written as early as Solomon's time, for the purpose of being used in the dedication of the temple.

" O Lord, remember David,
And all his affliction!
How he sware to Jehovah,
And vowed to the Mighty One of Jacob :
' I will not go into my house,
Nor lie down on my bed ;
1 will not give sleep to my eyes,
Nor slumber to my eyelids ;
Until I find a place for Jehovah,
A habitation for the Mighty One of Jacob.'
Behold, we heard of it at Ephratah ;
We found it in the fields of Jaar.
Let us go into his tabernacle ;
Let us worship at his footstool !
" Arise, O Jehovah, into thy rest,

---

he shall be my son. If he commit iniquity, I will chasten him with the rod of men, and with the stripes of the children of men ; but my mercy shall not depart away from him, as I took it from Saul, whom I put away before thee. And thine house and thy kingdom shall be established for ever before thee ; thy throne shall be established for ever." (Comp. 1 Kings ii. 4 ; viii. 25 ; ix. 5.)

The eighty-ninth Psalm was probably written long before the Books of Samuel and Kings. (Comp. Vol. II. pp. 240, 241, Vol. III. pp. 45, 46.) When the writer of the history and the writer of the poem used language so much the same in the texts referred to, did they both draw from a tradition which had descended to them, respecting a communication made by Nathan to David? Perhaps so. But what seems to me more probable is this. The origin of this language of God's *oath*, &c., respecting a perpetuity of greatness in the royal family of David, is poetical. It is the form in which the authors of the Psalm before us and of other Psalms clothed their opinion, and the opinion of their nation and time, that God *designed* to make David's family permanently illustrious. (Comp. Pss. lxii. 11, lxxxix. 49, xcv. 11, cx. 1, 4, cxxxii. 11 ; 1 Sam. xxiv. 4.) But in all times except the most modern, the poems of an earlier period have become in a later the materials of history. And as the ballads of primitive Rome became incorporated into Livy's history, so what was originally only a natural and legitimate expression, in a Hebrew lyric, of the writer's belief that it was God's settled purpose to make the dynasty of David dignified and lasting, may not improbably have given rise to the prose narrative, of after times, which represented him as having acquainted David with that purpose through Nathan.

Thou, and the ark of thy glory!
Let thy priests be clothed with righteousness,
And thy servants shout for joy!
For the sake of thy servant David,
Reject not the prayer of thine anointed! *
Jehovah hath sworn in truth unto David,
And he will not depart from it :
' The fruit of thy body will I set upon the throne.
If thy children keep my covenant,
And my statutes, which I teach them,
Their children also throughout all ages
Shall sit upon thy throne.'
For Jehovah hath chosen Zion;
He hath desired it, as his dwelling-place.
　　" ' This is my rest for ever ;
Here will I dwell, for I have chosen it.
I will abundantly bless her provision ;
I will satisfy her poor with bread.
I will also clothe her priests with salvation,
And her servants shall shout aloud for joy.
There will I exalt the power of David ;
I will prepare a light for mine anointed.
His enemies will I clothe with shame,
And the crown shall glitter upon his head." — cxxxii. 1 - 18.

In the latter part of this Psalm there is a remarkable peculiarity of expression. David is identified with his lineage. Their glory is to be his glory.

" If thy children keep my covenant,
And my statutes, which I teach them,
Their children also throughout all ages
Shall sit upon thy throne." — 12.

And then, not during David's lifetime, but in that of his distant posterity, will the promise be fulfilled.

" There will I exalt the power of David;
I will prepare a light for mine anointed.
His enemies will I clothe with shame,
And the crown shall glitter *upon his head*." — 17, 18.

The prevailing conception of the prince who was expected to spring from the royal line of Judah is largely and magnificently expressed in the seventy-

* With cxxxii. 8, 9, 10, comp. 2 Chron. vi. 41, 42.

second Psalm. The title of the Psalm (of uncertain genuineness) is " Of [or *for*] Solomon." *For* Solomon, — that is having Solomon for its subject, — it can scarcely have been, unless it were written by some one who before or in the early part of Solomon's reign believed that he would turn out to be the great personage predicted by Moses, and now (in a different character from what Moses had intimated) looked for by the nation. *Of* Solomon, — that is, having Solomon for its author, — it may well have been. If his songs were not as many as " a thousand and five," * it may be presumed from that statement in the history, that he wrote lyrics, and he would be quite as likely as any other person to employ his poetical talent in celebration of the splendid monarch whom he, as well as others, expected to spring from his line. The language of the latter half of the seventeenth verse (" all nations shall call him blessed ") appears to me in a very striking manner to connect the person described in the Psalm with the person expected by the Jews from an early age of their history.†

> " To the king, O God, give thy justice,
> And to the son of a king thine equity !
> Yea ! he shall judge thy people with righteousness,
> And thine oppressed with justice.
> For the mountains shall bring forth peace to the people,
> And the hills righteousness.
> He shall defend the oppressed of the people ;
> He shall relieve the destitute,
> And break in pieces the oppressor.
> They shall fear thee as long as the sun and moon shall endure,
> From generation to generation.
> He shall be like rain descending upon the shorn mead ;
> Like showers, which water the earth.
> In his days shall the righteous flourish,
> And great shall be their prosperity, as long as the moon shall endure.
> He shall have dominion from sea to sea,

---

* 1 Kings iv. 32.   † Comp. Gen. xii. 3; xxvi. 4; xxviii. 14.

And from the river to the ends of the earth.
The inhabitants of the desert shall bow before him,
And his enemies shall lick the dust.
The kings of Tarshish and of the isles shall bring presents;
The kings of Sheba and Seba shall offer gifts.   ·
Yea, all kings shall fall down before him;
All nations shall serve him.
For he shall deliver the poor, who crieth for aid,
And the oppressed, who hath no helper.
He shall spare the weak and the needy,
And save the life of the destitute.
He shall redeem them from deceit and violence,
And their blood shall be precious in his sight.
He shall flourish, and to him shall be given the gold of Sheba;
Prayer also shall be made for him continually,
And daily shall he be praised.
There shall be an abundance of corn in the land;
Even on the tops of the mountains its crops shall shake like Lebanon,
And the citizens shall flourish as the grass of the earth.
His name shall endure for ever;
His name shall be continued as long as the sun.
Men shall bless by making mention of his name;
All nations shall call him blessed.

———

" Praised be God Jehovah, the God of Israel,
Who alone doth wonderful things!
Praised be his glorious name for ever;
May his glory fill the whole earth! Amen! Amen!" — lxxii. 1 - 19.

I think it probable that the same is the significance of the forty-fifth Psalm, in which (if that was its theme) the writer has introduced into the conception of the Messiah, as popularly entertained, an element not apparent in any of the earlier representations; namely, that he would form a splendid conjugal alliance. It may be, however, that this was only a courtly ode, partly martial, partly *epithalamial*, addressed to some Jewish prince.*

---

* Of course I do not forget the quotation of Psalm xlv. 6 in the Epistle to the Hebrews, i. 8. But of that in its place. I will but say here, that I do not consider the anonymous writer of that (so-called) Epistle to be an authority in respect to a question of Old Testament interpretation, or to any thing else.

" My mind is full of a pleasant theme ;
I will address my song to the king ;
May my tongue be like the pen of a ready writer !
Thou art the fairest of the sons of men ;
Grace is poured upon thy lips ;
For God hath blessed thee for ever !
 " Gird on thy sword, O hero,
Thy glory and ornament !
In thy glorious array ride forth prosperously
On account of thy truth, and mildness, and justice ;
And thy right hand shall teach thee terrible things !
Thine arrows are sharp ;
Nations shall fall before thee ;
They shall pierce the hearts of the king's enemies.
 " God is thy throne for ever and ever ;
A sceptre of righteousness is the sceptre of thy sway.*
Thou lovest righteousness, and hatest iniquity ;
Therefore, O God, thy God hath anointed thee
With the oil of gladness above thy fellows !
 " All thy garments are myrrh, aloes, and cassia ;
From ivory palaces stringed instruments delight thee.
Daughters of kings are amongst thy chosen women ;
On the right hand stands the queen
In gold of Ophir.
Listen, O daughter ! consider, and incline thine ear ;
Forget thy people and thy father's house !
For the king is captivated with thy beauty ;
He is now thy Lord ; honor thou him !
So shall the daughter of Tyre seek thy favor with gifts ;
The rich among the people.
 " All glorious is the king's daughter in her apartment ;
Her robe is embroidered with gold.
In variegated garments shall she be led to the king ;
The virgin companions that follow her shall be brought unto thee.
With gladness and rejoicing shall they be brought ;
They shall enter the king's palace.
Instead of thy fathers shall be thy children,
Whom thou shalt make princes through all the land.
 " I will make thy name memorable throughout all generations ;
So shall the people praise thee for ever and ever ! " — xlv. 1 – 17.

In the same vein is a Psalm, the one hundred and

---

* I have changed Dr. Noyes's translation above of verse 6, to conform it to the Septuagint and Vulgate, which I believe to present a correct representation of the Hebrew. It is equally literal, and it brings out that parallelism which is the characteristic device of Hebrew poetry.

tenth, which our Lord, in remarkably express terms,* ascribes to David as its author, and interprets as having in view the coming Christ; that is, of course, the coming Christ as the character of that personage was understood by David.

" Jehovah said to my lord,
' Sit thou at my right hand,
Until I make thy foes thy footstool.'
Jehovah will extend the sceptre of thy power from Zion;
Thou shalt rule in the midst of thine enemies!
Thy people shall be ready, when thou musterest thy forces, in holy splendor ;
Thy youth shall come forward like dew from the womb of the morning.
Jehovah hath sworn, and he will not repent.
' Thou art a priest for ever,
After the order of Melchisedeck! '
The Lord at thy right hand
Shall, in the day of his wrath, crush the heads of kings.
He shall execute justice amongst the nations ;
He shall fill them with dead bodies,
He shall crush the heads of his enemies over extensive fields.
He shall drink of the brook in the way ;
Therefore shall he lift up his head." — cx. 1 - 7.

All is quite intelligible here, and in accordance with the statement of our Lord, when, perplexing the Pharisees who had attempted to perplex him, he showed them how vague, ill-considered, and inconsistent were those views of the Messiah which they undertook to derive from the words of the Messiah's great ancestor. David, in this Psalm, did speak of the great personage expected by him and his countrymen. He spoke of the Messiah, agreeably to the prevailing conception, as one who was to spring from his own line. He spoke of that illustrious descendant as one greater than himself, calling him " my lord," and in poetical language, significant of the power and greatness to which he would be raised, described him as being placed by Jehovah at his own right hand. He described him as concen-

---

* Matt. xxii. 43, 44 ; Mark xii. 36 ; Luke xx. 42, 43. Comp. Acts ii. 34, 35.

trating in himself the venerable powers and attributes
of the ancient royal priest, Melchisedeck.*   But still,
even in David's mind, the leading idea of the Messiah
was of one who should "crush the heads of kings,"
and heap the earth "with dead bodies," and slay till
he was exhausted with weariness and thirst.

The correctness of the ascription, by the disciples
at Jerusalem,† of the second Psalm to David as its
author, I take to be confirmed by its place in the
Psalter, and by the tenor of its contents.

> " Why do the heathen rage,
> And the nations meditate a vain thing ?
> Why do the kings of the earth rise up,
> And the princes combine together,
> Against Jehovah, and against his anointed king ?
> ' Let us break their bonds asunder ;
> Let us cast away from us their fetters.'
>   " He that sitteth in heaven laugheth,
> The Lord hath them in derision.
> Then shall he speak to them in his wrath,
> And confound them in his hot displeasure.
> ' I myself have anointed my king,
> Upon Zion, my holy hill.'
> I will declare the decree of Jehovah ;
> He hath said to me : ' Thou art my son ;
> This day I have begotten thee.
> Ask of me, and I will give thee the heathen for thine inheritance,
> And the ends of the earth for thy possession.
> Thou shalt break them with a rod of iron ;
> Thou shalt dash them in pieces like a potter's vessel.'
>   " Be wise, therefore, O ye kings !
> Be admonished, ye rulers of the earth !
> Be subject to Jehovah with awe,
> And fear with trembling !
> Kiss the son, lest he be angry, and ruin come upon you ;
> For soon shall his wrath be kindled !
> Happy are all they who seek refuge in him." — ii. 1-12.

---

* Comp. Ps. xlv. 4 ; Gen. xiv. 18-20. Perhaps the point of similarity intended to be indicated in the words "after the order of Melchisedeck " was,
that the seat of government of both was to be the same. Melchisedeck was
" king of Salem," afterwards called Jerusalem. Comp. Ps. cx. 2.

† Acts iv. 25, 26.

It may be that in this Psalm David intended to represent the expected prince as speaking, and using language which would be suitable for him, supposing the conceptions entertained by his nation respecting his character and office to have been correct. Imagine it to be a modern poem, with the title prefixed, " The Future Messiah's Defiance to his Enemies," and we see how easy and natural that interpretation would be.* But, considering the inartificial character of old poetry, the absence of such a title is nothing to influence our exposition of the piece.

I think it, however, very doubtful whether David in this Psalm referred to any thing beyond the greatness which he understood that Jehovah designed him to attain in his own royalty. "The plots of hostile nations," we may understand him as saying, "are all vain. They conspire against Jehovah, when they oppose the king whom he has caused to be anointed and enthroned upon Mount Zion; against the Almighty Jehovah, who in his resistless sovereignty derides, and in his hot displeasure will confound them.† Jehovah has determined, as by a positive decree, to adopt me for his son; ‡ to extend my sway over distant regions, and give me triumphant success against every foe. Take warning, and be peaceable. Submit yourselves

---

* See Vol. II. pp. 415, 416. Comp. Is. lxiii. 1, &c. On this construction we have (ii. 2) one instance in the Old Testament (additional to Dan. ix. 25, if that were another) of the application of the name מָשִׁיחַ (" Messiah," *anointed*) to the expected Jewish prince.

† " I myself have anointed my king " (6); the Septuagint and Vulgate read, " I am constituted king by him." — " He that sitteth in heaven laugheth " (4); Jehovah *derides* his enemies in the words (1–3) which precede (comp. lii. 6, 7); and he *threatens* them, " speaks to them in his wrath " (5), in the words (6–9) which follow.

‡ Elsewhere David is represented as God's son, in the sense, of course, of being a person peculiarly favored and distinguished by him ; e. g. Ps. lxxxix. 26, 27 (comp. 2 Sam. vii. 14).

27*

to Jehovah, and propitiate him by doing homage to me, his son. So shall you escape his destructive anger, and find the happiness of those who seek refuge in him." Assuming this construction to be correct, if anywhere in the Psalm David referred at all to the time of his expected descendant, the Messiah, it was in the seventh, eighth, and ninth verses. In a not unnatural interpretation of the words, and without any transition whatever, we may understand him as there alluding to a greatness which was to be attained by himself, because it was to be attained by his offspring. The glory of David's family would be the glory of David. A dynasty being permanently established, with high destinies, in his person, its future distinctions would be his own. The representation is the same as that which has been already remarked upon in the hundred and thirty-second Psalm.*

The inscription to the sixteenth Psalm entitles it "a Psalm of David"; and the contents confirm that statement. In it the writer expresses, in the following terms, his confidence in Jehovah, purpose of devotion to his service, sympathy with and attachment to his friends, and gratitude for his great mercies, present and to come.

> "Preserve me, O God, for to thee do I look for help!
> I have said to Jehovah, Thou art my Lord;
> I have no happiness without thee!
> The holy that are in the land, and the excellent,
> In them is all my delight.
> They who hasten after other gods shall have multiplied sorrows;
> Their drink-offerings of blood I will not offer,
> Nor will I take their names upon my lips.
> Jehovah is my portion and my cup;
> Thou wilt maintain my lot!

---

* *Vide supra*, pp. 310, 311. Comp. Pss. xxi. 3, 4, 6, 7; lxi. 6, 7; lxxxix. 30 – 37.

My portion hath fallen to me in pleasant places ;
Yea, I have a goodly inheritance.
"I will bless the Lord, who careth for me ;
Yea, in the night my heart admonisheth me.
I set the Lord before me at all times ;　·
Since he is at my right hand, I shall not fall.
Therefore my heart is glad, and my spirit rejoiceth ;
My flesh also shall rest in hope.*
For thou wilt not give me up to the grave ;
Nor wilt thou suffer thy holy one to see the pit.
Thou wilt show me ʼhe path of life ;
In thy presence is fulness of joy ;
At thy right hand are pleasures for evermore." — xvi. 1 – 11.

I conceive that in this Psalm we have an expression of the sentiments, purposes, and hopes of David, and that he speaks not at all in the person of the Messiah, but in his own person. At the same time, I think that in the latter part of the Psalm he had in view the expected advent of his greater successor, and that accordingly the Apostles Peter and Paul put the natural and correct construction upon his words in their original meaning, when they declared him to have referred therein to the "raising up"† of the future Messiah.‡ I take the case to have been this. Possessed with the opinion, current in his nation, that the splendid fortunes understood to await it were to be enjoyed through the instrumentality of an illustrious monarch of his own line, David, in expressing his grateful sense of the various goodness of God which

---

* Mr. Noyes's version of this Psalm, given above, reads in the second clause of the ninth verse, "My flesh also dwelleth in security." I restore the rendering of King James's translators, as being at once more literal, and more accordant, in my view, with the sense of the context.

† So the word ἀνάστασις should be translated, rather than "resurrection," the original word being more generic than *resurrection*, and this translation not being suitable, on any interpretation of the passage, at least in part of the places where the original is used. The *advent* of the Messiah is what is intended. Comp. Deut. xviii. 18; Heb. vii. 11, 15.

‡ Acts ii. 25 – 31; xiii. 34 – 37.

had distinguished him, is led especially to rejoice that
his glory is not to pass away with his life; but that
he is to enjoy a virtual immortality in his greater
offspring. Recognizing Jehovah as being on his right
hand, his immovable champion, he feels that his prosperity is perennial and secure. His heart is glad,
and his spirit rejoices, in the thought, that death, the
universal leveller, cannot prostrate him. He will lay
down his body to its last rest in hope, for he knows
that he is not to lie down to nothingness and oblivion.
He will not be wholly abandoned to the grave; the
greatness of David will not be all swallowed in the
pit. He will revive in his magnificent son; a living
branch will be made to spring from the dead root;
and thus, though compelled, like others, to undergo in
his own person the sentence of mortality, God will
lead him, in the person of his descendant and representative, along the ways of life and action. Full, therefore, shall be his joy in Him who is thus present with
him at all times; endless his satisfactions in the Divine Protector for ever at his right hand.* This conception (by no means violent, or transcending very
narrow limits of the license of poetry) of life renewed
and prolonged in one's descendants, is the same which
has been already remarked upon as expressed in other
Psalms.†

Of the ten Psalms upon which I have commented
as containing references of some kind to the times and
office of the expected Messiah, only five are quoted
from by the New Testament writers.‡ There are,

---

* Ps. xvi. 8 – 11.   With 11 comp. 8.

† *Vide supra*, pp. 311, 318; also, comp. 2 Sam. vii. 12 – 16; 1 Kings
xi. 36; 2 Kings viii. 19.

‡ Pss. lxviii. 18 (comp. Eph. iv. 8); xlv. 6, 7 (comp. Heb. i. 8, 9);
Ps. cx. 1 (comp. Matt. xxii. 44, Acts ii. 34, 35, Heb. i. 13, x. 12, 13); Ps.

however, in the New Testament, very numerous quotations from other Psalms. Before closing this lecture, I will present a few specimens of cases in which the careful reader finds himself compelled to allow, either that he entirely mistakes the meaning of the writer of a Psalm, or else that the manner of quoting it in the New Testament cannot be so understood as to intimate that the quoted language was intended by its author to express a prediction.

As far as an inference can be drawn from language literally construed, no stronger case can be produced of apparent assertion by a New Testament writer, that a passage which he quotes from a Psalm was intended as prediction, than the following words of Matthew, occurring at the close of his recital of several of the parables of Jesus: —

" All these things spake Jesus unto the multitude in parables, and without a parable spake he not unto them; *that it might be fulfilled which was spoken by the prophet,* saying, ' I will open my mouth in parables, I will utter things which have been kept secret from the foundation of the world.' " *

We search in the Old Testament Scriptures for the words here said to have been spoken by the prophet, or poet, and we find them to be inaccurately quoted from the second verse of the seventy-eighth Psalm, where it is said: —

> " I will open my mouth in a parable [or, *poem*];
> I will utter sayings of ancient times."

The meaning of this Psalm is perfectly clear. It relates not at all to the future, but to the past. It con-

---

cx. 4 (comp. Heb. v. 6, vi. 20, vii. 17, 21); Ps. ii. 1, 2 (comp. Acts iv. 25, 26); Ps. ii. 7 (comp. Acts xiii. 33, Heb. i. 5, v. 5); Ps. xvi. 8 - 11 (comp. Acts ii. 25 - 28, xiii. 35).

* Matt. xiii. 34, 35.

tains a recapitulation of the principal events in the Jewish history, from the earliest times to the reign of David. This epitome the writer prefaces by saying that he intends to give it in a poetical form.* It is impossible that we should misunderstand what he meant in these words. It is impossible that Matthew should have misunderstood him. Nothing can be plainer than that Matthew, when he spoke of these words of the Psalmist being *fulfilled* by Jesus when he spoke in parables, meant simply to say, that this proceeding of Jesus reminded him of the Psalmist's words, and might be aptly described by them. It is equivalent to the familiar form of expression which is used in one of the New TestamentEpistles, where, aft er a description of the backsliding of certain professed penitents, it is said: "It is happened unto them according to the true proverb, 'The dog is turned to his own vomit again'; and 'The swine that was washed to her wallowing in the mire.'" †

The Evangelists Matthew and John relate that the Roman guards, at the crucifixion of Jesus, " parted his garments, casting lots, that it might be fulfilled which was spoken by the prophet, ' They parted my garments among them, and upon my vesture did they cast lots.'" ‡ The words quoted occur in the eighteenth verse of the twenty-second Psalm, where the writer (whether David, as the inscription declares, or not) was clearly speaking of his own distresses and persecutions, and not of those of any other person, of a past, present, or future age. It was merely by such a verbal accommodation as I have described, that the Evangelists applied the words to an incident of their Master's death.

---

* לֶשָׁמ signifies a *parable*, an *apothegm*, a *proverb*, or a *poem*.

† 2 Pet. ii. 22.   ‡ Matt. xxvii. 35; comp. John xix. 24.

"I speak not of you all," said Jesus at his last supper with his disciples; "but that the Scripture may be fulfilled, 'He that eateth bread with me hath lifted up his heel against me.'"* The sentence is taken from the ninth verse of the forty-first Psalm, where the writer complains of the perfidy of his "own familiar friend, in whom he trusted." Jesus, in an affecting accommodation of the words, represents himself as being the object of a like ungrateful and treacherous hostility.†

When Jesus had chased the traffickers from the temple, "his disciples remembered that it was written, 'The zeal of thine house hath eaten me up.'"‡ It is so written in the ninth verse of the sixty-ninth Psalm; but without any reference whatever to that act of Jesus. The writer of that Psalm, whether David (as the inscription imports) or some other person, is obviously speaking only of himself. To the Evangelist the language appeared naturally applicable to the (so to speak) consuming zeal of Jesus for the honor of God's house, as evinced in his expulsion from it of its profane occupants; and he made a rhetorical accommodation of it accordingly.

St. Peter is related to have made similar use of the same and of another Psalm. "It is written," said he to the one hundred and twenty disciples, "in the Book of Psalms, 'Let his habitation be desolate, and let no man dwell therein'; and, 'His bishopric let another take.'"§ This language was very suitable to the use in which Peter employed it; namely, his proposal for the deposition of Judas from the apostleship. But

---

* John xiii. 18.

† See John xv. 25 (comp. Pss. lxix. 4, cix. 3) for a passage evidently requiring a similar interpretation.

‡ John ii. 17.   § Acts i. 20; comp. Pss. lxix. 25, cix. 8.

it is difficult for one who reads the Psalms from which
it is taken, to suppose that their writers had in view
the crime and degradation of Judas, or that Peter
could have intended to attribute to them that sense.
Though I have thus very briefly hinted at the sense
which is to be put upon the references which we find
in the New Testament to some of the Psalms, any discussion of that subject would here be premature. No
more belongs to the course of inquiry in which we are
now engaged, than to show that the Psalms themselves
afford no indication of the possession, on the part of
their writers, of supernatural knowledge relative to the
Gospel dispensation, or to the life and character of
Jesus. Whether, in quotations in the New Testament
books from any of the Psalms, such a construction as
would imply supernatural foreknowledge on the part
of their writers is rightly or wrongly put upon those
poems, is a question strictly of New Testament interpretation.* I am perfectly well satisfied that nothing
of the kind, in relation to those Psalms, is taught by
any language of the New Testament, as well as that
the poems in the Psalter itself afford no ground for
ascribing supernatural endowments to any of their
authors, or, in respect to King David,† add any thing
to our knowledge upon this point, already obtained
from the history of his reign. ‡

---

* An outline of my views on the very important subject of the object and
meaning of quotations in the New Testament from the Old, may be found
in my "Lowell Lectures on the Evidences of Christianity," Vol. II.
pp. 224 – 244.

† See Vol. III. p. 41.

‡ The following list of passages quoted in the New Testament from the
Psalms may aid the reader in an examination of this subject : — v. 9 (comp.
Rom. iii. 13); viii. 2 (comp. Matt. xxi. 16) ; viii. 4 – 6 (comp. Heb. ii. 6 - 8);
viii. 6 (comp. 1 Cor. xv. 27); x. 7 (comp. Rom. iii. 14); xiv. 1 – 3 (comp.
Rom. iii. 10 – 12); xviii. 49 (comp. Rom. xv. 9) ; xix. 4 (comp. Rom. x.

18) ; xxii. 1 (comp. Matt. xxvii. 46 ; Mark xv. 34) ; xxii. 8 (comp. Matt. xxvii. 43) ; xxii. 22 (comp. Heb. ii. 12) ; xxiv. 1 (comp. 1 Cor. x. 26) ; xxxi. 5 (comp. Luke xxiii. 46) ; xxxii. 1, 2 (comp. Rom. iv. 7, 8) ; xxxiv. 12 – 16 (comp. 1 Pet. iii. 10 – 12) ; xxxvi. 1 (comp. Rom. iii. 18) ; xl. 6 – 8 (comp. Heb. x. 5 – 7) ; xliv. 22 (comp. Rom. viii. 36) ; li. 6 (comp. Rom. iii. 4) ; lxviii. 19 (comp. Eph. iv. 8) ; lxix. 9 (comp. Rom. xv. 3) ; lxix. 22, 23 (comp. Rom. xi. 9, 10) ; lxxviii. 24 (comp. John vi. 31) ; lxxxii. 6 (comp. John x. 34) ; xci. 11, 12 (comp. Matt. iv. 6 ; Luke iv. 10, 11) ; xciv. 11 (comp. 1 Cor. iii. 20) ; xcv. 7 – 11 (comp. Heb. iii. 7 – 11, 15 ; iv. 3, 7) ; xcvii. 7 (comp. Heb. i. 6) ; cii. 25 – 27 (comp. Heb. i. 10 – 12) ; civ. 4 (comp. Heb. i. 7) ; cxii. 9 (comp. 2 Cor. ix. 9) ; cxvi. 10 (comp. 2 Cor. iv. 13) ; cxvii. 1 (comp. Rom. xv. 11) ; cxviii. 6 (comp. Heb. xiii. 6) ; cxviii. 22, 23 (comp. Matt. xxi. 42 ; Luke xx. 17 ; 1 Pet. ii. 7) ; cxl. 3 (comp. Rom. iii. 13).

LECTURE LXIV.

THE CANTICLES, AND THE GNOMOLOGICAL BOOKS.

CLASSIFICATION OF LYRIC POEMS. — THE CANTICLES A COLLECTION OF
EROTIC BALLADS. — THEORY OF BOSSUET. — DIVISIONS OF THE BOOK
BY DIFFERENT CRITICS. — THE WORK OF ONE AUTHOR, IN OR NEAR
THE TIME OF SOLOMON. — ALLEGORICAL INTERPRETATIONS, DESIGNED
TO GIVE IT A RELIGIOUS SIGNIFICANCE. — NOT REFERRED TO IN THE
NEW TESTAMENT. — TITLE OF THE BOOK OF PROVERBS. — ANALYSIS
OF ITS CONTENTS. — QUESTION OF ITS AUTHORSHIP. — QUESTIONS CON-
CERNING AGUR AND LEMUEL. — THE BOOK ILLUSTRATIVE OF JEWISH
MORALS AND MANNERS. — QUOTATIONS IN THE NEW TESTAMENT. —
SUBJECT AND DESIGN OF THE BOOK OF ECCLESIASTES. — TIME OF
ITS COMPOSITION. — ITS STRUCTURE NOT THAT OF A DIALOGUE. — ITS
CYNICAL AND EPICUREAN DOCTRINE. — REMARKS ON SOME PASSAGES.
— NO QUOTATION FROM IT IN THE NEW TESTAMENT. — AUTHOR AND
TRANSLATOR OF ECCLESIASTICUS. — ORIGINAL IN THE HEBREW TONGUE.
— VERSIONS. — TIMES OF THE COMPOSITION AND TRANSLATION. —
ANALYSIS OF THE CONTENTS. — VALUE OF THE BOOK IN ITSELF, AND
AS ILLUSTRATIVE OF THE INFLUENCE OF JEWISH INSTITUTIONS. — REF-
ERENCES TO IT IN THE NEW TESTAMENT. — THE WISDOM OF SOLOMON
THE WORK OF AN EGYPTIAN JEW. — DATE OF ITS COMPOSITION. — ITS
DOCTRINE OF RETRIBUTION. — ANALYSIS OF ITS CONTENTS. — ITS UNI-
TY. — COINCIDENCES OF LANGUAGE BETWEEN IT AND THE NEW TESTA-
MENT.

A COLLECTION of lyric poems, of a very different description from those embraced in the Book of Psalms,
next comes under our notice.   Horace says,

> " Gods, heroes, conquerors, Olympic crowns,
> Love's pleasing cares, and the free joys of wine,
> Are proper subjects for the lyric song." *

And Dr. Blair, following a common modern classifica-

---

* " Ars Poet.," vers. 83 – 85.

tion, divides lyrics into, — 1. Sacred Odes; 2. Heroic
Odes; 3. Moral and Philosophical Odes; and 4. Festive and Amorous Odes; * — his third class being additional to those specified by the Roman bard.

To the fourth class belong the Canticles, otherwise
called the Song of Solomon. They are *amatory poems*,
a class of lyrics of which we have specimens from
Anacreon, Horace, and other classical writers, and in
which the Arabian, Persian, and other Oriental poets,
have always abounded.

I have called the Canticles a *collection* of amatory
poems. Some critics have understood the book to
consist of a single poem; and Bossuet went so far as
to represent it as an *Epithalamium*, or Marriage Song,
of a sort of dramatic structure, and divided into seven
parts or *acts*,† corresponding to the seven days during
which the nuptial festivity continued among the Jews. ‡
But this method of interpretation I regard as merely
fanciful. I can discern no other unity in the book
than that which belongs to the same class of topics,
treated in the same style. It seems to me that it
would be easy to select a portion of the Odes of Anacreon, and arrange them together so as to present a
more probable appearance of having originally constituted one whole, than is presented by these poems.

While the frequent breaks in the continuity of the
sense repel the idea of unity in the composition, there
is room for great difference of opinion as to the proper

---

* " Lectures on Rhetoric," &c., Lect. XXXIX., *juxta fin.*

† See Bossuet, " Præfat. in Canticum Canticorum," § III. The days,
as he distinguished them, were as follows, viz. : — (1.) i. 1 – ii. 6; (2.) ii.
7 – 17; (3.) iii. 1 – v. 1; (4.) v. 2 – vi. 9; (5.) vi. 10 – vii. 10; (6.) vii.
11 – viii. 3; (7.) viii. 4 – 14. The seventh day he considered to be indicated
as the Sabbath, by the circumstance that the bridegroom is not therein represented as having gone abroad, as on the other days. See his note on viii. 5.

‡ Gen. xxix. 27; Judg. xiv. 12, 17.

manner of analyzing the book so as to separate the respective pieces. Eichhorn imagines that the collector (whether the same person with the author, or not, he does not decide) arranged the single compositions in four *books*, each having a general scheme similar to the rest, and a similar beginning and close; and that he then disposed as an appendix what did not admit of being placed in either of these sections.* Jahn finds in the book eight distinct compositions.† Dr. Noyes designates twelve pieces, dividing into two each of the first four indicated by Jahn. Dr. Good makes the ·same number as our learned countryman, with a different division as to all but one of the last eight poems. ‡

That all these compositions are the work of the same author appears in the highest degree probable, from their universal similarity of style, both of thought and language. Who he was, we have no means of knowing. The title, which ascribes them to Solomon,§ cannot have been written by himself; he would not have pronounced his composition to excel all others of the kind, which is the meaning of the Hebrew words. Nor, by whomsoever else written, is it of any value in determining the question of the authorship. Any anonymous compositions were likely to have that

---

* Eichhorn, "Einleitung," u. s. w., Band III. § 649. Eichhorn's division into books is as follows, viz.: — (1.) i.–ii. 7; (2.) ii. 8–iii. 5; (3.) iii. 6–v. 2; (4.) v. 3–viii. 4; throwing three short passages into the Appendix; viz. viii. 5–7, 8–12, and 13, 14.

† He separates them as follows ("Einleitung," Th. II. § 204), viz.: — (1.) i. 1–ii. 7; (2) ii. 8–iii. 5; (3.) iii. 6–v. 1; (4.) v. 2–vi. 9; (5.) vi. 10–viii. 3; (6.) viii. 4–7; (7.) viii. 8–12; (8. a fragment) viii. 13, 14.

‡ Dr. Good's classification is as follows, viz.: — (1.) i. 1–8; (2.) i. 9–ii. 7; (3.) ii. 8–17; (4.) iii. 1–5; (5.) iii. 6–iv. 7; (6.) iv. 8–v. 1; (7.) v. 2–vi. 10; (8.) vi. 11–13; (9.) vii. 1–9; (10.) vii. 10–viii. 4; (11. the same as Dr. Noyes's 10) viii. 5–7; (12.) viii. 8–14.

§ i. 1.

inscription prefixed by a copyist who wished to do them honor, and the record respecting that famous king, that "his songs were a thousand and five," * would easily suggest the statement. That it was without foundation seems to be sufficiently indicated by different portions of the contents.† There appears, however, to be good evidence from the same source, that the book was written in, or not long after, Solomon's time. ‡ On the other hand, it is said that the strong Aramæan tinge of the phraseology indicates a much later origin. § But to this De Wette well replies, that this peculiarity may not have belonged to the original compositions, but may have been superinduced upon them in the course of their transmission to later times, as current songs of the people.

I do not think it worth while to spend many words upon these poems. They are not at all suitable to be consulted for spiritual edification ; so far from it, that even the Jews forbade them to be read by any person under the age of thirty years. || Nor do I perceive that they are capable of affording any gratification even to a literary taste, or serving any other use than that of a reader who might be curious to know how the poets of an ancient nation, in the state of society and culture that belonged to the Jews, dealt with this class of subjects. In order to explain their introduction into the Bible, which was assumed to be a collection of religious books alone, it has been necessary, by

---

* 1 Kings iv. 32.

† Cant. i. 4, 5, 12 ; iii. 6 – 11 ; vii. 5 ; viii. 11, 12.

‡ i. 5 ; iii. 7 – 11 ; iv. 4 ; viii. 11, 12.

§ For instance, the prefixed שׁ, and the insertion of י in דָּוִיד. On this point, see Eichhorn, " Einleitung," Band III. § 646, and De Wette, " Einleitung," § 277, a. 1.

|| Hieron., " Prolog. ad Explan. in Ezek.," " Opp.," Tom. III. p. 697 (edit. Martianay).

means of *allegorical interpretations*, to put a sense upon them entirely different from that which their plain language indicates them to have been intended to express.* By the male and female collocutors respectively, the Jewish commentators have understood to be meant God and the Church; and the mutual love existing between those parties is the subject which they have considered to be illustrated by the book. Among Christian expositors, the doctrine generally supposed to be enforced under its glowing images has been that of the reciprocal affection of Christ and his Church; and in elucidating this view, Origen, in the third century, displayed so much ingenuity, as to cause Jerome to say of him, that "in others of his works he outdid other men; in this he outdid himself, discoursing so magnificently and perspicuously as to fulfil that saying, 'The king hath led me to his chamber.'" †

There is no decent pretence of argument in favor of either of these interpretations, or of any other belonging to the same class, while it is true that, as to particulars of a just interpretation, the reader is sometimes at a loss. No book, ancient or modern, can be mentioned, bearing more manifestly on its face the general character of the meaning it was intended to convey. No book can possibly be more free from the faintest intimation that it has reference to any matter within the wide compass of religious thought. Indeed, the theory of any connection between the sensual images of this book and the subjects of the love of God or of Christ towards good men, or of theirs to-

---

* For remarks on the subject of allegorical interpretations of the Bible, see Vol. II. pp. 332 – 342.

† Hieron., "Opp.," Tom. II. p. 807 (edit. Martianay). Jerome's expression above, in regard to the *fulfilment* of Cant. i. 4, elucidates my remarks in the last Lecture (pp. 321 – 324) respecting the form of quotations from the Old Testament.

wards their Creator or Redeemer, appears to me so objectionable, — not to say; so offensive, — that I rejoice to be dispensed from refuting it by the fact, that there is not a shadow of positive argument in its behalf. The only basis for it, is reasoning like this: If the book does not mean something religious, how came it in the Old Testament? Men of sense will reverse the argument, and ask, With such matter as this in the Old Testament, how can it be pretended that the Old Testament is throughout a collection of inspired, or even of grave or useful writings? This book is canonical, no doubt; that is, it belonged to the collection of ancient compositions, known to the Jews by such names as "The Scriptures," or *writings*, before the Christian era. But that it is in any sense authoritative as a religious document, or that it has any relation whatever to religious faith or practice, I hold to be about as wild an opinion as even Biblical interpreters have ever entertained.

The New Testament contains no allusion to it.

The Hebrew word translated *proverbs*, in the title of the book called the " Proverbs of Solomon," is of more comprehensive sense than the English term denotes. If it meant no more than that term, there is a large part of the contents of the book to which it would not be applicable. It also signifies any figurative or poetical expression or discourse. Our translators have often rendered it *a parable;* * and this frequently in cases where the word *poem* would better express the meaning.†

The Book of Proverbs is made up of several independent parts. First occurs a passage embracing

---

* Ezek. xvii. 2; xxiv. 3.

† As Numb. xxiii. 7, 18; Job xxvii. 1; xxix. 1; Ps. xlix. 4; lxxviii. 2.

panegyrics on wisdom, and inculcations of the practice of virtue; in particulâr, of the virtue of purity.*
This section is in a higher strain of poetry than any
other part of the book. Prefixed to it is an inscription attributing its composition, or that of the whole
book, to "Solomon, the son of David, king of Israel."
Next follows a collection of sentences, for the most
part such as are properly called *proverbs*. It bears
the inscription, "The Proverbs of Solomon," and extends through fifteen chapters. It consists, for the
most part, of weighty sentences, instructive as to the
right conduct of life, and each consisting of a single
distich, framed according to the laws of the Hebrew
poetical parallelism.† At the close of this section,
however, there is a portion in which this structure of
the sentences is abandoned, and they become longer; ‡
and the separate title of its last twelve verses, "these
are the words of the wise," § seems to indicate for
them an independent origin. The third principal
division consists mainly of proverbs, properly so
called,|| like the greater part of the second, and cast
in the same mould of distiches containing a parallelism; it bears the inscription, "These also are proverbs
of Solomon, which the men of Hezekiah, king of
Judah, collected." Each of the last two chapters has
an inscription of its own. The former is as follows:
"The words of Agur, the son of Jakeh, even his sayings; the solemn declaration of the man to Ithiel,
even to Ithiel and Ucal." The other is: "The words
given to King Lemuel; the sayings which his mother
taught him." But only the eight verses immediately
following appear to correspond in sense to this title.

---

* Prov. i. 1–ix. 18.
‡ xxii. 17–xxiv. 34.
|| xxv. 1–xxix. 27.

† Comp. Vol. II. p. 311 *et seq.*
§ xxiv. 23.

The remaining twenty-two verses of the chapter constitute an acrostic poem,* descriptive of a good housewife. It appears to be a separate composition, complete in itself.

Thus the contents of the book, with the exception of the last two chapters, are referred to Solomon as their author. But we have already seen satisfactory reason to distrust these statements, in many instances, and to admit that internal evidence, as far as we can gather it, is the best guide in the decision of this question; and the ascription to some single distinguished individual of the wise and pithy sayings current among a people has been common in all times; so the Greeks represented Pythagoras as the author of their popular apothegms, the Arabians, Lochman and others, and the Scandinavians, Odin. The first part of the book, which seems to have been originally one whole, may well have been written by Solomon, who in the history is said to have spoken "three thousand proverbs," or verses.† To this view it has been objected,‡ that the royal polygamist, and offspring of an adulterous union, would scarcely have written as this writer has done in praise of conjugal fidelity.§ But I think the remark has no great weight. The strongest rebukes of sin not uncommonly come from those who have had the best reason to be acquainted with its consequences.

The chief objection to ascribing to Solomon the whole body of apothegms in the second part is their very great number. It is less likely that so many striking sayings should have proceeded from one author, than that men in later times, making a collection

---

* See Vol. II. pp. 306, 307.   † 1 Kings iv. 32.
‡ See Bertholdt, "Einleitung," Th. V., § 505.
§ Prov. v. 15 – 20; vi. 24 – 33; vii. 4 – 27.

of such sayings from various sources, should erroneously attribute them to one author, who was renowned for
his genius in that department. That many of the
maxims comprehended in this division were Solomon's, there is no reason to doubt. That all were his,
cannot positively be denied. But certainly many of
them bear more the appearance of being the observations of persons conversant with common life, than of
being the fruit of the reflections of a king, however
wise.* That the collection thus far was made before
the time of Hezekiah, who lived three centuries after
Solomon, may be inferred from the inscription to the
third part. But how long before Hezekiah's time it
should be dated, and whether early enough for the
compilers to have any trustworthy information concerning Solomon's authorship, is a question respecting
which we must be content to remain in ignorance.
That it was not made with great care appears from
occasional repetitions of the same maxim, — repetitions
sometimes made more than once.†

Nor have we means of determining whether the
alleged collectors in the time of Hezekiah were right
in attributing to Solomon, as they have done, the matter contained in the five chapters beginning with the
twenty-fifth. It must be owned that they lived at too
distant a period to have any personal or certain knowledge on the subject. But, on the other hand, I cannot
allow much force to representations which have been
made, that certain parts appear to be respectively

---

* As a mere specimen of such passages, which the attentive reader observes to be numerous, see x. 15, xi. 14, 26, xii. 4, xiv. 1, 21, xv. 25,
xvi. 9 - 15, xvii. 2, xviii. 8, 23, xix. 13, 14, xx. 2, 10, 14, 23, 26, 28, xxii.
29, xxiii. 6 - 8, xxiv. 21, 22.

† Comp. x. 8 with x. 10; xiv. 31 with xvii. 5; xix. 5 with xix. 9; xix.
12 with xx. 2; xx. 10 with xx. 23; xxi. 9 with xxi. 19; xxii. 28 with
xxiii. 10; xiv. 12 with xvi. 25, xxi. 2.

rather the production of a courtier,* a teacher of youth,† a censor of courtly manners,‡ or a keeper of herds and flocks,§ than of the famous king and sage of Israel. I add only, in respect to this part, that several repetitions occur of matter contained in the preceding.||

We know nothing respecting "Agur, the son of Jakeh," whose sayings are said to be preserved in the thirtieth chapter. They consist of a prayer, of moral precepts and reflections, and of remarks of a half-facetious nature.

As little do we know of King Lemuel, to whom, according to the inscription at the beginning of the thirty-first chapter, were addressed by his mother certain instructions relating to personal habits and a just administration of his government. No monarch of that name is mentioned in the Jewish history. Perhaps he was a foreign prince, the son of a Jewish mother. Perhaps the name was only fictitious, and assumed by the writer in giving expression to his views of the proper character of a young ruler.

The piece appears to be a fragment, and to have had originally no connection with the alphabetical poem, describing a model mistress of a family, which next follows and closes the book. Its acquaintance with the employments and interests of a common household betokens an author in no exalted condition of life.

In short, the book, whether more or less of it actually proceeded from the distinguished personage to whom most of it is ascribed, may not unfitly bear the title which a German critic has proposed, that

---

* xxv. 2-7.　　† xxvii. 11.　　‡ xxviii. 16.　　§ xxvii. 23-27.
|| Comp. xxv. 24 with xxi. 9; xxvi. 15 with xix. 24; xxvi. 22 with xviii. 8; xxvii. 12 with xxii. 3; xxvii. 13 with xx. 16.

of the *Gnomological Anthology* of the ancient Hebrews.*

It is, at all events, a book of special interest; not
because its authors claimed, or because there is any
appearance of their having possessed, any degree of
supernatural endowment; — there is nothing of the
kind; but because, more than any other which the
Hebrew nation have bequeathed to us from the times
of their independent nationality, it throws light on
their morals and manners in common life. It is true
that in great part the morality has no more elevated
character than that of a shrewd worldly wisdom. It
is the morality of experience, prudence, calculation,
rather than that of sentiment and faith. It is the
morality of Franklin much more than of Fénelon.
Not seldom the profound knowledge of human nature
which is evinced expresses itself in the tart language,
or with the sportive allusions, with which modern
apothegms invest some weighty sense. But there is
also much in a different vein, presenting the true view
of human duty, in its high character of obedience to
God, — identifying the fear of God with wisdom, the
knowledge of the Holy One with understanding. The
moral doctrine of the Proverbs is not Christian doctrine. It never refers to the retributions of another
life; it never appeals to the human agent as to one
acting for eternity. But it does frequently and im-
pressively present the great idea of God's constant
watchfulness and providence, and set forth the safety
of the good as enjoying his protection, and the danger
of disobedience as provoking his displeasure.

Six texts from this book are quoted by the New
Testament writers.†

---

* Bertholdt, " Einleit.," Th. V. § 503.

† Viz. iii. 11, 12 (comp. Heb. xii. 5, 6) ; iii. 34 (comp. James iv. 6)

The Book of Ecclesiastes, or "The Preacher," is a
discursive treatise on the worthlessness of all human
objects and pursuits. Notwithstanding the ingenious
attempts which have been made to trace in it a religious moral, I am unable to interpret it otherwise than
as the cynical expression of the feelings of a sated
and disappointed voluptuary. It is Johnson's "Vanity
of Human Wishes," divested of the philosophy and
good temper of that poem. "The Hebrews," says Jerome, "say, that whereas it might seem that this
book should not have escaped the destruction which
was the doom of other writings of Solomon, inasmuch
as it declares that every thing is worthless, and that
food, drink, and transient enjoyments are preferable to
all else, nevertheless it deserved to be retained in the
sacred collection on account of its ' conclusion of the
whole matter'; namely, that ' to fear God and keep
his commandments is the whole duty of man.' " *

The writer, very suitably for his purpose, assumes
the character of Solomon, the great king of Israel, at
that period of his life, when, having drunk deep of all
the joys of power, pleasure, knowledge, and fame,
he finds them to be all "vanity and vexation of spirit."† That Solomon was not really the author is ren-

x. 12 (comp. 1 Peter iv. 8); xxv. 21, 22 (comp. Rom. xii. 20); xxvi. 11
(comp. 2 Peter ii. 22); xxvii. 1 (comp. James iv. 13, 14).

* "Annot." ad Eccles. xii. 13 (Tom. II. p. 788, edit. Martianay).

† I think it quite unnecessary to go into the question of the various interpretations which have been proposed of the word קֹהֶלֶת, rendered in our
version, *the preacher*. The feminine termination for a masculine noun is not
out of analogy. פֶּחָה, קֶנֶת, סֹפֶרֶת, פֹּכֶרֶת, מָפִי־בֹשֶׁת, are examples. It is
evident from i. 1, 12, who was meant to be designated by the term, and that
it could not have been intended, as some critics have inferred from its etymology, to denote an *academy* of philosophers. There is one instance (vii.
27) in which the word is connected with a feminine verb. But this difficulty
is at once relieved by an easy change in the division and vowel-pointing of
the two words; אָמַר הַקֹּהֶלֶת instead of אָמְרָה קֹהֶלֶת. Not improbably the

dered entirely clear by the character of the style, which
belongs to a much later age,* not only abounding in
Chaldaisms † more than any other Old Testament book,
but containing a Persian word,‡ and even, it has been
thought, a word borrowed from the Greek language.§
Some critics have supposed that they detected allusions
to the sects of the Pharisees, Sadducees, and Essenes,‖
indicating the composition of the book at a time subsequent to the rise of those sects; or, at least, to the
origin of opinions which distinguished them. On the
whole, it is probably to be referred to a period not far
from that of the Macedonian conquest.

I think it is quite impossible to discern in the
book any two such distinct alternate strains of remark
as would justify the opinion of some commentators,
that it contains a dialogue between two parties, an
inquirer and a teacher.¶ A worse constructed dia-

---

radical verb קָהַל may have had the meaning, of which there is now no other
vestige, of *he spoke*, kindred to the common word קוֹל. At all events קָהַל,
in common Hebrew use, signifies *he assembled;* and the preacher (he who
moralizes in speech) *assembles* an audience (comp. xii. 9).

* This circumstance is so decisive, as to make it superfluous to dwell on
other considerations. I may, however, mention that Solomon could scarcely
have said of himself that he was "king over Israel *at Jerusalem*" (i. 12),
— an expression which seems to point to a time after there had been kings
of the northern tribes, — or that he was wiser, richer, and greater than all who
had gone before him at Jerusalem (i. 16 ; ii. 7, 9), when he had had only one
predecessor there, viz. his father David. I do not attach much importance
to the argument that remarks on the public administration indicate an observer who looked upon it from a private condition rather than from the
throne (iv. 13 – 16 ; v. 8, 9 ; viii. 2 – 5 ; ix. 13 – 18 ; x. 4 – 7, 16 – 20).

† For examples, see De Wette, "Einleitung," § 284 ; Eichhorn, "Einleitung," B. III. § 658.

‡ פַּרְדֵּסִים (ii. 5).

§ פִּתְגָם (viii. 11) has been thought to represent the Greek φθέγμα ; but
this is doubtful.

‖ See Bertholdt, "Einleitung," § 516.

¶ The book has been variously distributed on this hypothesis. Eichhorn's
scheme ("Einleitung," Th. III. § 661) is as follows, viz.:—The Disciple,
i. 1 – iv. 16 ; v. 12 – vi. 12 ; vii. 15 ; vii. 23 – 29 ; viii. 9 – ix. 6 ; ix. 11 –

logue, assuming it to have been one, could hardly be. In no manner does it appear that the two supposed interlocutors reply to one another's assertions or arguments. The successive use of the pronouns of the first and second person, which seems to have been chiefly what suggested this theory of interpretation, is nothing uncommon for a preacher, and is indeed the proper expedient of any writer who throws his thoughts into the form of an address. And the panegyric at the conclusion on Solomon, one of the speakers, presents (if genuine) a further objection to this scheme.

The doctrine of the writer is, that there is no satisfaction to be found in any thing that men possess or struggle for.*

Every thing is in perpetual fluctuation; nothing is constant but change.† Pleasure cloys and disgusts.‡ Power, wealth, and praise are hard to obtain, and worthless when obtained.§ When ambition has prospered, loneliness, envy, and hatred are all its meed.‖ Wisdom, which might seem to be the best of human possessions, is beyond human reach.¶ The whole system of things is a riddle.** Death is the only thing that

---

18; x. 5-7. The Teacher, iv. 17-v. 11; vii. 1-14; vii. 16-22; viii. 1 -8; ix. 7-10; x. 1-4; x. 8-xii. 7. Conclusion, xii. 8-14.

* " Two sisters by the goal are set,
    Cold Disappointment and Regret;
    One disenchants the winner's eyes,
    And strips of all its worth the prize,
    While one augments its gaudy show,
    More to enhance the loser's woe.
    The victor sees his fairy gold
    Transformed, when won, to drossy mould;
    But still the vanquished mourns his loss,
    And rues, as gold, that glittering dross."
                        Rokeby, Canto I. Stanza xxxi.
Here is the precise theme of Ecclesiastes.
    † Eccles. i. 1-11; iii. 1-9.   ‡ ii. 1-11.
    § iv. 13-16; v. 9-vi. 12.   ‖ iv. 4-12.
    ¶ i. 12-18; vii. 23, 24; ix. 11-x. 1.   ** viii. 14-ix. 6.

is certain, and, on the whole, the only thing to be desired; and that is a refuge for the wicked as well as for the good.* Death is better than life, and not to have lived is better than either; still, while life lasts, it is well for a man to seize all that it has to bestow, and that is enjoyment, — to "rejoice in his labors." † Such, half Cynical, half Epicurean, is the moral of the book. Pleasure is very little worth having; still it is all that is to be had, and a wise man will get the most of it.‡

As one might expect in so ill-compacted a composition, remarks are interspersed which the interpreter finds hard to weave into the general unity of the work. There are two long passages, which seem as if they had fallen out of their proper place in the Book of Proverbs, or rather as if they were a designed imitation of that book.§ Like the greater part of it, they consist mainly of apothegms relating to the prudent and safe conduct of life, constructed in the form of the poetical parallelism; but even in these the skeptical and sardonic temper of the writer occasionally finds vent.‖ In one passage, which has a very devout semblance, I seem to myself to perceive an under-current of ridicule.¶ The writer appears to be giving a serious caution against hasty vows, and to be warning too zealous devotees against the danger they are incurring of the Divine displeasure. But I cannot escape the impression, from the turn of the phrase, and a certain light and playful character which marks it, that he is amusing himself with the forwardness of will-worship-

---

* Eccles. viii. 6 – 8.   † iii. 16 – iv. 3.
‡ ii. 12 – 26 ; iii. 10 – 15; v. 9 – vi. 9 ; ix. 7 – 10 ; xi. 7 – xii. 8.
§ vii. 1 – viii. 10 (observe vii. 6, 15, 23, 25, 27, viii. 10, in which are remarks seemingly intended to make a connection between the passage and the rest of the book) ; x. 1 – xi. 6.
‖ vii. 15 – 17.   ¶ v. 1 – 7.

pers, a class of persons with whom he has no sympathy, and professing to give them a caution in an ironical use of their own pretending phraseology.

There are two passages in a quite different spirit from the rest of the work.* They are the following: —

"Because sentence against an evil work is not executed speedily, therefore does the heart of the sons of men become bold within them to do evil. But, though a sinner do evil a hundred times, and have his days prolonged, yet surely I know that it shall be well with them that fear God, that fear before him. But it shall not be well with the wicked ; he shall be like a shadow, and shall not prolong his days, because he fears not before God." †

"Let us hear the end of the whole discourse. Fear God, and keep his commandments, for this is the duty of all men. For God will bring every work into judgment, with every secret thing, whether it be good, or whether it be evil." ‡

The latter passage, and the four next preceding verses, with which it stands connected in the same paragraph, have — I think on very good grounds — been regarded by some critics as no part of the original composition, but a spurious continuation from some later hand. It is "The Preacher" that has been discoursing, in his own name, in all the previous part of the book. But here he is spoken of in the third person,§ and a glowing panegyric is pronounced upon

---

* I do not understand iii. 17 – 19 to be a passage of this description. On the contrary, I interpret the writer as here saying, that when, in the contemplation of prevailing wickedness (iii. 16), he ventured to promise himself that there would, after all, be a righteous retribution (17, 18), he found himself contradicted by experience (19 – 22). יְכִּ, at the beginning of verse 19, I would translate *but*, instead of "for."

† Eccles. viii. 11 – 13.   ‡ xii. 13, 14.   § xii. 8 – 10.

him, such as can scarcely be imagined to have proceeded from his own lips or pen, or to have been ascribed to him by a writer who had assumed his character, and was speaking in his name. We may suppose, with a high degree of probability, that some one, who — like others of his countrymen, according to Jerome's statement * — observed the wholly unedifying character of the book, added this last paragraph by way of pointing it with a moral, which, however opposed to its general contents, might do something to redeem its character. The original book ended as it began, with the dismal declaration that all was vanity, — that even the most beautiful of all earthly things, youthful piety, was no exception.† A well-intentioned officiousness applied itself to take out this sting, and bequeathed to us the wholesome, but inappropriate, paragraph which is appended.

And I think it probable that the other passage quoted on the last page had a similar origin. To me it bears strongly the appearance of a gloss, intended to contradict — as it does, categorically — the hurtful statement, in the verse which next follows, that there was no difference as to good fortune between the wicked and the righteous. If genuine, however, the passage does but show the wholly unsettled state of the writer's mind; and the denial of a righteous providence, which is the latter of the two contradictory declarations, is of course rather to be taken as the true representation of the writer's opinion, than the affirmation of such a providence, which goes before.

The book has but one use for us Christians; — the use of exhibiting the miserable disgust and despondency into which the reflecting mind will fall,

---

* See above, p. 337.   † Eccles. xii. 1 – 8.

when not enjoying the help of the Christian revelation of immortality to unriddle the problem of life.

It is not quoted in the New Testament.

"The Wisdom of Jesus, the Son of Sirach," has come down to us in a Greek version from the original work, made by the grandson of its author.* In a prologue, the translator states that, travelling into Egypt in the thirty-eighth year of King Ptolemy Euergetes, he found there "a book of no small learning," written by his grandfather Jesus, and that he "thought it most necessary to bestow some diligence and travail to interpret it, ... and set it forth for them also, which in a strange country are willing to learn, being prepared before in manners to live after the law." Another prologue, prefixed to this in some editions, is of uncertain origin, but is commonly ascribed to the pseudo-Athanasius, among whose works it first appears.† It declares that the translator's name was also Jesus, and that his father's name too was Sirach. The fact may have been so, but the statement is of small authority.

This is all that we know of either author or translator. Some critics, by reason of the respect which the author expresses for the medical profession, and some supposed indications of his being versed in the science, have imagined him to have been a physician.‡ Others, because of his zeal for the Law, have supposed him to have been a priest,§ and even to have

---

* The title "Ecclesiasticus" in our Bible is borrowed from the Latin version, in which it was probably adopted to distinguish the book from that of Ecclesiastes.

† "Synopsis," "S. Athanas. Opp.," Tom. II. p. 173 (edit. Paris).

‡ Ecclus. xxxviii. 1 - 17 ; comp. xxx. 24, xxxi. 20 - 22, 25, 30.

§ vii. 29 - 31 ; xlix. 1 - 13.

been high-priest. Carrying out still further this idea, and influenced by the similarity of name, some have been inclined to identify him with Jason, who, in the reign of Antiochus Epiphanes, usurped the high-priesthood from his brother Onias.* But, other objections apart, no characters could be more unlike than that of the wise and devout author of this book, with his profound reverence for righteousness and the Law, and that of the profligate courtier who at once introduced idolatrous usages among his people, and subjected them to foreign oppression. And with what decency — not merely to say with what truth — could the author of the prologue have ventured to apply to such a traitor as Jason the commendations which he bestows on the author of the book?

According to the translator's prologue, the original of the work was in the Hebrew tongue. Jerome says that he had met with it in that form,† and the fact of such an original is put beyond question by the structure of the composition. A large part of it is cast in the shape of that *parallelism*, which is the distinguishing costume of Hebrew poetry. The work bears every appearance of being an extremely literal translation, abounding in Hebrew constructions throughout, sacrificing perspicuity to the object of being literal, and presenting not a few clear instances of misapprehension, on the translator's part, of the text from which he was rendering. It has, however, been questioned, whether, by the *Hebrew* of the original, we are to understand the ancient language of the chosen people, or that Syro-Chaldee dialect which came into common use between the time of the Captivity and the Christian

---

* See above, p. 190.

† "Jesu, filii Sirach liber; . . . . . Hebraicum reperi." "Præfat. in Lib. Salomon.," "Opp.," Tom. L p. 938 (edit. Martianay).

era, and which is called *Hebrew* in the New Testament.* Jerome's statement of the name of the book, which is pure Hebrew, has some weight in confirmation † of the former opinion.

The Council of Carthage declared this book to be canonical.‡ The Greek fathers called it the " Treasure of all the Virtues"; and quoted it under the name of " Scripture," " Divine Scripture," and " Prophecy." ‖ It has come down to us in manuscripts of the Septuagint, and in translations into Latin, Syriac, and Arabic, the two former of which appear to have been also made from the Hebrew original, and the latter from the Syriac.¶ The Latin version, incorporated into the Vulgate, was not made by Jerome, but belongs to a much earlier time, being quoted literally by the Latin fathers of the second and third centuries.

The Latin and Syriac versions differ materially from the Greek, and from each other; and they present a different arrangement after the twenty-fifth verse of the thirtieth chapter, which arrangement is also followed in the Complutensian edition of the Septuagint.

The translator describes himself as "in the eight-and-thirtieth year coming into Egypt, when Euergetes was king." Now there were two Ptolemies, kings of Egypt, surnamed *Euergetes;* the one, successor of Philadelphus, who filled the throne from the year 246 to 221 B. C.; the other, also called Physcon, who reigned from 169 to 116. The writer greatly extols one " Simon the high-priest, the son of Onias." ** But

---

* Comp. Vol. I. p. 4, note.

† מְשָׁלִים. "Opp.," *ubi supra.*

‡ See Vol. I. p. 38.

‖ For examples, see Eichhorn, " Apokryph. Schrift.," pp. 76, 77.

¶ See Bertholdt, " Einleitung," § 541. Eichhorn, however, thinks they were made from the Greek (" Einleit. in die Apokryph.," s. 84).

** Ecclus. l. 1 *et seq.*

there were also two Simons, sons of Onias, of whom
the former died forty-six years before the accession of
the first Ptolemy Euergetes, the latter twenty-six years
before that of Ptolemy Physcon. The first Simon,
called Simon the Just, is one of the very eminent men
of that period of Jewish history. Accordingly, the
warm panegyric of the son of Sirach is thought to
be more applicable to him than to that Simon, of a
later age, of whom nothing equally meritorious is
known; and some critics, assuming the book to have
been written in the first Simon's time, or soon after it,
have proceeded to place the journey into Egypt of the
author's grandson and translator in the reign of the
first Ptolemy. But the statement of the journey's
having been made "in the eight-and-thirtieth year,
when Euergetes was king," appears to me to refer its
date conclusively to the time of Ptolemy Physcon,
who reigned over part of Egypt during his brother's
lifetime, twenty-four years, and over the whole, after
his death, twenty-nine years, while the other reign
lasted only twenty-five or twenty-six years.* The
thirty-eighth year of Ptolemy Physcon was the year
131 B. C. Should we allow fifty years for the space
of time between the translator's journey and his grandfather's composition of this book, we should refer the
composition to about the year 180 B. C., fifteen years
after the death of Simon II., whom the author may
probably have known, and have had some special
reason to commend. I, however, see not at all why
the adoption of this date for the work compels us to
understand that it is Simon II. who is celebrated,
since it was entirely fit that the writer, after extolling

---

* Jahn gets rid of this argument by understanding "the eight-and-thirtieth
year " to denote that year of the translator's age ("Einleitung," Th. II.
§ 249). But this is merely arbitrary.

Zerubbabel and Nehemiah,* as well as more ancient
worthies, should go on to celebrate the illustrious Simon the Just, who, though his predecessor by a century or more, was still much nearer to him in time
than those others. The time of the composition of this book appears
to have been also a time of trouble and persecution,†
which that of the first Ptolemy Euergetes was not;
while with the reign of Antiochus Epiphanes, from
the year 176 B. C., began one of the most sorrowful
passages in Jewish history. And there is nothing to
prevent our placing the composition as late as five, or
even ten, years after the accession of Antiochus; for
the latest of these dates would interpose thirty-five
years between the translator's journey into Egypt in
the thirty-eighth year of Ptolemy, and the composition
of that "book of no small learning" by his grandfather, which, after "continuing there some time," he
found. The whole case considered, I think there can
be little question about referring the completion of
the original work to a late year in the first half of
the second century before Christ.

No better division can be made of the book than
that which we find in the second prologue, above
named. "It containeth wise sayings, dark sentences,
and parables, and certain particular ancient godly
stories of men that pleased God; also his [the author's] prayer and song." "This Jesus did imitate
Solomon," the prologue further states, "and was no
less famous for wisdom and learning." The part
which contains matter bearing a certain resemblance
to the book known as Solomon's Proverbs, occupies
the first forty-three chapters; the subject of the seven
chapters next following is the merits of the patriarchs

---

* Ecclus. xlix. 11, 13.   † xxxv. 15 - 19 ; xxxvi. 1 - 17 ; li. 1 - 12.

and other worthies of Jewish history; a prayer, and exhortation to the pursuit of wisdom, in the fifty-first chapter, conclude the book.

It is a work of great value, excelling, in my judgment, the Proverbs of Solomon, in all the merits appropriate to that class of compositions to which the two books belong. The writer had been a careful and keen observer of the movements of society. He had pried "into the ways of men with sharpened, sly inspection." He had rare powers of generalization to class his observations, and of wit to illustrate them with brilliant similitudes. His vein of thought was wise, generous, and calm, as well as original. For sagacious, comprehensive, and, for the most part, benignant views of life, for copiousness, aptness, and force of illustration, and for general felicity of phrase, his book challenges the reader's admiration. This is its general character; it has its obscure portions, owing apparently, in part, to the translator's misapprehensions of the sense of the original.

There is yet another point of view, independent of its abstract merit, in which a very peculiar interest attaches to this work. It presents itself to us as an exponent of Jewish intellectual and moral culture in the second century before the advent of Jesus Christ. The author was a "Hebrew of the Hebrews"; a Jew by ancestry, by birth,* by culture, by sentiment. A highly cultivated man, he shows not the slightest indication, from first to last, of being acquainted with the Gentile literature and philosophy of his time. Whatever he was, that he appears to have become under national influences alone, — the influence of the Jewish faith, of Jewish learning, of Jewish society, and Jewish habits of thought and life.

---

* Ecclus. l. 27.

Accordingly, in his intellectual and moral condition, as far as his book discloses it (and that is very far), he presents to us a specimen of the result which, at the time when he lived, had been wrought out by the Law, which, thirteen centuries earlier, Moses had delivered to his nation, and by the institutions of every sort which that Law established. It is profoundly interesting to place the writer of this book by the side of the semi-barbarians for whom Moses first legislated, and to consider how his Law had operated to effect such a change in the style of character and thought.

To form a just idea of the agency which such influences, by their operation on successive generations, had proved at last capable of exerting on a mind and heart favorable to their operation, one must acquaint himself familiarly with the contents of this book. A mere description of its contents conveys the idea but faintly. The careful reader will recognize it as breathing the spirit of a man who had attained to all of religious wisdom that was attainable without the help of Christianity, and who, as plainly, had stopped far short of the standard which Christianity prescribes. He had noble conceptions of the Deity.* His morality by no means consisted in external service, but acknowledged the paramount obligation of a sense of duty within, kept in view the perpetual superintendence of the Searcher of hearts,† and traced all righteous conduct to its true source in the religious sentiments.‡ It taught our Lord's own lessons, that it is the forgiving man who may hope for forgiveness from God,§ and that the most secure and profitable treasure is that which is laid up with Him. ‖ On the other hand, it did not

---

* Ecclus. xliii. 26 – 33.　　† xxxvii. 13 – 16; xxi. 6 – 11; xxiii. 19.
‡ xxv. 10 – 12.　　§ xxviii. 2 – 7.
‖ xxix. 11.

reach the high conception of that charity, of Christ's enjoining, which does good to the unthankful and the evil; * and the great Gospel sanction, founded on immortality and retribution, is at best but faintly and doubtfully disclosed.† Life and immortality were not yet brought to light, and the hopes of the most enlightened and devout for an existence beyond the tomb had as yet no foundation of assured faith. Judaism had done its appropriate work in educating the minds of some of its disciples to a state of mature preparation for a better discipline; but the very accomplishment of its work showed how much a better discipline was needed. ‡

If there are no formal quotations from this book in the New Testament, there are occasional instances of the use of its language, showing, as far as they go, the estimation which it enjoyed as a book of authority and salutary doctrine. §

The book of "The Wisdom of Solomon" has been thought to bear a resemblance to Ecclesiastes, analogous to that of Ecclesiasticus to the Proverbs, but I think without much reason, except as in both Solomon is represented as speaking.

To all appearance, this book was not, like the one last remarked upon, from a Palestine, but an Egyptian

---

* Ecclus. xii. 4.   † xix. 19; comp. xli. 3, 4.

‡ If the common text of li. 10, rendered, "I called upon the Lord the father of my Lord," is correct, it may contain a reference to the expected Messiah, in language borrowed from Ps. cx. 1 (comp. ii. 7, 12)]; but it is probable that the word κυρίου, which is wanting in the versions, is an interpolation, and that the genuine reading was that which would be rendered, "I called unto the Lord my Father."

§ v. 11 (comp. James i. 19) ; xxiv. 21 (comp. John vi. 35); xxvii. 6 (comp. Matt. vii. 20); xxix. 11 (comp. Matt. vi. 20) ; xxxv. 12, 13 (comp. Acts x. 34, Rom. ii. 11, Gal. ii. 6, Eph. vi. 9, Col. iii. 25, 1 Pet. i. 17) ; xxxv. 18 (comp. 2 Pet. iii. 9) ; xliv. 16 (comp. Heb. xi. 5).

source, and the Greek text in our hands is not a translation, but the original work. " It is not found among the Hebrew books," says Jerome, "nay, its very style is redolent of Greek eloquence, and some ancient writers say that its author was Philo the Jew." * The author's name may have been Philo; but he could not have been that Philo the Jew, contemporary with the Apostles, whose copious writings are in our hands; for the respective works, with a general resemblance in their philosophy, differ widely from each other in respect to particular views, as well as in style.† Nor could he have been the Philo (mentioned by Josephus) who wrote in the time of Caligula;‡ for that Philo was a heathen, while the whole strain of the book before us determines its author to have been a Jew.

From the time of the conquests of Alexander, Judaism had two principal seats, Jerusalem, and Alexandria in Egypt. The Egyptian Jews cultivated the Greek philosophy, and particularly the Platonism which was then the favorite doctrine of the Greek schools; and their speculations presented a singular sort of eclecticism, — a combination of philosophical ideas of Grecian origin with those derived from the Jewish Scriptures, — which is throughout apparent in this work.

Respecting its date, nothing can be determined with any exactness, — not even so much as whether it was composed before or after the Christian era. It must have existed some time before the close of the second century, for it is referred to by Clement of Alexandria and Tertullian.§ Eichhorn thought it was known to

---

* " Pref. in Libb. Solom.," " Opp.," Tom. I. p. 938 (edit. Martianay).

† For a full argument on this subject, with ample quotations, see Eichhorn's " Einleit. in die Apocryph. Schrift. des A. T.," ss. 172 – 177.

‡ " Cont. Apion.," Lib. I. § 23.

§ " Stromat.," Lib. V. p. 583 (edit. Paris); " Adv. Valent.," c. 2; " De Præscrip. Hæret.," cap. 7.

St. Paul; * but, granting that passages of the two writers have such a resemblance as to show them not to be of independent origin, it remains uncertain which of the two referred to the other, or whether the expressions of both have a common source. Lowth says: " I agree with those critics, who suppose this book to be a much more modern production than that of the son of Sirach." †

This uncertainty respecting the date of the work is the more to be regretted, because of the allusions which occur in it to some kind of immortality and retribution, such as have not presented themselves in any book which has hitherto come under our notice. ‡ To whatever time we should refer them, an important question would arise, how far they present a sense higher than that of earthly retribution and the immortality of favorable or unfavorable remembrance on earth ; § and as far as they might be found actually to refer to a future life, a further question would occur as to their accordance with Egyptian ‖ or Greek doctrines on the one hand, and with those of the New Testament on the other. Some of the best critics, beginning with Grotius,¶ have been of the opinion that the work has been wrought over by Christian hands, and has experienced interpolations and changes. Nothing of this kind can now be proved; but it may well have taken place, in the time previous to the appearance of the

---

* Rom. i. 20 – 23 (comp. Wisdom xiii. 1 – 10); Eph. vi. 13 – 17 (comp. Wisd. v. 18 – 20).

† " Sacred Poetry of the Hebrews," Lect. XXIV. p. 345.

‡ Wisd. ii. 23 – v. 15 ; viii. 13 ; xv. 3.

§ Our translation of ii. 23 is altogether more definite than the original, in respect to accordance with the Christian doctrine of immortality. ψυχαί (iii. 1) means *lives* as well as *souls*. It is earthly retribution that is spoken of in iii. 11 – iv. 6. But I have no occasion to pursue this inquiry.

‖ Comp. viii. 19, 20.

¶ " In Lib. Sapient. Solom. Proœmium."

book in the quotations of the Fathers, at the close of the second century.

The work, like that of Ecclesiastes, is thrown into the form of a discourse on the part of ·the wise King Solomon, who, as in the other case, is described without naming him.* It begins with a panegyric on religious wisdom, especially recommending it to kings and governors, and expatiating largely on its excellent attributes and uses.† Then follows a prayer for its possession, ‡ which slides into another eulogium upon it, extending to the end of the book with copious illustrations, mostly drawn from the Jewish history, of its use in protecting and honoring its votaries, and the miserable condition of those who reject it, and especially who substitute for it the impious absurdities of idolatry. The conclusion is abrupt, though the closing words, "In all things, O Lord, thou didst magnify thy people, and glorify them, neither didst thou lightly regard them, but didst assist them in every time and place," are a sort of generalization of many of the particulars which have been produced, and concise statement of the *thesis* which they sustain.

An opinion has been common, and been very elaborately defended, that the book, as we have it, was made by a union of at least two parts, the productions either of different writers, or of the same writer at different periods of his life.§ I can only express my surprise, that the opinion has gained favor in such quarters. I can find no reason for such a division as is proposed, in any diversity of subject, opinion, representation, or style. Nor do I think that the book admits of division

---

* Wisd. vii. 1–22; ix. 5–12.   † i. 1–viii. 21.   ‡ ix. 1–18.
§ Eichhorn ("Einleit. in die Apocryph. Schrift.," ss. 90–162) understands the first part to end at xi. 1; Bertholdt ("Einleit." § 526), at xii. 27; *alii, alias.*

in any place which has been proposed. The end of the eighth chapter introduces a prayer or address to God. A prayer, properly so called, begins the ninth chapter. A commendation of the wisdom which is prayed for — still in the form of a devotional appeal — occupies the residue of that chapter; and the same form of address to God is continued through the illustrations of the excellence of wisdom, and the mischief of its opposite, to the end of the book.

There are three old translations of the book, — into Syriac, Arabic, and Latin, — all believed to have been made from the Greek text. The Latin is known, from Jerome's own statement, to be more ancient than the time of that Father.*

We cannot speak of references in the New Testament to this book, inasmuch as we do not know whether it was composed earlier or later than the books of that collection.†

---

* *Ubi supra.*

† Instances of resemblance in language are such as follow, viz. : — iii. 7 (comp. Matt. xiii. 43) ; vii. 26 (comp. Heb. i. 3); ix. 13 (comp. Rom. xi. 34) ; xviii. 15 (comp. John i. 1).

LECTURE LXV.

TOBIT, PRAYER OF MANASSEH, AND JUDITH.

ABSTRACT OF THE NARRATIVE IN THE BOOK OF TOBIT.—ITS DESIGN
AND PLAN THAT OF A ROMANCE.—ITS MORAL INSTRUCTIONS.—SIG-
NIFICANCE OF SOME OF ITS PROPER NAMES.—ITS AUTHOR, AGE, ORIG-
INAL LANGUAGE, AND PLACE OF COMPOSITION.—CANONICAL AUTHORITY.
—VERSIONS.—COINCIDENCES OF PHRASE BETWEEN IT AND THE NEW
TESTAMENT.—THE PRAYER OF MANASSEH, SUGGESTED BY THE NAR-
RATIVE, IN THE CHRONICLES, OF THAT MONARCH'S CAPTIVITY.—THE
GREEK TEXT, IN OUR HANDS, PROBABLY THE ORIGINAL COMPOSITION.—
CHARACTER OF THE PIECE.—ABSTRACT OF THE NARRATIVE IN THE
BOOK OF JUDITH.—TIME TO WHICH THE RELATION IS TO BE RE-
FERRED.—CONFUSION OF GEOGRAPHY.—THE BOOK A ROMANCE.—
TIME OF ITS COMPOSITION.—ORIGINAL LANGUAGE.—VERSIONS.—
CANONICAL AUTHORITY.—NOT REFERRED TO IN THE NEW TESTA-
MENT.

ALL the remaining books of the Hagiographa and
Apocrypha are, in whole or in part, historical and
biographical. I shall take them up in the order of
the times to which they appear respectively to refer.
The title of the Book of Tobit is as follows:—
"The Book of the Words of Tobit, son of Tobiel,
the son of Ananiel, the son of Abdiel, the son of Gabael, of the seed of Asael, of the tribe of Naphtali,
who in the time of Enemassar, king of the Assyrians,
was led captive out of Thisbe, which is at the right
hand of Kadesh of Naphtali in Galilee above Aser."
It is a life of Tobit and his son Tobias, cast in the
form of an autobiography through the first two or
three chapters of the Greek text, after which the narrative is conducted, for all the characters, in the third
person.

Tobit is represented as a pious and charitable Jew,
who, while he lived in Palestine, refusing to have any
participation in the irreligious practices which had
prevailed in his tribe after the revolt of Jeroboam,
was in the habit of going to Jerusalem with his offerings at the great festivals, as the Law required, and of
devoting another large portion of his wealth to hospitality and charity. He married his kinswoman Anna,
and by her had a son named Tobias. They were carried captives to Nineveh, where his brethren "did eat
of the bread of the Gentiles"; but, from a sense of
religious duty, he refrained. Having been promoted
by Enemassar to be his "purveyor," he "went into
Media, and left in trust with Gabael, the brother of
Gabrias, at Rages, a city of Media, ten talents of silver." *

Enemassar being dead, the disordered state of affairs
which ensued in the reign of his son prevented Tobit
from going into Media, to look after his deposit. Continuing his course of alms-giving, and attending to the
pious duty of burying the dead of his nation, especially those who had fallen victims to the tyranny of
the king, he incurred the royal displeasure, and was
stripped of all his property, and reduced to find safety
in flight. Sennacherib having been assassinated, his
successor, Sarchedonus, promoted a relative of Tobit,
by whose friendly offices he obtained permission to
return to Nineveh. Having contracted ritual unclean-
ness by burying another dead body, he slept in a place
apart, where he was exposed to a singular accident, in

---

* Tobit i. 1–14. — "Kadesh of Nephthali" (2); comp. Josh. xx. 7;
Judges iv. 6. — "All the tribe of Nephthali my father fell" (4); rather, *had
fallen*, for the apostasy took place two centuries and a half before the Assyrian captivity. — "The first tenth part of all increase . . . . . another
tenth part . . . . . and the third" (7, 8); comp. Vol. I. p. 456, note ‡.

consequence of which he lost his sight. In this helpless condition, he was supported by the industry of his
wife and the bounty of his relative, the king's favorite.
His wife having received the present of a kid, he
charged her with having stolen it. A retort of hers
distressed him, and he offered a prayer that he might
die. It so happened, that at the same time a prayer of
the same tenor was offered at the distant city of Ecbatana in Media, by one Sarah, daughter of Raguel, who
had been "reproached by her father's maids, because
that she had been married to seven husbands, whom
Asmodeus the evil spirit had killed" on the nuptial
night, being himself enamored of her. Both suppliants returned at the same time to the apartments
which they usually occupied, and "the prayers of them
both were heard before the majesty of the great God,
and Raphael was sent to heal them both," in the ways
related further on.*

"In that day Tobit remembered the money which
he had committed to Gabael in Rages of Media." He
called his son Tobias, and, having enjoined on him the
observance of filial duties, and given him abundance
of judicious counsel respecting a life of uprightness,
beneficence, chastity, temperance, docility, and piety,
directed him to go to Media to reclaim the deposit,†
and gave him a written instrument containing authority to transact the business. By his command the
young man went in search of a guide, and "found
Raphael, that was an angel; but he knew not." To

---

* Tobit i. 15–iii. 17. — "Remembering that prophecy of Amos," &c.,
(ii. 6); this form of introducing a quotation from a prophet, where no fulfilment of prediction was intended to be alleged, illustrates the New Testament quotations from the Old. See above, pp. 321–324. — With iii. 6, comp.
Jonah iv. 8. — With iii. 8, comp. vi. 14, where the motive for the murders
by Asmodeus is explained.

† iv. 1–21.

Tobit's inquiry respecting his name and kindred, Raphael, after first evading the question with some petulance, replied that his name was Azarias; his family connection, which he also disclosed, was approved by Tobit; a compensation was agreed upon; and, the opposition of Anna being quieted, the travellers proceeded on their way, "and the young man's dog with them." *

"They came in the evening to the river Tigris, and they lodged there." Tobias, going to the river's bank for his ablutions, was attacked by a fish which "leaped out of the river." By the angel's direction, he "laid hold of the fish, and drew it to land," and together they cooked and ate it. Asking his companion of what use were the entrails, which he had been directed to keep, he was told, "Touching the heart and the liver, if a devil or an evil spirit trouble any, we must make a smoke thereof before the man or the woman, and the party shall be no more vexed; as for the gall, it is good to anoint a man that hath whiteness in his eyes, and he shall be healed." Arrived at Ecbatana, the angel told Tobias that he meant to lodge him there in the house of Raguel, and to propose a marriage for him with Raguel's daughter, Sarah, to whom she was due by the levirate law of Moses. Tobias objected, on account of what he had heard, as before related, of the fate of her former seven husbands. The angel, however, overruled his scruples, partly with commendations of her merit, partly with references to the last counsels of Tobit; and gave him directions how to proceed in order to a happy termination of the affair.†
They came to Raguel's house, and, having made known their relation to Tobit, were generously entertained.

---

* Tobit v. 1 – 22. † vi. 1 – 17.

Raphael made his proposals, which were accepted by the host, after a frank explanation of the attending danger, and the ill-boding nuptials were formally solemnized.*

Left alone with his weeping bride, Tobias proceeded to execute the directions he had received from Raphael. He " took the ashes of the perfumes, and put the heart and the liver of the fish thereupon, and made a smoke therewith; the which smell when the evil spirit had smelled, he fled into the utmost parts of Egypt, and the angel bound him"; after which Tobias called upon Sarah to join him in a prayer for Divine protection. Raguel, expecting none but a fatal event, " went and made a grave," which, when the bridegroom was found to be still alive, he caused to be filled, and offered thanks for the preservation. Raguel insisted on detaining his son-in-law for a wedding festivity of a fortnight's duration,† during which time Raphael, with " a servant and two camels," proceeded to Rages, and returned thence safe with the money collected from Gabael, and accompanied by that faithful trustee. ‡ Tobit meanwhile anxiously counted the unexpected days of their long absence; and his wife, still more impatient, "went out every day into the way which they went, and did eat no meat on the daytime, and ceased not whole nights to bewail her son." §

The nuptial holidays being over, Tobias, resisting the entreaties of Raguel for a further delay, set out on his return with his wife, dismissed with the affectionate benedictions and counsels of her parents, and with half their property for her dowry. As they approached Nineveh, Raphael proposed to him that they, with the dog, should precede Sarah to the city, taking

---

* Tobit vii. 1 – 18.   † viii. 1 – 21.
‡ ix. 1 – 6.   § x. 1 – 7.

with them "the gall of the fish," with which to anoint
his father's eyes, and cure his blindness. Anna was
the first to discern their approach, and to welcome her
son, declaring that she was now "content to die." As
Tobit, to whom she had given notice, advanced to meet
him, the application of the gall was made; "the whiteness pilled away from the corners of his eyes, and when
he saw his son, he fell upon his neck." He offered
a devout thanksgiving, and "went out to meet his
daughter-in-law at the gate of Nineve, rejoicing and
praising God." He welcomed her with a blessing on
herself and hers; his patron, the great courtier Achiacharus, with another kinsman, paid a visit of congratulation to the happy family; and amidst the rejoicings
of "all his brethren which were at Nineve," "Tobias's
wedding was kept seven days." *

The guide having been called, by an agreement between Tobias and his father, to receive not only his
stipulated wages, but the additional donative of one
half the property which had been brought from Media,
in requital of his great services, "took them both
apart," and after some appropriate, devout suggestions,
announced himself as "Raphael, one of the seven
holy angels, which present the prayers of the saints,
and which go in and out before the glory of the Holy
One." In this character he said that he had been an
approving witness of the good works of Tobit, and
had presented "before the Holy One" those prayers
which he and Sarah, in distant places, had offered at
the same hour. He directed them to "give God
thanks," and "write all things which are done in a
book." They had prostrated themselves in fear before
him; "and when they arose, they saw him no more."

---

* Tobit x. 7 – xi. 19.

"Then Tobit wrote a prayer of rejoicing," composed of topics relating more to national concerns than to his own.*

Tobit "was eight-and-fifty years old when he lost his sight, which was restored to him after eight years." He persevered in his religious and benevolent course of life; "and when he was very aged, he called his son," and his six grandsons, and telling Tobias that he believed what Jonas the prophet had predicted of the overthrow of Nineve, and that Jerusalem too would be desolated for a time, and afterwards restored to a condition of great glory, accompanied by a conversion of all mankind to the worship of Jehovah, advised him to betake himself with his family to Media for a more quiet residence. He bade him "keep the law and the commandments," and show himself "merciful and just," illustrating the latter lesson by two or three personal anecdotes. "Bury me decently," he said, "and thy mother with me." Finally, "when he had said these things, he gave up the ghost in the bed, being an hundred and eight-and-fifty years old, and he buried him honorably. And when Anna his mother was dead, he buried her with his father; but Tobias departed with his wife and children to Ecbatane, to Raguel, his father-in-law, where he became old with honor, and he buried his father and mother-in-law honorably, and he inherited their substance, and his father Tobit's. And he died at Ecbatane in Media, being an hundred and seven-and-twenty years old. But before he died, he heard of the destruction of Nineve, which was taken by Nabuchodonosor and Assuerus; and before his death, he rejoiced over Nineve." †

---

* Tobit xii. 1 – xiii. 18.   † xiv. 1 – 15.

Who does not see that this book is a romance?
How could it bear more distinctly the characters of a
fictitious narrative, — a class of composition which, as
we have heretofore seen, was considered to be legitimate among the Jews as well as other nations?* Regarded in this light, it is a production by no means
destitute of merit. With all its grotesque machinery,
it has passages of genuine pathos, and the prayers are
conceived in a spirit of true devotion. Tobit was a
man, like Cornelius in the New Testament, whose
" prayers and alms had come up as a memorial before
God"; and the efficacy of such a life as his to propitiate the Divine favor, to give support under affliction,
and to invoke prosperity, is illustrated in an entertaining and not unimpressive manner.

In the condition and character of Tobit, a godly
and prosperous man, reduced to such distress, and so
disturbed by the reproaches of his wife, that he was
tempted to curse God and die,† the writer seems to have
had in view the history of Job. Some of the proper
names appear to be significant, as befits the plan of such
a fiction. Thus, Tobit, in its original Hebrew form,
means *my good man;* Tobias, *the Lord is good;* Azariah, *help of the Lord;* Gabael, *the Lord is a bulwark;*
Achiacharus, *my nephew is the second,* that is, after
the king; ‡ Raphael, *God has cured.* §

Of the author we know nothing. Prideaux, with
others of that school of commentators who have
dreamed of its being a true history, says that the book
" seems, in its original draught, to have been the me-
moirs of the family to which it relates, first begun by
Tobit, then continued by Tobias, and lastly finished
by some other of the family, and afterwards digested

---

* Vol. III. p. 469; Vol. IV. pp. 126, 127. † Tobit ii. 14 – iii. 6.
‡ Comp. i. 22. § Comp. vi. 8; xi. 11 – 13.

by the Chaldee author into that form in which we now have it. Jerome translated it out of the Chaldee into Latin." * But the very basis for this division is imaginary; for though, in our Greek copies, the writer speaks in the first person through the first three chapters, it appears from Jerome's version, that in the Chaldee text, from which he translated, the narrative was conducted in the third person from beginning to end.

For any thing that we know, it may have been written later than the Christian era. It is thought that Clement of Alexandria, about the year 200, refers to it; † and if so, this is the earliest reference. Neither Josephus nor Philo makes any allusion to it; but, as it is not clear that they had any occasion to do so, this is imperfect evidence of its not having been in existence in their time. The mythology of a divine council of seven angels ‡ is believed to have had its origin in the attendance with which the Persian king, Darius Hystaspis, surrounded his throne. § But however this might be, it was a doctrine of the Persians, ‖ with which people the Jews had no intimate relations till the time of the capture of Babylon by Cyrus; and several generations must be supposed to have passed before the Jews incorporated into their own popular faith an article so peculiar, and so foreign to their national theology. "Rages, a city of Media," is the scene of some of the transactions related; ¶ but the foundation of Rages is attributed by Strabo ** to Seleu-

---

* "The Old and New Testaments connected," &c., Part I. Book I. An. 612.
† Viz. to Tob. iv. 15, in "Stromat.," Lib. II. p. 503 (edit. Potter.), and to Tob. xii. 8, in "Stromat.," Lib. VI. p. 791.
‡ Tobit xii. 15.
§ Eichhorn, "Einleit. in die Apokryph. Schrift.," s. 408, anm. h.
‖ Bertholdt, "Einleit.," § 582.
¶ Tobit i. 14; ix. 2.					** "Geog.," Lib. XI. p. 524.

cus Nicator, about 300 B. C.; and supposing this statement to be correct, we can scarcely place the date of the book earlier than the year 100 or 150 B. C., since this seems allowing little time enough for the origin of Rages to have been so far lost sight of as that the writer should have supposed it to have been a place of resort so early as the time which he indicates. These considerations conduct to no definite result; but they afford all the light we have.

The book bears no marks of the style of thought of an Egyptian Jew. We are probably to look for the writer in Palestine, where stood the city and temple for which he had so much reverence,* or in Babylon, where he has placed the scene of his story. In either case, he probably wrote in the Hebrew language. Possibly the Chaldee text, from which Jerome says that he translated,† was the original, though, if so, it was a text materially different from that which was used by the author of the Greek version in the Septuagint.‡ Origen, a hundred and fifty years before Jerome, knew the book only in a Greek copy,§ and it might thence appear probable that the same was true of the Jews of his time. But several instances have been pointed out, in which obscurities in the Greek are cleared up, and apparent errors corrected, by supposing mistakes of the Greek translator in respect to the reading or the sense of a Hebrew word.‖

The Book of Tobit was declared canonical by the Council of Carthage in the year 397.¶ It does not appear in the earlier lists of canonical writings.

---

* Tobit i. 4 – 7; xiii. 9 – 18.
† "Præfat. in Tob." ("Opp." Tom. I. p. 1158)
‡ For examples, see De Wette, "Einleit.," § 310.
§ "Epist. ad African.," § 13 (Tom. L p. 26, edit. Delarue).
‖ Bertholdt, "Einleit.," § 583.
¶ Vol. I. p. 38.

There is a Syriac translation, which follows the
Greek as far as through the first half of the seventh
chapter, from which point it differs frequently both
from that and from the Latin. A Latin version, earlier
than any of these except the Greek, differs from them
all, though having more affinity with the Greek than
with the Latin of Jerome. There are also extant two
Hebrew versions, one made from the Greek, the other
from the Greek and Vulgate Latin combined. Neither
is of any critical value.

Some instances are pointed out of resemblance between the language of the New Testament and of this
book. But they are not such as to authorize us to
say that the New Testament ever refers to it.[*]

The history in the Books of Kings bears no trace
of any captivity of Manasseh.[†]   In the Second Book
of Chronicles we read that " the Lord spake to Manasseh and to his people, but they would not hearken ;
wherefore the Lord brought upon them the captains
of the host of the king of Assyria, which took Manasseh among the thorns, and bound him with fetters,
and carried him to Babylon; and when he was in
affliction, he besought the Lord his God, and humbled
himself greatly before the God of his fathers, and
prayed unto him; and he was entreated of him, and
heard his supplication, and brought him again to Jerusalem into his kingdom.   Then Manasseh knew
that the Lord, he was God."[‡]   " Now the rest of the
acts of Manasseh, and his prayer unto his God, ...
behold, they are written in the book of the kings of
Israel; his prayer also, and how God was entreated of

---

* E. g. Tobit iv. 15 (comp. Matt. vii. 12, Luke vi. 31) ; xiii. 16 (comp.
Apoc. xxi. 18).

† 2 Kings xxi. 1 - 18.   ‡ 2 Chron. xxxiii. 10 - 13.

him, ... behold, they are written among the sayings of the seers." *

This narrative appears to have suggested the idea of the short composition which has been transmitted to us in some copies of the Greek of the Septuagint, and in the Latin of the Vulgate, and thence adopted into our English Apocrypha, under the title of " The Prayer of Manasses, King of Judah, when he was holden captive in Babylon." It is not included in any ancient catalogue of canonical writings, nor even in the Canon of the Council of Trent. The first notice which occurs of it is in a copy in the Apostolical Constitutions, a work referred to the fourth century of our era.† It bears no marks of having been translated from the Hebrew or Chaldee; and probably the Greek, which the Vulgate closely follows, is the original text. The form of the invocation, " O Lord, Almighty God of our fathers, Abraham, Isaac, and Jacob, and of their righteous seed," and the similar language, " Thou, therefore, O Lord, that art the God of the just, hast not appointed repentance to the just, as to Abraham, and Isaac, and Jacob," have been thought to indicate the author to have been a Jew; but though such may well have been the fact, I cannot think the argument good, as, for one writing in Manasseh's name, even if he were a Christian, it required very little art to place himself so far in that monarch's place. Though the sentiments of the piece are well conceived and well expressed, the fiction is not skilfully preserved throughout. According to the history, Manasseh had now lost his throne and his liberty, which were afterwards restored. But he is not here represented as praying for their restoration;

---

* 2 Chron. xxxiii. 18, 19.   † Lib. II. cap. 22.

while, on the other hand, he is represented as being
" bowed down with many iron bands," and unable to
lift up his head, or draw his breath, particulars which
have an appearance of being due to the writer's imagination.   The Jews had a story that, when Manasseh
uttered his prayer, he was inclosed in a brazen globe,
around which the Chaldees kindled a fire; that, in
this deplorable condition, he prayed to his idol gods,
but they did not hear; that when he turned to Jehovah, angels shut up all the windows of heaven,
so that Jehovah should not hear; but that Jehovah
made a way for the ascent of his prayers directly under his own throne, and that, the prayer being thus
heard, a spirit came from between the wings of the
cherubim, and blew Manasseh home to his capital
city.*   According to others, as Manasseh prayed, his
iron fetters snapped, and he flew away from Babylon.†

The author of the Book of Judith has been thought
by some critics to have intended to refer his narrative
to the time of Manasseh, after that monarch had been
restored to his freedom and throne.

The book relates, that " in the twelfth year of the
reign of Nabuchodonosor, who reigned in Nineve,
the great city," that prince made war upon Arphaxad,
who " reigned over the Medes in Ecbatane," and who
had fortified his capital with walls of great solidity
and magnificence.   Numerous forces mustered under
the standard of Nabuchodonosor from the countries
bordering on the Tigris and Euphrates, and others,
but his summons to the tribes of Persia, Asia Minor,
Egypt, and Syria (including Palestine) was disregard-

* Targum on 2 Chron. xxxiii. 11 (apud Bertholdt, " Einleit.," § 615).
† " S. Johan. Damasc. Opp.," Tom. II. p. 463 (edit. Le Quien).

ed; "they were not afraid of him; yea, he was before them as one man," and they sent away his ambassadors from them without effect, and with disgrace. Deferring his threatened vengeance for this slight, he "in the seventeenth year" prosecuted a successful war against Arphaxad, whom he put to death, and took and sacked his capital; after which, returning to Nineve, "he took his ease and banqueted, both he and his army, an hundred and twenty days." *

The following year the king, proceeding, by the advice of his nobles, to execute his unappeased displeasure against his disobedient tributaries, "called Holofernes, the chief captain of his army, which was next unto him," and bade him invade "all the west country" with an army of a hundred and twenty thousand infantry, and twelve thousand horse, demand of the inhabitants "earth and water," the tokens of submission which the Persians were accustomed to exact,† spoil and put to the sword all who resisted, and reserve those who submitted themselves for the king's own disposal. Holofernes, with the force specified, and with ample provisions and equipments, proceeded on his conquests, which are described with a singular confusion of geography. He invaded Egypt and Arabia, then recrossed the Euphrates "and went through Mesopotamia," then ravaged a portion of Asia Minor, and having traversed "the south, over against Arabia," and "compassed also all the children of Midian," ended his present exploits by burning the fields, destroying the flocks and herds, spoiling the cities, and putting to death all the young men of "the plain of Damascus." ‡

"Therefore the fear and dread of him fell upon all

---

* Judith i. 1 – 16.   † Comp. Herod. Lib. VII. § 133.   ‡ ii. 1 – 27.

the inhabitants of the sea-coasts, which were in Sidon and Tyrus, and them that dwelt in Sur and Ocina, and all that dwelt in Jemnaan; and they that dwelt in Azotus and Ascalon feared him greatly." Receiving an embassy from them, with an unconditional surrender of themselves and their property to his mercy, he moved his forces towards the sea-coast, garrisoning the cities, impressing men, destroying the idol groves, and being everywhere received with a simulated joy, "with garlands, with dances, and with timbrels." *

Approaching the Jewish frontier, "he pitched between Geba and Scythopolis, and there tarried a whole month, that he might gather together all the carriages of his army." The Jews, who "were newly returned from the captivity," with their worship just restored, "were troubled for Jerusalem, and for the temple of the Lord their God." They "possessed themselves beforehand of all the tops of the high mountains, and fortified the villages that were in them, and laid up victuals for the provision of war." By the advice of Joacim, the high-priest, they occupied "the passages of the hill country; for by them there was an entrance into Judea, and it was easy to stop them that would come up, because the passage was strait, for two men at the most." The people "cried to God with great fervency, and with great vehemency did they humble their souls." They clothed themselves and their families, their guests, their servants, and even their cattle, in sackcloth. At Jerusalem, all the inhabitants prostrated themselves at the temple, and "put sackcloth about the altar," while they sent up their agonized entreaties for deliverance. "The people fasted many days in all Judea and Jerusalem, before the sanc-

---

* Judith ii. 28 – iii. 8.

tuary of the Lord Almighty; and Joacim the high-
priest, and all the priests that stood before the Lord,
. . . . . had their loins girt with sackcloth and offered
the daily burnt-offerings, with the vows and free gifts
of the people, and had ashes on their mitres, and
cried unto the Lord with all their power, that he
would look upon all the house of Israel graciously."
An unhoped for deliverance was to come. " God heard
their prayers, and looked upon their afflictions." *

At the intelligence that the Jews had closed the
passes of the hills, and made other military preparations, Holofernes " was very angry, and called all
the princes of Moab, and the captains of Ammon, and
all the governors of the sea-coast," and made inquiries
of them respecting this rebellious people, who they
were, what was their government, what their resources,
and what the occasion of their obstinacy. " Achior,
the captain of all the sons of Ammon," replied with
a very correct account of the early fortunes of the
nation. " Whilst they sinned not before their God,"
he said, " they prospered, because the God that hateth
iniquity was with them. But when they departed
from the way which he appointed them, they were
destroyed in many battles very sore, and were led
captives into a land that was not theirs, and the
temple of their god was cast to the ground." From
this captivity they had returned, and he gave it as his
opinion, that, if they were now sinning against their
God, they might be successfully attacked; otherwise
it was better to " pass by "; they would be found un-
conquerable, and their assailants would " become a
reproach before all the world." † This discouraging
language excited great indignation in the officers of

---

* Judith iii. 9 – iv. 15.   † v. 1 – 21.

Holofernes, and his Moabite and Phœnician allies.
They urged him to give it no attention, and even
threatened Achior's life. Holofernes, having severely
rebuked him for the treason of doubting the irresistible might of Nabuchodonosor, and declared that his
life should pay the penalty when he should again fall
into the conqueror's hands, for the present " commanded his servants that waited in his tent to take
Achior, and bring him to Bethulia, and deliver him
into the hands of the children of Israel." Left bound
near Bethulia, he was brought by some Israelites before the magistrates of that city, who, in a great assembly of ancients, youth, and women, proceeded to
their investigation. Achior told them of his counsel
to Holofernes, and of the arrogant resolution of that
commander. The people, having prostrated themselves in a prayer for deliverance, " comforted Achior,
and praised him greatly; and Ozias," a Simeonite,
one of the magistrates, " took him out of the assembly unto his house, and made a feast to the elders, and
they called on the God of Israel all that night for
help." *

The next day Holofernes advanced his camp towards Bethulia, and prepared for a vigorous inroad
into the Jewish country, his infantry having received
an increase of fifty thousand men, " besides the bag-
gage, and other men that were afoot among them, a
very great multitude." The citizens were in consternation, but not in despair. " Every man took up his
weapons of war, and when they had kindled fires upon
their towers, they remained and watched all that night."
Holofernes reconnoitred the city, and, by the advice
of his allies from the neighboring country, secured the

* Judith v. 22 – vi. 21.

springs of water from which it was supplied, that so
he might win a bloodless victory. The blockade was
formed; thirty-four days passed; the distress from
thirst was extreme, and there remained only a scanty
supply of water for one day. The people, men,
women, and children, presented themselves before
Ozias with clamor and tears, and earnest entreaties
that he would surrender them to the conqueror's mercy; and that steadfast magistrate hardly persuaded
them to hold out for five days longer, in the feeble
hope that in that time their God would "turn his
mercy" towards them, and open a way of deliverance.*

There lived at this time at Bethulia, a young, rich,
noble, and beautiful widow, named Judith, whose husband had died of a sun-stroke three or four years before. She passed her secluded days in fasts and mourning, and enjoyed universal esteem; " there was none
that gave her an ill word, for she feared God greatly."
" She sent her waiting-woman, that had the government of all things that she had," to invite an interview with the magistrates, and rebuked them for their
ignorant and presumptuous distrust of God's power
and willingness to give his people rescue. She reminded them that the idolatries which had in past
time provoked him to anger, had in their better days
passed away. She bade them consider that he would
hold them responsible for that desolation of the sanctuary, and for the slaughter, captivity, and shame,
which would follow on a surrender to the barbarous
infidel. She told them that it was for such as they
to set an example of constancy, and not give way to a
popular rage. She called to the aid of her lofty lesson
the teachings of old history. And finally she an-

---

* Judith vii. 1 – 32.

nounced her purpose to undertake with her woman's
craft and courage an enterprise for the deliverance of
her nation, the nature of which she refused to dis-
close. So, having excused themselves for their want
of her valiant spirit, and bespoken her prayers, they
blessed her, and "returned from the tent and went to
their wards." *

"Judith fell upon her face, and put ashes upon her
head, and uncovered the sackcloth with which she was
clothed; and about the time that the incense of that
evening was offered in Jerusalem in the house of the
Lord, Judith cried with a loud voice," imploring the
Divine help to her brave undertaking.† Then, having
put off her mourning weeds, and attired herself magnificently, "she gave her maid a bottle of wine, and
a cruise of oil, and filled a bag with parched corn, and
lumps of figs, and with fine bread," and they proceeded
together to the gate.   There she found "the ancients
of the city," who "wondered at her beauty very greatly," and renewed their prayers for her safety and success.   They ordered the gates to be opened at her request, and watched her as with her maid she descended the hill, and till she passed into the valley out of
sight.   Presenting herself at the first Assyrian out-
post, she desired to be led to Holofernes, declaring
herself to be a Jewish woman, come to betray her
countrymen into his hands, by acquainting him with
a path over the hills.   With a guard of a hundred
men she was conducted to the commander's tent, while
crowds of his troops stood around admiring, and saying to each other, "Who would despise this people,
that have among them such women?"   Holofernes, informed of her approach, rose from his "canopy, which

---

* Judith viii. 1 – 36.   † ix. 1 – 14.

was woven with purple, and gold, and emeralds, and precious stones," and advanced to meet her " before his tent, with silver lamps going before him." With his attendants, he "marvelled at the beauty of her countenance; and she fell down upon her face, and did reverence unto him." *

Holofernes, affirming that it was the people's own rashness that had brought them into their present straits, for he "never hurt any that was willing to serve Nabuchodonosor, the king of all the earth," inquired of Judith the reason of her flight. Asserting her own perfect frankness and sincerity, and professing great reverence for his sagacity and valor, so well known to her own people, she told him that they had heard from Achior what he had said in the council of war, and that it was all true; that their God would effectually protect them, until they should offend and estrange him by their sins, — but that this they were about to do; that, pressed by famine and thirst, they were meditating " to spend the first-fruits of the corn, and the tenths of wine and oil, which they had sanctified and reserved for the priests that serve in Jerusalem, before the face of God, the which things it is not lawful for any of the people so much as to touch with their hands"; that they had sent messengers to Jerusalem, where the same thing had been done, " to bring them a license from the Senate"; that, dissatisfied with such proceedings and anticipating their fatal result, she had withdrawn herself; that, being a religious person, serving " the God of heaven day and night," God would make known to her the time when the proposed profanation was committed, in answer to the prayers which she asked permission to make nightly

---

* Judith x. 1 - 23.

in the valley; that then there would be no longer any
power of resistance, and she would guide him through
the country to Judea, and establish his "throne in
the midst thereof," and he should "drive them as
sheep that have no shepherd"; and that, finally, she
was sent to give him this information.*

"Her words pleased Holofernes, and all his servants, and they marvelled at her wisdom"; and he
made her flattering compliments and promises. He
conducted her into his tent, and invited her to his
table; but she excused herself on the ground of a religious scruple, and said that she had brought provision of her own, enough to last till all her errand
was done. Having retired to repose, "she arose when
it was towards the morning watch," and sent to Holofernes to ask permission, which was granted, to "go
forth unto prayer." This she continued to do for three
days. On the fourth, Holofernes made a banquet for
the immediate attendants on his own person, and sent
one of them to bid Judith as a guest. When the
hour arrived, "decked with all her apparel, and her
woman's attire, ... Judith came in and sat down."
Urged by Holofernes to share in the feast, she assented
so far as that "she took and ate and drank before him
what her maid had prepared; and Holofernes took great
delight in her, and drank much more wine than he had
drunk at any time in one day since he was born." †

The feast being over, and the weary attendants dismissed, Judith was left alone with Holofernes, who
lay upon his bed, overcome with his excess. "Judith
had commanded her maid to stand without her bed-
chamber, and to wait for her coming forth, as she did
daily; for she said she would go forth to her prayers,

---

* Judith xi. 1 - 19.   † xi. 20 - xii. 20.

and she spake to Bagoas according to the same purpose." Having fortified her stern purpose with a short prayer, "she came to the pillar of the bed which was at Holofernes's head, and took down his fauchion from thence, and approached to his bed, and took hold of the hair of his head, and said, 'Strengthen me, O Lord God of Israel, this day'; and she smote twice upon his neck with all her might, and she took away his head from him, and tumbled his body down from the bed, and pulled down the canopy from the pillars; and anon she went forth, and gave Holofernes's head to her maid, and she put it in her bag of meat; so they twain went together, according to their custom, unto prayer; and when they had passed the camp, they compassed the valley, and went up to the mountain of Bethulia, and came to the gates thereof." To the elders, summoned by the porters upon whom she had called "afar off" for admission, she proclaimed her success, and exhibited the trunkless head by the firelight. At her instance, the people bowed themselves in adoration before God, their deliverer. Ozias besought for her every blessing in recompense of her patriotic service, "and all the people said, 'So be it, so be it.'" *

Judith advised that they should hang the head in a conspicuous place on the city wall, and at sunrise marshal their armed array, as if they would give battle, saying that the leaders of the Assyrian army would seek their commander, and when they came to know the truth would be struck with a panic, which would make them an easy prey. First, however, she showed the head, and in the hearing of the exulting people related the circumstances of her exploit, to Achior,

---

* Judith xiii. 1 – 20.

who, when he "had seen all that the God of Israel
had done, believed in God greatly, and was joined to
the house of Israel." *

Bagoas, having entered his master's chamber to call
him to the battle, which the citizens seemed to provoke, rushed forth, and, with gestures of horror,
told the host of the bloody work which had been
there transacted. "And fear and trembling fell upon
them, so that there was no man that durst abide in
the sight of his neighbor, but, rushing out all together, they fled into every way of the plain, and of
the hill-country." The Bethulians pursued, and, re-
inforced by numbers of their countrymen who gathered at a summons from Ozias, "chased them with a
great slaughter, until they were past Damascus, and
the borders thereof." The citizens left behind, and
others when they returned from the pursuit, pillaged
the hostile camp, and greatly enriched themselves with
its spoils. "Joacim the high-priest, and the ancients
of the children of Israel that dwelt in Jerusalem,"
made a ceremonious visit of congratulation to Judith;
the spoilers of the camp gave her the tent of Holofernes, "and all his plate, and vessels, and all his stuff";
and "all the women of Israel ran together to see her,
and blessed her, and made a dance among them for
her; and she took branches in her hand, and gave also
to the women that were with her; and they put a
garland upon her, and her maid that was with her,
and she went before all the people in the dance, leading all the women; and all the men of Israel followed
in their armor, with garlands, and with songs in their
mouths." †

A spirited triumphal ode is then recorded, of which

---

* Judith xiv. 1 - 10.   † xiv. 11 – xv. 13.

it is said that "Judith began to sing this thanksgiving
in all Israel, and all the people sang after her this
song of praise." "As soon as the people were purified, they offered their burnt-offerings, and their free-
offerings, and their gifts," and "continued feasting in
Jerusalem before the sanctuary, for the space of three
months, and Judith remained with them." The treasures of the tent of Holofernes which had been given
to her, she dedicated "for a gift unto the Lord." Returning to her home when the people dispersed, she
rejected many suitors, and passed the rest of her days
unmarried. "She increased more and more in honor,
and waxed old in her husband's house, being an hundred and five years old, and made her maid free; so
she died in Bethulia; and they buried her in the cave
of her husband Manasses. And the house of Israel
lamented her seven days; and before she died, she did
distribute her goods to all them that were nearest of
kindred to Manasses, her husband, and to them that
were the nearest of her kindred. And there was none
that made the children of Israel any more afraid in
the days of Judith, nor a long time after her death." *

As far as the writer of this book can be understood
to have had any definite purpose as to time, the opinion of Prideaux and others appears, on the whole,
probable; that he intended to refer the events therein
related to the reign of King Manasseh, after the time
of his supposed detention at Babylon.† But if so, he

---

* Judith xvi. 1 – 25.

† "That Arphaxad in the said book of Judith was Deioces, and Nabuchodonosor Saosduchinus, appears from hence, that Arphaxad is said (i. 1, 2)
to be that king of Media who was the founder of Ecbatana, which all other
writers agree to have been Deioces; and the beginning of the twelfth year
of Saosduchinus exactly agreeth with the last year of Deioces, when this
battle of Ragan is said to have been fought (i. 15). And there are several
particulars in that history, which make it utterly inconsistent with any other

has contradicted the history in material particulars. The history knows no high-priest of the name of Joiakim in the time of the kings.* The temple was not " cast to the ground " † till sixty years after Manasseh's death. Manasseh, restored to his kingdom thirty years before, was conducting its administration at the period indicated, a fact irreconcilable with the total silence of the book concerning any regal government. The heroine, whom it could not have been intended to represent as old at the time of her adventure, is said to have lived to be " an hundred and five years old," during all which time, and " a long time after her death," " there was none that made the children of Israel any more afraid." But the period between Manasseh's reign and the Captivity by no means cor-

times ; for it was while Nineveh was the metropolis of the Assyrian empire (i. 1) ; it was while the Persians, Syrians, Phœnicians, Cilicians, and Egyptians were subject to them (i. 7 – 10) ; it was while the Median empire was in being, and not long after the building of Ecbatana (i. 1, 2) ; none of which could be after the captivity of Judah, where some would place this history. For, before that time, Nineveh had been long destroyed, and both the Assyrian and Median empires had been wholly extinguished, and the Persians, instead of being subject to the Assyrians, had made themselves lords over them, and over all the other nations of the East, from the Hellespont to the river Indus ; for so far they had extended and established their empire before the Jews were returned from the Babylonish captivity, and settled again in their own country. And therefore we must go much higher than the times after that captivity, to find a proper scene for the matters in that book related ; and it can be nowhere laid more agreeably both with Scripture and profane history, than in the time where I have placed it." — Prideaux, " Old and New Testaments connected," &c., Part I. Book I. An. 655.

* Judith iv. 6 ; xv. 8. — There was first a high-priest of this name in Nehemiah's time ; comp. Neh. xii. 26.

† Judith v. 18 ; comp. iv. 3. — These statements are wanting from Jerome's version ; but this is no reason for doubting their genuineness, considering the degree of care he bestowed on it. " I put aside," he says, " the engagements with which I was pressed, and devoted to it the study of one night, discarding the vicious variety of readings found in many copies, and preserving the sense, rather than following verbally the original." — " Præfat. ad Jud." (Tom. I. p. 1170).

responds to this description, and it was less than sixty
years after his death when the latter event took place.

The geography is as much in fault as the history,
presenting in different places the most heterogeneous
mixtures of names, and indicating the most incredible
movements backwards and forwards.* And I might
name other particulars, some of them singly decisive,
as it appears to me, against the supposition of a true
narrative of events. But I conceive this would be only
wasting words. Clearly, the book will not bear the
test of any such hypothesis. Judged by its legitimate
standard, it has no small merit. It is a well-conceived
romance. The story is skilfully elaborated, and told
in a lively style, not without passages of pathetic
eloquence. The national deliverance related bears a
certain resemblance to those which make the subjects
of the Book of Esther and the Third Book of the
Maccabees.

The time of its composition is quite uncertain. The
first reference to it is found in a passage of Clement of
Rome, about the year 96.† The total silence of Josephus and Philo respecting it, particularly considering
the large use made by the former writer of the similar
book of Esther,‡ has inclined some critics, not without
reason, to the opinion that it was written since the
Christian era. The scheme of Grotius is plausible,
who refers it to the age of the persecution of Antiochus Epiphanes, and thinks its design was to rouse
the Jews, in that dismal state of their affairs, to a
hope of deliverance through Divine aid.§

---

* Judith i. 6 - 10 ; ii. 21 - 27.

† "Epist. Prior. ad Corinth.," cap. 55 (Coteler. "SS. Patr. Apostol.
Opp.," Tom. I. p. 178). Clement's reference, however, is to the story, rather
than to the book.

‡ "Antiq. Jud.," Lib. XI. cap. 6.

§ "Annott. in. V. T." (Tom. III. "Proœm. ad Jud."). Grotius sug-

It is equally doubtful whether we have the original work, or whether our Greek text is a translation from the Hebrew or Chaldee. According to information which Origen had from Jews,* they did not possess the book in their own language, while according to Jerome, writing two hundred years later, it was " written in Chaldee," † and from a Chaldee text he made the version now included in the Vulgate. The reference to " the eves of the Sabbaths," and " the eves of the new moons " ‡ has been thought to denote a writer acquainted with local customs of modern origin in Palestine. On the other hand, not only do expressions occur which belong to the classical Greek,§ but the Greek style is throughout free and easy, and without those indications which almost infallibly betray a translation.‖ And the method of the Greek historians is pursued, in developing characters and events by the fiction of set speeches ascribed to the actors.

Two ancient versions are extant, besides that of Jerome; — one into Latin, older than his, made from the Greek, but from a text frequently differing from that now in our hands; the other into Syriac, following our Greek very closely, though not without occasional

---

gests that many of the names were significant ; as Judith (יְהוּדִית), meaning *the Jewish nation ;* Bethulia (בֵּית אֶל יָה), *the house of God the Lord* (a city named Bethulia is never mentioned elsewhere) ; Holofernes (הַלּוֹפֶר נָחָשׁ), *the serpent's servant ;* and Joacim (יְהוֹיָקִים), *God will restore.*

* " Epist. ad African.," § 13 (" Opp.," Tom. I. p. 26).

† " Præfat. ad. Jud." (" Opp.," Tom. I. p. 1170).

‡ Judith viii. 6; comp. Mark xv. 42. Mark's προσαββάτον is the first notice we have of any such observance, except the text in Judith. There is no other reference to it in any Old Testament book, canonical or apocryphal. Partly on the strength of this fact, Bertholdt inclines to refer the composition of this book to a period so late as that of the Roman operations in Judea (Einleitung," Th. V. § 601).

§ ix. 2; xvi. 7.

‖ On this point, however, De Wette dissents from the opinion of every other critic with whom I am acquainted (Einleitung," § 308).

deviations. An important addition to the Latin version is that of the last verse: "The day of the feast commemorating this victory is esteemed by the Hebrews among their holy days, and has been celebrated by them from that time to the present."

Judith appears as a canonical book in the catalogue of the Council of Carthage.* Augustine, about the year 400, speaks of it as a canonical writing.† And Jerome mentions its being "said to be reckoned among Sacred Scriptures by the Nicene Council;"‡ a statement, however, which the record of that council does not sustain.

I suppose there is no reference to the book in the New Testament.§

---

* See Vol. I. p. 38.

† "De Doctrinâ Christ.," Lib. II. cap. 8 ("Opp.," Tom. III. p. 25, edit. Basil).

‡ "Præf. ad Jud." (*ubi supra*).

§ Comp., however, Judith xiii. 18 with Luke i. 42; viii. 25 with 1 Cor. x. 9, 10.

LECTURE LXVI.

BARUCH AND DANIEL.

Origin of the Book of Baruch, and Effect produced by it. — Missive to the Jews remaining at Jerusalem after the Captivity.
— Panegyric upon Wisdom. — Prospect of the Future Ruin of
Babylon, and Glory of Jerusalem. — Letter ascribed to Jeremiah. — Probably written in Greek by an Egyptian Jew. — Authorship of the preceding Chapters. — Ancient Versions of the
Book. — Its Canonical Authority. — Not quoted in the New Testament. — Abstract of the Contents of the Hebrew and Chaldee
Portions of the Book of Daniel. — Account of the Contents of
the Greek Portions of the Book.

IN the Book of Jeremiah we read of one Baruch,
his scribe,* who, after the capture of Jerusalem by the
Babylonians, accompanied the prophet into Egypt.†
In the composition before us, this same Baruch, " the
son of Nerias, the son of Maasias," is said to have
written a book at Babylon, " in the fifth year, and in
the seventh day of the month, what time as the Chaldeans took Jerusalem and burned it with fire," ˙and to
have read it in the hearing of the captive king Jechonias, of his nobles, and of his people of every rank,
" that dwelt at Babylon, by the river Sud."   On hearing it, " they wept, fasted, and prayed before the Lord;
˙they made also a collection of money, according to
every man's power, and they sent it to Jerusalem unto
Joachim the high-priest, the son of Chelcias, son of

---

* Jer. xxxii. 12, 16; xxxvi. 4, 10, 14, 26; xlv. 1.
† xliii. 6, 7.

Salom, ... at the same time when he received the
vessels of the house of the Lord that were carried
out of the temple, to return them into the land of
Juda, the tenth day of the month Sivan, namely, silver vessels which Sedecias, the son of Josias, king of
Juda, had made, after that Nabuchodonosor, king of
Babylon, had carried away Jechonias and the princes,
. . . . . and brought them unto Babylon." *

Whether or not the writer meant to represent "the
book" written by Baruch as beginning immediately
after these statements, is a question.   If not, the passage which next follows was intended as a recital of
a letter from the Jews in Babylon to their brethren
in Judea, written to accompany the book, which itself
begins further on.   Whether letter or "book," this
passage informs the persons addressed that their
friends had sent them the means of presenting the accustomed offerings on Jehovah's altar; invites them to
pray for the life of Nabuchodonosor and his son, that
so the conquerors might regard their captives with
favor, and to intercede for the captives with God,
against whom they had sinned; and recommends to
them to read the "book" which was transmitted, and
to "make confession in the house of the Lord, upon
the feasts and solemn days." †   A form for such confession and prayer is next proposed, embracing a full
acknowledgment of the sins of the nation, accompanied with a recital of divine judgments by which
they had in time past been visited, and with professions of repentance and supplications for forgiveness·
and for that restoration and reëstablishment which
God had promised to Moses.‡

---

* Bar. i. 1 – 9.   † i. 10 – 14.
‡ i. 15 – iii. 8. Of those critics who do not understand " the book " to

Then comes a long address, in which Israel is exhorted to "give ear to understand wisdom," for want of which it had been afflicted with exile, "the princes of the heathen" had "vanished and gone down to the grave," and "giants famous from the beginning . . . . . were destroyed." * This wisdom, it is said, fully possessed by God alone, "he hath given unto Jacob his servant." It is the substance of "the book of the commandments of God, and the law that endureth for ever." Happy are God's people in possessing it, for "all they that keep it shall come to life"; and if they have been punished for their sins, it was not that they might be finally destroyed. Let them hearken to the expostulation which Jerusalem addressed to her children, for whose sins she was "left desolate." Let them listen to her again, when in other accents she said, "Be of good cheer, O my children, cry unto the Lord, and he shall deliver you from the power and hand of the enemies." Jerusalem should herself "take a good heart," for she should be comforted by him that gave her her name, while the city which received her captive sons should be struck with fire "from the Everlasting," and "be inhabited of devils for a great time." Let Jerusalem "put off the garment of her mourning and affliction, and put on the comeliness of the glory that cometh from God for ever." Her dispersed children are to be "gathered from the west unto the east," and "God shall lead Israel with joy in

---

begin at i. 10, some place its beginning at i. 15, and some at iii. 9; and what intervenes between i. 9 and these places respectively, they regard as constituting a letter sent along with the "book" from the Jews at Babylon to those in Jerusalem. — "The dead that are in the graves, whose souls are taken from their bodies, will give unto the Lord neither praise nor righteousness" (ii. 17); a text which betrays the same ignorance of a future life, which we have observed in the earlier books.

* Bar. iii. 9 - 28.

the light of his glory, with the mercy and righteousness that cometh from him.*

With the fifth chapter ends the Book of Baruch,
properly so called. It is followed, in one chapter, by
what is entitled, " A copy of an epistle which Jeremy
sent unto them which were to be led captives into
Babylon, by the king of the Babylonians, to certify
them as it was commanded him of God." In the introduction, Jeremiah is represented as saying to the
exiles, " Because of the sins which ye have committed before God, ye shall be led away captives into
Babylon, by Nabuchodonosor, king of the Babylonians. So when ye be come unto Babylon, ye shall remain there many years, and for a long season, namely,
seven generations; and after that I will bring you
away peaceably from thence. Now ye shall see in
Babylon gods of silver, and of gold, and of wood,
borne upon shoulders, which cause the nations to fear."
And the rest of the piece consists of a diffuse satire
on the nothingness of idols and the folly of their votaries, framed upon the model of some previous passages of Scripture.†

---

* Bar. iii. 29 – v. 9. — " Afterward did he show himself upon earth, and
conversed with men " (iii. 37) ; this text appears to be but an expression of
the idea in Prov. viii. 31 ; Grotius, however (" Annott." *ad loc.*), supposes
it to be an interpolation by some Christian. The fourth and fifth chapters
contain a compend of the doctrine respecting the future glories of the chosen
people, which we have seen so largely expounded through the whole series
of the Later Prophets. The fifth, especially, is a sort of *cento* from Isaiah.
The writer often uses the language of Daniel (whichever may have used it
first), and of Nehemiah ; comp. Bar. i. 15 – 19 with Neh. ix. 32 – 35, Dan.
ix. 7 – 15 ; ii. 1, 2 with Dan. ix. 11, 12 ; ii. 7 with Dan. ix. 13 ; ii. 9 with
Dan. ix. 14 ; ii. 11 with Neh. ix. 10, Dan. ix. 15 ; ii. 15 with Dan. ix.
19 ; ii. 19 with Dan. ix. 18.

† Comp. Is. xl. 18 – 20 ; xliv. 9 – 20 ; xlvi. 5 – 7 ; Jer. x. 1 – 8 ; Ps.
cxv. 1 – 8. — " When ye be come unto Babylon, ye shall remain there *many
years and for a long season*, namely, seven generations ; and after that I
will bring you away peaceably from thence " (vi. 3) ; the letter in which

This chapter was not written by Jeremiah, but is in form an imitation of a letter from him to the Babylonish exiles, preserved among his acknowledged works.* It bears no marks of being a translation, nor is any thing known of a Hebrew original. It was probably written in Greek and (judging from the purity of its style) by an Egyptian Jew, and had originally no connection with the Book of Baruch. Some manuscripts of the Septuagint place it after the Lamentations. The time of its composition is uncertain. In the Second Book of Maccabees † is a notice of Jeremiah's warnings against idolatry, which has been thought to refer to this piece, but it may equally well be understood as a reference to the recognized works of that prophet.‡ The superior style, as compared with that of the preceding chapters, indicates a different author.

Nor is there good reason to believe that the preceding chapters were written by that Baruch, servant and scribe of Jeremiah, to whom they have been attributed. Jerome knew nothing of a Hebrew original.§ The Greek in our hands bears no marks of having been translated from a text in another language, as must have been the case had Baruch been the author, and there are historical inaccuracies not easy to reconcile with that supposition. By some, however, of those commentators with whom, on the whole, I agree on

---

these words are found is ostensibly a letter of Jeremiah; it is plain that the writer, who was acquainted with the works of that prophet, and here refers to his words, did not understand what he had said of a captivity of seventy years in the sense which has been put upon them by later commentators. See Vol. III. p. 344, note †.

* Jer. xxix. 1 - 23. Comp. Vol. III. pp. 359 - 361.

† 2 Mac. ii. 1, 2.

‡ E. g. to Jer. x. 2 - 4.

§ " Librum autem Baruch notarii ejus, qui apud Hebræos nec legitur nec habetur." (" Prolog. in Jerem.," " Sanct. Hieron. Opp.," Tom. I. p. 554, edit. Martianay.)

this point, I must own that I think it has been too
easily disposed of. Baruch may have made a journey
to Babylon,* and Nebuchadnezzar may have had a
son named Belshazzar,† who might even, while he
lived, have been heir-apparent to the throne, though
the history does not inform us of either of those facts.
Jechoniah is related to have been present with his
people at the reading of " the book," ‡ while the statement in the history is that he was released from close
confinement on the accession of Nebuchadnezzar's successor.§   But in the early period of his exile his imprisonment may not have been strict.   A stronger fact
is that, at the time referred to, " Joachim, ... the
son of Chelcias, son of Salom," is said to have been
"high-priest . . . . . at Jerusalem "; while that name
of a high-priest does not occur in the accredited lists
till nearly a hundred years later.‖

The strong local feelings of the author, in respect
to the present depression and expected greatness of
Jerusalem, have been thought to afford some indication
of his having been an inhabitant of Palestine.   Nothing definite can be said respecting his time.   A reasonable conjecture might be, that its object was, like
that of the Book of Judith, to confirm the faith and
hopes of the Jews during the period of their troubles
with their masters of Syria or Egypt.

---

* Bar. i. 3, 4 (comp. Jer. xliii. 5 – 7). — He is said (Bar. i. 2) to have
been in Babylon " in the fifth year, and in the seventh day of the month,"
without any designation of the month. De Wette thinks (" Einleit.," § 321)
that there may here be a false reading, and that the true one would be " in
the fifth month," the reference being to the same date as that in 2 Kings
xxv. 8, when Nebuzaradan is said to have burned the city and temple.

† Bar. i. 12.

‡ i. 3.

§ 2 Kings xxv. 27

‖ Bar. i. 7. — Also, how could " burnt-offerings and sin-offerings," &c.,
have been presented " upon the altar of the Lord," after the destruction of
the city ! (i. 10). But as to this point, see Jer. xli. 5.

In Walton's Polyglot are Syriac and Arabic versions of this book, which exhibit a few variations from
the Greek text. The Paris Polyglot has a different.
Syriac translation. The version in the Vulgate was
made earlier than the time of Jerome. In Walton's
and the Paris Polyglot there is also, in the Syriac
language, a different work, purporting to be an epistle
from Baruch to the ten tribes. Of this no Greek original is known.

The Book of Baruch has a place in Origen's list of
canonical writings. It was also recognized as canonical in the fourth century by Athanasius, Cyril, Epipha-
nius,* and the Council of Laodicea.†

The New Testament nowhere quotes it, nor, as I
think, refers to it.‡

The Book of Daniel, as it stands in our Hebrew
Bibles, begins with an account of the first appearance
of that personage at the Babylonian court. " In the
third year of the reign of Jehoiakim, king of Judah,
came Nebuchadnezzar, king of Babylon, against Jerusalem, and besieged it. And the Lord gave Jehoiakim,
king of Judah, into his hand, with part of the vessels
of the house of God; and he carried them into the
land of Shinar, to the house of his god; and he
brought the vessels into the treasure-house of his
god." He directed one of his household, named Ashpenaz, to select some comely, vigorous, and intelligent
youth from among the Israelites of the royal family,
" to stand in the king's palace, and be taught the writing and the language of the Chaldeans." And he or-

---

* Comp. Vol. I. pp. 35, 37.

† Prideaux, " Connection," Vol. I. p. 206, an. 595.

‡ The language in 1 Cor. x. 20 (comp. Bar. iv. 35) is rather a reference
to Deut. xxxii. 17; comp. Ps. cvi. 37.

dered a provision to be made for them from his own table for "three years, that at the end thereof they might stand as servants before the king." *

"Among these were, of the sons of Judah, Daniel, Hananiah, Mishael, and Azariah," whose names were altered respectively, by the officer who had them in charge, to Belteshazzar, Shadrach, Meshach, and Abednego. Unwilling to taste food which might be of a description forbidden by the Law, Daniel applied to Ashpenaz, whom his deportment had conciliated, for a dispensation for himself and his companions. That officer having expressed his reluctance to the arrangement, lest their inferior appearance on account of their spare living should endanger him with his master, Daniel, with better success, repeated the request to a subordinate, with a proposal to try the experiment of a diet of pulse and water for ten days. "And at the end of ten days their countenances appeared fairer and fatter in flesh than, all the youths who ate the portion of the king's meat; so the steward took away the portion of their meat, and the wine which they should drink, and gave them pulse. And God gave these four youths knowledge and skill in all learning and wisdom; and Daniel had understanding in all visions and dreams." In due time, they were presented before Nebuchadnezzar, who attached them to his person, and found them to be superior to any of his attendants of the same rank, and even "ten times better than all the scribes and magicians that were in all his realm. And Daniel," it is here added, "lived even to the first year of Cyrus, the king." †

In the second year of Nebuchadnezzar's reign, having had a dream which disturbed him, he summoned

---

* Dan. i. 1 – 5.　　　　　　† i. 6 – 21.

"the scribes, and the magicians, and the sorcerers, and
the Chaldeans." They asked to know what the dream
was, before they should pronounce its interpretation,
but the king told them, that, if they did not acquaint
him with the one as well as with the other, they should
be cut in pieces, and their houses be overthrown, while,
if they did as he demanded, they should have a liberal
reward. When they said that it was impossible, "the
king was angry and very furious, and commanded to
destroy all the wise men of Babylon." Under this
commission, search was made for Daniel and his Hebrew associates. "Then Daniel went in, and desired
of the king, that he would give him time, and that he
would show the king the interpretation"; and he engaged his three companions to pray to God to interpose for their rescue by revealing the secret.*

The prayer was heard. The matter was "revealed
to Daniel in a night vision," and he expressed his
gratitude in appropriate terms. Introduced by "Ari-
och, the king's captain," again into the royal presence, he told Nebuchadnezzar what his dream had
been, professing to speak not through any wisdom of
his own, but by revelation from the "God in heaven
that revealeth secrets." The king, he said, had dreamed
of seeing a tall, bright, terrible image. "The head
of this image was of fine gold; his breast and his
arms of silver; his belly and his thighs of brass; his
legs of iron; his feet, part of iron and part of clay."
There came a stone, "cut out without hands, which
smote the image upon his feet, that were of iron and
clay, and broke them to pieces," and all the solid me-
tallic materials of the statue were swept away before
the wind, "like chaff from the summer threshing-

* Dan. ii. 1 – 18.

floors," while "the stone that smote the image became a great mountain, and filled the whole earth." All this Daniel interpreted to mean, that there were to be five successive monarchies, that of Nebuchadnezzar being the first; that the fourth should be "a divided kingdom," made up of ill-compacted parts of different degrees of strength; while, as to the fifth, he declared, "in the days of these kings shall the God of heaven set up a kingdom which shall never be destroyed; and the kingdom shall be left to no other people; but it shall break in pieces and consume all these kingdoms, and it shall stand for ever." Having heard him out, "King Nebuchadnezzar fell upon his face, and worshipped Daniel, and commanded that they should offer an oblation and sweet odors to him." He magnified Daniel's God, "made Daniel a great man, and gave him many great gifts, and made him ruler over the whole province of Babylon, and chief of the governors over all the wise men of Babylon." And, at the prophet's request, he set his three friends "over the affairs of the province." *

"Nebuchadnezzar the king" is then related to have "made an image of gold, whose height was sixty cubits, and whose breadth was six cubits. He set it up in the plain of Dura, in the province of Babylon," and summoned all the great men of his realm and provinces to be present at its inauguration. A herald proclaimed that, at a signal from instruments of music, the whole assembly should prostrate themselves before it, and that whoever should fail to do so should "the same hour be cast into the midst of a burning, fiery furnace." The command was obeyed, except by the three friends of Daniel. They were brought into the

---

* Dan. ii. 19–49.

royal presence, where, being interrogated as to the
meaning of their contumacy, and told that it was not
too late to repair it, they replied that they had nothing
to explain or to alter; that they looked to the God
whom they served for deliverance, and that, at all
events, they would do homage to no idol. The king
commanded the heat of the furnace to be increased
seven-fold. It was so hot, that the mighty men who
threw the Jewish confessors into it were themselves
scorched to death. The amazed king presently broke
out into an exclamation that he saw Shadrach, Meshach, and Abednego walking unhurt in the fire,
and with them a fourth, who looked "like a son of
God." He called them out of the flames, and they
were found unhurt, without "a hair of their head
singed," or so much as "the smell of fire." Nebuchadnezzar praised the God who had delivered them,
made a decree that any one who spoke against him
should be "cut in pieces," and again "promoted
Shadrach, Meshach, and Abednego in the province
of Babylon." *

Next follows, without any preface, a proclamation, in
which King Nebuchadnezzar makes known "to all people, nations, and languages, that dwell upon the whole
earth," that he had had a dream; that, having baffled
the skill of the Chaldean wise men, it was interpreted
by Daniel; that the event corresponded to his interpretation; and that now the king, having experienced
what it foretold, found himself moved to "praise, and
extol, and honor the king of heaven; all whose works
are truth and his ways justice, and those that walk in
pride he is able to abase." He had dreamed of seeing
a high, fair, spreading, and fruitful tree, and of hear-

---

* Dan. iii. 1 – 30.

ing a heavenly " watcher, even a holy one," sentence
it to be hewn down, and cut in pieces, while " the
stump of its roots," was to remain in the ground,
clamped with " bands of iron and brass," to " be wet
with the dew of heaven," and to share " with the beasts
in the grass of the field." And then, with an abrupt
change of the imagery, the decree went on: " His
heart shall be changed, and be no more that of a man,
and a beast's heart shall be given him, and seven times
shall pass over him." Daniel's interpretation, when he
had stood " amazed for one hour," was, that the tree
typified Nebuchadnezzar himself, against whom had
gone forth a decree that he should be driven from
among men, and dwell with the beasts, and " eat grass
as oxen, and be wet with the dew of heaven," and
have " seven times," pass over him, till he should
" know that the Most High ruleth in the kingdoms of
men, and giveth them to whomsoever he will"; but
that still, as was indicated by leaving the stumps of
the tree, his kingdom should not be irrevocably withdrawn from him. The proclamation proceeds to relate
that, a year after, as Nebuchadnezzar, of whom it now
speaks in the third person, " was walking in the palace
of the kingdom of Babylon," and musing on his own
greatness, " there fell a voice from heaven " pronoun-
cing a sentence according to the dream, which sentence was presently fulfilled, with the addition that " his
hairs were grown like eagle's feathers, and his nails
like bird's claws." The proclamation concludes with
Nebuchadnezzar's declaration, in his own person, of
his restoration to sanity and to his throne, and of
his sense of the glorious attributes of " the king of
heaven." *

---

* Dan. iv. 1 – 37.

Belshazzar was the fourth king after Nebuchadnezzar, and he reigned seventeen years. The narrative before us overleaps the intervening history, to
relate some circumstances of the time of his dethrone-
ment and death. He had invited " his thousand lords "
to a great feast. The beauties of his harem graced the
table; the drinking-cups were " the golden and silver
vessels which his father, Nebuchadnezzar, had taken out
of the temple at Jerusalem "; and " they drank wine,
and praised the gods of gold, and of silver, of brass,
of iron, of wood, and of stone; in the same hour
came forth fingers of a man's hand, and wrote over
against the candlestick upon the plaster of the wall
of the king's palace; and the king saw the hand that
wrote." In abject terror he sent for his magicians,
and promised them great rewards if they would read
and interpret the words. But the task was beyond
their art. The queen came into the banqueting-house,
and said that there was one Daniel whom Nebuchadnezzar had distinguished for his skill in this department; and for him she advised Belshazzar to send.

He did so, and repeated to him the offers of promotion. These Daniel rejected, but proceeded to solve the
riddle. After reciting the punishment which had come
upon Nebuchadnezzar for his pride, as related in the
last chapter, he told the king that by similar impiety
he too had provoked " the Lord of heaven," who had
caused the mysterious hand to announce his doom in
the words written on the wall; and that their sense
was, that, for his ill-deserts, his reign was presently to
be brought to an end, and his dominions to be shared
between the Medes and Persians. Daniel received the
compensation he had declined, and was made " the third
ruler in the kingdom "; and " in the same night was
Belshazzar, king of the Chaldeans, slain, and Darius,

the Mede, took the kingdom, being about sixty-two years old." *

" It pleased Darius to set over the kingdom a hundred and twenty satraps, which should be over the whole kingdom, and over these three presidents, of whom Daniel was one, that the satraps might give accounts to them, and the king should have no damage; then this Daniel was preferred above the presidents and satraps, because an excellent spirit was in him, and the king thought to set him over the whole realm." Such eminence could not be viewed without envy; but it was justified by a character without fault, so that they who plotted his ruin found themselves forced to the conclusion, " We shall not find any occasion against this Daniel, unless we find it against him concerning the law of his God." They shaped their course accordingly. The presidents and satraps went in a body to Darius, and told him that they had " consulted together to establish a royal statute," forbidding every one, for thirty days, to " ask a petition of any god or man," except the king, on pain of being " cast into the den of lions "; and they prayed him to ratify that law with his signature, so that, according to the practice of the Medes and Persians, it might be beyond repeal. " Wherefore King Darius signed the writing and the decree."†

Daniel, however, had been in the habit of praying three times every day, " his windows being open in his chamber toward Jerusalem "; and this practice he did not discontinue. The conspirators found him praying, and accused him to the king. Darius would have spared him, but the unchangeable law allowed no discretion. So " the king commanded that they

---

should bring Daniel, and cast him into the den of lions ; and the king spake and said to Daniel, ' May thy God, whom thou servest continually, deliver thee!' and a stone was brought and laid upon the mouth of the den ; and the king sealed it with his own signet, and with the signet of his lords." Darius, having passed a wakeful night, " arose very early in the morning, and went in haste to the den." Daniel answered his call with an assurance that he was safe, for his God had " sent his angel, and shut the lions' mouths." He " was taken up out of the den" unhurt. "And the king commanded, and they brought those men which had accused Daniel, and cast them into the den of lions, them, their children, and their wives ; and the lions had the mastery of them, and broke all their bones before they came to the bottom of the den." Upon this " Darius wrote to all people, nations, and languages, that dwell in all the earth," commanding them to " tremble and fear before the God of Daniel." And " Daniel prospered in the reign of Darius, and in the reign of Cyrus, the Persian." *

" In the first year of Belshazzar, king of Babylon, Daniel had a dream," which he is represented as relating in his own person. While " the four winds of heaven burst forth upon the great sea," he saw " four great beasts" come up from it. " The first was like a lion, and had eagles' wings ; . . . . . his wings were plucked from it, and it was lifted up from the earth, and made to stand upon the feet as a man, and a man's heart was given to it. And, behold, another beast, the second, like to a bear, and it stood up on one side, and it had three ribs in its mouth between its teeth, and they spake thus to it: 'Arise, devour much flesh!' . . . . .

---

* Dan. vi. 10-28.

And lo, another, like a leopard, which had upon its back four wings of a bird; the beast also had four heads, and dominion was given to it. After this, ... behold, a fourth beast, dreadful, and terrible, and exceedingly strong; and it had great iron teeth; it devoured and brake in pieces; . . . . . and it had ten horns.'" From these horns proceeded " another little horn, before which three of the first horns were plucked up by the roots." It had "eyes like the eyes of man, and a mouth speaking great things." Then was seen the fiery throne of " an aged person," surrounded by myriads of attendants. " And because of the great words which the horn spake, ... the beast was slain, and his body destroyed, and given to the burning flame. As to the rest of the beasts, they had their dominion taken away, for the duration of their lives had been appointed for a season and a time. . . . . . And behold, one like a son of man came with the clouds of heaven, and came to the aged person, and they brought him near before him. And there was given him dominion, and glory, and a kingdom, that all people, nations, and languages should serve him; his dominion is an everlasting dominion, which shall not pass away, and his kingdom shall not be destroyed." *

A by-stander, of whom Daniel distressfully inquired, explained to him these symbols. The four beasts, he said, represented four successive kings, or monarchies, after whose time " the saints of the Most High" were to " possess the kingdom for ever "; and from the kingdom typified by the fourth beast, ten kings should arise, and after them yet another, who should " subdue three kings." Into his hand the saints should be given " a time, and times, and half a time "; but finally,

---

* Dan. vii. 1 – 14.

" the tribunal" would "sit, and his dominion be taken away, ... and power over all kingdoms under the whole heaven be given to the people of the saints of the Most High." Daniel was much agitated and terrified by these visions, but he made no disclosure.*

With the beginning of the eighth chapter, the use of the Hebrew language is resumed. In it Daniel is represented as describing a vision which he saw "in the third year of the reign of King Belshazzar, ... in Shushan, in the palace, which is in the province of Elam." There appeared to him, "by the river Ulai," a ram with two horns, of unequal height. The animal butted " westward, and northward, and southward," and "did according to his will, and became great." Then a horned "he-goat came from the west, over the face of the whole earth, without touching the ground." He "smote the ram, and broke his two horns, ... and he cast him down to the ground." But when the he-goat "was strongest, the great horn between his eyes was broken, and instead of it grew up four conspicuous ones toward the four winds of heaven ; and out of one of them came forth a little horn which became exceedingly great toward the south, and toward the east, and toward the glorious land. And he exalted himself even to the host of heaven, and some of the host and of the stars he cast down to the ground, and stamped upon them ; yea, he magnified himself even to the prince of the host, and the daily sacrifice was taken away from him, and the place of his sanctuary was cast down ; and a host set itself against the daily sacrifice with impiety, and it cast down the law to the ground, and it accomplished its purpose and prospered." And Daniel heard a " holy one" inquire, "'To how

* Dan. vii. 15 - 28.

long a time extends the vision concerning the daily sacrifice, and the impiety of the destroyer, that both the sanctuary and the host shall be trodden under foot?' And he said to me," Daniel continues, " 'To two thousand and three hundred evenings and mornings; then shall the sanctuary be cleansed.' " *

" When I, Daniel," so the narrative proceeds, " had seen the vision and sought for the meaning, behold, there stood one before me having the appearance of a man," who called aloud and said, " Gabriel, make this man to understand the vision." As the form approached him, Daniel fell senseless to the ground, but was lifted to his feet to have the vision explained. The ram with two horns, he was told, denoted " the kings of Media and Persia," and the goat " the king of Greece," " the great horn between his eyes " being the first monarch of the Greek line. From the kingdom which he ruled, four less powerful states were to arise; and " when the transgressors have filled up the measure of their iniquities," a fierce and cunning king should appear, who would " destroy the mighty, and the people of the holy ones," and " stand up against the prince of princes," but should himself finally " be broken without hand." The excitement of the vision, of which he had no further explanation, caused Daniel to faint, and continue " sick some days." †

" In the first year of Darius, the son of Ahasuerus, of the race of the Medes, who became king over the realm of the Chaldeans," Daniel " attentively considered in the books the number of the years, concerning which the word of Jehovah came to Jeremiah, the prophet, that Jerusalem should remain in ruins, till they were accomplished, namely, seventy years." He sought a

---

* Dan. viii. 1 – 14. † viii. 15 – 27.

relief to his perplexity through prayer and fasting.*
Avowing that the people's sins had been the cause of
their calamities, he earnestly entreated of the divine
mercy their pardon and restoration. †　And the narrative proceeds : —

"While I was speaking in prayer, the man Gabriel,
whom I had seen in the former vision, came, weary with
running, and reached me about the time of the evening
oblation, ... and said, ... ' At the beginning of thy
supplication the commandment went forth, and I am
come to show thee; for thou art greatly beloved; therefore give heed to the words, and consider the prophecy.
Seventy weeks are appointed for thy people, and for
thy holy city to complete the iniquity, and to fill up
the measure of sins, and to expiate the guilt, and to
bring in the righteousness of ancient times, and to seal
up the vision and the prophet, and to anoint the most
holy place. Know, therefore, and understand ! From
the going forth of the word that Jerusalem should
again be built, to an anointed prince, are seven weeks ;
then shall the streets and moats of Jerusalem again
be built sixty-two weeks, yet in troublous times. And
after sixty-two weeks shall an anointed one be cut off,
without deliverance, and the city and the sanctuary
shall be destroyed by the people of the prince that shall
come, whose end shall be as by a flood ; yet to the end
of the war is desolation appointed. And he shall establish a covenant with many for one week, and during
half a week he shall cause the sacrifice and the oblation
to cease, and upon the battlement [of the temple] shall
be the abominations of the destroyer, until the appointed destruction is poured out upon the destroyer.' " ‡

---

* Comp. Jer. xxv. 11, 12, xxix. 10, and my remarks thereupon, Vol. III.
pp. 339 - 353, 360, 361.
† Dan. ix . 1 - 20.　　　　　　　　　‡ ix. 21 - 27.

"In the third year of Cyrus, king of Persia," Daniel, having mourned and fasted three weeks, saw, on "the four-and-twentieth day of the first month," "by the side of the great river Hiddekel," "a certain man, clothed in linen, and his loins girded with gold of Uphaz; his body was like chrysolite, and his face had the appearance of lightning, and his eyes were as torches of fire, and his arms and his feet like polished brass, and the sound of his words was as the sound of a multitude." Daniel saw the vision alone, for his attendants fled from it in terror. The form raised him from the ground, to which he had fallen overpowered by his alarm, and bade him give heed to its words. It told him that it would have appeared to him from the first day of his having set his "heart to understand," but that it had been obstructed for three weeks by "the prince of the kingdom of Persia"; that Michael, one of the chief princes, had come to its aid; and that, having thus obtained a victory, it had come to make known to him what should befall his "people in future days." Daniel bowed his head and was dumb, till "one having the appearance of the sons of men" touched his lips. Then he spake a few words explaining his emotion, but again was overpowered and was silent. Again, "the appearance of a man" encouraged him, and, recovering strength to speak, he entreated the vision to go on. It told him that it was about to return "to fight with the prince of Persia"; that "the prince of Greece" should then come; that, in the conflict which it had on hand, its only auxiliary was Michael; and that Michael's aid was a just requital of services of its own, for it "also, in the first year of Darius the Mede," had "stood up to confirm and strengthen him." *

---

* Dan. x. 1 – xi. 1.

It proceeded to inform him that there would "arise yet three kings in Persia," after whom the fourth would be far the richest, and would "stir up all against the realm of Greece." "A mighty king" should then arise, "and rule with great dominion, and do according to his will." His kingdom would not descend to his posterity, but "be plucked up, and divided amongst others besides those." "The king of the South" would "become strong," but would be supplanted by "one of his princes," with whom at length he would make an alliance. The king of the North would espouse "the daughter of the king of the South," to confirm their alliance; but her power would be short-lived; her offspring would not succeed, and she and her adherents would be "given up." "Out of a branch of her roots" would arise a conqueror who would make successful war "against the fortresses of the king of the North"; he would "carry into captivity into Egypt" a spoil of gods, and images, and "precious vessels of silver and gold"; he would "prevail for many years against the king of the North," who would make a fruitless expedition against him, and "return into his own land." A new irruption would be undertaken by his sons, over whom the king of the South would obtain a victory. But presently the tide would turn. The king of the North would advance, "after certain years, with a great army and with great riches"; the part which "violent men" among the Jews would take, would only hasten the troubles denounced against their nation; he would "stand in the glorious land" of God's chosen, and his conquering arms would meet with no effectual resistance. With a perfidious pretence of friendship, he would give his daughter in marriage to the king of the South, but the plot would not succeed. Then he would

" turn his face to the isles, and take many." He would
encounter a commander who would " put an end to
his scorn," and he would " turn his face to the fortresses of his own land, and stumble, and fall, and
not be found." †

In his place would arise one who would collect a
tribute in Judea, and " within few days " would die an
inglorious death. After him would " arise a despised
person," who, in a quiet time, would " come in and
obtain the kingdom by flatteries." But he would establish his power on the ruins of adversaries and allies,
and, by cunning arts and lavish distributions, would
become powerful from a small beginning. With great
military preparation, and with the help of treachery,
he would overcome the king of the South, and after
communications with him, false and profitless on both
sides, would " return into his land with great riches,"
meditating outrages " against the holy covenant." Attempting another expedition " against the South," and
frustrated therein by the arrival of " Chittæan ships,"
he would turn to the safer enterprise to " pollute the
sanctuary, the stronghold, and take away the daily
sacrifice, and set up the abomination of the destroyer."
Many would " he lead to apostasy by flatteries." But
the faithful would " be strong, and do exploits "; the
wise would instruct and exhort; and brave confessors
would " fall by the sword, and by flame, by captivity,
and by spoil, many days "; while there would be back-
sliders even among " some of them of understanding."
The king would " do according to his will," insulting
Heaven by his horrible idolatries and blasphemies, and
securing his followers by dividing " the land amongst
them for a reward." Again would a stand be made

* Dan. xi. 2 – 19.

against him, but again in vain. He would pour out his conquering battalions over Palestine and Egypt, and though Edom, Moab, and a portion of Ammon would escape, distant Lybia and Ethiopia would "be in his train." In this career of conquest, "tidings out of the East and out of the North" would arrest and "trouble him," and he would "go forth with great fury to destroy, and utterly to make away many." He would "pitch his palace-tents between the sea and the glorious holy mountain"; but he would "come to his end, with none to help him." *

"And at that time," concludes the visionary speaker, "shall Michael arise, the great prince that standeth up for the sons of thy people; and there shall be a time of trouble, such as never was since there was a nation even to that time; but at that time shall thy people be delivered, every one that shall be found written in the book. And many of them that sleep in the dust of the earth shall awake, some to everlasting life, and some to shame, to everlasting contempt. And they that are wise shall shine as the brightness of the firmament; and they that turn many to righteousness, as the stars for ever and ever. But thou, O Daniel, shut up these words and seal this book even to the time of the end. Many shall run eagerly through it, and much knowledge shall be gained." †

Daniel "looked, and behold, two others stood there, one on this side of the bank of the river, and the other on that side of the bank of the river; and one of them said to the man clothed in linen who was upon the waters of the river, 'How long shall it be to the end of these wonders?'" The reply, confirmed by an oath, was, "that in a time, times, and a half, and when

---

* Dan. xi. 20–45.　　　　　　　† xii. 1–4.

the dispersion of the holy people should be at an end,
all these things should be fulfilled." Daniel asked
for information concerning events still more remote
in the future, and was denied; but was told, by way
of further explanation of what had been disclosed,
" From the time when the daily sacrifice shall be taken
away, and the abomination of the destroyer set up,
there shall be a thousand two hundred and ninety
days. Happy is he, that waiteth and cometh to a
thousand three hundred and five-and-thirty days!
But go thou thy way even to the end; for thou shalt
rest, and rise up for thy portion at the end of the
days." *

Such are the contents of the Book of Daniel, as
it is preserved partly in the Hebrew language, and
partly in the Chaldee. In the Greek text of the
Septuagint, and in the Vulgate Latin, it contains considerably more matter, in three passages, one prefixed,
one inserted, and one added to the book as it stands
in our Hebrew Bibles. By the authors of our version,
in their Apocryphal collection, the first is called, " The
History of Susanna"; the second, " The Song of the
Three Holy Children"; the third, " The History of
the Destruction of Bel and the Dragon."

The first information that we have of Daniel from
the Greek text, relates to his intervention in the case
of Susanna, the beautiful and chaste wife of Joacim,
a rich and honorable Jew living at Babylon. I shall
not rehearse the story. The conspiracy of the two
wicked elders against the character and life of the
woman whom they failed to corrupt either by seductions or threats was all but successful. She had al-

* Dan. xii. 5 – 13.

ready been condemned by the assembly to death, when the Lord, hearing the voice of her supplication, caused " a young youth, whose name was Daniel," to interpose in her behalf. By a skilful examination of the accusers apart, he caused them to contradict each other. Their guilt was manifest; and the people, "according to the law of Moses, did unto them in such sort as they maliciously intended to do to their neighbor; and they put them to death; thus the innocent blood was saved the same day; . . . . . from that day forth was Daniel had in great reputation in the sight of the people."

The passage entitled " The Song of the Three Holy Children" is inserted in the Greek immediately after the twenty-third verse of the third chapter. Its contents are not merely such as its title indicates. In the first place, in twenty verses, is recited a prayer which Azarias, or Shadrach, and his companions, are said to have uttered, while they walked in the midst of the fire. Its topics are those of praise to God for his righteousness and truth, acknowledgment of national sins, retrospect of national calamities provoked by those sins, and entreaty for national deliverance and for retribution on such as do the Lord's servants hurt.* Then follows a statement that " the king's servants that put them in ceased not to make the oven hot with rosin, pitch, tow, and small wood, so that the flame streamed forth above the furnace forty-and-nine cubits; and it passed through and burned those Chaldeans it found about the furnace; but the angel of the Lord came down into the oven, together with Azarias and his fellows, and smote the flame of the fire out of the oven, and made the midst of the furnace as it had been

---

* Song, 3 – 22.

a moist whistling wind, so that the fire touched them not at all, neither hurt nor troubled them." [*] The rest of the piece represents them, in the expression of a course of thought even less suitable to their singular position than that of the former prayer, as blessing the Lord at much length, and calling upon men, beasts, and numerous objects and agents of nature, to "praise and exalt him above all for ever." [†] Finally, they call upon themselves and one another to bless him, because, say they, "he hath delivered us from hell, and saved us from the hand of death, and delivered us out of the midst of the furnace and burning flame; even out of the midst of the fire hath he delivered us." [‡] The ode is constructed on the model of the hundred and thirty-sixth and hundred and forty-eighth Psalms.

"The History of the Destruction of Bel and the Dragon," which closes the book in the Greek copy, is referred to the time of Cyrus, when "Daniel conversed with the king, and was honored above all his friends." [§] The Babylonians, it is said, set out every day for their idol, Bel, a sumptuous repast of flour, sheep, and wine. The king worshipped him daily, but "Daniel worshipped his own God." The king asked Daniel why he did so, who implied in his answer that Bel was not a "living God." Cyrus. asked him how that could be, when day by day he consumed so much food. The prophet said it was not so, but that jugglery was practised; that Bel was only clay and brass, "and did never eat or drink any thing." The king sent for his priests, and charged them, on pain of death, to confess the fraud, if there was one, declaring at the same time that Daniel should die for his blas-

---

[*] Song, 23 – 27.   [†] Ibid. 28 – 65.
[‡] Ibid. 66 – 68.   [§] Bel, 1.

phemy, if they could prove that the idol consumed
the provisions. Daniel consented to these terms, and
went with the king to the temple. At the instance
of the priests, who were in number "threescore and
ten, beside their wives and children," Cyrus "set on
the meat, and made ready the wine, and shut the door
fast, and sealed it with his own signet; . . . . . and
they little regarded it, for under the table they had
made a privy entrance, whereby they entered in continually, and consumed those things." Daniel knew
or suspected this, and took his measures accordingly.
Before the door was closed, "he had commanded his
servants to bring ashes, and those they strewed throughout all the temple, in the presence of the king alone."
"In the night came the priests with their wives and
children (as they were wont to do) and did eat and
drink up all." In the morning, taking Daniel with
him, who owned that the seals were unbroken, the
king, looking in at the door, and seeing that the provisions had disappeared, broke out with a loud ascription of glory to Bel. "Then laughed Daniel, and held
the king that he should not go in, and said, 'Behold
now the pavement, and mark well whose footsteps are
these.'" The tracks of men, women, and children in
the ashes revealed the imposture. "Then the king
was angry, and took the priests with their wives and
children," and "slew them, and delivered Bel into
Daniel's power, who destroyed him and his temple." *

"In that same place there was a great dragon, which
they of Babylon worshipped." Cyrus bade Daniel
worship the dragon, reasoning with him that he could
not say this was "no living god," as he had said of
Bel. Daniel refused, and said he would slay the beast

* Bel 2 – 22.

410 DANIEL. [LECT.

"without sword or staff," which Cyrus gave him leave
to do. "Then Daniel took pitch, and fat, and hair,
and did seethe them together, and made lumps thereof; this he put in the dragon's mouth, and so the
dragon burst in sunder." This occasioned a popular
commotion. The people "came to the king, and said,
'Deliver us Daniel, or else we will destroy thee and
thine house.'" Cyrus yielded, and "delivered Daniel
unto them, who cast him into the lion's den, where
he was six days; and in the den there were seven
lions, and they had given them every day two carcasses
and two sheep, which then were not given them, to
the intent they might devour Daniel." At the time
"there was in Jewry a prophet called Habbacuc, who
had made pottage, and had broken bread in a bowl,
and was going into the field for to bring it to the
reapers; but the angel of the Lord said unto Habbacuc, 'Go, carry the dinner that thou hast into Babylon,
unto Daniel, who is in the lion's den'; and Habbacuc
said, 'Lord, I never saw Babylon, neither do I know
where the den is'; then the angel of the Lord took
him by the crown, and bear him by the hair of his
head, and through the vehemency of his spirit set he
him in Babylon over the den; and Habbacuc cried,
saying, 'O Daniel, Daniel, take the dinner which God
hath sent thee.'" Daniel "arose, and did eat," after a
proper acknowledgment of God's goodness; "and the
angel of the Lord set Habbacuc in his own place again
immediately. Upon the seventh day the king went
to bewail Daniel"; but, finding him alive, he glorified
the prophet's God, and "drew him out, and cast those
that were the cause of his destruction into the den, and
they were devoured in a moment before his face." *

---

* Bel 23 – 42.

LECTURE LXVII.

GREEK AND CHALDEE PORTIONS OF THE BOOK OF DANIEL.

QUESTIONS RESPECTING THE IDENTITY OF DANIEL, — THE AUTHORSHIP OF THE BOOK, — THE TIME OF ITS COMPOSITION, — AND ITS ORIGINAL LANGUAGE. — DIFFERENT PORTIONS TRANSMITTED FROM THE JEWS, IN GREEK, HEBREW, AND CHALDEE. — PORPHYRY'S TESTIMONY TO A GREEK ORIGINAL OF THE WHOLE. — PHENOMENA ACCORDING WITH THAT STATEMENT. — THE BOOK A COMPOSITION OF THE AGE OF ANTIOCHUS EPIPHANES. — DESIGN OF PORTIONS OF IT, THE SAME AS THAT OF THE BOOK OF JUDITH. — GREEK PORTIONS OF THE BOOK. — CHALDEE POR-TIONS. — FICTITIOUS NARRATIVES IN THE SECOND AND FOUR FOLLOW-ING CHAPTERS. — GREEK INSERTION IN THE THIRD CHAPTER. — INTER-PRETATION OF THE HISTORIES IN THE FORM OF PREDICTIONS, IN THE SECOND AND SEVENTH CHAPTERS. — ILLUSTRATIONS OF THIS FORM OF COMPOSITION, FROM MODERN LITERATURE. — THE IMAGERY IN THE SECOND AND SEVENTH CHAPTERS SIGNIFICANT OF EVENTS WHICH HAD OCCURRED BEFORE AND DURING THE TIME OF ANTIOCHUS, AND OF THE MESSIAH'S EXPECTED REIGN.

THE name of Daniel occurs six times in other books of the Old Testament. David is said to have had a son so called.* There was a Daniel, of the priestly family of Ithamar, who accompanied Ezra on his jour-ney from Babylon to Jerusalem "in the reign of Ar-taxerxes," † and perhaps it is the same person who is represented to have been "sealed" along with "Nehe-miah the Tirshatha." ‡ Ezekiel, more than a hundred years before Ezra, speaks of a Daniel in a connection significant of the extraordinary wisdom ascribed to the personage so named, but without indicating the time when he lived, or any other particular of his charac-

---

* 1 Chron. iii. 1.   † Ezra viii. 1, 2.   ‡ Neh. x. 6.

ter or position.* Whether the Daniel referred to by
Ezekiel, or some other person of the same name or of
a different name, in that age or in a later age, was
author of the book before us, — these are all open
questions. According to the statement of the book
itself, those adventures and visions of Daniel which
it records extended through a period of seventy-three
years, from the third year of Jehoiakim to the third
year of Cyrus; † and by the use of the pronoun of
the first person in the latter half of the book, the
hero and the writer of that part are represented as the
same person.

But the judicious critic at once observes various phenomena of the book unfavorable to the supposition
of such an authorship. He remarks occasional manifestations of a style of thought which had its origin
in a later age.‡ The hero of the piece can hardly be
supposed to have extolled himself in such terms as are
employed by the writer.§ The style of the Hebrew
portions indicates a later age for their composition than
that of any other book of the Old Testament.‖ There
are historical errors and incongruities into which no
contemporary could have fallen.¶ The peculiar *an-
gelology*, or mythology of angels,** belongs to the period

---

* Ezek. xiv. 14–20; xxviii. 3.   † Dan. i. 1; x. 1.

‡ E. g. iv. 13; viii. 15, 16; ix. 21; x. 13; xii. 1.

§ i. 19, 20; v. 11, 12; vi. 4; ix. 23; x. 11.

‖ For examples, see De Wette, "Lehrbuch," § 255, anm. *f*; Lengerke, "Daniel," "Vorwort," § 11. Eichhorn ("Einleitung," § 615, *b*)
characterizes the Hebrew style of the last chapters as being not only more
modern than that of the books of Ezra, Nehemiah, and Esther, but as sink-
ing into rabbinical forms.

¶ For instance, in Dan. i. 1, Nebuchadnezzar is said to have besieged
Jerusalem " in the third year of the reign of Jehoiakim," in contradiction
to Jer. xxv. 1, 9; xxxvi. 1, 9; 2 Chron. xxxvi. 5, 6. (Comp. Vol. III.
p. 344.) For other examples, see Lengerke, " Daniel," § 13 (5); Bertholdt,
" Daniel," Band I. s. 34.

** Dan. iv. 13; viii. 16; ix. 21; x. 13–20; xii. 1.

of Persian, and not of Babylonian sway; * and instances occur of what appear to be but Greek words
set down in Hebrew letters.† The son of Sirach does
not mention Daniel.‡ It does not appear how the
correctness of the common opinion respecting the origin of the book is to be reconciled with the place assigned to it by the Jews in the collection of their
Scriptures. Had it been of the character and authority which has been supposed, it would seem that they
would have given it a place among the Prophets, instead of referring it to the later and inferior collection of Hagiographa, and placing it almost at the end
of that. And if, at the time (probably during the
persecutions of Antiochus Epiphanes) when they arranged passages from the writings of the prophets
for reading-lessons in the synagogues,§ they had had
our Book of Daniel, and regarded it in a similar light
to that in which they did regard the writings of Jeremiah and Ezekiel, prophets of the time of the Captivity, there appears no reason why that book should
not have been treated in the same way, which however was not done.

Josephus says that, on the visit of Alexander the
Great to Jerusalem, the priests showed him Daniel's
prophecies.|| But it was four centuries after the Sy-
rian conquests of Alexander that Josephus wrote, and
his unsupported testimony to such a point at so re-

---

* See Corrodi's " Versuch," u. s. w., Band I. ss. 89 – 91.

† E. g. קִיתָרוֹס, κίθαρις ; סַבְּכָא, σαμβύκη ; סוּמְפֹּנְיָה, συμφωνία ; פְּסַנְתֵּרִין,
ψαλτήριον. For other examples, and a discussion of the question what inferences are to be drawn from such forms, see Eichhorn's " Einleit.," § 614
(2); Bertholdt's " Einleit.," § 388 (3) ; Bertholdt's " Daniel," Band I. s.
24 ; Lengerke's " Daniel," " Vorwort," § 11.

‡ Ecclus. xlix.

§ הַפְטָרוֹת, *Haphtaroth.*

|| " Antiq. Jud.," Lib. XI. cap. 8, § 5.

mote a time is entitled to no confidence.* The author
of the First Book of Maccabees refers to occurrences also related in our Book of Daniel,† but without
any intimation whatever of its existence in his time, or
that it was not from some other source — whether
writing or popular tradition — that he derived his information. Our Lord, in one of his discourses, is made
by our translators to say that an expression employed
by him had been used " *by* the prophet Daniel." ‡ But
this is not what he did say, according to a true translation of the preposition in the New Testament Greek.
Supposing the words of the clause in which Daniel is
named to have been part of the discourse of Jesus
(which I have no inclination to dispute, though they
may well be understood as a parenthetical comment
of the historian who records it), the true rendering of
them is, " spoken of *in* the prophet Daniel." § The
phrase " in the prophet Daniel," according to a well-
established and familiar use, was equivalent to " in the
prophecy of Daniel." ‖ Our Lord, in using it, did but

---

* It may be added, that the manner in which Alexander is mentioned in
the book is not such that those who wished to pay court to him would do
well to call his attention to it.

† 1 Mac. ii. 59, 60.

‡ Matt. xxiv. 15. — The words " spoken of by Daniel, the prophet," in
the parallel text in Mark xiii. 14, are spurious, and, as such, are cancelled
by Griesbach in his edition.

§ The preposition is not ὑπό, which the rendering of our translators would
require, but διά. Of course, I am not unaware of the pains to which the
lexicographers have put themselves to show that, in the New Testament,
διά, in such cases, denotes the *instrumental cause*. But one has only to turn
over a few pages of the Septuagint to see how frequently it is used, in the
Hellenistic dialect, as simply equivalent to the Hebrew ב, *in*. The excellent Syriac translator has rendered διά by that prefix in the present instance.
But suppose we give διά the rendering claimed for it, what follows? For an
answer see Luke xvi. 18. " Hear what the unjust judge saith," said our
Lord, certainly without meaning to declare that the unjust judge was an historical character. and had really spoken the words ascribed to him.

‖ Comp. Vol. II. p. 387, note. The form of expression is the same as
that of " *Moses* is read," in Acts xv. 21.

refer to the book in which the expression "the abomination of desolation" was found, calling that book by the name, "the prophet Daniel," by which, whether the name was correct or not, the book was commonly known.

About one quarter part of the book, as the Christian era found it in the hands of the Jews, existed only in the Greek language. Of the residue, one part (more than two fifths) was extant in Greek and Hebrew, and the other in Greek and Chaldee.* Of the portion which, according to the notation of our Bibles, precedes the eighth chapter, only one short passage is in the Hebrew tongue.†

Porphyry, in the third century, referred the composition of the book to the time of Antiochus Epiphanes, and said that the original was in Greek. It is true that Jerome, from whom we have this fact, (for the polemical writings of Porphyry have perished,) gives us to understand that he inferred the Greek origin of the book from two passages, each containing a *paronomasia* in the Greek language; ‡ both which passages occur in one of the narratives now esteemed apocryphal, and accordingly do not furnish an argument applicable to the canonical parts of the book.§

---

* The proportion of the Chaldee to the Hebrew in quantity is not far from that of 19 to 14.

† Dan. i. 1 – ii. 4.

‡ Susan. 54, 55, 58, 59.

§ " Contra Prophetam Danielem duodecimum librum scripsit Porphyrius, nolens eum ab ipso, cujus inscriptum est nomine, esse compositum ; sed a quodam, qui temporibus Antiochi, qui appellatus est Epiphanes, fuerit in Judæa ; et non tam Danielem ventura dixisse, quam illum narrâsse præterita. Denique quidquid usque ad Antiochum dixerit, veram historiam continere ; si quid ultra opinatus sit, quia futura nescierit, esse mentitum. . . . . . Sed et hoc nôsse debemus inter cætera, Porphyrium de Danielis libro nobis objicere, idcirco illum apparere confictum, nec haberi apud Hebræos, sed Græci sermonis esse commentum, quia in Susannæ fabulâ contineatur, di-

But it is not safe to trust Jerome for accuracy in the statement of an opponent's reasoning, nor does he even affirm that this was Porphyry's only argument. Porphyry was a very able and learned disputant, as abundantly appears from the pains which were taken to refute him.* He knew, as well as Jerome did, that the passages referred to did not exist in Hebrew, and it is by no means probable that he relied alone upon an argument drawn from them, to establish a conclusion relating to the whole book. It is altogether likely that Jerome has given us only a part of his testimony and reasoning on the subject; — in other words, that Porphyry had other grounds for his belief of a Greek, and accordingly modern, origin of the book.

The present peculiar condition of the book is not only entirely consistent with that supposition, but is most easily explained by it. Supposing it to have been originally written in Greek, it would have been very natural that some Jew should translate into Hebrew a portion of it, which particularly struck his fancy. Some other person, or the same person, for a

---

cente Daniele ad presbyteros, ἀπὸ τοῦ σχίνου σχίσαι, καὶ ἀπὸ τοῦ πρίνου πρίσαι, quam etymologiam magis Græco sermoni convenire, quam Hebræo." ("Prœm. ad Comment. in Dan.," Tom. III. pp. 1071 - 1074.)

* He was answered by Methodius, Eusebius, and Apollinarius. For some account of the controversy, see the author's " Lowell Lectures," Vol. II. pp. 48 - 59. The loss of these answers to Porphyry is much to be regretted. Had they been preserved, we should, no doubt, be much better able to judge of the credibility of his assertion concerning the origin of the book. In the midst of the Hebraisms which pervade the Greek text, and which are to be looked for on any hypothesis, — since, in whatever language composed originally, the work was written by a Jew, — I think I have observed, in the canonical portion, some instances of a turn of phrase belonging to the Greek idiom, and not to the Hebrew or Chaldee. If there are such, they are of course so many important indications that the Greek was the original language. But as this is a line of argument quite subtle as well as new, and as it only occurred to me while carrying these last pages through the press, I forbear to propose it till after further consideration.

similar reason, or for any one of a variety of reasons that might be imagined, rendered another portion into Chaldee.* Those portions of the book which had thus come to be expressed in the forms of the Hebrew or (what was the same) the Chaldee alphabet, were in a shape suitable to be received into the Old Testament collection, which was itself wholly written in that letter. The parts which remained extant only in the Greek language were not in a shape to be so admitted, and, coming down to us in only this condition, have taken their place in our modern versions as *Apocrypha.*

If the Hebrew and Chaldee medley now in our hands was not derived from a Greek original, but was the original itself, I know no plausible way of explaining its present state on the supposition of its having proceeded from one author, or, indeed, on any other supposition. But, in whatever language or languages originally composed, (for the supposition of the late origin of the book by no means necessarily involves that of a Greek original,) I conceive that all the facts of the case go to sustain the opinion that its composition is to be dated in the age of Antiochus Epiphanes.

Availing himself of a perfectly legitimate rhetorical

---

* The Chaldee passage begins at ii. 4, with the words, "Then spake the Chaldeans unto the king in their own language." This fact suggests the reason why a Chaldee translator may have chosen to begin his task here. When begun, it would be idle to conjecture what circumstances determined the place at which it should close. The writer, having proceeded for a while, may have become weary of a dull task, and have chosen to bring it to an end at the place where the Chaldee passage terminates (vii. 28), or to continue his version in the Hebrew, a language written in the same character, and with which he may have been more familiar. The word אֲרָמִית, "in Syriac" (ii. 4), is brought in in a singular manner. It has sometimes struck me that it was originally only a marginal note, containing a memorandum to the translator that here his version into Hebrew was to end, and that into Chaldee to begin.

artifice, such as we have seen to have been used by the author of the Book of Jonah and of the Second Book of Esdras,* the writer (supposing there was but one) has for the purposes of his fiction adopted the name of an eminent countryman of his in former times, of whom (with the exception of Ezekiel's passing notices) only tradition had preserved the renown, and has cast his thoughts into the mould of adventures described as having been experienced, and visions described as having been seen, four centuries before his own time, by Daniel.

The minute acquaintance of the writer with the state of affairs in his nation as far down as to the persecutions under Antiochus Epiphanes, and no further, shows him to have lived in the time of that prince. A large part of his book appears to have been composed on the same plan, and with the same purpose, which I have ascribed to the Book of Judith; namely, to ex- cite the people to a spirit of constancy under their great sufferings at that period, by inspiring in them the hope of Divine protection and support. The au- thor of the former book had shown, in the example of Judith, how patriotic courage will avail under the most disastrous circumstances, and how faithful God will be to grant his people rescue, if they will but be faithful in their allegiance to him. By the equally fictitious examples of the Three Holy Children con- demned to the flames, and of Daniel twice thrown into a lion's den, for their loyalty to Jehovah, but all of them delivered by his Divine power, and extorting by their heroism the homage of heathen to his holy name, the writer of the book before us enforced the same weighty and seasonable lesson. The history of Susan-

* Vol. III. p. 473; Vol. IV. p. 126.

na (though perhaps mainly indebted for its place in the compilation to its being a legend commemorative of the early wisdom of that sage who was selected for the hero of the book) has yet a certain bearing on the same moral, as showing that innocence, however persecuted with wrong and embarrassed by malicious artifices, has only to refuse to yield, and it may promise itself a providential vindication. And the same is to be said of the prosperous condition of health and vigor in which the four pious youth found themselves, when, refusing to partake of heathen dainties, they trusted to God, and lived on ascetic fare.

The stories in the fourth and fifth chapters respecting Daniel's having predicted an insanity of Nebuchadnezzar, the conqueror of Judea, and, some thirty or forty years later, the capture of Babylon by the Persians and Medes, were not improbably legends which had come down to the author of this book from an earlier age. If so, they may have suggested to him the idea of presenting Daniel in the character of a prognosticator of events more remote from his own time, an idea which he has followed out in the second chapter, and in the last six chapters of his book.

These are but general observations. What claim they have to be regarded as well founded can be better judged as I proceed with some particular comments on the different sections of the book.

The three stories extant only in Greek afford occasion for very little remark beyond what has been already made. The books of Jonah, Tobit, and Judith, the Third Book of the Maccabees, the account of Zerubbabel's introduction to Darius in the First Book of Esdras, are specimens, at less or greater length, of that kind of fictitious narrative to which I understand these portions of the Book of Daniel to belong.

They are all of that character that they appear very likely to have been oral traditions circulating among the people, before they were committed to writing; but, however this may have been, the character of the Greek style in which they are written renders it probable that, when first committed to writing, it was in the Greek language. If composed earlier than the time of the persecution under Antiochus, they at all events acquired an additional interest at that period, from the lessons they conveyed of the folly of idolatry, and of the power and willingness of Jehovah to protect the innocent and loyal; and this, independent of the fact that they relate to Daniel, was a good reason for their being inserted at that time in the book which took his name.*

That portion of the book which we find in the Biblical Chaldee begins with the words, "O king, live for ever! Tell thy servants the dream, and we will show the interpretation." † It seems safe to infer, from the abruptness of this commencement, that the passage must have been, not an independent composition, but a continuation of what precedes, and originally in the same language. What was that original language? Certainly it may have been the Hebrew, — the language in which the fragment that precedes and introduces the Chaldee passage is now found. But, if so, would the Hebrew original of what we now have in a Chaldee translation have been lost? This, too, may have been; we have an example of such

---

* "The same year were appointed two of the ancients of the people to be judges, *such as the Lord spake of*, that wickedness came from Babylon from ancient judges," &c. (Susan. 5); this appears to be a reference to Jer. xxix. 22, 23, in the manner of the New Testament quotations from the Old which I have lately remarked upon. See above, pp. 321 – 324.

† Dan. ii. 4.

a loss in the Wisdom of the Son of Sirach. But it seems less probable than that both the Hebrew and Chaldee were translations of parts of a Greek original which remained entire, and has been transmitted to our times.

The narrative which occupies the second chapter, relating how Nebuchadnezzar ordered an indiscriminate massacre of the wise men of Babylon, because they could not tell what he had been dreaming, as well as give its interpretation, and how, when Daniel, in answer to the prayers of his three friends, had been instructed in a vision concerning the dream and its meaning, they were " set over the affairs of the province of Babylon," and he was made " chief of the governors over all the wise men," I take to be a composition of the same character as the passages in Greek upon which I have remarked ; — that is, to be a fable, an *Aggada.*[*]   The remarks which I have to make on the prediction of future events alleged to have been extracted.from the dream, I reserve till the same subject presents itself again in connection with the seventh chapter.

The four chapters next following contain each another fictitious history of the same description.[†]

The story in the third chapter, of the miraculous preservation of Shadrach, Meshach, and Abednego, when they had refused to obey the impious mandate of an idolatrous king, conveyed a moral eminently ap-

---

[*] See above, p. 127.

[†] In these chapters, considerable diversities of reading occur between the Greek and Chaldee texts, besides the long Greek insertion of the " Song of the Three Holy Children." For instance, the passage iv. 3 - 6 is omitted in the Greek copy. Additions are made to iii. 48, iv. 15 and 33. The language is condensed in v. 17 - 25, 26 - 28. It is altered in iii. 1. In iii. 31 - 33, it is partly abbreviated and partly enlarged. See also iv. 10 - 12, 28 - 31, 69.

propriate to the time of Antiochus Epiphanes, who
had commanded his Jewish subjects, on pain of death,
to abstain from the worship of Jehovah, and take a
part in heathen rites.* It is between the twenty-third
and twenty-fourth verses of this chapter that the Greek
copy introduces the passage entitled in the English
Apocryphal collection, " The Song of the Three Holy
Children." The evident chasm in the sense between
those verses — which deficiency the Greek supplies
— favors the opinion that the Greek was the original
work; though the topics of the song of Azariah and
his companions appear no more appropriate to the
peculiar situation of the suppliants, than those of the
psalm ascribed to the prophet Jonah under circumstances somewhat similar.†

In the piece in the fourth chapter, the form of a
proclamation of Nebuchadnezzar " to all people, nations, and languages that dwell upon the whole earth,"
is not strictly preserved. The story of his dream, of
the transformation which, according to Daniel's interpretation of it, followed, and of his restoration to himself and his throne in the devout frame of mind created
by his calamity, is partly told as if by a third person.‡
On account of the extravagances of his temper, An-

---

* See above, pp. 136, 137, 195.

† See Vol. III. p. 467. — The Song of the Three Holy Children is a
sort of expansion of Ps. cxlviii. The prayer of Azariah, which precedes it,
resembles that of Ezra in Ez. ix. 5 – 15. — It is scarcely worth while to remark on such things as the extraordinary proportions of a statue with a
height ten times its diameter, or the exposure of such a mass of precious
metal as composed it in an open plain (iii. 1); the command to increase
the heat of the furnace seven times (19); its scorching to death the men who
threw the faithful Jews into it (22) ; or the sudden change in the religious
policy of Nebuchadnezzar for all parts of his wide empire (29). — The " son
of God " seen by him " in the midst of the fire" (25) is explained (28) as
an " angel."

‡ Dan. iv. 19, 28 – 33.

tiochus Epiphanes was sometimes called *Epimanes*, "the madman." * Not improbably the piece had a reference to this fact, and was intended to intimate that the infirmity of Antiochus was a judicial visitation from Jehovah, and that then only might he hope for relief, and "a lengthening out of his tranquillity," when he should "break off his sins by righteousness, and his iniquities by showing mercy to the poor," † — that is, by desisting from his cruelties to the helpless Jews.

The story in the fifth chapter was one of easy construction. That Babylon had been taken by the Medes, was an historical fact. What was supplied from imagination was, that the city was taken on a night when the king had been putting the sacred vessels of the ravaged temple of Jerusalem to a profane use, and that "in the same night," in the interpretation of a vision which confounded the sorcerers of the court, Daniel had predicted the catastrophe as a punishment of the king's impiety. Antiochus, too, in the writer's time, had pillaged the temple of its precious utensils.‡ How just would it be, should Jehovah commission the enemies of Syria to avenge that awful sacrilege!

The moral of the story in the sixth chapter is the same as of that in the third. Nebuchadnezzar in the one case, and Darius in the other, are represented as having commanded their Jewish subjects to disown their God, as Antiochus did in more recent times. But Shadrach and his friends defied Nebuchadnezzar, and came harmless from the flames; and Daniel without disguise disobeyed Darius, and passed a night untouched in a den of hungry lions. In both cases, the persecuted were the conquerors. True and constant

---

* See Vol. III. p. 170.   † Dan. iv. 27.   ‡ See above, pp. 135, 194.

in the tremendous trial of their faith, the three friends were " promoted in the province of Babylon," and the accusers of Daniel, with " their children and their wives," were cast into the den, where " the lions had the mastery of them, and broke all their bones"; while in both cases the worship of Jehovah, instead of the disgrace which had been meditated, obtained honor, through a royal proclamation to all the world to reverence his name. Who could tell but that, with a loyalty on the part of his people like that related of Daniel and his associates, Jehovah would be equally ready now to protect and glorify his worshippers and his cause against the proud Syrian oppressor?

We come to the seventh chapter, in which Daniel is represented as having foretold, " in the first year of Belshazzar," the rise of four successive empires, to follow after that of Babylon. In connection with it, I recur to the second chapter, in which the same subject is treated with less precision.

The Jewish nation, after the loss of its independence, fell successively under the government, — 1. of Babylon; 2. of Persia; 3. of Macedon; 4. of the conflicting Greek monarchies of Egypt and Syria. Daniel, in the time of the Babylonish and Persian kings, is represented as predicting this series of revolutions with great exactness. But I understand the writer to have lived at the last stage of the series, in the time of Antiochus Epiphanes. Down to that time, he clearly appears to have been perfectly well acquainted with the course of events. To him they were historical, though he puts them, in the form of prediction, into the mouth of a Jewish worthy of four centuries before his day. At the time of Antiochus his knowledge ends. He makes his hero predict nothing definitely, subsequent to the period when he himself was writing. What was known to himself as past, he makes Daniel, a personage of four centuries before, predict as future. And where his own knowledge of what in his own time was past ends, there he arrests Daniel's descriptions of what was to come.

This is a perfectly well understood form of composition, and never leads to any error, except in connection with that task of commenting upon Scripture, which, more than any other, seems suited to divest men of their common sense. Virgil lived when the ages of the Roman republic had come to an end, and the empire was established indespotic tranquillity under Augustus. In the sixth book of his Æneid he represented the fabulous founder of the Roman state as listening to an outline of the history, terminating with the writer's time, expressed in the form of prediction of what in the founder's time was future. Horace's "Prophecy of Nereus"* is constructed on the same plan. Gray, in his poem of "The Bard," represents a Welsh minstrel in the reign of Edward the First as sketching the course of English history (future to the minstrel) nearly down to the time when Gray lived. What was known to the writer as fact is put into the mouth of a fabulous ancient as prediction. Macaulay, in his "Prophecy of Capys," and our countryman, Holmes, in that magnificent lyric in which he represents one of the Plymouth settlers as relating his vision of future national greatness to

> " The pilgrim child, whose wasting face
> Was meekly turned to hear,"

have given specimens of a rhetorical device, so natural, familiar, and expressive, that none but Scriptural interpreters are in any danger whatever of being

---

* Lib. I. Ode 15.

perplexed by it. When one of the native sovereigns
of England suffered cruelty and indignity from the
Roman conquerors, a Druid of the time of Nero is
represented by Cowper as consoling her with a prediction of those calamities of Rome and great fortunes of
Britain which the poet knew to have signalized the
intervening centuries. I copy the piece as a specimen
of this form of composition, selecting it simply as the
shortest, in English, that I call to mind.

" When the British warrior queen,
    Bleeding from the Roman rods,
    Sought, with an indignant mien,
    Counsel of her country's gods ;

" Sage beneath a spreading oak
    Sat the Druid, hoary chief ;
    Every burning word he spoke
    Full of rage, and full of grief.

" ' Princess ! if our aged eyes
    Weep upon thy matchless wrongs,
    'T is because resentment ties
    All the terrors of our tongues.

" ' Rome shall perish, — write that word
    In the blood that she has spilt ;
    Perish, hopeless and abhorred,
    Deep in ruin as in guilt.

" ' Rome, for empire far renowned,
    Tramples on a thousand states ;
    Soon her pride shall kiss the ground, —
    Hark ! the Gaul is at her gates !

" ' Other Romans shall arise,
    Heedless of a soldier's name ;
    Sounds, not arms, shall win the prize,
    Harmony the path to fame.

" ' Then the progeny that springs
    From the forests of our land,
    Armed with thunder, clad with wings,
    Shall a wider world command.

" ' Regions Cæsar never knew
Thy posterity shall sway ;
Where his eagles never flew,
None invincible as they.'

" Such the bard's prophetic words,
Pregnant with celestial fire,
Bending, as he swept the chords
Of his sweet, but awful lyre.

" She, with all a monarch's pride,
Felt them in her bosom glow :
Rushed to battle, fought, and died ;
Dying hurled them at the foe : —

" ' Ruffians, pitiless as proud,
Heaven awards the vengeance due ;
Empire is on us bestowed,
Shame and ruin wait for you.' " *

It is precisely this form of poetical representation
that the writer now under our notice has adopted in
the second, and in the last six chapters of his book.
He lived when the Babylonian, the Persian, the Macedonian, and the divided Greek-Egyptian and Greek-
Syrian empires had successively borne rule over the
Jews.   He selected, for the chief figure in the pageant
which he designed, a sage of his nation, who had
lived, or whom he feigned to have lived, in the time of
the Babylonish conqueror of Judea.   That monarch
he represented as having dreamed of seeing a majestic
image, with the head made of gold, the breast and

---

* Other examples occur in the Æneid, I. 261-296, VIII. 626-731;
Ovid's " Metamorphoses," XV. 813-842 ; Tasso's " Gerus. Liber.,"
XVII. Stanz. xlvi. - xciv. ; Voltaire's " Henriade," Chant VII. ; Milton's
" Paradise Lost," XII. 1-544 ; Shakspeare's " King Henry the Eighth,"
last scene ; Scott's " Marmion," Canto II. Stanza xxxi., and " Lord of
the Isles," Canto II. Stanzas xxx. - xxxiii.   Dante, in his " Inferno,"
furnishes numerous examples, as in Cantos I., VI., X., XXIV.   Barlow's
" Columbiad " and Scott's " Vision of Don Roderick " are instances of
long poems constructed wholly upon this plan.

arms of silver, the loins and thighs of brass, and the
nether limbs of iron and clay, which image was smitten, and scattered into dust, by a stone " cut out without hands," which itself " became a great mountain,
and filled the whole earth."   This dream Daniel is
said to have interpreted to Nebuchadnezzar as fore-
boding what, except in the last particular, was known
by the writer to have actually taken place between
Nebuchadnezzar's time and his own.   The Babylonish
empire had been symbolized by the golden head, the
Persian by the silver breast, the Macedonian by the
brazen thighs, and the Greek power over Palestine —
divided, after Alexander's death, between the Lagidæ
in Egypt and the Seleucidæ in Syria — by the feet of
mixed iron and clay.   So far, the writer was proceeding
on sure ground.   The imagery which he used was suitable to describe the course of public events which had
taken place before his day.   He invented it, as being
thus suitable.   When, having thus traced down that
course of events as far as history gave him warrant, —
that is, as far as to his own time, — he proceeded further to make Daniel predict, " And in the days of
these kings shall the God of heaven set up a kingdom
which shall never be destroyed, and the kingdom shall
not be left to other people, but it shall break in pieces
and consume all these kingdoms, and it shall stand for
ever," he did but put into Daniel's mouth, as an oracle, the expression of a thought which had been up-
permost in the mind of patriotic Jews from David's
time to the writer's own, — the thought of the destined
establishment of the Messiah's reign.*

---

* " This image's head . . . . . his breast . . . . . his belly and his thighs
. . . . . his legs . . . . . his feet " (ii. 32); the descent from early to later events
is represented by that from the upper to the nether extremities of the body. —
" A stone was cut out without hands " (34); that is, as I understand, the

The topics of this passage are again presented in the seventh chapter; namely, the succession of four empires known to the writer to have held sway over Judea, to be succeeded, as he hoped, by the more illustrious kingdom of the Jewish Messiah.

The representation of the Babylonish power under the figure of a lion with eagle's wings was probably intended to denote the fierceness and fleetness at once, with which that monarchy moved on in its career of conquest. The plucking of the beast's wings, its standing upright and still, and its being endowed with a man's heart, may signify the reduced dominion, the more inoffensive administration, and superior humanity of the Chaldean power under Nebuchadnezzar's successors.*

By the three ribs in the mouth of the bear, which typified the power of Cyrus and his successors, I presume was signified the union of the Babylonian, Persian, and Median empires to constitute their dominion. The beast's standing " on one side," † Jerome said that the Jews of his time understood to mean the Persian monarchs' keeping themselves apart from Judea, and not disturbing it by invasion or oppression. ‡

The four wings and four heads of the leopard, the symbol of the Macedonian power, § appear to me to

---

fifth empire would be one, not " set up " by human power, but by " the God of heaven " (comp. 44). — " Another kingdom inferior to thee," &c. (39); the Persian empire did not include, like the Babylonish, the Mediterranean coast of Africa; and it was of less extent than the Macedonian, both to the east and west. — " They shall mingle themselves by marriage " (43); Antiochus Theos married a daughter of Ptolemy Philadelphus; Antiochus the Great gave his daughter to Ptolemy Epiphanes; and Alexander Balas of Syria espoused Cleopatra, an Egyptian princess. Comp. Vol. III. pp. 165, 166, 168; Vol. IV. p. 162.

* Dan. vii. 3, 4. Jeremiah (iv. 7, 13, xlviii. 40) uses similar imagery in application to the Babylonians.

† vii. 5.

‡ Hieron., " Comment. in Dan.," *ad loc.*   § vii. 6.

have been designed to indicate those four sections, or
dynasties, of the empire created by Alexander, with
which, as I pointed out in the history of the time,*
the Jews were brought into important relations.†

The description of the "fourth beast, dreadful and
terrible, and exceedingly strong," which "had great
iron teeth," and "devoured and brake in pieces, and
stamped the residue with its feet," was such as might
have been expected from one who had himself seen
and experienced the oppressions of the tyranny thus
typified. The "ten horns" of that beast represented
the succession of ten sovereigns, of Greek race, who
had preceded Antiochus Epiphanes in the government
of Syria.‡ The "other little horn" which "came up
among them," in which "were eyes like the eyes of a
man, and a mouth speaking great things," and "before which three of the first horns were plucked up by
the roots," was that vigilant, arrogant, and ambitious
monarch himself, who usurped the thrones of his
brother Seleucus and his nephew Demetrius in Syria
and his nephew Ptolemy Philometor in Egypt. What
in fiction was foretold of the person typified by "the
little horn," that he should "speak great words against
the Most High, and harass the saints of the Most High,
and resolve to change times and laws," — that is, to
abrogate the Jewish institutions, — was precisely what
the writer knew to have been actually done by Anti-
ochus Epiphanes.|| Agreeably to the most natural
interpretation, " a time, and times, and half a time"

---

* Vol. III. p. 161.

† Prideaux thinks ("Connection," &c., Vol. II. pp. 343, 393) that Ptolemy, who possessed himself of Egypt, Seleucus of Babylon, Cassander of
Greece, and Lysimachus of Thrace, were intended. Grotius ("Annot."
ad loc.) supposes the reference to be to Perdiccas, Seleucus, Ptolemy, and
Meleager. Alii, alias.

‡ See Vol. III. pp. 162–170.

|| See above, pp. 134–137, 193–195.

means three years and a half, and this appears to have been the duration of the sharpest Syrian persecution.*

To that time the ostensible prediction of Daniel, as far as it has any thing of a circumstantial character, extends. Soon after that time, the author wrote; and that kingdom of the Messiah, which he makes Daniel further predict in merely vague terms, as coming to terminate the horn's "war with the saints," and exalt them to "possess the kingdom," he, like every Jew of his time and of earlier times, expected would speedily ensue. This is what he accordingly dilates upon, in striking poetical imagery, through the rest of the chapter; representing the Almighty as seating himself in imperial pomp on his tribunal, surrounded by "ten thousand times ten thousand" ministers, and condemning the profane beast to death, and his body to the flames; † the Messiah coming "with the clouds of heaven," to assume the sublime investiture of his universal and everlasting sway; ‡ and "the saints," or holy people, established in perpetual "sovereignty, and dominion, and power over all kingdoms under the whole heaven." ||

---

* Dan. vii. 7, 8; comp. 19, 20, 23 - 25. — Josephus says ("De Bel. Jud.," Lib. I. cap. 1, § 1) that Antiochus put a stop to the daily sacrifices in the temple "for three years and six months." In another place ("Prœm. in Bel. Jud.," § 7), he says that Antiochus held the city "three years and three months." And in another ("Antiq. Jud.," Lib. XII. cap. 7, § 6), he states the "desolation of the temple" to have lasted exactly three years.

† vii. 9 - 12.

‡ vii. 13, 14.

|| vii. 18, 21, 22, 26, 27. — "I came near to one of them that stood by, and asked him the truth concerning all this, so he told me" (16); the machinery is the same as that of the Second Book of Esdras (comp. 2 Esd. ii. 44 - 48; iv. 1 - 52, &c.).

LECTURE LXVIII.

HEBREW PORTIONS OF THE BOOK OF DANIEL.

AGGADA IN THE FIRST CHAPTER. — DANIEL REPRESENTED AS THE
WRITER OF THE LAST FIVE CHAPTERS. — VISION IN THE EIGHTH
CHAPTER, REPRESENTING THE PERSIAN AND GREEK EMPIRES, AND THE
PERSECUTIONS UNDER ANTIOCHUS EPIPHANES. — PROPHECY (SO CALLED)
OF THE SEVENTY WEEKS IN THE NINTH CHAPTER. — ERRONEOUS EX-
POSITIONS OF USHER, — PRIDEAUX, — LLOYD, — BLAYNEY, — WINTLE,
— AND OTHERS. — THE WRITER'S MEANING TO BE SOUGHT IN THE CIR-
CUMSTANCES OF HIS OWN TIME AND THAT OF ANTIOCHUS EPIPHANES.
— EXAMINATION OF THE PASSAGE ON THIS BASIS. — INTRODUCTION IN
THE TENTH CHAPTER TO A SKETCH, IN THE ELEVENTH, OF THE HIS-
TORY FROM XERXES I. TO THE DEATH OF ANTIOCHUS. — PROGNOSTIC
OF THE SPEEDY ESTABLISHMENT OF THE MESSIAH'S KINGDOM. — DIF-
FERENT RECKONINGS OF THE DURATION OF THE EXISTING TROUBLES.
— DIRECTION TO SECRETE THE BOOK, AND INFERENCE THEREFROM AS
TO THE DATE OF ITS PRODUCTION. — ITS RECEPTION INTO THE CANON
FACILITATED BY THE FAVOR OF THE REIGNING FAMILY. — REFERENCES
TO IT IN THE NEW TESTAMENT.

IT remains to remark upon those portions of this
book which have been transmitted to us in the Hebrew language. Concerning that passage, beginning
with the first chapter and ending with the fourth verse
of the second, which contains a relation of the circumstances of the introduction of Daniel and his three
companions at the Babylonish court, I have nothing
further to suggest than that it belongs to that same
class of fictitious narratives to which I have referred
the stories already considered in the Greek and Chaldee portions; and that its moral was eminently appropriate and opportune at the time when the Syrian gov-

ernment was endeavoring to seduce its Jewish subjects into heathen practices.*

From the beginning of the eighth chapter to the
close of the book, Daniel is represented, in the use of
the pronoun of the first person, as being himself the
writer.† The vision in this chapter takes up the history at the period of the Macedonian conquests. There
is no mistaking the main sense of the imagery
which is employed, since its explanation is given in
the context. The strong ram, butting towards all
quarters except the east, with its two horns, of which
the one that sprouted last was longest, is declared
to represent the Medo-Persian power, which pushed
its conquests in the directions of Egypt, Syria, and
Greece, and in which the Persian, the later in origin,
was the stronger element.‡ The he-goat with "a conspicuous horn between his eyes," which, coming "from
the west, over the face of the whole earth, without
touching the ground," "smote the ram, and brake his
two horns," and "cast him down to the ground, and
stamped upon him," is in like manner interpreted as
typifying the far-seeing ambition and rapid conquests
of "the king of Greece." §   "But when he was strong-

---

* See above, pp. 136, 195.

† Dan. viii. 1, 15, 27; ix. 2, 20; x. 2, 12; xii. 5.—This cannot properly
be said of the seventh chapter, since, though Daniel is there represented
as relating his own experiences (vii. 2, 6, 7 *et seq.*), he is introduced by a
passage which speaks of him in the third person (vii. 1).

‡ viii. 1 - 4; comp. 15 - 20.—The ram is said to have been the ensign
of the Persians, as the lion, in these days, of the English, and the eagle, of
the Americans. (See Ammianus Marcellinus, "Res Gest.," &c., Lib. XIX.
cap. 1.) In the ruins of Persepolis, Sir John Chardin saw sculptured ram's
heads with horns of unequal length. ("Voyages en Perse," &c., Planche
LXVII.) These appear to be indications of a peculiar propriety in the imagery here employed. — "This vision relates to the time of the end" (17);
the writer supposed that presently after the revolutions described the Messiah's reign was to begin.

§ viii. 5 - 7; comp. 21. — The goat is said to have been the Macedonian

est, the great horn was broken"; at the height of his
prosperity, Alexander died. "And instead of it grew
up four conspicuous ones towards the four winds of
heaven, indicating, as is explained, "four kingdoms"
to "arise out of the nation," and answering, as I
understand, to those four divisions of the Greek monarchy which I have specified as having had more or
less influence over the Jewish affairs.* "And out of
one of them came forth a little horn"; a repetition of
the imagery in the last chapter, and with the same significance.   What is represented in the rest of this
chapter as having been foretold to Daniel, had taken
place just before the book was written (if my view of
its origin is correct), in the reign of Antiochus Epiphanes.   That prince "became exceedingly great toward the south, and toward the east, and toward the
glorious land" of Palestine. "And he exalted himself
even to the host of heaven, ... yea, he magnified
himself even to the prince of the host, and the daily
sacrifice was taken away from him, and the place of
its sanctuary was cast down.   And a host . . . . .
cast down the law to the ground, and it accomplished
its purpose and prospered." †   To the inquiry heard
by Daniel, "To how long a time extends the vision
concerning the daily sacrifice, and the impiety of the

---

emblem (see Justin. "Hist. Philip.," Lib. VII. cap. 1), and one of the
national names was Ægeades, *quasi* from *αἴξ*, a goat. — " Over the face of
the whole earth, without touching the ground " (5); " Such bribes the *rapid*
Greek o'er Asia whirled," says Johnson.

    * Dan. viii. 8, 22 ; comp. Vol. III. p. 161.

    † viii. 9 – 12 ; comp. 23 – 25 ; see also above, pp. 134 – 137, 195, 196. —
" The glorious land " (9) ; comp. Ezek. xx. 6, 15. — " The prince of the
host " (11) ; that is, God, who is elsewhere called the " Lord of Hosts,"
as in Pss. xxiv. 10 ; xlvi. 7, 11 ; xlviii. 8. — " Taken away from him "
(ibid.) ; that is, from " the prince of the host." — He shall be broken without hand (25) ; that is, apparently, he shall not fall by human violence ;
comp 1 Mac. vi. 8, 16 ; 2 Mac. ix. 5, 28.

destroyer, that both the sanctuary and the host shall
be trodden under foot," it was replied, " To two thousand and three hundred evenings and mornings; then
shall the sanctuary be cleansed," * as it was by Judas
the Maccabee.† Two thousand three hundred evenings and mornings make one thousand one hundred
and fifty days, or three years and nearly two months.
We have before seen that Josephus in one place states
the duration of the desolation of the temple at three
years; in another, the cessation of the daily sacrifices
at three years and a half; and in yet another, the
occupation of the city by Antiochus at three years
and three months.‡ Probably the time admitted of
being differently reckoned, according as its beginning
was identified with one or with another of the successive acts of Syrian profanation.

After the prayer of Daniel, in the beginning of the
ninth chapter, in which he is represented as deploring
the ungrateful and sinful course of his people through
all the past generations, acknowledging the justice of
the fate which had overtaken them in their dispersion
in foreign countries, and entreating that, not on account of their righteousness, but on account of his
great mercy, God would behold their desolations, and
the city called by his name, and cause his face to shine
upon his desecrated sanctuary, § " the man Gabriel" is
related to have made to him a communication, in words
recited in a previous Lecture in the version of Dr.
Noyes, ‖ which, under the mistaken name of " The
Prophecy of the Seventy Weeks," has probably been
the cause of more pedantic waste of learning, and
more ostentatious violence to common sense, than any

---

* Dan. viii. 13, 14.   † See above, pp. 144, 199.
‡ See above, p. 431, note *.   § Dan. ix. 1 – 20.
‖ See above, p. 401.

other equal number of words recorded in any language.*

Supposing the writer to have really intended to speak prophetically of Jesus the Messiah in this passage, common readers would have to conclude that he was in error. Literal "weeks" of seven days are out of the question in respect to the computation intended. Periods of seven years must have been meant.† From the "going forth of the commandment to restore and to rebuild Jerusalem," in the first year of Cyrus, viz. in the year B. C. 536, neither a term of sixty-two times, nor of sixty-nine times, nor of seventy times seven years would terminate at the date of the advent or of the crucifixion of Jesus, or at that of the destruction of Jerusalem by the Romans, to say nothing now of further insuperable difficulties attendant upon each of these hypotheses in an interpretation of the context.

Abandoning the date of the decree of Cyrus as unmanageable for the purposes of this kind of exposition, Archbishop Usher ‡ proposed to understand "the going forth of the commandment to restore and build Jerusalem" as signifying an incident recorded in the Book of Nehemiah, ‖ and there referred to the twentieth year of Artaxerxes Longimanus. This, according to the common reckoning, was the year 444 B. C., from which date seventy weeks of years extend to

---

* "The history of the exposition of this passage presents one interpreter always in conflict with the rest. And the most satisfactory part of each successive essay has hitherto always been the exposure of the arbitrary assumptions and calculations of previous critics. Then has followed the proposal of some new scheme, equally chargeable with the same errors that had been deplored in the earlier explanations."— "Allgem. Bibliothek," Band III. ss. 782, 783.

† Comp. Gen. xxix. 27.

‡ "Annal. V. T." ad ann. Per. Jul. 4260. Usher's scheme had before been proposed by Petau.

‖ Neh. ii. 1-8.

A. D. 46. But to favor his scheme, Usher proposed to date the beginning of the reign of Artaxerxes ten years earlier.

Prideaux proposed to identify " the going forth of the commandment," &c., with the commission said to have been granted to Ezra by Artaxerxes Longimanus, in the seventh year of that prince's reign.* The difficulties accompanying this theory he attempted to surmount in detail, in a discussion occupying some sixty pages of his work.†

Bishop Lloyd, in order to make out a satisfactory computation, thought it necessary to understand the writer as having intended to express his periods of time in lunar years, of three hundred and sixty days each. Like Archbishop Usher, he began the computation from the twentieth year of Artaxerxes. From this date, four hundred and eighty-three (or seven times sixty-nine) lunar years extend to the year thirty-two of our era, in which year, or the year following, he supposes Jesus to have been crucified. The week of years that remains to make up the number of seventy, he separates from the rest, and proposes to begin in the year 63, seven years before the destruction of the city and temple of Jerusalem by the Romans.‡

Blayney, the translator of Jeremiah, dissatisfied with these schemes, suggested one which would be much

---

* Ezra vii. 1–8.

† " Old and New Testaments," &c., Part I. Book V. An. 458.

‡ Bishop Lloyd's scheme was developed in the " Chronological Treatise " of his chaplain, Mr. Marshall. I have not seen the book ; I take my account of it from Lowth, Prideaux, Blayney, Wintle, &c. Bishop Chandler, who has written skilfully and learnedly in defence of the common views of the Book of Daniel, has presented the theories of Usher, Prideaux, and Lloyd as plausible ; but without deciding for either. (" Defence," ch. ii. § 1, p. 132, *et seq.* " Vindication of the Defence," &c., Vol. I. p. 308.) Samuel Chandler (" Vindication of the Antiquity and Authority of Daniel's Prophecies," &c., p. 154 *et seq.*) follows Prideaux.

more plausible, provided his bold translation, and yet bolder treatment of the text (partly on the authority of the Chigian manuscript of the Septuagint), could be defended. The following is his rendering of the passage : —

" Weeks sufficient have been terminated (or completed) upon thy people and upon thy holy city, to check the revolt and to put an end to sins, and to make atonement for iniquity, and to bring again the righteousness of ancient times, and to seal (that is, authenticate) the divine oracle and the prophet, and to anoint (that is, sanctify anew) the most holy things.

" And thou shalt know and understand, that from the going forth of a decree to rebuild Jerusalem unto the Messiah the Prince shall be seventy and seven weeks, and three score and two years; it shall be rebuilt, still enlarging itself, and becoming more and more considerable, even amidst times of distress.

" And after the times seventy-seven and threescore and two, Messiah shall cut off from belonging to him both the city and the sanctuary; the prince that shall come shall destroy the people; and the cutting off thereof shall be with a flood (that is, a hostile invasion) ; and unto the end of a war carried on with rapidity shall be desolations.

" But he shall confirm a covenant (or make a firm covenant) with many for one week; and in the midst of the week he shall cause the sacrifice and meat-offering to cease; and the abomination of desolation shall be upon the border (that is, encompassing and pressing close upon the city and the temple); and an utter end, even a speedy one (or, even until an utter end, and that a speedy one), shall be poured upon the desolated." *

---

* " Dissertation," &c., in the Appendix to Blayney's " Jeremiah," pp. 56, 57.

By the "seventy and seven weeks," Blayney understands weeks of years, extending from the date of the
decree of Cyrus, and including in the last week the
date of our Saviour's birth ; and by the "threescore
and two" he understands single years, ending with
the breaking out of the war (A. D. 66) in which the
city and temple of Jerusalem were destroyed by the
Romans. His argument, for text and for exposition,
is a notable specimen of what may be done with the
most unpromising materials to sustain a foregone conclusion.

In the main features, of the date reckoned from, and
the computation by lunar years, the scheme of Wintle
(the last English laborer in this field of whom I know
any thing) accords with that of Bishop Lloyd. His
paraphrase of the passage is as follows : —

"Seventy weeks of precision (or precise weeks) remain upon thy people and upon thy holy city, Jerusalem, to restrain their rebellion or apostasy from God,
and to put an end to sins and expiate iniquity (or to
bring to a conclusion their sufferings and the punishment that occasioned them), and to introduce the righteousness of ancient times, and to seal the vision of the
prophet Jeremiah, and to restore the religious rites and
holy things to their proper uses. This first deliverance
from the captivity shall be accomplished within seventy weeks of days ; but this term shall be typical, or
a prelude to another more glorious deliverance, which
from its commencement to its full and final period
shall be comprehended in the same number of sevens
or weeks, yet not of days, but of times or years. And
this longer period shall be distributed into three portions, of seven weeks, and then of sixty-two weeks,
and lastly of one week, each of which will be distinguished by extraordinary events, as the prophecy now
proceeds to show.

" For know and understand (this interesting business induces me thus solemnly to recall your attention), that from the passing of an edict to rebuild your city, Jerusalem, that had been destroyed by fire, until Messiah the Prince (or from the 20th of Artaxerxes Longimanus when this edict will be delivered to Nehemiah, till that important hour when the Messiah shall be offered up, and thereby triumph as a prince over death and hell and all his enemies), shall be seven weeks and threescore and two weeks, or sixty-nine weeks of years. And the term is thus divided because the former part shall be distinguished by the building of the city, which shall be fully completed, with its streets and walls, in that narrower limit of the times.

" Then after the threescore and two weeks (or at the Passover next following their termination) shall Messiah be cut off by an ignominious death, and a total desertion. Yet though none shall be for him (or he shall be altogether forsaken at that time), his princely authority will still be manifested; for the people of the prince that shall come (or the Roman army in the service of the Messiah, when his business upon earth is completed, and the Gospel fully published) shall destroy both the Jewish city and sanctuary; and they shall come up against it like an inundation, and shall cut down with a general ruin, and to the end of a war decisive of the nation of the Jews there shall be desolations.

" Yet the one week of years that remains to complete the number typified in the former deliverance, this space of seven years shall make firm a covenant of security and protection to many, when those who are in Judea will escape to the mountains; and in the midst of the week the sacrifice and meat-offering (or the whole ritual of the Jewish worship) shall cease;

and when upon the borders of the temple, represented by an expanded wing, shall be the abomination of desolation (either the dead bodies of the slain, or the idolatrous ensigns, together with the Roman armies encompassing Jerusalem), then the desolations shall presently follow, and shall continue till a full accomplishment of the decided fate of this devoted people shall be poured upon the desolate (or until the times of the Gentiles shall be fulfilled)." *

All this, and much more of the same sort, — for I have only ventured to give a specimen, — I take to be merely learned babbling. The commentators started on a wrong track, and the further in their different directions they followed it, the further they wandered from sound judgment and from the truth. They have exhausted every trick of ingenuity, and every resource of erudition, to bring the words into harmony with their theories, — changes of text, changes of punctuation, changes of translation, conjectures in chronology, assumptions of dates, computations of years by different lengths. But all in vain. The stubborn text mocked at the labor of each; and the collected labor of all was, as Jortin said of ecclesiastical history, " a Briareus with a hundred hands, each smiting against the others."†

It is much easier to satisfy one's self of the incorrectness of that sort of exposition upon which I have been remarking, than to determine what was really the meaning of the author in this passage. The difficulty of arriving at a conclusion would be great enough, did it only consist in a translation of the words, and an explanation of the allusions ; but when, in addition to

---

* " Notes on Daniel," pp. 155, 156.

† Bertholdt (" Daniel," Band II. ss. 567 et seq.) gives thirteen different termini a quo, proposed by different critics.

this, we consider the extreme uncertainty of the text,
the problem is greatly complicated.* When, besides
the vagueness of words of indefinite meaning, and
equivocal references to events past and present, or
future, we are in doubt as to those precise words of
the author which are necessary to lay the basis for an
argument, it is plain that any exposition which may
be proposed must be merely hypothetical.   In what I
have further to say upon the subject, I shall assume
the correctness of the received Hebrew text,† and the
general correctness of the translation of Dr. Noyes.

A natural construction of the passage would be, that
the writer understood a duration of seventy times seven
years, divided into unequal periods of forty-nine years,
four hundred and thirty-four years, and seven years
(the last still unexpired), to have intervened between
"the going forth of the word" and his own time.
But if he thought so, he was in error, supposing him
to have lived at the time of the desecration of the tem-

---

* In the twenty-fifth verse the text of the Chigian manuscript (thought to
represent the original Septuagint version, in the place of which that of
Theodotion stands in the printed copies) bears a very faint resemblance to
the Hebrew, and especially says nothing of either "seven weeks," or
"sixty-two weeks," or of "an anointed one," or of "troubled times." In
the twenty-sixth verse, instead of "after sixty and two weeks," the same
manuscript reads, "after seven, and seventy, and sixty-two." The twenty-
seventh verse is almost entirely different from the Hebrew, and in particular,
instead of "during half of the week," it reads, "at the end of the week."
In the twenty-sixth verse, the Arabic version, representing yet another text,
reads, "after seven weeks and sixty-two weeks the anointing shall cease."
A glance at the versions in Walton's Polyglot is sufficient to show how unsettled is the text of a passage, to a satisfactory interpretation of which an
exact knowledge of the text is the first requisite.

† Of course, I refer here only to the different ways in which the four verses
(ix. 24 – 27) are exhibited in the versions and in the Greek manuscripts.
In Löwenheim's "Critical and Exegetical Inquiry," &c., the writer denies
the authenticity of the whole passage, and gives several critical reasons for
his opinion, some of them not contemptible. (See Eichhorn's "Allgemeine Bibliothek," Band I. s. 790.)   But I do not take this ground.

ple by Antiochus Epiphanes. From the destruction of the temple under Nebuchadnezzar to the desecration of its successor by Antiochus, only four hundred and twenty-one years intervened; from the decree of Cyrus, giving permission to rebuild, only three hundred and sixty-nine. Could the author of this book have been so ignorant of the history of his country, or so careless in relating it, as to make this false computation, of a century, more or less? Considering the character of his composition, and particularly considering other historical errors into which he has fallen, it would not perhaps be safe to deny, that he may have been thus ignorant or thus careless.*

But I am disposed to look for some explanation of the writer's words, independent of the supposition of such an erroneous chronology. In proposing one, I desire to have it constantly remembered that we are exploring a field in which close reasoning and satisfactory conclusions are scarcely to be looked for.

Let us understand the author, writing in the time of Antiochus Epiphanes, to represent Daniel as having, three hundred and seventy-five years earlier ("in the first year of Darius"†), called to mind the language of Jeremiah (committed to writing sixty years before that) respecting a seventy years' " desolation " of Jerusalem,‡ and proposing to himself to put a sort of cabalistic

---

* " It must be agreed that the author, according to his reckoning of the time passed since Jeremiah, really believed that it amounted to about seventy times seven years." (Bleek, " Ueber Verfasser und Zweck des Buches Daniel," in "Theologische Zeitschrift," Band III. p. 292.) Bertholdt's theory (" Daniel," Band II. s. 613, u. s. w.), that the writer, deducting from seventy weeks of years seven for the time to the decree of Cyrus, and one for the operations of Antiochus Epiphanes, used the round number of sixty-two (the remainder) as only an indefinite expression for the duration of the series of intervening events, has a certain affinity with this.

† Dan. vii. 1.

‡ Jer. xxv. 8 – 11; xxix. 10 – 14.

sense upon it. The sense which Daniel is represented as finally attributing to it corresponds with this description. It is an arbitrary, imaginative, mystical sense. It is through an error of our own, if we look for a logical interpretation from such a writer; and it is proved to be an error by the ill-success which has invariably followed the numerous attempts to devise an interpretation constructed upon that plan.

The author, writing, as I understand, in the year 163 or 164 B. C., — that is, four hundred and twenty-four or four hundred and twenty-five years after the destruction of Jerusalem, — knew that the complete national restoration of which Jeremiah had spoken, and of the nature of which (as he himself paraphrased it) he gives a glowing description,* had not only not taken place within seventy years after that catastrophe, but that it had not taken place even down to his own time. On the other hand, he thought he saw it rapidly approaching at the time when he wrote, through the victories of Judas the Maccabee. And he knew from history, that long before his day, in the first year of the reign of Cyrus, — that is, about seven times seven years after the destruction of Jerusalem, — had been issued that permission for the rebuilding of the city, which seemed to correspond to the sense of part of those words of Jeremiah which he was considering.

On the basis of these facts he proceeds in his fanciful exposition. I understand, we may conceive him as saying, two things to be referred to by Jeremiah, and not merely one. These two things are, the rebuilding of the city, and the reëstablishment of the nation in independence, virtue, and prosperity; and to regard those events as contemporaneous, experience has shown

---

* Dan. ix. 24.

to be an error. The first of them has long ago taken place. Assuming for its date — as with a sufficient approach to exactness may be done — the establishment of that Persian dynasty which authorized it immediately after its own accession to power, it took place seven times seven years after the city was sacked by Nebuzaradan. Accordingly, Gabriel is represented as saying to Daniel: " Know, therefore, and understand! From the going forth of the word to the rebuilding of Jerusalem, even to the advent of the anointed prince, shall be seven weeks." *

" And the streets and moats of Jerusalem shall again be built † sixty-two weeks, but in troublous times." ‡ If the computation of these sixty-two weeks of years should be begun at the end of the forty-nine years previously spoken of, it would reach to the year 105 B.·C., which time was in fact followed by nothing of that kind which, according to the writer, was to take place after sixty-two weeks. But the writer by no means intimates that it was his intention to have the computation so begin. Further on, as to the last period specified, he says that the reckoning of the one week is to be begun " *after* sixty-two weeks." § But he does not in like manner say that the reck-

---

* Dan. ix. 25. — Instead of Dr. Noyes's translation, I adopt so far that of the Syriac version (or rather of Walton's rendering of it, for the version is not unequivocal), which I think perfectly well represents the Hebrew text in our hands. Supposing it to be correct, " the rebuilding of Jerusalem " simultaneous with " the advent of the anointed prince " (viz. Cyrus, comp. Is. xliv. 28, xlv. 1, 13) is the *terminus ad quem* for the seven times seven years, more or less. And the *terminus a quo* is " the going forth of the word." But what " word " went forth half a century before the rebuilding ! I think the expression may in such a connection be very properly understood of that divine sentence, or that decree of the king of Babylon, in obedience to which Jerusalem was destroyed.

† Or, " again *stand* built."
‡ ix. 25.
§ ix. 26.

oning of the sixty-two weeks is to begin after the seven.*

I propose to understand him as having intended to have the reckoning of the second period specified — namely, that of the sixty-two weeks of years — begin at such a point as to end with the beginning of the third period, namely, that of one week; and as having intended to have that third period begin in the year 167 B. C., that is, three years and a half before the re-institution of the temple worship by Judas. During half of the last week of years "the sacrifice and the oblation" were "to cease" † (which they no longer did after Judas restored them), and that last week was to come "after the sixty-two weeks." Reckoning back the sixty-two times seven years from the year preceding by half a week of years the purification of the temple, we arrive, in a precise computation of the time, at the year 601 B. C., which appears to have been the year of, or the year before, the rebellion of Jehoiakim.‡

But since, in the reckoning of the first-named period of seven weeks of years, the destruction of Jerusalem in the year 588 B. C. furnished the *terminus a quo*, why, upon this scheme, should it not perform the same office as to the second period, that of sixty-two weeks? Why should the writer begin the computation of the second period at a date thirteen years earlier?

I repeat the remark, that it is in vain to demand a

---

* " *Then* shall the streets and moats," &c. writes Dr. Noyes. But the word corresponding to "then" is the copulative conjunction ?. — My placing the seven weeks within the sixty-two, instead of making the sixty-two succeed the seven, may seem a violent method of interpretation. Which is most so, — this, or the orthodox schemes of Lloyd and Wintle, which separate the one week by a long interval from the sixty-two? There is, besides, the great difference that they and writers of their class suppose the author to have had in view an exact chronology. I suppose nothing of the kind.

† Dan. ix. 27.

‡ Comp. Vol. III. p. 346; Prideaux, " Old and New Testaments," &c., Vol. II. p. 197, An. 603.

logical account of that to which no logical charactei belongs. The whole conception of the passage belongs to the province of the imagination. The expansion of Jeremiah's seventy years (intended by him for an indefinite time) into seventy times seven years, and the distribution of that period into different classes, was a mere conceit, — a plan arbitrary and lawless, and conforming to no rules of interpretation except such as should be suggested by the terms of the conceit itself. It appears to me to be enough to say, under such circumstances, that, the writer having deducted from his assumed period of four hundred and ninety years forty-nine years for one purpose, and seven years for another, there remained just four hundred and thirty-four years, and as, to carry out his plan, they must be made to end at the date of the abrogation of the temple ritual by the Syrian tyrant, he had to let them begin at that point of time to which the computation would carry them, be that point where it might. And, himself understanding what a free kind of composition he was indulging in, and supposing that his readers would understand it just as well, it is not likely that he dreamed of their holding him to a close arithmetical calculation, or of their raising a question about an inexactness of half or three quarters of a score of years in a space of four or five centuries.

Still, if we will hold him to such exactness, I think that there is something to be said in his behalf. The subject of his meditations had been that term of " seventy years," " whereof the word of the Lord came to Jeremiah the prophet." Now Jeremiah had twice used that expression; — once, of the *destruction* of the land by Nebuchadnezzar; * once, more particularly,

———————————

* Jer. xxv. 9 – 12.

of a return of the people "back from captivity." *
These might, for such a use as that in the passage before us, be not unfitly regarded as two independent
subjects. The captivity from which the people returned was coincident with the sack of Jerusalem;
and with that event, accordingly, the writer dates the
beginning of the seven times seven years which expired at the time of the Persian conquest. The series
of heavy national calamities did not, however, then begin. It might suitably be regarded as beginning with
the time of Jehoiakim's rebellion and subjugation, to
which time the backward computation of sixty-two
times seven years from the fourth year preceding the
reëstablishment of the temple worship by Judas in
fact conducts us.

"After sixty-two weeks shall an anointed one be cut
off, without deliverance." † It is no longer "an anointed *prince*" that is spoken of, as in the preceding verse.
The omission of that word here is significant, and may
well be understood as indicating a reference to an
anointed personage not of princely character. Priests,
as well as princes, were instituted in their office by
the ceremony of unction. Onias the Third, the last
worthy representative of the ancient line of priests,
was put to death in or about the year 170.‡ He was
"cut off without deliverance," or, as the words perhaps would better be rendered, "without any *successor*," i. e. fit to be called such. To him, accordingly,
these words have been thought to refer. I incline to
think, however, that the "cutting off" and abandon-
ment§ are rather to be interpreted of the discontin-

---

* Jer. xxix. 10 – 14.   † Dan. ix. 26.
‡ See above, pp. 190 – 192.
§ The literal translation of the words rendered " without deliverance "
(לוֹ אֵין) is " and not [or *nothing*] to it [or *him*]."

uance of the high-priest's functions at the time of the pollution of the temple by Antiochus.

"And the city and the sanctuary shall be destroyed by the people of the prince that shall come, whose end shall be as by a flood; and to the end of the war is desolation appointed." The times of desolation by Antiochus began in the year 169 B. C., at his first visit to Jerusalem, and became more grievous two years after, when he ordered the temple to be desecrated, and the worship to cease.

"And he shall establish a covenant with many *in the* [not, *for*] one week," that is, the covenant of the Jewish apostates to adopt Gentile customs.* He did not establish it for one week, or for any precise length of time. But he established it in that time, which, according to the scheme of the passage, constituted the only remaining week of years.

"During half a week he shall cause the sacrifice and the oblation to cease, and upon the battlement of the temple shall be the abominations of the destroyer, until the appointed destruction is poured out upon the destroyer." † According to the history in the First Book of the Maccabees, it was on "the fifteenth day of the month Casleu in the hundred forty and fifth year" (that is, of the Seleucidan era), that the Syrians "set up the abomination of desolation upon the altar," and it was on "the five-and-twentieth day of the ninth month, which is called the month Casleu, in the hundred forty and eighth year," that the Jews again "offered sacrifice according to the law." ‡ The interval is three years and ten days. But Josephus, as we have already seen, § makes statements of the

---

* See above, pp. 134, 190.   † Dan. ix. 27; comp. xi. 31; xii. 11.

‡ 1 Mac. i. 54, 59; iv. 52, 53; vi. 7.

§ See above, p. 431, note *.

time still more closely corresponding to that in
Daniel.

In the tenth chapter we see only the machinery employed to introduce the contents of the eleventh, in
which, in the form of a prediction uttered to Daniel
by a visionary person, we have a summary of the history from the time of Cyrus (to whose third year the
revelation is referred), to the death of Antiochus Epiphanes.* The " three kings in Persia," successors of
Cyrus, are Cambyses, Smerdis, and Darius Hystaspis.
The fourth, " richer than they all," who, " relying
upon his riches," should " stir up all against the
realm of Greece," is Xerxes the First, whose invasion
was repelled at Salamis.† The " mighty king " who
should " arise, and rule with great dominion, and do
according to his will," but whose kingdom should be
" broken," and not pass to his posterity, is Alexander
the Great. ‡ The course of events during the reigns
of the Greek kings " of the North," or Syria, and
" of the South," or Egypt ; the accessions respectively
of Ptolemy Lagus and Seleucus Nicator ; § the family alliance between Ptolemy Philadelphus and Antiochus Theos, and its consequences ; ‖ the successes of
Ptolemy Euergetes against Seleucus Callinicus ; ¶ the
renewal of the war by the sons of the latter, namely,
Seleucus Ceraunus and Antiochus the Great, against
Ptolemy Philopator, and the changing fortunes of
that war ; ** the treacherous betrothal of the daughter

---

* With xi. 2–4, comp. Vol. III. pp. 152–154, 157, 161–170; IV. 134
–148, 187–199. But, for further particulars of the history thus sketched,
the English reader, who may be curious on the subject, will do well to consult Wintle and Prideaux. — It will not fail to have been observed, that
the four professed prophecies in chaps. ii., vii., viii., and xi. all relate to the
same general series of events, and each is more full than the preceding.

† Dan. xi. 2.   ‡ xi. 3, 4.   § xi. 5.
‖ xi. 6.   ¶ xi. 7–9.   ** xi. 10–16.

of Antiochus to Ptolemy Epiphanes; * the stop put
to that monarch's ambitious movements by the Romans, and his death; † the unimportant reign of Seleucus Philopator, and his secret murder; ‡ and much
more particularly the whole series of transactions in
the time of Antiochus Epiphanes, § as we have already
become acquainted with them from the Books of the
Maccabees, including the circumstances of his rise to
power, his negotiations and wars with Egypt, his ostentatious impieties, his oppression of the Jews and
profanation of their temple, and the anxieties and furious passions which disturbed his last days, — are
portrayed with a detailed precision and correct sequence which are historical in all but the form.

With the death of Antiochus, the particularity of
the professed prediction ceases, the course of events
having been followed as far down as to the writer's
time, and as far as his knowledge extended. He passes
off into a declamatory strain, seemingly designed to
encourage those of his countrymen who had been faithful in the recent troubles to persevere in their righteous course, confiding that, by Michael's agency, and
through another struggle of yet unparalleled severity,
the day of glory long expected by their nation, the
day of their Messiah's government, was presently to
dawn. What was his precise meaning, or whether
there was any definite meaning in his mind, when he
spoke of the awaking of those that slept " in the
dust of the earth, ... some to everlasting life, and
some to shame, to everlasting contempt," and of the
promotion of those " that are wise," and " that turn
many to righteousness " to " shine as the brightness
of the firmament," and " as the stars," may admit of

---

* Dan. xi. 17.   † xi. 18, 19.   ‡ xi. 20.   § xi. 21 – 45.

doubt. But those commentators seem to have reason on their side who consider these expressions to be but strongly descriptive of the national and political revival which was looked for, accompanied, as it was expected to be, by a moral reform, and containing in itself the elements of perpetuity.*

As to the periods of time which the writer makes "the man clothed in linen" specify to Daniel, I suppose it is impossible to satisfy ourselves that we ascertain the sense in his mind. First, it is said that in a time, times and a half, and when the dispersion of a portion of the holy people should be at an end, all these things should be fulfilled; that is, apparently, in three years and a half from the re-dedication of the temple, thus completing a week of years from the beginning of the worst outrages of Antiochus; or, possibly, the three years and a half to come before the fulfilment of all things in the safe reëstablishment of the Jewish state, may have been designed to date from the death of that prince. Then it is said that "*from* the time when the daily sacrifice shall be taken away, and the abomination of the destroyer set up, there shall be a thousand two hundred and ninety days," or thirteen days over three years and a half. With what event this series of days, beginning with the abolition by Antiochus of the daily sacrifice, was to end, is not stated; probably we are to understand its end to be with the restoration of the sacrifice by Judas. And then it is added, "Happy is he that waiteth" six weeks after that, "and cometh to a thousand three

---

* Dan. xii. 1-3; comp. Is. xxvi. 19; Ezek. xxxvii. 1-14.—Grotius thinks ("Annot." *ad loc.*) that the reference is to the reappearance of those who, in the troubles of the time, had been driven into concealment "in dens and caves of the earth." (Comp. 1 Mac. ii. 28, 29; 2 Mac. v. 27; x. 6; Heb. xi. 38.) — With Dan. xii. 10 comp. xi. 35.

hundred and five and thirty days." Possibly this expression denotes the precise time when the author was writing this verse, and when, in the course which affairs were taking, he seemed to himself to discern a fair prospect of better things.*

The command to " shut up these words and seal this book even to the time of the end,"† if it signifies a direction to conceal the book till the time of Antiochus Epiphanes, when the events to which it relates should come to pass, accords with the opinion of its having been written in that prince's time, and with the plan of that class of fictions to which I understand it to belong. Its contents, so agreeable to the Asmonæan family, which occupied the throne down to the time of the usurpation of Herod, would naturally facilitate its attainment of that popular estimation which is indicated by its possession of the place in the Jewish canon which we find it occupying at the time of our earliest authorities in respect to that collection of writings.

There is nothing in the New Testament which can be called a quotation from this book, except that to which I have referred in one of the discourses of our Lord.‡ There are apparent references to its language, particularly in the Apocalypse, § but also in other books.||

---

* Dan. xii. 5 – 13. Grotius (" Annot." *ad loc.*) and Lardner (" Credibility," &c., Part II. chap. xxxvii. § 3) suppose that these forty-five days were intended to " reach to the time of the death of Antiochus."

† xii. 4; comp. 9; viii. 26.

‡ See above, p. 414.

§ ii. 44 (comp. Apoc. xi. 15); vii. 9, x. 5, 6 (comp. Apoc. i. 14, 15); vii. 10 (comp. Apoc. v. 11, xx. 12); vii. 11, 26 (comp. Apoc. xix. 20); vii. 13 (comp. Apoc. xiv. 14) ; vii. 22, 27 (comp. Apoc. xx. 4); vii. 24 (comp. Apoc. xvii. 12) ; vii. 25 (comp. Apoc. xiii. 5, 6) ; viii. 26, xii. 4 (comp. Apoc. x. 4, xxii. 10) ; x. 13, 21 (comp. Apoc. xii. 7). Much of the machinery of the Apocalypse appears to have been suggested by the Book of Daniel.

|| ii. 34, 35, 44 (comp. Matt. xxi. 44,' Luke xx. 18); vii. 13 (comp.

I have spent an amount of time upon the study of comments on this book, altogether disproportioned to its importance, and which has contributed but little fruit to the remarks which I have made. The piece being of the irresponsible character which I have ascribed to it, I might perhaps have been justified in passing it over as lightly as I have done another composition which is not entirely unlike it, namely, the Second Book of Esdras, and contented myself with merely describing its contents, without attempting to ascertain the sense which lay beneath them in the author's mind. But I have thought that both the importance which has been attached to it through the various incorrect interpretations which have prevailed, and the facilities which it furnishes for arriving at its author's meaning in most parts, entitle it to a different treatment. I close this Lecture with a few sentences from a letter of Dr. Arnold, as high an Episcopalian authority, I suppose it will be allowed, as any of the present century: —

"I have long thought that the greater part of the Book of Daniel is most certainly a very late work, of the time of the Maccabees, and the pretended prophecy about the kings of Grecia and Persia, and of the North and South, is mere history, like the poetical prophecies in Virgil and elsewhere. In fact, you can trace distinctly the date when it was written, because the events up to the date are given with historical minuteness, totally unlike the character of real prophecy; and beyond that date all is imaginary. It is curious that, when there was so allowed a proof of the existence of apocryphal writings, under the name of the Book of Daniel, as the stories of the apocryphal

Matt. x. 23, xvi. 27, xxiv. 30, xxvi. 64) ; vii. 18 (comp. 1 Cor. vi. 2) ; xi. 36 (comp. 2 Thes. ii. 4).

Esther [?], Susanna, and Bel and the Dragon, those should have been rejected, because they were only known in the Greek translation; and the rest, because it happened to be in Chaldee, was received at once in the lump, and defended as a matter of faith.   But the selfsame criticism which has established the authenticity of St. John's Gospel against all questionings, does, I think, equally prove the non-authenticity of great part of Daniel ; that there may be genuine fragments in it, is very likely." *

---

* Arnold's "Life and Correspondence," Letter 222.

LECTURE LXIX.

THE BOOK OF ESTHER.

Relation of the Book to the Feast of Purim.—Its Contents.—
Account of a Feast made by King Ahasuerus,—of the Divorce
of Vashti,—of the Promotion of Esther,—of the Malice of
Haman,—of the Royal Decree for an Extermination of the
Jews,—of Honors done by the Royal Command to Mordecai,—
of the Intercession of Esther for her People,—of the Execution of Haman,—of the successful Self-defence of the Jews,
—of the Institution of the Feast of *Purim* to commemorate
the Transaction,—of the Imposition of a Tribute by Ahasuerus,—and of a Registration by Mordecai of the Transactions of his Reign.—Apocryphal Portions.—Dream of Mordecai.—His Disclosure of a Conspiracy against the King.—
Proclamations of Artaxerxes.—Authorship of the Book.—Time
and Place of its Composition.—Question as to its Historical
or Fictitious Character.—Alexandrine Arrangement of the
Apocryphal Parts.—Canonical Authority of the Hebrew Portion.—No Quotation from it in the New Testament.—Comparison with the Books of Tobit and Judith.

The Book of Esther professes to relate the occasion
of the institution of the Feast of Purim, or *Lots*, the
Saturnalia of the Jews, celebrated yearly on the fourteenth and fifteenth days of the month Adar, which
nearly corresponds to our September.

According to the statement in this book, " Ahasuerus, who reigned from India even unto Ethiopia,
over an hundred and seven and twenty provinces,"
" made a feast unto all his princes and his servants " at
his Persian capital, Shushan, " in the third year of
his reign." It lasted six months; " and when these
days were expired, the king made a feast unto all the

people that were present in Shushan the palace, both unto great and small, seven days." The furniture was of the richest description; the drinking-vessels were of gold, the couches of gold and silver, and the other appointments of corresponding magnificence. Wine was abundant, but no guest was compelled to drink.*

" On the seventh day, when the heart of the king was merry with wine," he sent the officers of his household to summon his beautiful queen, Vashti, who meanwhile was keeping similar hospitality for the women, to come and display her charms before the revellers. With womanly and queenly dignity she refused, and the offended monarch consulted his chamberlains respecting a proper punishment for her contumacy. They advised him that it was of bad example; that it would encourage other women to "despise their husbands in their eyes"; that thence would " arise too much contempt and wrath"; and that the proper course for their master was to divorce Vashti, and supply her place with " another better than she." " And the saying pleased the king, and . . . . . he sent letters into all the king's provinces, into every province according to the writing thereof, and to every people after their language, that every man should bear rule in his own house." †

Ahasuerus acceded to the proposal of his courtiers to collect young women from all the provinces of the empire, from whom the king should make his choice of one to " be queen instead of Vashti." There was at Shushan at the time " a certain Jew, whose name was Mordecai, the son of Jair, the son of Shimei, the son of Kish, a Benjamite, who had been carried away from Jerusalem with the captivity which had been carried

* Esther i. 1-8.   † i. 9-22.

away with Jechoniah, king of Judah, whom Nebuchadnezzar, the king of Babylon, had carried away ; and
he brought up Hadassah (that is, Esther) his uncle's
daughter ; for she had neither father nor mother ; and
the maid was fair and beautiful ; whom Mordecai
(when her father and mother were dead) took for his
own daughter." Esther was one of those who were
brought into the royal harem, where she refrained
from disclosing her lineage, agreeably to the caution
of Mordecai, who came every day to the precincts of
her abode, to inform himself of her welfare and prospects. Presented to the king, "she obtained grace
and favor in his sight more than all the virgins, so
that he set the royal crown upon her head, and made
her queen instead of Vashti," celebrating her coronation with "a great feast," a remission of taxes, and a
distribution of presents. She was further endeared
to Ahasuerus by making known to him a conspiracy
(of which she had information through Mordecai) of
two of his chamberlains against his life.*

With the promotion of his kinswoman, Mordecai
had been advanced to a service about the royal residence. Haman, an Amalekite, was distinguished by
the king's favor "above all the princes that were with
him." By the royal command, all "the king's servants, that were in the king's gate," did him homage
as he passed, — all but Mordecai, who, whether from
knowledge of his character, or from hereditary national
antipathy, greeted him with no token of respect. His
associates, having remonstrated with him to no purpose, called the attention of Haman to his discourtesy,
at the same time making known his Jewish birth.
Furiously incensed, Haman "thought scorn to lay

* Esther ii. 1 – 23.

hands on Mordecai alone," and "sought to destroy all
the Jews that were throughout the whole kingdom."

Having "cast *Pur*, that is, the lot," and been directed by this divination to the month Adar for the
execution of his bloodthirsty purpose, he informed
Ahasuerus that there was a disorderly people dispersed
through his provinces, whom it was "not for the king's
profit to suffer"; and he proposed to the king to give
orders for their extirpation, engaging on that condition to pay ten thousand talents of silver of his own
into the royal treasury. The king assented; with his
signature and seal, "letters were sent by posts into
all the king's provinces, to destroy, to kill, and to
cause to perish all Jews, both young and old, little
children and women, in one day, even upon the
thirteenth day of the twelfth month (which is the
month Adar) and to take the spoil of them for a prey;
. . . . . the posts went out, being hastened by the
king's commandment; . . . . . and the king and Haman sat down to drink, but the city Shushan was perplexed." *

The decree carried consternation into every settlement of the Jews. Clothed in "sackcloth with ashes,"
and weeping bitterly as he passed through the streets,
Mordecai came to the palace gate. Informed by her
household of his presence and of his squalid attire,
Esther "sent raiment to clothe Mordecai, ... but
he received it not." Through an attendant sent to inquire the cause of his forlorn appearance, he conveyed
intelligence to her of the desperate condition of their
people, and charged her to intercede for their deliverance with her royal husband. She returned him
word that it was impossible, for she had not lately

---

* Esther iii. 1 - 15. — "Haman, the son of Hammedatha, the Agagite"
(1); comp. 1 Sam. xv. 8.

been called into the king's presence, and whoever approached it unsummoned did it at the sacrifice of life,
unless the king should indicate his forgiveness of the
offence by extending the golden sceptre. He replied,
that it was no time for such considerations; that
her own fate was involved in the sentence proclaimed
against her kindred, and might overtake her, even if
safety for others should spring up from some other
source; and that perhaps it was for the very purpose
of delivering her nation in this strait that Providence
had raised her to the throne. Acknowledging her
mission, she desired Mordecai to cause the Jews in
Shushan to keep a fast of three days in her behalf,
while she should prepare herself for her dangerous
enterprise by a similar act of devotion. "If I perish,"
said she, "I perish." *

The king was sitting on his throne on the third day
after, when Esther, having " put on her royal apparel,"
stood before him. "She obtained favor in his sight,
and the king held out to Esther the golden sceptre
that was in his hand." He asked what she desired,
and promised that she should have it, were it half of his
kingdom. She replied, that she but wished to have the
king and Haman come that day to a banquet she had
made ready. Ahasuerus caused Haman to be summoned accordingly; at table he repeated the inquiry
what favor it was that Esther would have granted;
and was requested to allow her petition to be presented at another banquet, the next day, in the same
presence. As Haman, transported with such signal
honors, went " forth that day joyful, and with a glad
heart," he passed again by the stubborn and motion-
less Mordecai. Smothering his rage till he reached his

---

* Esther iv. 1 - 17.

home, he there " called for his friends, and Zeresh his
wife," and to them exposed his intolerable disquiet.
He " told them of the glory of his riches, and the
multitude of his children, and all the things wherein
the king had promoted him," and how he had sat with
the king and queen, and was to sit again, at their private banquet. " Yet all this," he said, " availeth me
nothing, so long as I see Mordecai the Jew sitting at
the king's gate." They advised him to have a gallows
erected fifty cubits high, and to apply the next day to
the king for an order to hang Mordecai upon it.
" And the thing pleased Haman, and he caused the
gallows to be made." *

The king that night was sleepless; and, to while
away the hours, he ordered " the book of records of
the chronicles " to be brought and read to him. Having listened to the narration of the disclosure by Mordecai of the design of his chamberlains against his
life, he asked how that service had been rewarded.
Being told that no requital had been made, he inquired what courtier was in attendance. Haman,
who was already in an ante-room, awaiting an opportunity to present his suit for Mordecai's execution, was
summoned into the royal presence, and commanded
to give his advice as to what should be " done unto
the man whom the king delighteth to honor." Supposing that it must be himself that was meant, Haman
advised that the person so distinguished should be
robed in " the royal apparel," and, wearing the king's
crown, and mounted on the king's horse, should be
conducted through the streets of the city by " one of
the king's most noble princes, making proclamation
before him, " Thus shall it be done to the man whom

---

* Esther v. 1 – 14.

the king delighteth to honor." The king took him
at his word, and directed him to confer these singular
distinctions on Mordecai the Jew. He did so, and
then, while Mordecai withdrew to his accustomed post,
returned, wretched with envy and baffled malice, to his
home.*

His wife and his friends had scarcely had time to
express their provoking solicitude for this cloud over
his fortunes, when the royal chamberlains appeared to
conduct him to Queen Esther's banquet. When the
king now repeated his inquiry of the preceding day,
Esther said that her suit was for her life and that of
her people, who had been sentenced to die, and for
whom, if only doomed to bondage, she might not have
ventured to intercede. " ' Who is he, and where is he,' "
demanded Ahasuerus, " ' that durst presume in his
heart to do so?' And Esther said, ' The adversary and
enemy is this wicked Haman.' " The king, enraged, rose
from table, and went into the adjoining garden, while
the trembling Haman sued for his life to the queen.
The king, returning to the apartment, was still further
incensed at what he construed as the offensive familiarity of Haman with Esther, and, being told of the
gallows erected in Haman's house for Mordecai, ordered that he should be hanged thereon. It was done,
and " then was the king's wrath pacified."†

Ahasuerus confiscated the property of Haman, and
gave it to his queen, appointing Mordecai to administer it, of whose relationship to Esther he was now informed, and on whom also he bestowed the ring which
had formerly attested the authority of his defeated
rival. But the decree which had been issued against
the Jews remained in force. With tears, Esther en-

---

* Esther vi. 1 – 12.   † vi. 13 – vii. 10.

treated the king to revoke it, but in vain. "The writing," said he, "which is written in the king's name,
and sealed with the king's ring, may no man reverse."
All that could be done to repair the injustice, he
did. He ordered Mordecai to send "letters by post
on horseback, and riders on mules, camels, and young
dromedaries, wherein the king granted the Jews which
were in every city to gather themselves together, and
to stand for their life, to destroy, to slay, and to cause
to perish, all the power of the people and province that
would assault them, both little ones and women, and
to take the spoil of them for a prey." "And Mordecai
went out from the presence of the king in royal apparel of blue and white, and with a great crown of
gold, and with a garment of fine linen and purple......
And in every province, and in every city, whithersoever
the king's commandment and his decree came, the
Jews had joy and gladness, a feast and a good day.
And many of the people of the land became Jews; for
the fear of the Jews fell upon them." *

It might have been anticipated that the two parties,
armed respectively with royal decrees of opposite tenor,
would have proceeded in a manner different from what
is related, and that the Jews would either have sunk
under the overwhelming onset of their adversaries
authorized by the first decree, or that those adversaries
would not, by an unnecessary assault, have provoked
that retribution on the part of the Jews which had
been authorized by the second. But such was not the
issue. When the thirteenth day of the month Adar
came round, the day fixed by Haman for their massacre, "the Jews gathered themselves together in their
cities, throughout all the provinces of the king, Ahas-

---

* Esther viii. 1 - 17.

uerus, to lay hand on such as sought their hurt; .....
and all the rulers of the provinces, and the lieutenants,
and the deputies, and officers of the king helped the
Jews, because the fear of Mordecai fell upon them."
They "smote all their enemies with the stroke of the
sword, and slaughter, and destruction, and did what
they would unto those that hated them." At the capital they "slew and destroyed five hundred men," and
the ten sons of Haman, besides "seventy and five
thousand men" in the provinces; "but on the spoil
laid they not their hand," though they had express
permission to do so.* Ahasuerus asked his queen
what further she would have, and gratified her by
allowing the slaughter to be renewed the next day
(when three hundred more lives were taken by the
Jews at Shushan), and by causing the bodies of Haman's dead sons to be suspended on their father's gallows. Accordingly, "the Jews of the villages, that
dwelt in the unwalled towns, made the fourteenth day
of the month Adar a day of gladness and feasting, and
a good day, and of sending portions one to another, and
gifts to the poor," while, in reference to their double
exploit, "the Jews that were at Shushan" having
"assembled together on the thirteenth day thereof,
and on the fourteenth thereof," kept their commemoration "on the fifteenth day of the same, and made it
a day of feasting and gladness."

At Mordecai's instance, they resolved to make this
celebration perpetual, from year to year; and "called
these days 'Purim,' after the name of Pur," because
Haman "had cast Pur (that is, *the lot*) to consume
them and to destroy them." And "the Jews ordained,
and took upon them, and upon their seed, and upon

---

* Comp. viii. 11.

all such as joined themselves unto them, so as it should not fail, that they should keep these two days, according to their writing, and according to their appointed time, every year; and that these days should be remembered and kept throughout every generation, every family, every province, and every city, and that these days of Purim should not fail from among the Jews, nor the memorial of them perish from their seed." And the queen lent her authority to confirm these arrangements of her kinsmen through the hundred and twenty-seven Persian provinces.*

The king " laid a tribute upon the land and upon the isles of the sea." Of the transactions of his reign, and of the greatness to which he had advanced Mordecai, a record was made " in the book of the chronicles of the kings of Media and Persia; for Mordecai the Jew was next unto King Ahasuerus, and great among the Jews, and accepted of the multitude of his brethren, seeking the wealth of his people, and speaking peace to all his seed."†

Here ends what is found of the Book of Esther in the Hebrew language and in the Protestant canon. The Septuagint interpolates in different parts a quantity of other matter, amounting in the whole to more than half as much as the canonical book; and it is remarkable that in these parts there is frequent reference to God, while neither the name of the Supreme Being, nor any allusion to him, once occurs in the canonical writing. In the Vulgate, these passages are all brought together at the end of the book, and this order is adopted in the Apocryphal collection in our English Bibles. For the English reader's convenience, I shall follow it in my remarks.

---

* Esther ix. 1 – 32.   † x. 1 – 3.

In the continuation, as it stands in the Latin and
English, Mordecai is represented as saying that the
events related had taken place in fulfilment of a dream
of his, in which Esther had been represented by a full-
flowing river springing from a little fountain and reflecting the sun, and himself and Haman by two dragons. He ascribes to God's gracious providence that
deliverance of the people which is to be commemorated
hereafter through all their generations; and he appears
to give a different explanation of the origin of the
name of the Feast of Purim, as being derived from lots
drawn before God to determine whether the Jews or
their adversaries should prevail.*

Of this dream, and of the events which ensued, the
writer proceeds to give an account, indicating the
channel through which it had reached him. " In the
fourth year," he says, " of Ptolemeus and Cleopatra,†
Dositheus, who said he was a priest and Levite, and
Ptolemeus his son, brought this epistle of Phurim,
which they said was the same, and that Lysimachus,
the son of Ptolemeus, that was in Jerusalem, had interpreted it." By the words " this epistle of Phurim,"
seems to be denoted the narrative which follows, of the
circumstances of the origin of the feast known by that
name.

Describing the lineage of Mordecai, and the circumstances under which he was at Susa, in a manner according with the previous statement,‡ it relates that
he dreamed of seeing two dragons " ready to fight ";
then, " all nations " roused by their cry to " fight

---

* Esther x. 4–13. With 10, 11 comp. iii. 7.

† Among the many Ptolemies and Cleopatras of the Greek-Egyptian history, it is impossible to determine which were intended, so as to fix this
date.

‡ With xi. 2–4 comp. ii. 5, 6.

against the righteous people"; then, when the righteous people called upon God, "a little fountain"
bursting forth, which "was made a great flood"; after
which "the light and the sun rose up, and the lowly
were exalted, and devoured the glorious." This dream
Mordecai remembered, and was curious as to its
sense.*

Lodging in the same apartment with two officers of
the king, Mordecai overheard a plot of theirs against
his life, which he hastened to make known. Being
put to the torture, they confessed and were strangled.
Artaxerxes and Mordecai both made a record of the
transaction. Mordecai was promoted in requital of
his service; and "Aman, the son of Amadathus the
Agagite, who was in great honor with the king, sought
to molest Mardocheus and his people, because of the
two eunuchs of the king." †

The narrative proceeds abruptly with a copy of the
proclamation addressed by Artaxerxes to the princes
and governors of his hundred and twenty-seven provinces, commanding them to put the Jews to death; ‡ then
follow prayers, said to have been offered by Mordecai
and Esther for their deliverance, while "all Israel in
like manner cried most earnestly unto the Lord, because their death was before their eyes." §

On the third day Esther is related to have changed

---

* Esther xi. 1-12. — " This epistle of Phurim, which they said was *the
same* " (1); that is, I think, containing substantially the same history, or a
history relating to the same institution, as that recorded in the previous
chapters of the book.

† xii. 1-6. — This account differs from the preceding in the names of
the conspirators, in the omission of the particular of their being informed
against through Esther, and in the statement of Mordecai's having given
offence to Haman, by his loyalty on this occasion. Comp. ii. 21-iii. 6.

‡ xiii. 1-7 (comp. iii. 12, 13). In xiii. 6, the royal proclamation calls
a month by its Jewish name.

§ xiii. 7-xiv. 19.

her mourning for sumptuous attire, and, attended by
two maids, to have presented herself in an agony of
terror before the king, who "was very dreadful," as
he "sat upon his royal throne." "He looked very
fiercely upon her, and the queen fell down, and was
pale, and fainted, and bowed herself upon the head of
the maid that went before her; then God changed the
spirit of the king into mildness," and he revived her
with caresses. But so agitating was the interview,
that, "as she was speaking, she fell down for faint-
ness; then the king was troubled, and all his servants
comforted her." *

The completion of the history is implied, rather
than related, in another royal proclamation, wherein
Artaxerxes, after some general remarks upon the perfidy of courtiers, informs the governors and subjects
of his wide empire, that "Aman, a Macedonian, the
son of Amadatha," had imposed upon his confiding
and generous nature, and, aiming to "have translated
the kingdom of the Persians to the Macedonians," had
induced him to consent to the destruction of his friends,
the faithful people of his "blameless Esther." Aman,
he informs them, had been "hanged at the gates of
Susa, with all his family"; and he advises them, not
only "not to put in execution the letters" ordering the
extermination of the Jews, but to "aid them, that . . . . .
they may be avenged on them who in the time of their
affliction shall set upon them; for Almighty God hath
turned to joy unto them the day, wherein the chosen
people should have perished." He directs them, therefore, among their "solemn feasts to keep it an high
day with all feasting, that both now and hereafter
there may be safety to" himself, "and the well-affected

---

* Esther xv. 1 – 16.

Persians"; and he denounces severe tokens of his displeasure against all who shall disobey.*

On the question of the authorship of this book we have no light, either from history, or from any part of its own contents. No opinion which has been expressed respecting it rests upon any thing better than mere unsupported conjecture.

To what time is the composition to be referred? As to this we can say nothing more definite, than that it was a time considerably subsequent to that of the king (whoever he was) designated by the name of Ahasuerus, and apparently later than that of the Persian dynasty. For the reigning prince is described as being that "Ahasuerus which reigned from India even unto Ethiopia, over an hundred and seven and twenty provinces";† and in two instances statements are made of ancient usages, of which, it would seem, readers of the author's time needed to be informed, in order to a full comprehension of the narrative.‡ The Hebrew style is that of the latest age of which any specimens exist in the New Testament. From his apparent familiarity with the customs and localities of Persia, it would appear that the writer was a Persian Jew.§ And it is likely that he wrote a considerable time after the Greek conquest of that empire. From the account of the bringing into Egypt of "the epistle of Phurim," "in the reign of Ptolemeus and Cleopatra," by "Dositheus, who said he was a priest and Levite," it appears highly probable that nothing was known in Egypt either of the book, or of the festival whose origin it professed to explain, till the Ptolemies reigned in that country.

---

* Esther xvi. 1–24.   † i. 1.   ‡ i. 13; viii. 8.
§ i. 1, 3–9, 14, 15, 19; ii. 9, 21, 23; iii. 7, 12, 13; iv. 6, 11; v. 4, 9; vi. 1; viii. 8.

Does the book contain a true history, or mere fiction, or a basis of true history with a superstructure of fable?

The numerous and great improbabilities in the history weigh against the supposition of its truth. Ahasuerus keeps a feast for six months together, assembling about him all his great men, and leaving their provinces deprived of government. Haman's malice against a single Jew for refusing to do him reverence demands the sacrifice of probably not less than two millions of people in one day, and the king easily agrees to that extravagant request. The savage decree is issued in the first month of the year, to be executed in the twelfth; what sane man, intending its execution, would have given this notice? But it was given; and what were the doomed race doing in the interval? Were they fleeing, or preparing to defend themselves? Neither, according to the history; but quietly waiting their fate. When the king alters his mind respecting their extirpation, he does not rescind his decree (a step which it is said he was precluded from taking by a fundamental law of his empire), but, in place of so doing, he authorizes the Jews, if molested, to massacre those native subjects of his whom he had before called upon to massacre them; and with a full knowledge of his last decree, those subjects proceed to provoke the legalized hostility of the Jews by assailing them agreeably to the tenor of the first. More than seventy-five thousand Persians, after eight months' notice, suffer themselves to be butchered in one day by the Jews; and, as if this were not enough, the king, at Esther's request, allows another day for this carnival of blood. On the occasion of the disobedience of his wife, the king is advised by his august conclave, and actually proceeds, with all solemnity, to send "letters into all the king's provinces, into every province according to the writing thereof, and to every people after their language, that every man should bear rule in his own house." Haman promises to the king, as the price of his revenge, a sum amounting, according to different calculations, to ten millions, or to more than twenty millions of dollars.* The king orders Haman to be hanged with as little deliberation or reason, as had prompted him before to take Haman's money and indulge his revenge.

I have not specified by any means all the statements of this description which a careful reader observes, but only some of the principal. But if, in view of such statements, we feel obliged to conclude that the work is not to be received as true history, it is to be admitted, on the other hand, to have probably had some historical basis. The Feast of Purim, though not mentioned in the New Testament, nor anywhere in the Old Testament † except in the Book of Esther, has been observed among the Jews, as their *Saturnalia*, from the earliest time of their having a place in profane history. From the narrative in this book, it seems reasonable to infer as much as this: that the Feast was instituted by the captive Jews in Persia, to commemorate their deliverance from a persecution, with which, at the instance of some powerful enemy of their race, they had been threatened by the government. The story was preserved by tradition, which treated it as usual, amplifying and embellishing very freely, and erecting on a narrow basis of truth a large structure of fiction. At length it was set down in writing, in the form in which it has been transmitted to our day.

---

* Prideaux, "Connection," &c., Part I. Book V. An. 453.

† It is referred to in 2 Mac. xv. 36, under the name of Mardocheus's day.

The question, who was meant by Ahasuerus, has of
course been largely discussed by critics who have interpreted the book as containing authentic history.
Josephus,* and after him Prideaux,† understood Artaxerxes Longimanus to be intended.   But such,
whatever was the writer's meaning, could not have
been the fact, inasmuch as that monarch ascended
the throne in the year 464 B. C., a hundred and thirty-
five years after that captivity of Jeconiah in which
Mordecai is said to have been carried to Babylon.‡
The Book of Nehemiah speaks of the queen of Artaxerxes,§ but without any hint that she was a Jewess.
Nor did his well-known character at all accord with
that which is attributed to the Ahasuerus of this book.

The same objection on account of the time when
Mordecai is said to have lived applies with nearly
equal force to Xerxes the First, supposed by Jahn
and others to have been meant; he was father of
Artaxerxes Longimanus, and preceded him on the
throne by only twenty-one years.   The immediate
predecessor of Xerxes was Darius Hystaspis, the first
Persian monarch whose government was as extensive
as that of Ahasuerus is said to have been ; and he,
according to Herodotus,‖ was also the Persian monarch who first levied a tax on his subjects,¶ and who
instituted a council of seven princes.** But Darius
came to the throne seventy-eight years after the captivity of Jehoiachin, when Mordecai, who shared in
that captivity, must have reached an extreme age, and

---

* " Antiq. Jud.," Lib. XI. cap. 6, § 1.
† " Connection," &c., Part I. Book V. An. 462.
‡ Esther ii. 5 – 7.
§ Neh. ii. 6.
‖ Lib. III. § 89.
¶ Comp. Esther x. 1.
** Herod. Lib. III. § 84 ; comp. Esther i..10.

his niece could no longer have been so distinguished as was Esther for personal charms.* Darius Hystaspis married daughters of Cyrus and of one of his associates in the conspiracy against Smerdis; he would hardly have dared ignominiously to divorce one of them. Not one of the names of his counsellors, preserved by Herodotus,† corresponds with the names of the same officers in this book; ‡ nor did his character or his treatment of the Jews § at all correspond with what is here reported of Ahasuerus. The Persian kings before Darius were Cyaxares, Cyrus, Cambyses, and Smerdis; but the longest of their reigns was of less than eight years' duration, whereas Ahasuerus is represented to have reigned at least twelve or thirteen years.‖ In short, it is in vain to undertake to show what Persian king the author had in his mind. It is not likely that the author himself entertained any such question. He set down what had reached him of the occasion of an ancient institution. As to time and characters, he was writing at a venture.

I have already remarked, that those portions of the Book of Esther which are not found in the Hebrew Bible are in the Septuagint interpolated in different parts of the canonical book, so as to make with it one connected whole.

The Greek copy opens with the account of the dream of Mordecai, and of the information conveyed by him

---

* To escape this inference, it has been suggested that it is not Mordecai, but his great-grandfather, Kish, who is related to have been carried to Babylon with Jehoiachin; with what probability, let the reader compare Esther ii. 5, 7, and judge.

† Lib. III. §§ 70, 84.

‡ Esther i. 14.

§ Comp. Joseph. " Antiq. Jud.," Lib. XI. capp. 3, 4.

‖ Esther iii. 7.

to Ahasuerus, of the conspiracy against his life.* Here are given the same statements as in a later place, of the descent of Mordecai, and of his transportation to Babylon with Jehoiachin; † a mere repetition without use, if both originally made parts of the same treatise. Here, also, the promotion of Mordecai to be "a great man, a servitor in the king's court," is represented to have been as early as "the second year of the reign of Artaxerxes," and antecedent to the transactions described in the narrative; ‡ contrary to other statements, that he was not advanced till after the accession of Esther, and after the seventh year of that monarch's reign.§ The names of the two conspirators are here differently given; ‖ Mordecai "certified the king," it is said, as if he had the means of doing so directly, without any necessity of having recourse to Esther's intervention; ¶ he is related to have been rewarded for his fidelity at the time, and not on an investigation long after; ** and Haman is called a *Bugæan*, instead of an Agagite, as in the Hebrew, or a Macedonian, as elsewhere in the Greek.††

What purports to be a copy of the royal proclamation for the destruction of the Jews, is inserted in the Greek between the thirteenth and fourteenth verses of the third chapter of the canonical book.‡‡ The narrative appears incomplete without it.

---

* Esther xi. 2 – xii. 6.

† xi. 2 – 4 ; comp. ii. 5, 6.

‡ xi. 3 ; xii. 1.

§ i. 3 ; ii. 16, 19 ; iii. 1, 2.

‖ xii. 1 ; comp. ii. 21, vi. 2.

¶ xii. 2 ; comp. ii. 22.

** xii. 5 ; comp. vi. 3, *et seq.*

†† xii. 6 (the English version, I know not on what authority, avoids the word "Bugæan," which is in the Vulgate as well as in the Greek); comp. iii. 1 ; xvi. 10.

‡‡ xiii. 1 – 7.

Between the fourth and fifth chapters are inserted prayers, said to have been offered by Mordecai and Esther after their conference on the perils encompassing their people; * after which follows an account of the same interview between Esther and the king which is related in the canonical book, but much more full and circumstantial than in the other account.† Indeed, these are so different, that they must be regarded as independent records of the same transaction, almost as much as the different accounts of the persecution under one of the Ptolemies. ‡

The proclamation in favor of the Jews, which is only related in the canonical book to have been issued, is in the Greek inserted in full in its place in the eighth chapter.§ In it, not only is Haman called ·" a Macedonian," but he is said to have plotted to reduce the Persians to the Macedonian sway, circumstances which sufficiently indicate the comparatively modern date of the composition.‖ What is further observable is, that in this decree the Persians are commanded by their king to keep a festival of rejoicing for the Jews' escape, instead of its being a merely national commemoration.¶

Finally, the Greek book closes with the statement, that Mordecai remembered the dream related at its beginning, and, in the light of the great transactions through which he had passed, he now clearly saw its significance.**

The Book of Esther belongs to the class of the Jewish *Aggadoth*, as that description of writings has been

---

* Esther xiii. 7–xiv. 19.   † xv. 1–16; comp. v. 1, 2.
‡ See above, pp. 213–215.   § xvi. 1–24; comp. viii. 13.
‖ xvi. 10, 14.   ¶ xvi. 1, 22–24; comp. ix. 20–22.
** x. 4–13.

heretofore defined.*   As to its canonical authority, it is not embraced in the catalogue of Melito, nor in those of Athanasius and the Council of Carthage.†   It is not quoted, or referred to, in the New Testament.

"The Books of Judith and Esther," says the cautious Corrodi, "are not unlike. The former, too, is a story representing a Jewish woman as extricating her people from imminent danger of destruction, and so giving occasion to the institution of a Thanksgiving Feast. To that book and the Book of Tobit undeserved honor has been accorded, in their reception into the canon by so large a portion of the Christian world. Yet in my opinion the Book of Esther is inferior to both, in a moral point of view, presenting no such rules of conduct, no such pieces of devotion, no such intimations of future retribution, no such views of Divine Providence, as abound in the other two books."‡

---

* See above, p. 127, note †.
† See Vol. I. pp. 32, 37, 38.
‡ "Versuch einer Beleuchtung," u. s. w., ss. 125, 126.

LECTURE LXX.

HISTORY OF THE LATER JEWISH KINGDOM, AND CONCLUSION.

REIGN OF JOHN HYRCANUS, — OF ARISTOBULUS I., — OF ALEXANDER JAN-
NÆUS, — OF ALEXANDRA, — OF HYRCANUS, — OF ARISTOBULUS II. —
DISTURBANCES EXCITED BY THE PHARISEES. — ARRIVAL OF POMPEY IN
SYRIA. — REINSTATEMENT OF HYRCANUS. — RISE OF ANTIPATER TO
POWER. — CAPTURE OF JERUSALEM, AND CHANGES IN THE GOVERN-
MENT, BY THE ROMANS. — VISITS OF POMPEY AND CRASSUS TO THE
TEMPLE. — HYRCANUS DEPOSED, AND ANTIGONUS PLACED ON THE THRONE,
BY THE PARTHIANS. — HEROD THE GREAT MADE KING OF JUDEA BY
THE ROMANS. — HIS ESPOUSAL OF THE ASMONÆAN PRINCESS MARI-
AMNE. — HIS FORTUNES AND CHARACTER. — BUILDING OF CÆSAREA,
SEBASTE, A ROYAL PALACE, AND THE TEMPLE. — BIRTH OF JESUS AT
BETHLEHEM. — DEATH OF HEROD. — REIGN OF ARCHELAUS. — JUDÆA
REDUCED TO A ROMAN PROVINCE. — ADMINISTRATION OF COPONIUS, —
OF AMBIVIUS, — OF RUFUS, — OF GRATUS, — OF PONTIUS PILATE. —
SECTS OF THE ESSENES, — THE PHARISEES, — AND THE SADDUCEES. —
INSTITUTION AND WORSHIP OF THE SYNAGOGUES. — CURRENCY OF THE
ALEXANDRINE VERSION. — BAPTISM OF JESUS. — DISPERSION OF JEWS
THROUGHOUT THE EMPIRE. — CIRCUMSTANCES IN THE STATE OF OPIN-
ION, AND IN THE POLITICAL AND SOCIAL CONDITION OF THE ROMAN
WORLD, FAVORABLE TO THE PROMULGATION OF CHRISTIANITY.

THE First Book of Maccabees brought down the
history to the death of Simon, high-priest and governor of the Jews, the last survivor of the Asmonæan
brotherhood.* His son John, surnamed Hyrcanus,
who had distinguished himself in the recent military
operations, was at this time at Gazara,† where, receiving immediate information of his father's fate, and of

---

* See above, p. 177.
† Gazara (comp. 1 Mac. xiv. 34 ; xv. 28) I take to be the same as Gezer
(Josh. xvi. 3, 10 ; xxi. 21 ; Judg. i. 29).

the further designs of Ptolemy against himself, " he laid hands on them that were come to destroy him, and slew them." *

The administration of John, who succeeded his father as prince and high-priest, lasted thirty years, and was on the whole a prosperous one, though it began under discouraging circumstances. Antiochus Sidetes, who was then king of Syria, besieged him in Jerusalem, and compelled him to a capitulation, in which he agreed to pay a large annual subsidy, to throw down the fortifications of Jerusalem, and to build a fort for the Syrians on Mount Zion. Thus Judæa was again reduced to a tributary province for nine years. At the end of that time, Antiochus was defeated and slain in a great battle with the Parthians, and John, who had rendered him important services in the progress of the war, availed himself of the opportunity to recover the independence of his country. He drove the Syrians out of Judæa, in which they never afterwards established their dominion. Extending his conquests north and south, he overran Samaria and Galilee, which had been Greek territory since the time of Alexander, and destroyed the temple on Mount Gerizim and the city of Samaria, laying the latter under water. The Idumæans he compelled to adopt the Jewish religion, on pain of banishment from their country. He sent two embassies to Rome, to renew and confirm with that formidable power the friendly relations which had been established by his father. The close of his life was disturbed by a quarrel with the Pharisees, which sect now appears for the first time taking a part in public affairs. He had himself always belonged to them, but having been insulted by one of their number, he became the more

---

* 1 Mac. xvi. 22

susceptible of influence from the rival sect, the Sadducees, to which at length he publicly attached himself.*
I shall presently have a few words to say of these two
famous schools.

John left five sons, but bequeathed the government
of Judæa to his wife.   Aristobulus, however, the oldest son, succeeded in dispossessing her, and, first of
all the Jewish rulers since the Captivity, assumed the
style and state of king.   He threw his mother and
his three youngest brothers into prison, where the
former died of starvation.   His brother Antigonus he
treated kindly, employing him in his army and liber-
ally rewarding his services; till at last, being made
jealous of him by an artifice of the queen, he caused
him too to be slain by his guards.†   The reign of Aristobulus lasted but a year.   He is said to have died of
remorse for his brother's murder.   His administration
was marked by no event of consequence, except that
he made some addition, by conquests in Cœle-Syria,
to the extensive possessions of his father.

Alexander Jannæus, the oldest surviving brother
of Aristobulus, passed from his prison to the throne
in the year 104 B. C.   His reign of twenty-seven years
was a constant series of tumults, foreign and domestic.
His harsh and impetuous character kept him perpet-

---

* Josephus says that he was a prophet, as well as prince and high-priest,
for he predicted that his two eldest sons would not survive him long, and
that the third would succeed to the government; and when his sons gained
a victory over the Syrians, he knew it instantly, though Jerusalem, where
he was, was two days' journey distant from the scene of the conflict.
("Antiq. Jud.," Lib. XIII. cap. 10, §§ 3, 7; cap. 12, § 1.)   Josephus was
himself of the Asmonæan blood, being great-great-grandson, in the male
line, of a daughter of the hero Jonathan (see above, pp. 157–171), uncle
of John Hyrcanus.

† Josephus has a very circumstantial account of a prediction of the death
of Antigonus by one Judas, an Essene. ("Antiq. Jud.," Lib. XIII. cap.
11, § 2.)

ually engaged in wars with the bordering nations and
with his subjects. He sustained disastrous defeats from
the Egyptians, the Arabians, and the Syrians; but by
pertinacity and policy he enlarged his dominions to the
north, east, and south. Eight years before his death,
he composed affairs at home by a course of brutal
severity. Harassed, throughout his administration, by
the hostility of the Pharisees, an inheritance from his
father, and fearful of its consequences to his posterity,
he on his death-bed charged his queen, Alexandra,
to whom he bequeathed the government, to make
peace with them by taking them to her counsels, and
by delivering to them his body, to be visited with whatever insults they might see fit. The device succeeded.
They gave him a magnificent burial, and professed a
loyal devotion to his family. In his reign broke out
the long war between the Romans and Mithridates,
king of Pontus, fruitful of important consequences
to the Jews.

Alexander left two sons, Hyrcanus and Aristobulus,
whose rival pretensions made the chief element in Jewish politics for the next forty years. Hyrcanus, of a
mild and unambitious temper and moderate capacity,
was installed in the high-priesthood by his mother,
who assumed the government, while the younger son
was placed in command of the army, a trust suited to
the development of his vigorous and active character.
The Pharisees, though jealously regarded by Aristobulus and his friends, controlled every thing during
the nine years' reign of Alexandra, who, dreading the
civil dissensions of which she had had such sad experience, submitted with patience to their assumptions
and annoyances. A threatened invasion by Tigranes,
king of Armenia, was arrested by the advance of the
Romans, under Lucullus, into the territories of that

monarch. A conspiracy of Aristobulus, encouraged
by a dangerous sickness of his mother, to seize the
government, had become formidable at the time of
her death in the seventy-third year of her age. Josephus characterizes her as a woman who "showed none
of the weakness of her sex, but on the contrary an
eminent capacity for governing"; but he adds, that
her masculine passion for command, and subordina-
tion to it of the parental feelings, entailed lasting
calamities upon her family.*

Hyrcanus nominally succeeded to the government,
but at the end of three months, in the sequel of a battle with his brother's forces near Jericho, surrendered
the crown and high-priesthood to Aristobulus, and
retired to private life. There it appears that he would
have contentedly remained, but for the solicitations of
a courtier who had obtained a controlling power over
his feeble mind. Antipater was the son of one Antipas, a noble Idumæan, who had been governor of that
province under Alexander Jannæus. Having been attached, during the reign of Alexandra, to the party
of the court and of the Pharisees, and accordingly
feeling that he had little favor to look for from Aristobulus, who was their enemy, Antipater wrought upon
the fears of Hyrcanus, and persuaded him to flee from
Judea, and throw himself upon the protection of Are-
tas, king of Arabia Petræa. That prince conducted
him back with a force of fifty thousand men, with
which he took possession of Jerusalem. But Aristobulus having obtained by a large present the aid of
Scaurus, a lieutenant of Pompey in the conduct of
the Mithridatic war, who then lay at Damascus, Are-
tas retired, and Aristobulus resumed the government.

---

* "Antiq. Jud.," Lib. XIII. cap. 16, § 6.

Pompey having arrived at Damascus, the brothers appeared before him to present their rival claims. He deferred a decision of the question till he should have more leisure. The impatient Aristobulus took up arms; was defeated, and compelled to abdicate; again tried the fortune of war; and was besieged at Jerusalem by Pompey, who took the Temple by storm in the year 65 B. C. The Roman general entered the Temple, profaning even the Holy of Holies with his presence, but withdrew without rifling it of its treasures, contenting himself with ordering its walls, and those of the city, to be thrown down. He reinstated Hyrcanus in the government, on condition of the payment of an annual tribute, and took Aristobulus and his two sons prisoners with him to Rome.

On the way, Alexander, the elder of the sons, escaped, and, returning to Judea, renewed the disturbances in that province. He was defeated by Pompey's lieutenant, Gabinius, who proceeded to provide for the future quiet of the country by changing the form of its government. He divided it into five districts, each governed by a council, holding their sessions respectively at Jerusalem, Jericho, Gadara, Hamath, and Sepphoris in Galilee. The dignity of the high-priesthood appears to be all that now remained to the inefficient Hyrcanus, for Pompey had before forbidden his wearing a crown. Aristobulus also, and his younger son, Antigonus, soon after made their escape, and appeared in Judea in arms. They met with no better success than before. Both were made prisoners by Gabinius, and sent back to Rome. Aristobulus gave no further disturbance. He obtained the favor of Julius Cæsar, and was by him discharged from his captivity; but was presently after poisoned by the adherents of Pompey, by whom also Alexander, about the same time, was publicly executed at Antioch.

The government of Syria having, by the arrangements of the first Triumvirate, been assigned to Crassus, he came to Jerusalem in the year 54 B. C., and
plundered the temple of gold, says Josephus, to the
amount of ten thousand talents.* The next year he
was defeated and slain by the Parthians. Cæsar acted
a friendly part towards the Jews. He abolished the
aristocratic institutions of Gabinius, restored Hyrcanus
to his hereditary authority, and caused the Jews to be
declared by the Senate the allies of Rome. Antipater,
intrusted by Cæsar with the actual administration of
affairs, gave the government of Jerusalem to his son
Phasael, and that of Galilee to his younger son, Herod,
afterwards known as King Herod the Great.

After the battle of Philippi, the condition of things
in Judea depended on the will of Antony. Antipater
had the address to make him, too, his friend, and the
government of Hyrcanus remained unquestioned till
the time of the successes of the Parthians during Antony's voluptuous retirement in Egypt. Orodes, king
of Parthia, to whom Antigonus, younger son of Aristobulus, had retired after the death of his father and
brother, sent an army with him into Judea, which met
with no effectual resistance in placing him upon the
throne. Antipater had been poisoned by a rival courtier; Herod had fled to Rome; Hyrcanus and Phasael
fell into the hands of Antigonus; the latter escaped
threatened crucifixion by suicide; the former was sent
into banishment in Seleucia, his ears having been first
cut off, to render him for ever incapable of exercising
the functions of high-priest.

Meantime, Herod, who, by the favor of Hyrcanus,
had been betrothed to Mariamne, daughter of that

---

* " Antiq. Jud.," Lib. XIV. cap. 7, § 1.

prince's daughter Alexandra, and of Alexander, eldest son of Aristobulus, was pushing his interest at Rome. He asked no more than that the government and the high-priesthood might be confirmed to Aristobulus, brother of his bride, who united in his own blood the claims of the two rival houses; and that he himself might have such a subordinate place in the administration as had been filled by Antipater, his father. But the favor of Octavius and Antony marked him for a more splendid destiny. By a unanimous decree of the Senate, he was invested with the royal dignity, and was inaugurated at Rome, in the Capitol, one of the Triumvirs attending him in the procession on each side. Thus, in the year 37 B. C., was the Jewish royalty transferred, not only from the Asmonæan family, which had held it under different names for a hundred and thirty years, but to a person of foreign blood.

Herod, returning at once to Judea, prosecuted for three years his design upon the throne with doubtful prospects of success, for the party of Antigonus was in force, and the Roman armies found sufficient occupation with the Parthians. At length, with the help of a large force, commanded by Sosius, Antony's lieutenant in Syria, he took Jerusalem after a siege of six months. Antigonus surrendered himself, and was sent prisoner to Antioch, where he was put to death by Antony's order, at the instance of Herod.

The high-priesthood, which Herod's birth did not permit him to assume, belonged by hereditary right to Aristobulus, the young brother of the queen. Jealous of any thing which might give consequence to a member of the deposed family, Herod first promoted to that dignity an obscure person of the sacerdotal race, named Ananel, whom he brought from Babylon for

that purpose. After a while, yielding to the impor-
tunities of Mariamne and her mother, he made Aristobulus high-priest; but, disturbed by the favor which he
saw him winning with the people, he caused him to be
murdered by drowning, under circumstances intended
to make his death appear accidental. There remained
no member of the Asmonæan family to give him un-
easiness, except the old king, Hyrcanus, who, surrounded by a large population of his countrymen, was
living in a sort of royal state in Parthia. Herod invited him into Judea, and for a time treated him with
generosity and respect. But, after the reverses of his
friend Antony, his apprehension of being supplanted
in the government revived; and he found a pretence
for putting Hyrcanus to death, when that inoffensive
person had already passed his eightieth year. Repairing to Octavius when the fortune of Antony was seen
to have irrecoverably waned, he frankly avowed his
past hostility, and assured the conqueror that hence-
forward he was ready to serve him with the same constant and active friendship hitherto exercised towards
his rival. Octavius accepted the proposal, and continued ever after his fast friend.

Besides a magnificent palace on Mount Sion, Herod
built the cities of Sebaste (*Augusta*) in Samaria and
Cæsarea on the coast, giving them names in honor of
the emperor. But the work which had most interest
for his native subjects was the restoration of their
Temple, which, built under Nehemiah in an humble
style, had suffered much injury during the recent wars.
The rebuilding was begun in the year 17 B. C. In
less than ten years the edifice was ready for occupation, but it was still unfinished at the time of the
ministry of Jesus, when it was said to him, " Forty and

six years has this temple been in building." * Herod
appears to have designed this work to mitigate the
disgust which he had given to his people by freely
introducing Pagan customs, by the erection of a thea-
tre, and the institution of games in honor of Augustus.

Domestic troubles, often occasioned and always aggravated by his furious passions, made wretched the
declining days of Herod. In a fit of rage and jealousy
he put to death Mariamne, his favorite wife, and a
miserable remorse for that crime haunted him to his
grave. Alexander and Aristobulus, his sons by that
princess, he caused to be strangled, on an unfounded
suspicion of their aiming to supplant him in the kingdom. Antipater, a son by a former marriage, had,
like his brothers, been educated at Rome. Herod, re-
called him thence, and put him in prison. Falling
into a loathsome sickness, he attempted unsuccessfully
to commit suicide. He died at the age of seventy,
leaving directions in his will for the massacre of a
number of the principal men of the nation, in order,
as he said, that he might not die unmourned. One of
his last acts, carried into effect only five days before
his death, was an order for the execution of his son
Antipater. The deeds of frantic cruelty elsewhere
recorded of him fully prepare the reader for Matthew's account of his butchery of the infants of Beth-
lehem.

It was some time before the death of Herod, according to Matthew's narrative, that Jesus Christ was born.
Concerning the year when that event took place,
chronologists are not agreed. There is, perhaps, no
longer any dispute that our common era, which was
first established in the sixth century, fixes it too late;

---

* John ii. 20.

but how much too late — whether two, three, four, five, or even seven years — has been matter of discussion, and must be regarded as a point still undetermined.

Herod had ten wives. Four sons survived him; Archelaus and Herod Antipas, children of his sixth wife, Malthace, and Herod and Philip, born of Cleopatra of Jerusalem. By his last will, he bequeathed to Archelaus the sovereignty of Judea, Samaria, and Idumæa; Herod Antipas he made tetrarch of Galilee and Peræa; to Philip he gave Batanea, Trachonitis, and some other districts in the northeastern part of his dominions.

Archelaus went to Rome to present himself to Augustus, and after considerable opposition, made on the one part by the rival pretensions of his brother Antipas, who had been preferred to him in an earlier will of their father, and on the other by a disaffected portion of his subjects, instigated by the Pharisee leaders, he succeeded so far in his suit as to be authorized to administer the government under the title of *ethnarch*. He inherited his father's tyrannical disposition, without his great abilities. At the end of nine years, the complaints of his subjects had become so importunate, that the emperor deposed him from the government, and sent him into banishment to Vienne in Gaul, whence he never returned.

The independence of Judea, which, during all the later time of its relations with Rome, had been no more than nominal, was now at an end. It was constituted a province of the empire, and under the government of Coponius, as procurator, was attached to the prefecture of Syria, then administered by Publius Sulpitius Quirinius, or *Cyrenius*. Coponius, under whom Annas was made high-priest, was succeeded after two years by Marcus Ambivius, and he, after three more, by Annius Rufus, who was procurator at the time of the death of Augustus, in the fourteenth year of our era. Tiberius gave the place to Valerius Gratus, who, after a government of eleven years, was succeeded by Pontius Pilate. One of the last acts of Gratus was the appointment of Caiaphas, son-in-law of Annas, to the high-priesthood.

Of the three sects, spoken of by Josephus * and others as having arisen early during this second period of Jewish independence, the Essenes were a recluse, ascetic community, exerting no influence in public affairs. They observed celibacy, and in their several settlements lived upon a common stock, devoting themselves to agricultural industry. With them calmness and cleanliness were virtues, and they studied the medicinal properties of plants and minerals. They were the *Shakers* of Jewish antiquity.

The Pharisees are first mentioned by Josephus as taking a part in politics, in his history of the time of John Hyrcanus, whose administration they did so much to disturb. Their origin is uncertain. They have been sometimes connected — but, I think, without reason — with the Assidæans, of the time of the Asmonæan brothers.† Their name is equivalent to "separatists." ‡ They affected great strictness of doctrine, sanctity of life, and devotion to the Law. In some sense they were fatalists; and in some sense, apparently according to the Egyptian and Pythagorean doctrine of the transmigration of souls, they believed

---

* "Antiq. Jud.," Lib. XIII. cap. 5, § 9, XVIII. cap. 1, § 2-5; "De Bel. Jud.," Lib. II. cap. 8, § 14.

† See above, p. 138, note †.

‡ Apparently derived from פָּרַשׁ, otherwise פָּרַע, *he broke.*

in a renewed and retributory existence after death. They laid great stress upon ceremonies and upon traditions, especially upon the transmitted expositions of the Law, which they understood to have been communicated by an archangel to Moses during his forty days' seclusion on Mount Sinai, and from him handed down through an uninterrupted succession of holy men. They held that fasts, prayers, alms, and ablutions were efficacious to atone for sin; a doctrine which they even carried so far as to maintain, like the Romish Church in recent ages, that by such observances there might be laid up a supererogatory stock of merit.

To this sect was opposed that of the Sadducees, though I do not think it can be shown which of the two, by its earlier origin, gave occasion to the rise of the other. The Sadducees are said by some of the Rabbis to have owed their name to one Zadok, who lived in the first half of the third century before Christ,* and was a follower of Antigonus Socho, himself a pupil of Simon the Just.† They maintained the authority of the written Law, in opposition to that of glosses and traditions. They asserted the freedom of the will, and denied a future life. The rival sect charged them with laxness of manners, and in modern times it has been common to assert a resemblance between them and the Epicureans.

After the return from the Babylonish captivity, a method of religious service was introduced unknown to the Mosaic law. The institution of synagogues was

---

* See Vol. III. p. 166. — Others derive the name from צָדַק, *righteous*.

† For some remarks on the doctrine of this sect respecting the comparative authority of the Law and of the other Scriptures, see Vol. II. pp. 139 - 141. For some facts relating to the methods of Biblical interpretation in these times, see Vol. II. pp. 337, 338, 341, 342.

probably owing to the need which was felt of a more
systematic religious instruction for the people, when
the dialect in which the sacred books were written
had become to many a dead language; * and the addition of forms of social worship naturally followed.
According to the regulation of later times, synagogues
were to be erected in every place where there were
ten Jewish men, of full age, so circumstanced that they
might be relied upon to attend the synagogue service,
which, besides the Sabbaths, and the fasts and festivals,
was held three times on every Monday and Thursday
throughout the year. It consisted of prayers, chants,
and reading and commenting on the Scriptures, becoming thus the model for the ritual of Christian
churches. The superintendence of this service was no
function of the priestly family. The " rulers of the
synagogue," who maintained its order, and led in its
worship, might as well be of any other lineage as of
that of Aaron. The lessons were in number fifty-four †
from the Law, and fifty-four from the Prophets, one
of which was read and expounded every week.‡ This
reading of the Prophets in the same manner as the
Law, in the synagogue service, no doubt contributed
materially to the error, subsequently adopted by the
Christians from a portion of the Jews, of regarding
the Prophets as on a similar footing with the Law, in
point of authority.

The Chaldee was the language which the Jews who
returned with Zerubbabel, Ezra, and Nehemiah brought
back from their captivity, and into which accordingly
the Scriptures were rendered in the public instructions to the people. Not unreasonably these discon-

---

* Nehemiah viii. 1-8.
† To provide for the intercalated years, when a month was added.
‡ Acts xiii. 15, 27; xv. 21.

nected versions and comments have been thought to be the basis of the works, arranged long afterwards, which have come down to us under the names of the *Targums* of Onkelos, Jonathan, and others.*

But for more than three centuries, from the time of Alexander, the use of the Greek language had been extending among the Jews, and, though it had not superseded the Syro-Chaldee as the dialect of the common people, was understood by persons who pretended to any culture. The Alexandrine translation of the books of the Old Testament into that language was largely in use, and accordingly the New Testament quotations from them, as far as they are made with precision from any text, commonly represent the text of that version.

"In the fifteenth year of the reign of Tiberius Cæsar, Pontius Pilate being governor of Judea, and Herod being tetrarch of Galilee, and his brother Philip tetrarch of Ituræa and of the region of Trachonitis, and Lysanias the tetrarch of Abilene, Annas and Caiaphas being the high-priests, the word of God came unto John, the son of Zacharias, in the wilderness ; and he came into all the country about Jordan, preaching the baptism of repentance for the remission of sins." "Jesus also being baptized, and praying, the heaven was opened, and the Holy Ghost descended in a bodily shape, like a dove, upon him ; and a voice came from heaven, which said, ' Thou art my beloved son ; in thee I am well pleased.' And Jesus himself began to be about thirty years of age." † The purposes of the Mosaic discipline were accomplished. Another dispensation of miracle was to confer the blessings for which it had prepared the way. The

---

* See Vol. I. pp. 14, 65.　　　　† Luke iii. 1 - 3, 21 - 23.

Prophet like unto Moses was manifested. The glad
tidings of the Gospel were proclaimed. In the language of Eusebius, Christianity "flashed like a sun-
beam over the world." *

"When the fulness of time was come, God sent forth
his son."† In the early age of the Mosaic revelation,
the world, through all its borders, groaned under the
impious and bloody enormities of idol worship. For
weary centuries afterwards, that strange propensity of
the abused human understanding seemed unconquer-
able. But at length the Law did its work on the
chosen people, and after the return from Babylon,
though from time to time bad men apostatized for
ambitious ends, we read of no general relapse into the
follies of the Gentile nations. The sufferings and the
martyrdoms of the time of Syrian persecution at once
attested and confirmed the reformation which had been
wrought. Meanwhile, in the progress of a series of
revolutions, beginning at a time coeval with the Assyrian captivity of the ten northern tribes, the Roman
institutions had possessed the civilized world. The
civilized world was the Roman empire; and Judaism,
in the observance of its technical regulations, still more
in the profession of its essential principles, had spread
itself throughout the provinces of that vast dominion, "a light shining" everywhere in its dark places.‡
Nebuchadnezzar and Cyrus had been the unconscious
instruments for diffusing it in the East; Alexander, in
Greece and Egypt; § and the Roman conquerors, in

---

* "Hist. Eccles.," Lib. II. cap. 3.

† Gal. iv. 4.

‡ Comp. Vol. I. p. 94.

§ The famous library of Ptolemy Philadelphus made Alexandria the
resort of scholars from all quarters, thus bringing studious men especially to
the knowledge of the Jews in their principal colony, and of their Scriptures,
there existing in the universal language of the learned.

Africa and the West of Europe. So that Philo, soon
after the time of the crucifixion of Jesus, had occasion
to say, " One country does not contain the Jewish
people ; . . . . . they are found in all the best and most
flourishing countries of Europe and Asia, in the islands
and on the continents, all esteeming for their metropolis the holy city in which is the sacred temple of the
Most High God." *   And the report made by Agrippa
to Caligula, when he had ordered his statue set up
at Jerusalem, was, " It is the metropolis, not of the
country of Judea only, but of many others, on account
of the colonies which it has sent forth at different times, not only into the neighboring countries,
Egypt, Phœnicia, both the Syrias, but also into places
more distant, to Pamphylia, Cilicia, and many parts
of Asia, as far as Bithynia and the recesses of Pontus.
They are in the same manner in Europe, in Thessaly,
Bœotia, Macedonia, Ætolia, Attica, Argos, Corinth,
in the most and best parts of Peloponnesus.   Nor are
the continents only full of Jewish colonies, but also
the most celebrated islands, Eubœa, Cyprus, Crete ;
not to mention those which are beyond the Euphrates.
For excepting only a small part of Babylon, and some
lesser districts, scarcely any country of note can be
mentioned, in which there are not Jewish inhabitants." †   Josephus records, that the embassy which
came from Jerusalem to remonstrate with Augustus
against the pretensions of Archelaus to the throne, was
joined by more than eight thousand Jews of Rome." ‡
And on the day of the effusion of the Holy Spirit on
the disciples at the Pentecost, " there were at Jerusalem Jews, devout men, out of every nation under

---

* Philo, " Advers. Flac.," Vol. II. p. 524 (edit. Mangey).
† Idem, " Legat. ad Caium," Vol. II. p. 587.
‡ " Antiq. Jud.," Lib. XVII. cap. 11, § 1.

heaven," who said, "How hear we every man in our
own tongue wherein we were born, Parthians, and
Medes, and Elamites, and the dwellers in Mesopotamia,
and in Judea and Cappadocia, in Pontus and Asia,
Phrygia and Pamphylia, in Egypt and in the parts of
Lybia about Cyrene, and strangers of Rome, Jews and
proselytes, Cretes and Arabians?"*

Wherever, throughout the world, there were settlements of Jews, there was exhibited, in as many instances as their population consisted of, the striking
example of votaries of one God; there were maintained the worship and the instructions of the synagogue; and there were circulated copies of their sacred
writings, in that widely known language, the Greek,
into which, by the care of Divine Providence, they had
been translated before the age of the Roman conquests
in the East. It was in that language chiefly, in this
age, that the Jews themselves consulted their Scriptures. In that form, intelligible to the Gentiles around
them, they were able to appeal to the documents of
that faith, which, by the discipline of centuries, had
delivered them from the miseries of heathenism; and
therein, when the occasion came, the preachers of
Christianity were able to point to the ancient prediction of the "Prophet like unto himself," who was to
mature and complete the theology of Moses.†

The historians of the time, Jewish and Christian,
bear testimony to a consequence of this state of things,

---

* Acts ii. 5, 8 – 11.

† " Propter hoc enim illa gens regno suo pulsa est, et dispersa per terras,
ut ejus fidei, cujus inimici sunt, ubique testes fieri cogerentur." (Sanct.
Augustin. "Serm." 31, Tom. X. p. 626, edit. Basil.) " Reproba per in-
fidelitatem gens ipsa Judæorum, a sedibus extirpata, per mundum usque-
quaque dispergitur ut ubique portet codices sanctos, ac sic prophetiæ testi-
monium, quâ Christus et ecclesia prænuntiata est, ne ad tempus a nobis
fictum existimaretur, ab ipsis adversariis proferatur." (Ejusd. "Ep." 3,
Tom. II. p. 15.)

making it signally illustrative of that Divine wisdom, which, in its gracious condescension to the wants of men, had first revealed the Law of Moses, and then so ordered events as to make it the instrument of a universal benefit. "The multitude of mankind itself," says Josephus, "have had a great inclination for a long time to follow our religious observances; for there is not any city of the Greeks, nor of the barbarians, nor any nation whatsoever, whither our custom of resting on the seventh day has not come, and by which our fasts, and lighting up lamps, and many of our prohibitions as to food, are not observed. They also endeavor to imitate our friendly concord with one another, and the charitable distribution of our goods, and our diligence in our trades, and our fortitude in undergoing the distresses we are in, on account of our laws. And, what is here matter of the greatest admiration, our Law has no bait of pleasure to allure men to it, but it prevails by its own force; and as God himself pervades all the world, so has our Law passed through all the world also." * "When their Law," says Eusebius, "obtained celebrity, and like a fragrant odor was spread abroad among mankind, and by means of this Law the dispositions of men, even among most of the Gentiles, were improved by legislators and philosophers everywhere, who softened their wild and savage ferocity, so as to enjoy settled peace, friendship, and mutual intercourse; then it was, when men at length throughout the whole world, and in all nations, had been, as it were, previously prepared and fitted for the reception of the knowledge of the Father, that he himself again appeared." †

"The Jews," says Dr. Arnold, "were widely scattered over the Eastern provinces, and, as they adopted

---

* "Cont. Ap.," Lib. II. § 40.   † "Hist. Eccl.," Lib. I. cap. 2.

the language which was most prevalent around them, the Greek translation of the Old Testament, commonly known by the name of the Septuagint, was the form in which they were most familiar with their Scriptures. Intercourse with the Jews, and an acquaintance thus gained with the contents of their Law and of the writings of their Prophets, gave birth, throughout Syria and Asia Minor, to a class of persons who are called in our translation of the Acts by the name of 'the devout,' and who, without thinking themselves bound to conform to the national peculiarities of the Jewish worship, had yet acquired those true notions of the Divine nature and attributes, and of the duties which God demands of man, which are so largely contained in the Old Testament. The effect of this knowledge on those who profited by it was to produce the very virtues in which the world was generally most deficient, — devotion and charity; and by these means a large portion of the people was in some degree prepared for the doctrines of a still more perfect law, which were a few years afterwards introduced among them by the Christian Apostles." *

In the time of Augustus, philosophy had exhausted itself in endeavours, alike vigorous and vain, to solve the great problems of man's being. Through its defeats, it had been trained to be diffident and docile. This was a necessary step through which the human mind had to pass, before it could give up its hope of discovering, and be content to hear and believe. The questions which claim the most serious application of human intelligence had been discussed anxiously, acutely, and fruitlessly. Greek wisdom had tried its strength upon them, and ended where it began. Plato, who had compassed all the round and sounded all the depths

---

* "Later Roman Commonwealth," Vol. II. pp. 398, 399.

of speculation, had at last been fain to breathe a faint hope for "some easier and safer passage, upon some stronger vehicle," into this mysterious region of thought, than "the best and firmest human reason." * The Romans took up the unaccomplished task; but Cicero prospered in it no better than Plato. The experiment of ascertaining, by its own investigations, what the cultivated mind of man most longs to know, had been fully made, and had absolutely failed. And this, while the urgent need of that knowledge was disclosing itself more and more, in all the sad experience of society, — the experience of the discomfort of unsettled principles of action, and of the mischiefs of a gross prevailing immorality.†

Meanwhile the great polytheistic power of the world had been unconsciously bringing the conflicting idolatries of the world to an end, by the very growth of its own greatness. "Dragged in the train of political domination, the religions of the subject nations congregated in Rome. But what significancy could they retain, torn from the soil to which they were indigenous? The worship of Isis had perhaps a meaning in Egypt; it deified the powers of nature, such as they appear in that country; in Rome it was a senseless idolatry. The contact of the various mythologies was necessarily followed by their mutual hostility and destruction. No philosophical theory could be discovered, capable of reconciling their contradictions. . . . . . Independence fell; but with it fell the barriers of narrow nationalities. Nations were conquered, but by this very conquest they were united and incorporated. As the empire was called the world, so its inhabitants felt themselves a single connected race.

---

* "Phædo," § 78, "Opp.," Tom. IV. p. 127 (edit. Heindorf.).

† See the author's "Lowell Lectures on the Evidences of Christianity," Vol. I. pp. 74-97, for a course of remark upon these subjects.

Mankind began to be conscious of the common bond which unites them. . . . . . Thus, amidst a people which had hitherto held itself aloof from every other, arose, in all the force of truth, a faith which invited all and received all into its bosom. It proclaimed the Universal God, who, as St. Paul taught the Athenians, 'had made of one blood all nations of men for to dwell on all the face of the earth.' For this sublime doctrine the moment had arrived. A race of men had arisen, fitted to receive it." *

Wherever the disciples of Jesus went on their errand of evangelizing mankind, they found hearers already so far qualified to understand the offered truth, as that they were believers in the One True God; native Jews, and proselytes to Judaism.† And it may be presumed that here and there, at least, were persons of those rich attainments in religious wisdom, of which the son of Sirach had been so signal an example. But besides such persons, the preachers of Christianity found those who, from the other causes that have been named, were in a posture of mind not unsuited to offer access to the instructions of the Gospel.† It was a time of that high culture, when the soul, awakened to its needs, is capable of estimating the claims of what is offered to supply them; when it demands something better for its satisfaction than sophistry and fables; and when, once led into a right train, it finds in itself a sympathy with what is true, august, and generous.‡ It was a time of great intellectual activity. Science, letters, arts, commerce, war, and even the greed of vicious pleasure, permitted no stagnation of the faculties. And, with all its follies, it was a time of some sobriety of mind also, due to the dis-

---

* Ranke, " History of the Popes," chap. i. § 1.

† Acts xiii. 14, 42; xiv. 1; xvii. 1 - 4.

‡ " Greek cultivation and Roman polity prepared men for Christianity,

mal political troubles of three generations. If curiosity on the great questions of humanity had been baffled, it had not been silenced. With many, the habit of inquiry, so long and fruitlessly indulged, was still active, and looking for some better food. The deepest private wants of human nature never make themselves more felt, than in seasons of public disturbance and anxiety. Many must have been the minds which, at that period of the overthrow of liberty, and of wide-spread social calamities, felt with new force the need of some trustworthy tidings of another life.

Once introduced, the condition of the empire offered heretofore unparalleled facilities for the diffusion of the new faith. The civilized, that is, the Roman world, was now one vast community. Every subject state had easy communication with the capital; and from the capital, in turn, every thing that sought transmission found an easy way to the most distant provinces. When Peter and Paul brought the Gospel to the imperial city, it had already virtually made its way to Africa, Thrace, and Britain. "The permanent extension of the Roman empire broke down all the barriers of separation between the Eastern and Western worlds, united the Euphrates and the Thames under the same masters, and blended all the civilized states of Greece and Asia, of Africa and Europe, in one great commonwealth; in every part of which the Grecian language, now the language of the sacred records, became as it were the common tongue of the learned and the polite; while a perpetual intercourse

---

as Mohammedanism can bear witness; for the East, when it abandoned Greece and Rome, could only reproduce Judaism. Mohammedanism, six hundred years after Christ, justifies the wisdom of God in Judaism, proving that the Eastern man could bear nothing more perfect." (Arnold, "Life and Correspondence," Vol. II. p. 417.)

between the various parts of this mighty empire, the establishment of a firm and regular police through its whole extent, and, above all, that universal peace which its undisputed ascendency secured through the entire civilized world, when the Gospel of peace was first promulgated; all these circumstances secured to the teachers of that Gospel ready access to all the nations of the world capable of profiting by the sacred truths they taught, and gave men leisure to consider their unspeakable importance, and examine the evidence to which they appealed." * In the ages of the Babylonish and Persian dominion, commerce was so sluggish, and civilization so immature, that, for all purposes of the diffusion of opinion and sympathy, the subjugated, but not assimilated, nations might as well have retained their independence of each other. Nor were the conquests of Alexander ever consolidated into one social system. The iron hand of the Roman reduced to order, and symmetry, and cohesion, wherever he conquered, and brought every part into relations with all the rest. Like blood flowing back to the heart, and discharged again in a fuller flood through the arteries, every throb of life in any part of the body politic was destined to circulate through the whole frame. *To Rome and from Rome* was the sure course of every thing that had vitality; and thus it was that, under the gracious providence of Him, once revealed as the God of Abraham, now as Father of the human race, the doctrine of the Lake of Gennesaret so soon made its sound heard " through all the earth, and its words unto the end of the world."

---

* Graves, " Lectures," &c., Vol. II. pp. 348, 349.

THE END.

CPSIA information can be obtained
at www.ICGtesting.com
Printed in the USA
BVHW051514061218

534949BV00014BA/260/P

9 781330 105344